LETTERS FROM THE GREATEST GENERATION

LETTERS
FROM THE
GREATEST
GENERATION

WRITING HOME IN WWII

Edited by
HOWARD H. PECKHAM *&* SHIRLEY A. SNYDER

Foreword by
JAMES H. MADISON

INDIANA UNIVERSITY PRESS
Bloomington and Indianapolis

Originally published as *Letters from Fighting Hoosiers* by Howard H. Peckham
and Shirley A. Snyder, Indiana War History Commission, 1948.

This book is a publication of

Indiana University Press
Office of Scholarly Publishing
Herman B Wells Library 350
1320 East 10th Street
Bloomington, Indiana 47405 USA

iupress.indiana.edu

*Manufactured in the
United States of America*

*Library of Congress
Cataloging-in-Publication Data*

Names: Peckham, Howard Henry,
    editor | Snyder, Shirley A., editor.
Title: Letters from the greatest generation :
    writing home in WWII / edited by
    Howard H. Peckham and Shirley A.
    Snyder ; foreword by James H. Madison.
Other titles: Letters from fighting Hoosiers
Description: Bloomington : Indiana
    University Press, 2016. | Includes
    index. | "Originally published as Letters
    from Fighting Hoosiers by Howard H.
    Peckham and Shirley A. Snyder, Indiana
    War History Commission, 1948."
Identifiers: LCCN 2016019849 (print) |
    LCCN 2016021072 (ebook) | ISBN
    9780253024480 (print : alk. paper) |
    ISBN 9780253024602 (ebook)
Subjects: LCSH: World War, 1939-1945—
    Personal narratives, American. | Soldiers—
    United States—Correspondence.
Classification: LCC D769 .L45 2016 (print) |
    LCC D769 (ebook) | DDC 940.54/8173—dc23
LC record available at
    https://lccn.loc.gov/2016019849

1 2 3 4 5   20 19 18 17 16

Frontis:
Signal Corps photo from Acme
Sgt. John H. Parks, of Mill Creek, Indiana, was voted the "Man of the Year" by his fellow
G.I.s in the European theater of operations because his appearance typified the war-weary
soldier. As winner of this distinction, his picture appeared in *Stars and Stripes*, Dec. 22,
1944. The next day, the twenty-three-year-old tank man was killed in Luxembourg.

CONTENTS

vii   FOREWORD

1   Pearl Harbor and Bataan

15   Training Camps

43   North Africa

53   Italy

75   England

95   France

131   Germany

181   V-E Day and After

199   Alaska and the Aleutians

205   Southwest Pacific

235   Central Pacific and the Philippines

279   China-Burma-India

295   The Ryukyu Islands and Japan

333   After V-J Day

347   INDEX

FOREWORD

Here are the voices of fighting Hoosiers, the women and men who served overseas in World War II. Their letters home range from sophisticated insights to the tiny details of everyday life. They wrote of planes over Pearl Harbor "whipping down on us with the red sun of Japan on each wing tip," of the Normandy beaches and hedgerows—simply "a bad place," and of the kamikaze attacks off Okinawa where they "just sweated it out." Here are firsthand, moving accounts of war.[1]

World War II was the bloodiest war in human history. Letters home tended to be positive and hopeful, yet through them, twenty-first-century readers can still glimpse the brutality, which was not reported in newspapers at the time and was not always present in later public memories. There are vivid descriptions of the dead, including friends and comrades, and laments of rain and mud, cold and heat, the weeks without a change of clothing, the weariness of combat. Often it is the small things that stand out, as when Ernest Ellett told his parents a month after Nazi surrender that he was now gaining back the twenty pounds lost in combat.

Most of these writers were young, homesick Hoosiers. Many had not traveled outside Indiana, and their longing for family and home runs deep. "I'll bet I'm the only person in Decatur who has flown across the Atlantic," Jim Christen wrote from North Africa, as he asked his mother for news from the "little old town." Jim Rosenbarger regretted that he had not received a copy of the Corydon *Democrat* since arriving in France.[2]

Ordinary details of living fill the correspondence. Writers often mentioned food. Hubert Kress wrote that he couldn't stand to look at another can of Spam but also admitted he was part of "the best fed army in the world." This Clay County farm boy expressed his astonishment at seeing Italian farmers eating dark bread and washing it down with wine.[3]

One reason soldiers picked up their pens was to encourage responses from home. The mail they received was an essential morale booster in an age before long-distance telephones and electronic communication.[4] Complaints about not receiving letters were commonplace. Frank Woltman grumbled about slow mail but admitted that he had received twenty-three cards and letters in the two weeks after Christmas 1943. The American military was keenly aware of the importance of mail and worked hard to speed the flow. Improvement came with V-mail, short for Victory Mail, a process that photographed letters onto reels of microfilm. The reels were flown quickly overseas, where they were printed onto photographic paper and delivered to recipients. War propaganda posters encouraged home front and overseas correspondents to use V-mail and to write frequently. They did—soldiers received more than a billion V-mail letters.

While some letters were written in the voice of a loved one talking quietly in the kitchen or front room, censorship stood in the way of frank conversation. "I can't say anything about our engagements. The censor would just mark it out," Vernon Hobbs Jr. wrote from the Philippines to his parents. From the South Pacific, Charles Putnam Jr. lamented that he "couldn't write anything at all except, 'Hello, I'm fine, goodbye.'" Military men and women also self-censored not only to meet regulations but to spare loved ones the worst of horrors. Even love letters were often restrained. Writers also seldom noted instances of bad behavior by Americans. Historians now know that life overseas included drunkenness, sexual promiscuity, crime, and frequent use of profanity, with *chickenshit* and the f-word commonly deployed. These features of war were only hinted at, as in Red Cross volunteer Mary Sinclair's comment that there were "many wild raucous youths in the army." A leave to liberated Paris tended to elicit racy observations. For instance, Karl Price reported seeing nude female dancers in a city that "holds honors when it comes to immorality."[5]

There were traces, too, of Hoosier modesty. A. Ebner Blatt's description of parachuting with the 101st Airborne on the night before D-day was straightforward and full of telling details, though he did not boast of the genuine heroism and courage that we now know marked the Normandy landings. Similar was Kathryn Snyder's humorous description of abandoning a sinking ship with fellow nurses who used their helmets to bail out the lifeboat.

Mixed with the minutiae was the sense that these young Hoosiers knew what they were fighting for. "Gee, but I'm glad I'm an American," Laverta Baldwin wrote from India. Their patriotism often included a hatred of war. Many developed a deep bitterness toward the Japanese and Nazi enemies, though writers sometimes distinguished between Nazi leaders and ordinary German soldiers: "pretty much like the soldiers of any other army—flushed in triumph, bewildered by defeat," wrote Charles Bailey, who received a Silver Star for action at the Remagen bridge. The strongest feelings came from those who encountered the Nazi SS who were simply "killers," those captured by the enemy, and those who liberated the German camps. Dimly glimpsing what we understood later as the Holocaust, Myron Burkenpas wrote his father a description of bodies piled high. "That smell, Dad, is something I will not forget soon. . . . I don't tell you folks everything," he continued, but "I'm not exaggerating. . . . Tell the boys at the shop what it is all about."[6]

Some of the letters have sophisticated literary qualities. That's certainly true of the two examples of Ernie Pyle's writing included in this volume. World War II's greatest American correspondent penned a superb sketch of Tommy Clayton from Evansville with "the accumulated blur, and the hurting vagueness of being too long in the lines, the everlasting alertness, the noise and fear." Ordinary writers sometimes came close to Pyle.[7]

The Indiana War History Commission gathered and published these letters as part of a cooperative endeavor organized in 1942 by the Indiana University Department of History and the Indiana Historical Bureau to explore sources of both military and civilian life. The commission's work is an outstanding example of contemporary history that looked forward to the needs of future generations. *Letters from Fighting Hoosiers*, the original title of this collection, is one of ten volumes the commission planned and was the first to be published. It has the most enduring value, along with Max Cavnes's *The Hoosier Community at War*.[8]

The commission editors, Howard H. Peckham and Shirley A. Snyder, began with solicitations through Indiana newspapers. They received some 3,500 letters and selected 131. They chose to exercise "a free hand in editing"; that is, they cleaned up the writing. With living wartime memories all around them, it seemed wise to minimize embarrassments. But it also means today's reader misses some of the everyday language as well as, undoubtedly, some crude and less-than-patriotic writing.[9]

Almost certainly, the editors knew one or more of the ten thousand Hoosiers who died in this war. Among the most moving letters they selected are those by men who never made it home and one woman, Elizabeth Richardson of Mishawaka, now among those interred at the American Military Cemetery in Normandy.[10] There are also the words of Vernon Buchanan, a bombardier in the Pacific, who prepared a letter for his parents in Indianapolis to be sent only in the case of his death. "That's about all, folks," he laconically wrote near the end. "Don't feel too bad." The only illustration in the book shows John Parks of Mill Creek, a twenty-three-year-old killed at the Battle of the Bulge the day after his photograph was taken. War digs deep into our hearts and minds, never to be forgotten.[11]

Letters to Fighting Hoosiers earned praise when published, despite the small readership.[12] After all, Americans in the years after 1945 were focused on building families, homes, and careers. Later there would be time to look back, both for the aged fighting Hoosiers and for the generations to come.

James H. Madison

NOTES

1. Howard H. Peckham and Shirley A. Snyder, eds., *Letters from Fighting Hoosiers* (Bloomington: Indiana War History Commission, 1948), 2, 108, 353.

2. Ibid., 50.

3. Ibid., 82.

4. Note the very different nature of communication available to three Indiana women serving in twenty-first-century Iraq and Afghanistan. Helen Thorpe, *Soldier Girls: The Battles of Three Women at Home and at War* (New York: Simon and Schuster, 2015).

5. Peckham and Snyder, eds., *Letters from Fighting Hoosiers*, 13, 254, 101, 222. See Paul Fussell, *Wartime: Understanding and Behavior in the Second World War* (New York: Oxford University Press, 1989).

6. Peckham and Snyder, eds., *Letters from Fighting Hoosiers*, 335, 153, 218, 183–84.

7. Ibid., 126. Two historians of wartime correspondence comment on the good writing with a suggestion, perhaps exaggerated, that "the quality of public education in the 1930s and 1940s was far superior to that of today." Judy Barrett Litoff and David C. Smith, *Since You Went Away: World War II Letters from American Women on the Home Front* (New York: Oxford University Press, 1991), ix. Published wartime correspondence by Hoosiers includes Bruce C. Smith, *The War Comes to Plum St.*

(Bloomington: Indiana University Press, 2005); Frances DeBra Brown, *An Army in Skirts: The World War II Letters of Frances DeBra* (Indianapolis: Indiana Historical Society Press, 2008); and James H. Madison, *Slinging Doughnuts for the Boys: An American Woman in World War II* (Bloomington: Indiana University Press, 2007).

8. The Indiana War History Commission Papers at the Indiana State Archives, Commission on Public Records, Indianapolis, contain 259 boxes of the commission's work. The historian who led much of the work wrote an excellent description of the project. Lynn W. Turner, "Indiana in World War II—A Progress Report," *Indiana Magazine of History* 52 (March 1955), 1–20. For more context of World War II in Indiana, see Max Parvin Cavnes, *The Hoosier Community at War* (Bloomington: Indiana University Social Science Series, no. 20, 1961); and James H. Madison, *Indiana through Tradition and Change: A History of the Hoosier State and Its People, 1920–1945* (Indianapolis: Indiana Historical Society, 1982), 370–407.

9. Peckham and Snyder, eds., *Letters from Fighting Hoosiers*, xii.

10. Madison, *Slinging Doughnuts for the Boys*. The commission sent a copy of *Letters from Fighting Hoosiers* to Liz's parents and to the families of all the dead, as well as to all those writers who returned home. These complimentary copies added to the financial challenges of the War History Commission. See Lynn W. Turner to R. M. Fleischmann, 5 October 1949, War History Commission Papers, Box 17.

11. Peckham and Snyder, eds., *Letters from Fighting Hoosiers*, 265.

12. *Indianapolis Star*, September 18, 1949; and *Indiana Magazine of History*, 45 (December 1949), 421–23. In the twelve months after publication, the commission sold only 140 copies. Inventory, 25 August 1950, War History Commission Papers, Box 17.

LETTERS FROM THE GREATEST GENERATION

→ I ←

PEARL HARBOR AND BATAAN

EARLY in the morning of December 7, 1941, carrier-based Japanese planes attacked the United States naval base at Pearl Harbor, Hawaii, sinking or badly damaging the greater part of our Pacific fleet, including eight of the nine battleships, which were at anchor at the time of the attack. For two hours waves of Japanese planes continued pounding our fortifications, never meeting effective resistance from American forces. While this attack was being carried out against Pearl Harbor, similar strikes were made on small American owned and occupied islands in the Pacific. Garrisons at Midway, Wake, and Guam were attacked. Midway was the only one of the three islands to hold out successfully against the enemy. On December 9 the Japanese landed in the Philippines and swept down on Manila, which had been declared an open city. The American-Filipino forces that remained in the Philippines were withdrawn to Bataan, where they held out until April 8, 1942. On May 5 the forces on Corregidor, under Lt. Gen. Jonathan M. Wainwright, surrendered. Simultaneously troops on the other islands in the Philippines surrendered to the Japanese.

David Anderson, of Indianapolis, enlisted June 11, 1936, in Army Air Corps and received a direct commission in the field from the grade of master sergeant to 2d lieutenant Jan. 9, 1943, at Espiritu Santo. Anderson left the U. S. for Hickam Field,

Hawaii, Dec. 19, 1940, and was stationed subsequently on Christmas Island, Espir-itu Santo, New Zealand, New Caledonia, Norfolk Island and Guadalcanal. All his wartime duty was with the Army Airways Communications System. He was award-ed a unit citation (11th Bomb Group) for support of the Battle of Guadalcanal, and the Meritorious Service Ribbon for service between the Air and Airways Commu-nications Service and Headquarters Air Materiel Command at Wright Field from Apr. 1, 1945, to Jan. 1, 1947. Major Anderson is now stationed with the A. T. S. Command, Wright Field, Dayton, Ohio.

Dec. 1941
Hawaii

DEAR FOLKS:

Well, your wee yen has been through his first air raid. Sunday morning at 7:40, just as I was getting up for breakfast, I heard some dive bombers taking a pass at Pearl Harbor, which is in our backyard, so to speak. I remarked to Zuchalag, the sound man on the records I sent you, that some day that would be the real thing. I mean the dive bombers. Just then I heard an explosion. I looked out the window and saw clouds of smoke coming from the harbor. We all hurried and got dressed. Running outside we saw the planes whipping down on us with the red sun of Japan on each wing tip. I jumped into my car and rushed to the hangar, but by the time I got there the damned Japs had beat me to it.

There was a lull for a while and we started in on rescue work. Fowler and I (you will hear him on the records, too) hauled out about 10 wounded ourselves. We left the dead, and there were plenty of them. Oh, God, what a mess! We were both soaked with other fellows' blood. I lost many fellows that were good friends. The casualties are extremely high. Frank Bowen, who used to be at Schoen Field with me, got wounded in the hand. Zuchalag, my roommate, is missing. We received orders to disperse so I returned to my quarters. Just as I got back the damned so and so's came back again. The nearest one to me was about 150 feet, but it was only a light one, and a stick of bombs was coming to-ward me which I saw. I had time to throw myself on the ground. Boy, that is a sensation, to see a stick of bombs dropping toward you. Geysers of debris rush toward you.

We gave the Japs hell on the second go-round, though; several were shot down. They caught us with our pants down, but don't worry, it won't happen again. One reason is that we aren't taking our pants off any more. My address has been changed. There is no more Tow Target Detail—we have the real thing now. My address is now 327th Signal Company, 18th Bomb Wing, Radio, Hickam Field, Territory of Hawaii. I am glad, Mother, that this happened before you sailed. I wish I could see all of you. Well, I have to return to work. I will write later in more detail, so until then I will close with love to each and every one from the depth of my heart.

Your loving,
DAVID

P. S. Don't worry. I am not flying, and we will lick the devils in the end.

Arthur William Meehan, of Indianapolis, was graduated from the U. S. Military Academy in June 1928. He was on duty at Hickam Field, Hawaii, in Dec. 1941 with the Air Corps and was transferred one year later to Australia. He participated in many raids and made a night raid over Wake Island in June 1942. Promoted to colonel in May 1942, he was awarded the Distinguished Flying Cross for dangerous missions over enemy territory in Sept. Col. Meehan was reported missing in action Nov. 16, 1942, over Rabaul, New Britain, and was declared dead by the War Department Dec. 10, 1945. The Purple Heart was sent to his widow in 1947 with a note from President Truman.

Dec. 12, 1941
Hickam Field

DEAR FOLKS:

Since the surprise visit we received from our small yellow friends last Sunday I've been too busy to write. I knew how worried you would be, but I hoped that you would work on the old theory that "no news is good news."

When the raid hit I hurried to my office and I've been on duty almost continuously ever since. All of the families were evacuated from Hickam and other fields as soon as the first raid was quieted. Lucy left me a note telling me approximately where she was headed for. I finally located her late that night. She and Mrs. Lewis (another officer's wife) had moved in with their total of four kids on some people they knew in a peaceful valley. It is a lovely home and they are safe and comfortable. I don't know whether they will be allowed back to Hickam Field or not. I imagine that families may be evacuated to the mainland if safe passage can be arranged. Much as I hate the thought of separation, I'll be more relaxed about the whole thing when Lucy is safe somewhere in the U.S.A.

Now that the first bomb has been dropped we in the Army have a feeling of relief. It is nice to know exactly where we stand. Before it was all talk and uncertainties and we were in the position of waiting for someone else to fire the first shot. We don't have to wait any more. And, Mother, I'm lucky that you *did* raise your boy to be a soldier! I've waited around fourteen years preparing myself for this war—and, believe me, I'm ready.

I've almost forgotten about my trip home, it seems so long ago, but it was a wonderful trip, particularly in light of what has happened since.

Christmas is going to seem funny this year, but we'll celebrate it somehow. To show how Americans work, a load of Christmas trees from the mainland arrived yesterday—and they are selling like hot cakes. A gift I bought for Lucy—a very fetching evening gown—arrived on the same boat. I'll feel silly giving it to her now with a black-out on every night.

I'll try to write as often as I can but if letters are scarce don't worry. The mail will be irregular from now on. Best to everyone—and tell them that our chins are up, and out.

Love,
ARTHUR

Paul W. Franz, of Boonville, enlisted in the Army June 28, 1928, and served until May 15, 1942, when he was commissioned chief warrant officer, Schofield Barracks, Hawaii, in the quartermaster corps. Warrant Officer Franz participated in the defense of the Isle of Oahu, Hawaii, Dec. 7, 1941, at Wheeler Field. He also saw duty in Puerto Rico and Trinidad. Franz, who was awarded the Bronze Star, is now a master sergeant stationed at Camp Stoneman, Calif. The following account describes his experiences on Dec. 7, 1941.

On December 7, 1941, I was first sergeant of a unit on Wheeler Field, T. H., during the attack by the Japanese.

On this Sunday morning by some sixth sense I awoke early and was at the office doing some routine chores at 8 A.M., Hawaii time, when the attack began. Two other men were up working, too. As it was Sunday most of the men were still in bed. Some were housed in wooden barracks and some in tents. I immediately aroused everybody with my whistle and ordered all to scatter. The tents were strafed a few minutes after the men were evacuated.

Our first warning was the sound of machine guns. Low flying strafers were strafing the hangar line with incendiary bullets to put all planes out of commission. This they almost did. I believe three or four planes got into the air. Within the next five minutes I was to witness my first wartime casualty. I saw a pilot partly dressed running for the hangar line; a low flying strafer got him. I learned later it was Lt. Hans Christian Andersen (named after the poet). A bomber came over and let one loose which I believe was aimed at the garage nearby but hit the road 70 steps from where I was standing. Shrapnel flew in all directions. Within a few seconds another bomber came and dropped one on a warehouse full of bagged cement. It seemed that cement flew a half mile high. By this time a machine gunner had spotted me. I dove into a small hedge fence. Bullets flew all around me.

After about ten or fifteen minutes all enemy planes left (back to their carriers to reload). I decided to assemble the units. No officer was present but as I was the senior non-commissioned officer present I took over the unit and another QM unit, a truck company. While we were busy issuing arms and ammunition another wave of bombers and gunners came over. All we could do this time was scatter again. This wave left after about eight or ten minutes. The hangars were in shambles.

The units were really equipped this time. Trucks were moved from the vicinity of a burning vehicle (I was told the next day that I had saved the government $100,000 by this act). I dispatched an eight-man detail to remove dead and wounded from a nearby barracks that had been hit. I saw only one case of hysteria. A big, husky sergeant from the Ozarks knocked the man out. He came to an hour later and snapped out of it.

None of the enemy remained on the field at 10 A.M., to the best of my recollection. Our company officers arrived about this time, having been held up by nuisance attacks along the road from Honolulu to the field. I was recommended for an award that day but the award reached me only recently.

Guy Louis Vecera, of Richmond, enlisted in the Navy Sept. 14, 1937, as an apprentice seaman, and was assigned to the U.S.S. "West Virginia" until Dec. 7, 1941. For the next year and a half he served aboard the U.S.S. Y.P. 174; from June 1943 to Aug. 1945 he was on the U.S.S. "Huse" (DE 145); from Aug. 1945 to Jan. 1947 he was aboard the U.S.S. "Bailey" (DD 713). In March 1944 he was rated chief quartermaster, at which time he was aboard the U.S.S. "Huse" whose crew sank five German U-boats. With the rating of CQM (PA), Vecera has been stationed since Oct. 1947 at the U. S. N. Recruiting Sub-Station, Flint, Mich.

Dec. 25, 1941
[U.S.S. "West Virginia"]

December 7, 1941, Sunday, 7:55 A.M., I had the watch on the quarter-deck and was standing by the run-up "colors" when I sighted three bomb hits at the fork of the channel to Pearl Harbor. I ran forward and reported the fact to the Officer of the Day, Ensign Brooks, and as we both looked in that direction we saw a Japanese plane going across our bow with the emblem of the Rising Sun emblazoned boldly on her wings.

Immediately I ran to the deck officer and passed the word "all hands to general quarters" and "close all watertight doors." By this time a torpedo or two had already hit the ship amidships to port.

A few minutes, or possibly seconds after passing the word, the O.D. told me to go up to the bridge and find out if the captain was up there. As I started up the ladder to the boat deck, the O.D. grabbed my arm and told me to go there via the lower decks so as to escape the whistling machine gun fire from the Jap planes that were repeatedly dive bombing and strafing us, and to avoid interfering with our own antiaircraft gunners.

As I passed through the main deck another of several torpedoes hit the ship in approximately the same place as before. This occurred at about 8:15 A.M. and the ship started listing to port and it seemed as though it would capsize. But the first lieutenant and his damage control parties were on the job, and the ship was counterflooded and she returned to almost even keel although she was settling to the bottom fast.

All the while we were being bombed and strafed by the enemy planes. Along with our own antiaircraft fire going up, the din was terrific. One large 1,000-pound bomb hit the superstructure and smashed through the signal bridge, down into the galley and through into the commission issuing room, making a noise like a runaway train en route. The bomb did not explode, luckily for me, as I was standing just outside that compartment at the time. There were four or five men killed by the concussion alone.

Another heavy bomb of about the same size hit No. 3 turret and went down into the upper gun room where it stopped. It, too, did not explode but again the concussion killed several men. Fire was raging all over the topside to port and was completely out of control.

Our commanding officer, Capt. M. S. Bennison, who had been on the bridge since almost the beginning of the attack, was struck with a large fragment of the bomb and was fatally hurt. He did not die immediately and the grand old man that he was kept watching the action from his position lying on the deck, facing the sky. He continually asked how the battle was going and when several men attempted to move him he refused. I'm sure he died as he would have wished, on the bridge of the ship he loved, fighting her to the very last.

Meanwhile, I had attempted to get up to the bridge from the main deck, but all hatches were closed and I could not get through. I went down to the sound deck preparatory to going up through the conning tower, but the lights had all gone out and I could not see to pick my way along. The fuel tanks had been ruptured and the smell of oil was strong, so strong in fact that I was overcome by the fumes and collapsed. The next thing I remembered I was on the fo'c'sle, several shipmates having dragged me out.

By this time the ship was resting on the bottom, but the main deck was still above water. However, the entire forward part of the ship was in flames and the oil on the water around the ship was burning fiercely.

Then and only then came the order to "abandon the ship." Men dove over the side and swam to shore about 50 yards distant. I and a party of about 30 men climbed into a life raft and started paddling around the bow of the "Tennessee," which had tied up inboard of us, but we weren't making much headway and we realized that we would never make it, as the burning oil in the water was coming too close for comfort. Finally we gave up the raft and it was every man for himself. I still had on my shoes and I could hardly swim. I didn't think that I had time to take them off and several times I thought I was going down but managed to overcome my weariness enough to go a little farther. I finally reached the starboard side of the "Tennessee" and grabbed hold of her paravane chains to rest for a few minutes. By that time the oil fire on the water had spread so that I could not see the beach. That left me either to be burned by the oil, or drowned, or to attempt climbing up the chains over the bow of the "Tennessee."

I was so tired and weak I didn't believe it possible, but the strength a man has when fighting for his very life, hand over hand, inch by inch, foot by foot, forced me ahead. I crawled painfully up about 30 feet of chain where helping hands helped me down below. By this time the Japs had been beaten off, and I was so completely exhausted I didn't care what happened to me then.

Along with the heartbreaking damage I saw after returning to the topside again was the fact I had seen no sign of Eddie and I was worried about him. I had seen him lying on deck gasping for air as I ran through the main deck at about 9 A.M. I remembered telling him to get where he could get some fresh air. I did not see him after that time nor did I hear from him until three days later.

Well, that's still not quite all. It's not a pretty story, but that's the way it was and my one big regret is that I am not back on board the "West Virginia." She was the only ship in the world for me, and maybe some day I'll be back where I belong.

I don't know how I'm going to mail this, as our letters are supposed to be only two pages long, but I'll manage. Give my love to everyone back home and Merry Christmas.

GUY

William R. Evans, Jr., of Indianapolis, enlisted in the Navy Air Corps in July 1940, and was commissioned an ensign in Sept. 1941. His pilot's training and service was on the U.S.S. "Hornet" from Sept. 1941 to June 1942, and he was attached to Torpedo Squadron 8. Ensign Evans was killed in action in the Battle of Midway, June 1942. He was awarded the Navy Cross and the Purple Heart posthumously. Torpedo Squadron 8, which lost all but one man, was awarded the Presidential Unit Citation.

December 7, 1941
Norfolk, Va.

MY DEAR FAMILY:

What a day—the incredulousness of it all still gives each new announcement the unreality of a fairy tale. How can they have been so mad? Though I suppose we have all known it would come sometime, there was always that inner small voice whispering—no, we are too big, too rich, too powerful, this war is for some poor fools somewhere else, it will never touch us here. And then this noon that world fell apart. Even this business in the North Atlantic cannot be compared to the action now at hand. They still played it sort of as a gentleman's game, work during working hours, and plenty of play all the rest of the time. But now somehow all that is gone.

Today has been feverish, not with the excitement of emotional crowds cheering and band-playing, but with the quiet conviction of determination of serious men settling down to the business of the war. Everywhere little groups of officers listening to the radio, men hurrying in from liberty quickly changing clothes and reporting to battle stations. Scarcely an officer seemed to know why we were at war and it seemed to me there is a certain sadness for that reason. If the reports I've heard today are true the Japanese have performed the impossible, having carried out one of the most daring (and successful) raids in all history. They knew the setup perfectly—got there on the one fatal day—Sunday—officers and men away for the week end or recovering from Saturday night—the whole thing was brilliant. People will not realize, I fear, for some time how serious this matter is; the indifference of labor and capital to our danger is an infectious virus and the public has come to think contemptuously of Japan. And that, I fear, is a fatal mistake—today has given evidence of that—this war will be more difficult than any war this country has ever fought.

Our plans are as yet nebulous—tonight I put away all my civilian clothes—I fear the moths will find them good fare in the years to come—there is such a finality to wearing a uniform all the time—think that is the one thing I fear—the loss of my individualism in a world of uniforms—but kings and puppets alike are being moved now by the master, destiny. If I find out we're slated to leave soon I'll most probably sell my car, certainly so if we are sent across country to the West Coast (a persistent rumor).

It is growing late and tomorrow will undoubtedly be a busy day. Once more the whole world is afire—in the period approaching Christmas it seems bitterly ironical to mouth again the time-worn phrases concerning peace on earth—good will, with so many millions hard at work figuring out ways to reduce other millions to slavery or death. I find it hard to see the inherent kingdom. Faith lost—all is lost; let us hope tonight that people, big people, little people, all people throughout this great country have the faith to once again sacrifice for the things we hold essential to life and happiness; let us defend these principles to the last ounce of blood—but then above all retain reason enough to have "Charity for all and malice toward none." If the world ever goes through this again—mankind is doomed. This time it has to be a better world.

All my love,
BILL

Vernon D. Hobbs, Jr., of Richmond, was commissioned a 2d lieutenant on June 12, 1940, and was called to active duty June 25, 1941. The next month he left the U. S. and was assigned to the 2d Battalion, 24th Field Artillery, Philippine Scouts, on Luzon. On Jan. 1, 1942, he was promoted to 1st lieutenant. He served on Bataan until the surrender, survived the Death March, and spent almost two years in prison camps. Lt. Hobbs was aboard a prison ship in a Formosan harbor when it was bombed. He was mortally wounded and died a few days later on Jan. 23, 1945.

Dec. 9, 1941
Philippines

DEAREST FOLKS:

I wish there was some way to speed this letter on wings to let you know I am now on the front.

One day of war has passed. . . . We were eating lunch when the first heavy bombs hit. The Japs came over and knew exactly what they wanted. They bombed and strafed up the Clark Field area and strafed the upper post with heavy fire. Quite a few casualties, but I am O. K. We immediately moved out to the crater areas until nightfall, then moved to the jungle.

There were bombings, fires, and air battles all around and over us all night. I wasn't near a bed and it's now 7:30 A.M. the second day. Hope we don't move for a few hours, but I know we will. The whole battalion is dog-tired. . . .

It is now almost nightfall and we are in the same position. We've almost made ourselves at home. We have seen many planes today, but all ours, I guess. The news is very slow out here except by radio, and we do not know how much of that to believe. I went up the road to quiet down some white antitank groups who had nervous fingers and were firing on our own aircraft.

Later I found a pump and a bucket, and took a bath and shave. It does wonders for you, even in war. All the people have taken to the deep jungles, and it looks so funny to see open *bahis*, with chickens, pigs and carabaos around, but no people. Can't say I blame them. Awfully pitiful, though, to see them leave everything they have in the world behind.

My foxhole is very nice already. I have my bedding well in it, and it's very comfortable, except for mosquitoes.

Dec. 10

Up at 4:30 A.M. today. The roosters around here just won't let you sleep. Very quiet all night. I had the 8–12 watch, and it was very boring. Nothing at all. . . .

I guess we know less about what's happening than anyone in the States. All we know is what we see and hear. . . .

Finally resting a moment again. Just had our first parachute scare. A Jap bomber was shot down over to our right about 4,000 yards, and the crew of five bailed out. Immediately they were filled with lead. All reached the ground dead. . . .

Dec. 15

I seem to have found no time or inclination to write for several days. We have been constantly on the move. We just completed our last move about four hours ago, and when I ate, I fell asleep for an hour or so. . . .

The bombings are very regular on all the air stations, but do not get close to us here in the deep jungle. And I do mean jungle! Trees are over 100 feet high, tall underbrush, liana (vine trees), and even monkeys and parrots. . . .

We sure would like to know what is going on in this war. . . .

Dec. 23

I'm well and as happy as possible living in tropical jungle, although we are all on Filipino rations, rice and salmon, which gets very tiresome, to say the least.

I really can't say anything about our engagements. The censor would just mark it out. I wish I had a diary to keep. Hard enough to find paper though. I was the only one who brought even a little with me, and it's pretty low now. I have to go now. Will write tomorrow, Christmas Eve. Seems strange to be sweating in my boots on Christmas.

December 24 Christmas Eve.

Not much to make it seem like Christmas I'm afraid. It's very hot and dry. Beautiful bombing weather. I've seen quite a few Jap leaflets today, urging the Filipinos to go home and stop fighting. Even got hold of a surrender card. It guarantees safe conduct when the Japanese Imperial Navy takes over. I'm keeping it for a souvenir, in the event I ever get back.

Dec. 27 Saturday

All is quiet in the sector this morning. Not much bombing and the heavy guns haven't been heard from all day. Just got word most of Stotsenburg went up in flames, with all my worldly possessions. Sort of hard, losing everything. . . .

I've not received any Christmas presents yet, so have supposed they went to the bottom. . . . We're gradually reducing our lines back farther into the jungle. They will have to come and get me.

Jan. 5, 1942

Almost a month of war now. Still going strong and in perfect health. I've developed a slight case of jitters, but that's only natural, I guess, with so many bombs dropping every day.

I got my promotion over a week ago, but doesn't make much difference now. A little more money. . . . I have had no mail at all since the war. I've written about four times to you—hope you've received at least one. . . .

The days are hot and the nights cool and moonlit these past few nights. This is winter here, too, but you would never know it. I really enjoy the beauty of the huge forests and mountains around us, even when we know they (Japs) are coming closer each day. . . . I don't have time to write much any more. Just work, eat, sleep, and stay on the ball. . . .

There have been airplanes overhead constantly for four hours now, and the ground is always shaking from some bombing or another. Planes are so common they are not even scouted any more. We know whose they are. We just yell "cover" and jump into our foxholes. There are holes of all sizes all around. Some we have dug, and some, others have dug before us. They get deeper every time we are bombed.

Feb. 12

I know that I have not kept you informed of my well-being, etc., for the past six weeks, but I know that even had I written you probably would not get them for months, and also I haven't had time for writing.

I am well as can be, healthy and in good spirits. We have been through some very rugged times in these past weeks, with very little sleep, if any, and it becomes rather tiresome being on the constant alert dodging shells, bombs, and machine gun fire. You read enough of that in the papers I suppose, and anyway, I can't tell you anything about it, or my letters wouldn't stand a chance of getting through. . . .

We have gone through a lot of h—— in these few months, but have had surprisingly few casualties. One of my best friends from Richmond, Va., George Hardy, was killed by bombs. Gee, I hated to see him go. I've prayed to God each night to have great pity on the souls of those who are gone as they paid for their sins many times over in this h—— on earth.

I wonder if God is not only caring for ours, but for the thousands of young Japanese left lying in the jungles here in Luzon. We have taken a toll of lives many times what we have lost. I have seen what deadly effect my own firing has had among the ranks of the attackers in places where we have retaken the ground. They do not bury their dead except as an afterthought.

All my belongings are of course up in smoke. Even those I came into the field with were burned when my car was hit by a shell several weeks ago. The men gave me clothes and the officers gave me a razor and toothbrush and that's all I need, I guess.

I suppose this awful war has really just begun, but nine weeks has seemed an eternity. I'm so tired of killed men littering the jungle paths, of the stench of dead bodies being always in the air.

Will you please tell all the boys and girls I know that it's O. K. so far. Tomorrow isn't in our vocabulary.

$\rightarrow$ II $\leftarrow$

TRAINING CAMPS

As DEFENSE measures, the National Guard was ordered into active military service in September 1940, and the Selective Service sent young men to training camps for a year starting in November. After our declaration of war, December 8, 1941, both enlistments and inductions increased heavily, and new camps and especially air bases were built. The training period was disagreeable to almost all recruits, as the discipline was strange and the emphasis was laid on physical toughening. It was made more bearable by the USO canteens and the hospitality of nearby civilians. After basic training, soldiers and sailors were transferred to advanced training camps, specialist schools at colleges, military stations, or officer candidate schools. Crowded trains and troop trains passing in the night wove a web of intricate transportation throughout the war. Young women entered this masculine maze after the creation of the Women's Auxiliary Army Corps (WAAC) in May 1942, and the Women's Reserve of the U. S. Naval Reserve (WAVES) in July, as well as women's auxiliaries for the Marines, Coast Guard, and Air Force. Training camps capable of handling hundreds of thousands of young people were in operation by the end of the war.

Willis Read Davis, of Washington, enlisted in the Army Air Corps Nov. 13, 1940. He was a member of the 31st Army Reconnaissance Squadron, March Field, Calif. In the summer of 1941 he was sent to Chanute Field, Rantoul, Ill., for teletype training. Returned to March Field in Sept. 1941, he was transferred to the 307th Materiel

Squadron, Ferry Command, Long Beach, Calif. In June 1942 this command was renamed 348th Base Headquarters and Air Base Squadron, 6th Ferrying Group. Attaining the rank of technical sergeant on Sept. 14, 1942, and having just been called for officer's training, Davis died of nephritis in Santa Barbara, Calif., Oct. 4, 1942. Excerpts from several of his letters follow.

September 21, 1941
March Field, California

Now attached to the Ferry Command to service the planes leaving here for Britain. Field about two miles square. In one corner a new Douglas plant; known as a black-out plant; painted black and there isn't a window in any of the buildings. We are alongside the Naval Reserve hangars. At present we have only two small hangars.

September 28

Writing this from my own desk, believe it or not. Last Monday told to report to Col. Spake. He asked me what I'd been doing. Told him I was a teletype man so he put me to operating a machine. I explained I hadn't done any typing since I graduated from high school but that didn't bother him. Have been sending and receiving messages from all over the country for a week now and doing all right. The hardest job of all is keeping my mouth shut about the confidential messages from Washington.

November 9

Wearing two stripes now and proud of them as an old cat with five kittens.

Will try to tell you a little about the work here. To begin with, this is the newest and largest airport in the United States. There is a large monument erected here to Douglas Corrigan, as this is where he took off from when he made his nonstop flight to New York and thence to Ireland.

The outfit here is known as the "Western Division Air Corps Ferrying Command." It is from here that all planes take off on cross-country flights to Dorval Airport, Montreal, and then to Britain.

The operations office (in which I work) is the nerve center for the whole works. All the orders that send these ships on their flights are made up here.

At present I am in complete charge of the message center. My job is to send and receive messages and carry on the correspondence over the teletype machines. We have a Western Union and a Postal Telegraph machine for sending and receiving telegrams, a Bell Telephone machine for sending and receiving regular correspondence, also a Civil Aeronautics machine on which we get all weather data from every station west of Kansas City. We also receive all flight plans, notices to airmen, and emergency warnings.

December 8

Well, it looks as though we are going to have a little excitement at last. Second night of black-out. Working day and night as my department is short of personnel. Have had two hours sleep in the last thirty-six hours. Am working extremely hard, but at least my work is being appreciated. As of December 1 and thereafter I will be referred to as Sergeant Davis.

It is 9:30 P.M. and as yet nothing has happened, although we are certainly prepared for anything. The whole state of California is blacked out. All I have to work by is one little lamp. If we are attacked anywhere it should be in this area, as right here in the Los Angeles area is where most of our planes are manufactured. Here at Long Beach are the Signal Hill Oil fields. There are thousands of oil wells adjoining the field. The Douglas plant is also on this field. At present this place is harder for a soldier to get into than the Y.W.C.A. Sunday night I came home in a cab and was stopped and searched five times before I got into the field. They even searched the taxi.

December 11

Downtown last night when a black-out warning came. Sirens started screaming and police and soldiers were ordering lights out and cars parked. Very exciting, but no bombing.

This war has doubled my work but even so, I love it! Don't believe the West coast will ever be bombed, and if it is don't think those Japs could hit anything. If at any time there are any raids here, don't try to phone or wire me. We need to keep the wires open for more important communications. Each day it gets worse every time I try to put messages through. Will keep in close touch with you if anything should happen.

Ernest S. Maye, of Indianapolis, was inducted into the Army July 31, 1942, and was assigned to the 27th Quartermaster Battalion until July, 1944, and then was transferred to the 37th Quartermaster Battalion. Staff Sergeant Maye participated in the Sicilian campaign, and fought up through Italy from Naples to the Po Valley, winning five battle stars. Maye was discharged Nov. 6, 1945, and is a mail carrier in Indianapolis. The letter below was written to the staff of the State Library, where he had been employed.

[1942]
Camp Butner, N. C.

Hello Everybody:

In every man's life there comes a time when even his breathing seems to have a restriction on it. That time has come to me. Today has been my freest. I am making the most of it. Tomorrow will be another chapter. . . .

After doing a deal of riding hither and thither we finally found a resting place here. This camp is really full of opportunities for the ambitious. Every man here has an equal chance. Unfortunately there is no such thing as equal ability, therefore some of us go up and some down. I was fortunate. At present I am an acting top-kick; that is, first sergeant. If I make good I will get my stripes. It requires a lot of hard work on duty and off. A potential N.C.O. is required to stay at least a week ahead of his comrades. That means digesting your material ahead, reviewing for the class and instructing if called on to do so. There is no idle moment. I have made a 1,001 mistakes everyday and sometimes I wonder if I will ever get anything right. But I am sticking. The job must be done.

Chow is excellent. Had to loosen my belt today. I am brown from this sun and believe I am gaining weight. Plenty of showers and sleep. When night falls practically every soldier is ready for bed. We do not have to be coaxed. We just fall in.

As to my superiors, they are tough and I mean tough. They have to be or we would run things for them. I hope to never hear a whistle again someday. One day last week I walked in a semiprone condition from—falling in whistle—falling out whistle—chow whistle—this whistle—that whistle and the other whistle. But we are in the army now.

Do you recognize the paper? Yep, it is the paper you gave me. That "house-wife" is really a lifesaver. The pencil is in use every hour. The shoe brush every two hours. The comb and mirror six times a day. Everything sure came in handy. It won't be long until I can tell you in person—I hope. That billfold will be full soon. My first pay. Very shortly. Military secret. . . .

"My Life in the Service" (diary) is coming along splendidly. The first pages are very interesting to me. A lot of things I considered trivial then are important now. I read it as much as I write in it.

Please give my kindest regards to all of my former co-workers. I will write each one personally as soon as time permits. It is now time for chow and I must get this in the box.

> "'All actual heroes are essential men,
> And all men possible heroes.'"
>
> —E. B. Browning.

From first page, "My Life in the Service."

Sincerely,
ERNEST S. MAYE

John Stanley Popp, of Speed, was inducted into the Army Aug. 31, 1942, and was assigned to the air corps. He trained at Clearwater, Fla., and later entered radio school at Sioux Falls, S. D. In March 1943 he was assigned to the 81st Ferrying Squadron, 23d Ferrying Group of the Air Transport Command, Hamilton Field, Calif., as radio operator and mechanic. Discharged March 31, 1943, Pfc. Popp returned to Speed.

Dec. 5, 1942
Sioux Falls, S. D.

DEAR MR. DORSEY AND FRIENDS:

How is everything going back in my little home town? Things here are about the same except it is a lot colder than when I wrote you last. Only wish I could have canned some of that Florida sunshine and turned some of it loose up here. Don't see the sun very much up in this part of the country. We have had our first blizzard and it was frightening, as the wind blew very hard and the snow was so thick you couldn't see where you were going. The snow here is very dry and doesn't stick like it does down there.

Since being in the army I have been thinking of the many reasons for our being in this war. My conclusions are that it isn't for the times our toes have already been stepped on, but because we don't want them stepped on in the future and take a chance of losing our heritage. We have fought for our freedom before, but let's hope the armistice this time is not the first shot of the next war. I find that butchering the Japs and Germans isn't my real objective. I don't believe in killing, but there is something greater than the life or death of a freedom-grabber like Hitler and his puppets. I'm in here fighting for the things freedom stands for—our church bell ringing every Sunday, the truth on our radio and in our newspapers, our children going to school and learning something besides military tactics, everyone having the same privilege to get ahead, the gang on the corner doing and saying what they please, the Stars and Stripes waving in the office yard each day, all our competitive sports without worry of doing them Hitler's way, everyone happy because he is free and doesn't have to worry because of his race or creed, being able to have a car for cement dust to settle on. I know I could sit here all day and name the numerous freedoms we now have but wouldn't have should we let the enemy get the best of us. Everyone must do his utmost to assure himself that these little things aren't taken away from us. After all don't they all go together to spell *freedom*? Aren't they what our forefathers fought for? Does Hitler stand for any of them? I'm sure he doesn't and he is going to be mighty disappointed when he finds he can't take even one of them away from us. Also I'm sure any free man would rather die fighting for these things than to live the hell thereafter should we lose. Enough of this sermon.

School gets harder day by day. This only means harder work to assure myself that I will be better than any Jap or Nazi I ever encounter, and I want to always come out on top. I was the first to pass my sixteen words a minute code test in a class of about 200. Bragging a little, but I think you can understand how I feel about it. My theory class is some different; as a mechanic I guess I will make a good dishwasher. It's hard for me to get so much straight in the little time they give us.

Well, it's time to bring this to a close as I have some homework to do. I will do so wishing everyone a very Merry Christmas and *many* Happy New Years.

Sincerely,
Stanley Popp

Vivian B. Watson, of Waynetown, enlisted in the WAAC Sept. 1, 1942, receiving her basic training at Fort Des Moines, Iowa. She was commissioned a second lieutenant, Mar. 9, 1943. Lt. Watson was platoon commander of the 64th WAC Operations Company at Norfolk, Va., and attended the Basic Supply Officer's Class at Camp Lee, Va., early in 1944. In Mar. 1944 she became commanding officer of an Overseas

*Replacement Company, and departed for Africa April 3, 1944. While stationed over-
seas in Algiers, Italy, and Austria, Lt. Watson served as executive officer of the 6722d
WAC Communications Platoon, from June to Aug. 1944; as commanding officer of
the forward echelon, 6669th WAC Headquarters Platoon from Aug. 1944 to Aug.
1945, and as assistant secretary of General Staff of U. S. Forces in Austria from Aug.
to Sept. 1945. Awarded the Bronze Star, Lt. Watson was discharged Dec. 17, 1945,
and is now on the staff of the American Legion headquarters in Indianapolis.*

October 17, 1942
Des Moines, Iowa

DEAR JEAN:

It was so nice to get your newsy letter and it's also nice to know that you miss
me. Frankly it seems as if I've been away for months; any resemblance between
this career and my old one is purely coincidental. I go to bed at 9:30 and fall
asleep almost instantly and I hop out at 5:30 A.M. like a jack-in-the-box. Fran can
tell you that that is not at all like me. However, this morning I didn't get up until
7:00 and I felt like a plutocrat. It's really remarkable how well the women are
whipping into shape. A lot of them have had little more experience than sitting
at a desk all day, but they're right there with the best of them, marching three
or four hours a day, doing K.P. for 12 hours, etc. We've only had two or three out
of our company of 150 that couldn't take it and had to be sent to the hospital.

We finish our basic training next Saturday and will then be classified and
assigned to a specific brand of service for further training. It looks as though
I might be used to drill new recruits. I acted as platoon leader this week and
yelled, "Hut, two, three, four—right face, by the left flank, march" until you
could hear my echo all over the fort. I'll probably come into the library some day
and talk in a voice that can be heard all over the building.

We had an interesting experience on Wednesday. We paraded in review before Col. Hobby, Brig. Gen. Jean Knox of the British Women's Territorial Force,
and a Major of the Canadian Women's Army Corp. Then we heard Gen. Knox
speak to a graduating class of officers. She was simply marvelous. She spoke
very quietly and directly, no dramatics, etc., but you felt that every word came
from her heart. She has directed her women under fire and so spoke from her
own experience about the things we may be called on to do. When she had
finished speaking I don't believe there was a girl in the building who wouldn't
have walked into a barrage of machine gun fire if she had asked her to. When
one sees a person like Gen. Knox it makes you darned proud to be a woman.

And now for a less serious note—we paraded twice this week for the mov-ies—Joan Crawford and men from the M.G.M. studios were here filming scenes to use in her next picture. However, I'm afraid mine is a face never to be filmed—it seemed to me that every time I got within range the camera stopped turning. But I nearly stepped on a cameraman who was filming our feet—so if in Joan's next picture you see a pair of bowlegs marching by they are certain to be mine.

Phil Spitalney's "Hour of Charm" is to be broadcast from Des Moines to-night, the program to be dedicated to WAACs, and we are to be the guests for the broadcast and an additional hour and a half show. Needless to say I plan to be there.

I am at the beauty shop now having a hair cut for the second time and a permanent. They are very strict about one's hair so I decided to get it darned short. Every Saturday at inspection I fully expect my hair to fall down on my collar as the officer passes by. So far I have gotten by, but I wasn't going to trust my luck too far. If you are told to get your hair cut and don't do it an officer will personally take you to the barber shop and you are given a man's hair cut. None of that for me—I must keep my femininity (if any) at all costs.

I've met a lot of grand girls from all over the United States. If I don't come back with some kind of an accent I'll be surprised. And you should see how I look. My face is wind and sunburned with many additional freckles. My neck is red from the high shirt collars. My hands look like a scrub woman's, my nails are as short as I can possibly get them. We seldom have time for make-up except on week ends, so I'm definitely not a thing of beauty. But I really don't care for I'm thoroughly enjoying every minute, and every day brings new experiences. . . .

Loads of love,
Viv

Edward Fischer, of South Bend, became a volunteer officer candidate in the Army Oct. 5, 1942, and was commissioned a 2d lieutenant of infantry May 26, 1943. He took his basic training at Camp Croft from Oct. 1942 to Feb. 1943. For a year after being commissioned, he wrote training literature for the infantry school. He took an advanced officer's course and left the U. S. Nov. 10, 1944, serving in India, Burma, China, and Ceylon. He escorted 55 newspapermen on the first convoy across the Ledo-Burma Road (Stilwell Road). Capt. Fischer wrote the combat history of the

Burma campaigns, and assisted in writing the history of the India-Burma Theater. Discharged Mar. 16, 1946, Fischer is now assistant professor of journalism at the University of Notre Dame.

Christmas Day, 1942
Camp Croft, S. C.

DEAR PROFESSORS:

A year ago today I little dreamed that I would spend Christmas Eve and Christmas Day of 1942 in an army guard house. No, I haven't been misbehaving; my turn at sentry duty happened to come at this time.

From 5 P.M. Christmas Eve until 5 P.M. today we walked two hours and rested four; walked two and rested four. The walking part isn't too bad; but it is difficult to get any rest because we must keep all our equipment on when we turn in.

You might wonder what sentries thought about as they made their rounds on the darkest Christmas of our generation. Well, they hummed carols to themselves, and dreamed of Christmases past, and prayed that there would be more such Christmases in the years to come. Twenty-four hour guard duty on this day means a twenty-four hour lump in the throat for any soldier, because it gives him too much time for memories.

A fellow doesn't realize until he is in the army how dependent he is on "beauty." Here all the clothes are olive drab and all the walls are bare. And he catches himself staring at a Christmas tree just to get a "lift" from the colors of the lights. I didn't know until last night how rapidly the moon climbs into the sky. I had a big, yellow one for observation. And every time I made the round of my post it gained quite a bit of altitude. Another thing I noticed is that the roosters around here begin to crow at 3:55 A.M.

Even though rain did fall for about two hours, the weather as a whole was nice and balmy. Here's something you probably didn't know; when a soldier gets up in the morning he doesn't squint into the darkness or go outside to see if it is raining. He merely observes how a passing sentry carries his weapon. If the sentry has the rifle on his shoulder, muzzle skyward, it is not raining. But if he has the sling on his shoulder and muzzle pointing to the ground, then it's a damp day. Yes, you guessed it; he changes the position of his rifle to keep the rain from running down the barrel.

Christmas dinner was super-super. We thought the Thanksgiving meal couldn't be surpassed, but Christmas hit a new high. There were at least twenty-five things listed on the menu. As a reporter I covered many banquets, some of which cost quite a few dollars per plate. But none of them ever came near the Christmas dinner prepared in an army mess hall.

Last week we finished our work with the mortar. One day we left camp at 8:15; walked seven miles; fired on a deserted house till we blew it to bits, and then walked the seven miles back to camp, all by 1:15. That was a full five hours.

Now we are working on tactics. It entails a lot of field work. Sometimes at night we are given a map and a compass, and are told to locate the enemy and bring back a report of his activities. Of course we are supposed to do all this without being seen.

The "enemy" goes out in advance and begins to do such typical things as string barbed wire, dig trenches, set up machine gun nests, etc. Our job is to crouch in shadows; inch our way across patches of moonlight; slip past the sentries, and return again without being observed. It's tough, plenty tough.

I learned a valuable lesson one night; that is, never follow the line of least resistance. I spotted a sentry on a bridge which crosses a creek. So I took my squad well downstream to avoid him. But I made the mistake of selecting a spot where rocks jutted from the water and so facilitated the crossing. But the "enemy" knew that there is a human weakness that looks for the "easy way"; so we walked right into a machine gun nest.

Practically all of our work in these last three weeks of basic training will fall under the heading of tactics. After we finish this work, we will bide our time until Camp Croft is asked to fill its quota in an officer candidate school. That request may come in a week or it may take a month. Meanwhile, we will "prep" for the grind that awaits us.

Another physical exam last week saw more volunteer candidates pack their suitcases and return to civilian life. The government can't afford to put $8,000 into the training of an officer if it isn't practically certain that he will be able to stand the gaff physically.

More news of army life next week.

Sincerely,
ED FISCHER

Harold Sander, of Indianapolis, was inducted into the Army May 8, 1943, and was sent to Camp Croft, S. C., for basic training until Aug. 1943. Selected for language training, he was sent to Amherst College under the Army Specialized Training Program. Promoted to master sergeant, Sander was sent to England in June 1944 and was attached to headquarters of the 18th Airborne Corps as a photo interpreter for Military Intelligence. Sgt. Sander helped plan the Holland Airborne operation of Sept. 1944, and participated in the Battle of the Bulge, the Rhine Crossing at Wesel, the Ruhr Pocket cleanup, and the Elbe River crossing. Earning five battle stars, Sander was discharged Nov. 12, 1945, and is now a librarian in Indianapolis. The following letter was addressed to his colleagues at the State Library.

June, 1943
Camp Croft, S. C.

DEAR PUBLIC SERVANTS:

Sunday is truly a wonderful day. When the Lord created the earth, etc., in 6 days and rested the 7th He certainly set a precedent which is greatly appreciated by us buck privates. You will note that I have written *buck private* in small letters. This is proper.

Two weeks of my basic are now over. It has seemed like two months! At this point I can begin to see a few things that I overlooked before. First of all there is a war going on—we are in it and I am being trained to fight. Our training is no summer camp stuff or phys-ed class. It is tough. Of course this is as it must be, although it didn't sink in before. In two weeks' time we have covered a lot of ground. We have had everything from close order drill to bayonet practice and "dry shooting" of the M1 rifle. We are being toughened up gradually but steadily. Right now I feel better than I have for a year. Most of the soreness has gone from my aching muscles and I can see the results of our "toughening up" processes.

Last Monday I experienced one of the famous duties of a soldier—K.P. They usually take K.P.'s in alphabetical order and Monday was the day for Saban (I. U. football), Sander, Sanders, Schmidt, Schubert, Savarese, etc. You get up at 4 instead of 5—make your bed—get washed up—report to the kitchen. First we cleaned out the pantry and scrubbed it, then peeled potatoes, then washed the breakfast dishes. There are about 225 men in our company so you can calculate how many plates, cups, etc., there were. Then we had breakfast. After that we G.I.'d the floor. To explain—G.I. in this sense means getting down on your hands and knees with a stiff bristle brush—use G.I. soap, water and elbow grease. Most any floor will shine after being G.I.'d—otherwise you do it over. Then came inspection, of course our hands and nails had to be just so. Our mess sergeant was gigged because the inspecting officer found a speck of dust on a coffee pot that was back in the pantry—it hadn't been in use for six months! Then we again attacked the potatoes. After so much of that I was put on the can flattening detail. I guess I flattened and removed the paper from 200 tin cans. At this time we had our dinner (15 minutes). Now it was time to wash the dinner dishes plus pots and pans. This is about a two-hour job. Some carrots needed to be cleaned and scraped then. After the carrots came some more potatoes. Then we had supper, then came the supper dishes and a final cleaning up of the kitchen. I got back to the barracks at 8:15 P.M. During the day I had 15 minutes each for breakfast, dinner and supper. I smoked two cigarettes. Was on the go the rest of the time. Then, of course, you have to shine your shoes for the next day. After 16 hours of K.P. you can take my word, a person doesn't need to be rocked to sleep!

Fortunately, it was a rainy day, and not hot. The army cooks with coal ranges so you can imagine what it is on hot days.

On top of all this, we had to attend two hours of class the next evening to make up some of the work we missed because we were on K.P. the day before.

Usually our day runs from 5 A.M. to about 6 P.M. but frequently we have extra duties or details after supper. So you can see why we can't write as many letters as we would like. Camp Croft is an enormous place and pretty nice if you have an inclination to appreciate it.

I think I mentioned before that our company has a large contingent of I. U. and some Purdue R.O.T.C. boys. This is fortunate because I have made many fine friends out of this group. They are a high type. On the other hand, it seems to me that they are adjusting the pace and action of our drill to their qualifications. To a greenhorn like me this shows up my ignorance on military matters.

My chances of getting into O. C. S. are none too good now. From what I have learned, the quota of officers is fairly well filled now. However, I shall keep plugging and see what turns up. Anyway, 13 weeks' basic will take care of me for a long while.

Perhaps the hardest problem of any soldier is to make the social or even the emotional adjustment from civilian to army life. Army life is so much different from anything that a civilian has experienced that this adjustment becomes a problem. All the liberties, rights and freedom of action that the civilian has experienced are waived and the soldier learns to do as he is ordered. The chances are that your corporal, or sergeant, probably has an 8th grade or part of a high school education. Yet he is boss. He must live up to the orders given him by his higher-ups. For example, this is what happens. The other evening we were lined up for retreat and the corporal verbally burned us in hell by his language because one of the fellows had not buttoned his button on his shirt pocket. Yet, here stood the corporal in front of us with his own shirt button open. It's a job to keep your mouth shut on occasions such as this.

I hope I haven't sounded too morose in this letter. Really we are all getting along quite well. Of course none of us likes the army—nobody in it does—but we are working like hell to get this job done. I guess it will be finished more quickly if we all do our part. Believe me, it will be a great day in the morning when our job is done.

Since I have been "at attention" too long, I had better "fall out" and "take a break."

As ever,
Pvt. H. S.

John Alexander Griffin, of East Chicago, enlisted in the Army Air Cadet training program from Northwestern University, Dec. 14, 1942, and was called to active duty Feb. 20, 1943. He finished his advanced pilot training at Pecos, Texas, in May 1944. Sent overseas on Nov. 21, 1944, Griffin was killed on his first mission to Kassel, Germany, on Dec. 15, 1944. F/O Griffin was awarded the Purple Heart, a Citation of Honor by Gen. Arnold, and an accolade by President Roosevelt, all posthumously.

January 13, 1944
Cal-Aero Flight Academy

DEAR BOB:

I think I will write this one mainly to Bob in order to get him ready for what he has to face. Yes, it is undoubtedly the hardest part of the training. You may think that you are in good physical shape—and as a civilian you probably are—but you are not toughened for endurance like the army wants you to be. As you go away from the Basic Training Center the courses will actually be harder, the hours longer, and the freedom less. Still, after you have once become used to the army, these different stages of stepping up your activity will be made easily in comparison to this initial change that you are about to make. You and I have gone on long hikes together, for long bike rides, and for other such pleasure trips which required physical endurance. On the first two or three mile hikes it will seem more or less the same to you. It will probably be a pleasure. You will be a soldier for the first time, you will see yourself marching bravely into tough situations of the future; and you will be proud of your new uniform. After waiting in long lines for clothes, roll calls, shots and many other things, you will gladly welcome the activity of a long hike. But remember, when we did these things at home we took perhaps two or three in a summer and when we arrived home, although supper was perhaps cold because of our long delay, still it was waiting. And there was scarcely a time when we were asked to do further work after one of our long escapades to Wicker Park or the airport. In the army, however, you will find it different.

You will remember how you used to enjoy drilling in band during football season, so likewise, you will for a few weeks be eager about your drill. However, I doubt whether this enjoyment will last for so long a time if you are required, as in most basic training camps, to drill from 6:30 A.M. to 11:30 A.M. each day with ten minutes break every hour. Each week the drill in band is varied by new formations and enlivened by music, but in your first training, the drill will always be the same. It is especially true in basic training that the drill instructors are very dull and lacking in initiative so that you scarcely ever get a leader who has new ideas to liven up the task. And you will have student officers, who will be picked from the ranks, who will have trouble enough figuring out the correct foot for the command of execution much less any interesting drill. So you will have many hours of left flank, right flank, and to the rear march. I notice in your letter of today a note of eagerness about physical training. This is all good and well but be careful not to express this sentiment. You will want to march in step, and it will hurt you to be marching on the offbeat of the music. Still you will have to do this without question. At times I have become overly disgusted by this and have sounded off out of turn. On week ends I walked tours. You probably will do the same thing. Remember, you are always wiser than the one who is in front leading the outfit; so laugh at him to yourself while doing as he says, for he has the authority. Then later you will see him washed out with all the rest of his kind.

This idea of eagerness is very good in all things in the army, but as I said before, do not show it. Do as the majority of the fellows do in your actions. Don't try to be the first one out to formation or the one who marches the straightest, but just be average. In the classroom studies you can excell without prejudice.

But do not try to show off your knowledge. Just keep it to yourself and put down the right answers on the final exams. This will be what counts. In school and college the instructor always has quite a bit of personal contact with the students. In the army there is none, which makes you think that your efforts are not being noticed and that others who are not working at all are getting as much credit as you. You will think this more than ever as the dumb ones are always chosen for student officers. But on the contrary all your grades are being kept in an ever-increasing record. And if they are good you will have a better chance of success. Many fellows came to Cal-Aero simply because they had good grades in ground school at Santa Ana. This is really a break, since here there are more instructors than at the army-operated fields. Thus you have a better chance of success if you are sent to a good primary. About half the boys sent to Thunderbird washed out, not because they couldn't fly so well, but because the instructors cannot handle so many students as are sent to that field. However, do not work too hard. The army will make it rough enough that you won't have to push yourself in order to keep busy.

Anyway, in basic training you won't have to worry about this. All you will do there is drill in the morning and physical training and road runs in the afternoon. Sometimes you will get rifle drill, or obstacle course, or gas mask drill, or commando tactics, or lectures on the articles of war and hygiene, or orientation speeches, or sometimes you will wait in line to sign the payroll or get paid. In any case, you will not look forward to this time as an exciting adventure. You will trudge through it hoping for the time to pass swiftly so that you can get to the more interesting things of the future, and when you are long passed it you will look back at it with knowing what it is and will pray never to have to go through such a period again in your life.

At first when you come into the army you will be ignorant of rank to a certain extent. You will not notice much difference in uniforms. Then you will begin to notice the difference in the emblem on the officer's hat, and you will begin to notice how much better their clothes fit and how much darker their blouse is than yours. In a few months you will know all of the different ranks. You will notice how the G.I., regular soldiers, treat you when they find out you are a cadet. At Sheppard Field the G.I. privates and sergeants and all tried to make us feel that we were the lowest type person in the army. This is purely jealousy. But after two months of this type of treatment, you cannot help but feel that you are a higher type than they. After a time the word G.I. comes to mean a lower type of soldier. The cadets do not wish it this way at first, but it is forced upon them by this time at basic training. I could give you a lot of advice about what to do, but I shall not. I am just trying to present a picture of what might happen to you if the situation is still the same as when I came through.

I cannot picture everything clearly to you for I cannot send you a box of Texas dust to pour liberally over your whole body. I cannot send you a long hot road and a fine set of blisters or a pair of heavy G.I. shoes to be broken in. I cannot send you an overcoat which you will not be allowed to wear at reveille when it is freezing, but which you will be required to wear during the sweltering afternoon. I cannot send you aching muscles or a tired body which falls asleep each time it even gets near a bed. I cannot send you a shrill blasting whistle which will waken you each day at 5:30 A.M., nor the needles to stick yourself with in order to keep from getting some diseases. About half the men who go through basic training find it necessary to go to the hospital for a week or two to recover from the extreme change in life and climate. All of these things you will find out yourself, and you will do all right because I believe you have the spirit that is needed to bring you through a tough assignment. After a time that spirit will probably change to endurance, but nevertheless, you will be all right. . . .

JOHN

Harry B. Noon, of Indianapolis, enlisted in the Air Corps in July, 1942, and was commissioned a 2d lieutenant in Dec. 1943. He was sent to England in May 1944 and assigned to the 334th Fighter Squadron, 4th Fighter Group. On his fourth mission Lt. Noon was killed over France on June 11, 1944.

March 14, 1944
Bartow AAF, Fla.

DEAR FOLKS:

I'm about ready to take a big, long sleep. I'm really tired. Today I tangled with the "Great Iron Bird," the P-51. I feel I've been in a fight with a wildcat and run over by a steam roller at the same time. It scares the h—— out of you but handles swell. The first take-off and the first landing are the worst—or at least I hope so. I flew two different periods for a total of three hours, and I can truthfully say it's a whole week's work.

They devised a new traffic pattern for us to fly the first three times up—they say for safer and better flying. The army has lost one of the swellest boys it ever had. Rivers spun it on the 450-degree leg of the pattern from one thousand feet. There is no mysterious explanation of it. We all know what happened. Flying so low as to approach a stall, he poured the coal to it. She did a snap roll to the right, a split "S" from a thousand feet surely doesn't give one a ghost of a chance to recover. It happens too fast.

That's the way we'd all want it, if our number comes around, so short and sweet that we don't have time to think about it. It's hard to realize that the guys you joke with, play volleyball with, or drink a few brews with, could completely vanish from our midst. I know that Rivers wouldn't want anyone moping around for him. He'd just like you to drink a beer for him, break the glass, then dance on his coffin. I know it's none too pleasant to talk about, but that's just the way the boys feel.

It's a beautiful thought and a consolation we have in the old slogan of "Good pilots never die. They only fly away." Because I'm sure as the devil that old Rivers will be up there in pilot's heaven flying formation with Otley, Goodsen, Katy and P. M. Riley. God only knows how long it might be before we'll all join them. They're all swell fellows and I can't think of any better company.

Don't let my conversation worry you, because we all know how the odds are and what to expect when and if our number is due. I think that fliers are all sentimentalists at heart. We don't let any morbid thought keep us from what we love. There isn't one among us that wouldn't rather go that way than be grounded. We feel that we're doing something that's very special and the danger only gives us acceleration toward our great love—flying. You can call it the old theme of perhaps manifest destiny, but I think that it's only the spirit within a man which makes his body and soul free, when he raises his earthborn self into the blue above. There is something up there which calls you to indulge in endless ecstasy.

Your loving son,
HARRY

Raymond K. Mitchell, of Marion, enlisted in the Marine Air Corps Oct. 8, 1943, and took his boot training at San Diego, Calif., and later was transferred to Miramar, Calif. He was assigned to the aviation technical school at Norman, Okla., and from there was sent to Cherry Point, N. C., then back to Calif. Leaving the U. S. in Feb. 1945 as an aviation machinist, Mitchell saw duty on Hawaii, Eniwetok, Engebi,

Guam, Ulithi, Peleliu, Iwo Jima, and Okinawa, receiving the 4th Marine Air Wing for defense of Engebi. Promoted to the rank of corporal, Mitchell was discharged June 6, 1946, and is now employed at the Osborn Paper Co., Marion.

November 24, 1944
Mojave, California

DEAREST FOLKS:

There it goes again. That steady clickety-click, click of the train wheels. Now and then you can hear that lonesome moan of the whistle as we cross another road. Each one putting one more mile of distance between us and home. We are now in some little town in Georgia, approximately one hour out of Augusta. The scenery down here is beautiful but not near as lovely as the corner of 40th and Poplar Streets.

Everybody's indulging in something or other. Poker games, reading books, writing letters while still others are just thinking. Nobody knows what they are thinking about but 10–1 says it's that little girl in New York, Chicago, St. Louis or wherever he may be from. That's usually the thought on a young man's mind. We all know that what we have to do might not be so pleasant. That's why we think of the girls. I wonder whom she would marry if something happens to me? That's the exact words a guy asked me last eve. In my case I have no girl trouble. If I can't find one when I get back, it's just too bad.

This train is strictly G.I. No passengers aboard except Marines. We have only one destination, carrier duty in the South Pacific. No letters will be mailed, no telegrams sent or phone calls to be made while en route. Although we are going clear across the United States and passing thousands of towns we are still cut off entirely from civilians. People who haven't ridden a troop train can't understand this because it sounds a little, shall we say, fictitious. We have our own G.I. government aboard even though we are continually traveling. We have guards standing at every entrance so as to be sure no one or anything will either board or leave this train. These men are all trained, both for discipline and for their certain job. No chances can be taken. These men are vital and must be transported safely to their destination. We are the first to man a carrier. Sure we're proud, haven't we a right to be? We've been through many long months of schooling and training and we are very proud to execute our skill toward ridding the world of the enemy. We have everything aboard from truck drivers to the commanding officers. There are ten cars. Yes, ten cars of men who are waiting, impatiently, to do what they can against the enemy. Some with revenge in their eyes, others for the thrill and excitement of warfare and still others because it's their patriotic duty. It all adds up to one thing, peace and home once again to a peaceful and lasting endurance.

Most of the boys are just coming back from the diner now. I've already had chow myself. I was one of the lucky ones to be called first. We ate in Augusta this morning, but we picked up a diner somewhere and from now on we'll eat on the train. It's excellent chow, what there is of it. Maybe it won't be so long between meals now. There was eight hours between breakfast and dinner. Too long for a heavy eating squadron of Marines.

Still in Georgia. Steady rhythm of the wheels is deafening. Car is bouncing so I can hardly write. The men are quiet now. Heavy concentration. Probably thinking of their wives and kids and families. We've only been on the go twenty-four hours. A lot of them haven't ever made this trip before. Wait until the 5th or 6th day, they'll feel like tearing this train apart. Nothing to do but sit and watch and wait. Three of the hardest things to do when you know every minute you are being taken farther from your loved ones. Yes, we'll be ready to go aboard that carrier. Ready to settle up with the ones who are making us go through the misery of leaving home. We're out to get you, Tojo, each of us with our own secret weapon. Sure we'll tell you what it is; it's very common, a little thing called pride. We have our share, in fact your share too, because that's what you lack. We've enough pride to keep after you until you're downed, once and for all. Enough pride that no matter how difficult the problem is, we'll never turn back, because we are the United States Marines. We aren't glory boys. I know the papers and magazines state us as such, but we aren't; we just want to get this over with and get back to our homes. Home, where we can get up when we want to, sleep when we want to, enjoy the comfort and love which we should deserve. Lots of people think we are killers at heart but we aren't, we are just trained for warfare which is the exact opposite of what we have been brought up to believe. We might have complained a little when we first came in about how rough they treated us. At the time it seemed fantastic and unnecessary, but now we realize it was for our benefit and we are honored to know that we went through the ordeal and proved ourselves worthy of the name of a Marine.

Sunday afternoon and still riding. New Orleans just a couple of hours back. Louisiana is an odd sort of state to me. Marshes and swamplands every place. The climate is much the same as Indiana. The fields and trees remind me of southern Indiana. Passed a lot of different army and naval bases. As we ride determinedly ahead we pass many unusual and interesting sights. The shipyards at New Orleans, for instance. Fields of cotton. Many things which don't seem of importance to me. To me this is a business trip and I don't enjoy this scenery because I have no loved ones to share my pleasure. I've finally realized what the word love means. The most beautiful creature in the world is homely unless you have the one you love to share your ecstasy.

Expecting to hit California about Wednesday night. We are hoping to at least.

I'm wondering what you folks are doing right now. Sunday afternoon at approximately 2:00 P.M. (I just passed the Cotton Bowl football stadium.) It was beautiful. See if I can guess what you are doing. Maybe Rut and Ed are visiting or vice versa. Mom's clearing away dinner dishes. Dad's exercising his roosters. Right?

Just pulled into Baton Rouge. Beautiful city. Wish I could visit. Of course that kind of stuff is out, at least until the war ends. I think I'll take a little trip after the war, more for spite than pleasure. I want to be able to get off a train at a station and deliberately miss it. Maybe when the next one comes in I'll miss it too. Just to be able to have the feeling of freedom again. Probably send out a hundred telegrams announcing the time we leave, arrival and what route we are to take. Without worrying about a court martial. What a wonderful dream that is.

It is now about 9:30 A.M. Monday morning. Still clipping off the miles. Just came from breakfast. Had to wait until we picked up a couple of diners. We just passed Camp Hood. Sure is a big place. By the way, we are somewhere in Texas. Rolling plains are the scenery. Ranch houses off in the distance. The sun's shining bright but it's just a wee bit chilly. Frost still on the ground from last night. We had to catch a ferry from New Orleans to some little town. Loaded the whole train aboard. When we got on the other side we picked up a different engine and the engineer was one of the boys' father. What luck! He rode in the engine for two hundred miles with him. He sure was a happy lad.

Yep, it's still Monday, 5:50 P.M. to be correct. The scenery is changing quite a bit now although we are still in Texas. Pretty thickly wooded through this part. Lots and lots of cactus. Big as our whole house. This is typical western scenery. Looking for Indians to massacre us any moment now. Mountains are becoming more frequent now. Expect to be in New Mexico by midnight. Of course, that is, taken for granted that we don't have a flat tire. Ha!

You know something? I've been thinking things over. I figure it's going to take me a long time to get used to civilian life again. If and when I get back don't feel alarmed if I act strangely. Even on those four days I felt out of place. I guess what they say is right. Once a Marine always a Marine. You can't understand what I'm trying to say, I know, it's just something I've been thinking about.

Tuesday morning. Still trucking on down. Left New Mexico about one hour ago. Mountains are everywhere. Just pulled out of Holbrook, Arizona. I'm certainly glad we are getting closer. My back aches, my eyes hurt, I'm a complete physical wreck. I've ridden trains so much the last fourteen months I feel I should be drawing interest. New Mexico is 7,200 feet above sea level and even the desert has snow on the ground. Water was coated with ice. What a country! Just stopped at Winslow, Arizona, for chow. Wonderful place. I've been looking at the map. Here are the states I've seen on this trip—North Carolina, South Carolina, Georgia, Alabama, Louisiana, Mississippi, Texas, New Mexico, Arizona and California. These are the ones I've seen since October, 1943. Colorado, Oklahoma, Kansas, Utah, Missouri, Nebraska, Iowa, Illinois, Kentucky, Tennessee, Arkansas, West Virginia, Virginia, Maryland, Washington, D. C., Pennsylvania and Ohio. By the time I get back I will be able to name over as many islands in the South Pacific. By the way, I can tell you this now. Payday is just around the corner. Of the ten bucks I received from you just before I left I had exactly forty-two cents to make this trip. I had to pay a debt and spent the rest on clothes. I'll bet that's a record. Thirty-three hundred miles on forty-two cents. That's really being thrifty, eh? This trip would cost a civilian at least $300.

Sure am getting anxious to find out more about this carrier duty. Hope it's the "Shangri La." Sounds romantic. Have to have some kind of romance, because the real McCoy is going to be few and far between. Just passed over a canyon. Three hundred feet high. Nice place to commit honorable hara-kiri. I'm still on the lookout for Injuns. May be in California a little ahead of time. Made good time through New Mexico. Will send this out as soon as I get there.

Wednesday, November 29, 1944. Arrived in Mojave this morning at approximately 8:30 A.M. (Pacific time). The scenery surrounding us is really one of nature's loveliest. We are enclosed by snow-peaked mountains forming a half moon. The camp itself is situated right on the Mojave desert. When I get more time I will give the scenery more discussion. Just want you to know I'm positively O. K. and hope everything is the same at home. Little tired from the trip, but outside of that I'm tiptop. Don't worry about me.

Your son,
RAY

Norma F. Popp (Mrs. Charles Albert), of Speed, enlisted in the WAVES Nov. 16, 1944, and was sent to Hunter College, N. Y., for training. Achieving the rank of yeoman 1/c, Mrs. Albert was discharged July 19, 1946, and is now a medical stenographer at a hospital in Oneonta, N. Y., and resides in Sidney, N. Y.

16 Jan. 1945
Stillwater, Okla.

HELLO MR. DORSEY:

You won't believe it, but I have finally found time to sit down and write a letter to you. So much has happened that I believe I could write a book on it in order to cover everything. But I'll try to think of the most interesting points and forget the others.

The Navy doesn't waste any time in getting the new "boots" in good marching order because, upon arrival at Hunter, we were given these wonderful "G.I. nylon hose" (lisle) and hats and were immediately hupped to the mess hall. It was one sad sight to see everybody trudging along in the rain and at the same time trying to keep in step with the cadence which we had never heard of before. It sounds funny now, but we were in misery at the time.

As luck would have it, Frances and I were assigned the same apartment in which to live—she having the upper bunk, and me the lower. There were nine other girls in this apartment and we got along excellently, even though we would practically knock each other down during the morning rush and before mustering times.

Reveille was at 6 o'clock and we had until 7:30 to get dressed and to clean the apartment. An hour and a half may sound like ample time, but everything had to be in shipshape condition, and when I say shipshape I mean that there can't be a speck of dust or dirt anywhere nor could anything whatsoever be left lying around. Each thing had a specific place to be put. Each day our Specialist would inspect, and if anything was untidy, demerits were given, which you worked off each Friday night while the other girls had fun. Anyone with less than five demerits was excused and, since I had only three, I didn't have to work them off. Some of the girls really got their share of them though. Taps were at 9:30 on every night except Saturday when we had until 10:30.

From Saturday noon until Monday morning we had liberty. However, we were compelled to eat meals, and we couldn't go off the station grounds. Movies and variety shows were arranged for us so we usually went to them. On Sundays we all went to church in a group. Services were held in the auditorium and were very interesting.

Each day during "boot" was a full schedule in itself. Besides drilling, we also went to classes where we learned all about the different uniforms, ranks and ratings of the service. Educational movies and war orientation were given too—all of which was very interesting.

Going through the "Daisy Chain" was quite the stuff—if you know what I mean. We went in company formation and there we were, all 240 of us, waiting in line to be jabbed in the arm. Altogether we had three typhoid shots, one smallpox and a double tetanus shot. Believe you me, you continued with the daily routine too, even if you did feel as though you wanted to cry on mama's shoulder. You knew that she wasn't there so you struggled on.

Our mess hall was a half-mile away. It was a nice "little" walk on pretty days, but during the cold, slick weather it wasn't so good. Christmas at Hunter was as nice as it could be, being away from home. I'm sending a pamphlet which covers everything about Christmas at Hunter.

There were 360 of us who left Hunter on a Tuesday afternoon for Stillwater. On our way here we went through Canada, which was rather exciting. We had a thirty-minute layover in Moberly, Missouri. It was called ahead that we were to stop there, and as we got off the train, the American Legion served coffee, doughnuts and cakes to us. They had already served two troop trains that day, but we were the first group of WAVES they had served.

The WAVES live in one of the dorms here at A. & M. [Oklahoma Agricultural & Mechanical College]. Our barracks are very neat. I am very pleased with my roommates. The three of them are nice girls. The majority of the girls are nice. We are training to become yeomen, and will have a three months' course during which time we will take up shorthand, typing, history and navy correspondence. We have civilian teachers and they make the classes very interesting.

Well, Mr. Dorsey, I've rambled on and on and I had better close for now and do some studying. . . .

Sincerely,
NORMA

Arnold McKee, of Clay City, was inducted into the Navy as an apprentice seaman on Nov. 11, 1943. He was sent to Radar Operator's School at Virginia Beach, Va., and was rated radarman 3/c. Transferred to the Combat Information Center School at Little Creek, Va., McKee was later assigned to the U.S.S. "Scroggins" (DE 799), spending 19 months aboard this ship. RdM 2/c McKee was discharged Nov. 9, 1945, and is now a retail grocer in Clay City.

April 25, 1945
New York, N. Y.

DEAR HARRY:

As I begin this letter the radio announcer is trying to find new words and phrases to describe the Allied advance on Berlin. If this war lasts much longer the newspapers and radio newsmen are going to be in strait jackets, trying to outdo each other in describing the front line picture.

We came in last Sunday for a few days of recreation. We can really appreciate it, too, after a winter in the North Atlantic. We stumbled on a poor old lonely sub about 400 miles off Cape Cod, and proceeded to sink same. Up around Halifax and Newfoundland all winter, where the subs are supposed to be thick as hell and no luck. They sent us home and on the way in we accidentally found this one—just like rabbit hunting all day without getting any, and then as you cross the back yard one jumps up.

The damn subs had us screwy up north all winter. They would sink a merchant ship, or occasionally, an escort, and by the time we arrived they would be to hell out, or safely bottomed among the wrecks and rocks. The "sound men" went nuts trying to distinguish sub echoes from bottom echoes.

This one by himself really didn't have much of a chance. The hedgehogs were fired, they exploded, and about one-half minute later there was an underwater explosion that shook the hell out of us, and us on top, by that time 300 or so yards away. There was a lot of oil came to the surface, a lot of papers, plus a lot of other things—many of them with German markings. Most of the officers are under the impression that the navy will give it a Class B rating. For a Class A, I think you have to have the sub's skipper's autograph.

I noticed a headline in last night's paper that the army is to discharge all men over forty-two—so all I have to do is convince the navy to do the same—then serve ten more years and "lo and behold" I'm a civilian again. Simple. The forty-two ruling probably won't affect anyone from around home, but it is very cheerful news. Anyway, it's a step in the right direction.

We are tied at the 35th Street Pier, Brooklyn; you probably have a pretty good idea of about where that is. There is a newly commissioned hospital ship tied at the next pier—really a thing of beauty—if I thought I could find my way out of it, I would go over and ask to go aboard.

As always,
ARNOLD

P. S.—Someone just came in and said that a group of DE's were attacked by seven subs just off Norfolk—so we may see some more action ere long. I don't believe that the navy has announced this sinking as yet, so perhaps there shouldn't be too much said about it.

Frank A. Renneisen, of Jasper, was inducted into the Army July 24, 1943, and, qualifying for aviation cadet, was commissioned a 2d lieutenant Nov. 11, 1944. He was first stationed at Jefferson Barracks, then after attending A.A.F. Navigation School, Hondo, Tex., he was transferred to Great Bend A.A.F., Kans. From April to May 1945 Lt. Renneisen was stationed in the West Indies, and from July 1945 to Aug. 1946 he was on Okinawa. Discharged Aug. 31, 1946, Renneisen is an electrician in Lawrence, Kans.

July 17, 1945
Great Bend, Kans.

DEAR MOM:

Well, here I am. I haven't been particularly busy but was "sweating out" transfer to staging before writing. A watched pot never boils so I decided to write. We are still on the three-day routine which keeps us occupied but is not as bad as continuous flying. Trainers and ground school are routine but a resumé of a flying day might be interesting to a "paddlefoot" like yourself or the "hicks" [two younger brothers].

The day begins with getting up at 3:30 and rushing to the mess hall for quick breakfast and filling your coffee bottle. From here to squadron to pick up pencil clip-board and then to navigation office for logs before getting to briefing room at 0400. General briefing starts here at 0400 with entire crews together. C. O. gives latest info on squadron policy, S-2 reads the latest war news, operations officers go over the route, targets, requirements and formations to be flown, and the weather office gives the weather en route. This normally takes about 35 to 40 minutes.

Then the crews split up for special briefing. Gunners, Gunnery Officer; Radio, Communication Officer; Bombs, Bomb Officer; Navigation, Navigation Officer; Radar Operators attend one or both of the navigators' and bombardiers' briefing. At Navigation we get courses, distances, altitude, danger areas, E.T.A.'s (estimated time of arrival), and at Bomb, we get target charts, aerial photos, bomb types, bomb procedure, I.P.'s, etc.

From here we go to Personal Equipment, and get into our flying clothes and pick up Mae Wests, parachutes, harness and lunches, thermos jugs, life rafts, etc. Now it's about 5:30 and "Stations" is scheduled at 0620.

You carry your equipment out to the plane and begin preflight. For me, it's check the different radar sets, check the proper reports for signatures and obtain them if missing, assist bombardier in pre-flighting bomb racks and loading bombs, also loading and checking forward turrets, check cameras and camera hatches and leveling of cameras. Also store your equipment aboard.

Now the crews line up for inspection where the A/C checks parachutes, harness fit, Mae Wests and oxygen masks. It's now 0615, we hope. We take the dorm lock off the landing gear and bomb bay doors and get to our combat stations. Except the bombardier and myself, who ride the rear compartment on the take-off as the ship is nose heavy with a large gasoline load.

We start the engines at 6:25, taxi at 6:30 in the order of formation position. Take off at 0645. Start climbing on course to our first turning point. Now I crawl up through the tunnel to my position and get about my business as a Radar Observer. All this other is just incidental to the trade. From here on I'll describe a specific mission (our last one).

We leave Great Bend at 3000' flying on a 152° heading till we get to the coast west of New Orleans where we drop down to 500 feet and go on a dogleg over the Gulf to arrive at our first target at the briefed E.T.A. southwest of New Orleans. We come in over our first target, a river, and mine it (five mines per ship), and then start climbing to assemble the formation at 10,000 feet. At Alexandria, La., at 12:29. We've been flying as individual ships thus far. At Alexandria we found thunderstorm activity at 10,000 feet, so the leader changed the altitude to 20,000.

We are now about seven hours in the air. From here we go to Houston, Texas, in bomb formation (3 flights in train) on a convoy in the Gulf, 5 bombs per ship. While over the Gulf we practice firing the turrets. Now we reassemble in group formation and return to Great Bend arriving at 1800. The planes peel off at 12 second intervals and land. Now we clear the turrets, take out the guns, clean them, and lug our equipment back to squadron, fill out flight reports, report to

Interrogation, get out of our flying clothes and clean up. It's now 1930. You are now free to take care of your personal affairs, such as feeding your face. You had lunch (I forgot), 2 sandwiches and coffee and, if lucky, an orange or apple, at approximately 1200. The mess hall closed at 1900, so you go to the Snack Bar for a substantial meal of a hamburger and milk shake, or maybe a cheese sandwich. But then you have the next day off, except for trainers.

Here's the latest, won't guarantee it. Be leaving here Friday and going to Kearney, Nebraska. There about a week and then to California and out. Going to the 8th Air Force under Gen. Doolittle in Okinawa. Be the first B-29's to operate off Okinawa. Also first with the new radar. We were originally scheduled to go to the Philippines, but the war changed too quick.

Will send home quite a bit of junk. I'll write you what to do with it.

Love,
FRANK

→ III ←

NORTH AFRICA

WITH their first expeditionary force, the American and British troops invaded northwest Africa on November 7, 1942, landing near Oran and Algiers. A few hours later American forces landed at Casablanca, where the most vigorous resistance was met. Algiers surrendered on the 8th of November, Oran on the 9th, and Casablanca on the 11th. The German conquest of North Africa was brought to a halt by the defeat of Field Marshal Rommel at El Alamein in October 1942 at the hands of the British Eighth Army under Field Marshal Montgomery. The Germans retreated to Tunisia and again met the British at the German defenses along the Mareth Line, the border fortifications of Tunisia. Meanwhile American troops were fighting to the north, and together the British and American forces turned the Afrika Korps back. On April 7, 1943, the Americans entered Bizerte while the British were entering Tunis. Part of the German army trapped between these two Allied forces surrendered on May 8, while the remainder was driven into the Cape Bon peninsula and surrendered the next day.

John Hays Brown, of New Albany, was inducted into the Army Nov. 12, 1941, and was attached to the field artillery. He was sent to North Ireland, May 1942, and served there and in Scotland, England, North Africa, and Italy. He was attached to the 34th Division and later to the 85th Division, and rose to the rank of master sergeant, Dec. 20, 1944. Following the Tunisian campaign, he was landed at Salerno, Italy, and fought to the Swiss border. Discharged Aug. 30, 1945, M/Sgt. Brown returned to New Albany to work.

May 19, 1943
Tunisia

DEAREST FOLKS:

You've been wondering ever since I hit here just where I was and what I've been doing. Now it can be told, so get out your maps. We landed at Oran, about the third of January, and were bivouacked just outside of there at a little town called Assi-Ben-Okla about 10 days. We moved from there to another camp just outside of Tlemcen and remained here until February 7th.

On the 7th of February we started our trek to the front and we really covered some territory. The first night out we stopped at Sidi-Bel-Abbes, which by the way is the home of the French Foreign Legion. We proceeded from there to Orleansville, and on to L'Arba, Sidi Embarek, Ain M'Lila, Souk Ahras, and finally pulled into a bivouac area outside of Maktar, about 20 miles from the front lines.

We lay around this camp for several days and then went into position at Shiba; this was on February 18th and the next day we got our first taste of action. Jerry started an attack through the Kasserine Pass aimed at Tala and Tebessa. In two days of hot fighting we repulsed this attack and our artillery was credited with having knocked out several tanks. After this we just lay around for almost a month, while it rained and the weather hampered all movements.

On about the 26th of March we moved up to Hadjeh El Aouin and from there launched an attack on Fondouk. We were in this area for over a week and I believe it was here we took our worst beatings. We were under constant artillery fire and every day were either bombed or strafed by Stukas and Messerschmitts. However, a break-through was finally effected and contact was made with the British Eighth Army between Kairouan and Sousse. This was the 10th of April and the beginning of the end of Jerry.

After lying around this same spot for a few days we pulled out and went back to our bivouac area just out of Maktar. We stayed there for three or four days and then I left on a reconnaissance party to the north. We went through Maktar, Le Kef, Souk el Arba, Ain Draham, Tabarca, Djebel Aboid, and were attached to the 9th Division several miles east of Sedjenane. We stayed there for a couple of weeks and took part in the break through Baldy and Green Mountains at Jefna. This eventually led to the capture of Mateur and Bizerte.

We rejoined the 34th Division at Hill 609 just after they had captured it in some of the bloodiest fighting of this campaign. We then moved into position about 10 miles west of Tebourba and started in shelling Jerry once more. This was on about the 5th of May. At 3 A.M. on the morning of May 6th, we opened up with a terrific artillery barrage and the infantry advanced under the cover of it. We could see the flashes of the British 1st Army's artillery on our right flank and two days later we got the news that they had taken Tunis. That about winds everything up, as we are still in the same locality as we were when things wound up. All in all it's been rough and tough going and I've seen all of the bloodshed and killing I care for. However, it's been exciting as hell and we got plenty of laughs out of the whole thing.

I hope this puts you up to date on everything and clarifies a lot of things you've been wondering about. The wreck I mentioned being in happened just outside of Ain Draham when I was going north. Also our trip from Tlemcen, Algeria to Maktar, Tunisia was about 900 miles and took seven days in convoy. Bye for now. Write soon and often.

Love,
SONNY

James B. Christen, of Decatur, enlisted in the Air Corps, Sept. 4, 1941, and was commissioned a 2d lieutenant, May 20, 1942. He was sent to North Africa in November as a pilot with the 36th Troop Carrier Squadron, 316th Troop Carrier Group. After flying in the North African campaign, he was promoted to 1st lieutenant, Jan. 24, 1943, and participated in the invasion of Sicily. There Lt. Christen was killed in action, July 11, 1943. He was awarded the Air Medal posthumously.

Dec. 3, 1942
North Africa

DEAR MOM:

What goes on back in that little old town of Decatur? I'm really a long ways from there now. And how I'd love to be back! At least this has been an interesting experience. I'll bet I'm the only person in Decatur who has flown across the Atlantic. Except for being something new and different, the trip over here was routine and at times almost monotonous. Of course I can't tell you where we are or when we got here, but we've been here for quite some time, and I've been to Cairo, saw the Pyramids, Sphinx, the Nile and the Suez Canal.

It's rather fun to shop over here. Everyone—except us—seems to think that the Yanks are made of money and when it comes to buying anything you stand and argue for half an hour over the price. We haven't done a whole lot since we've been here, and we're all itching to get up to the front. Of course, we don't have any luxuries around here; but we manage to improvise a little bit on things we need—but we won't be able to improvise any snow for a white Christmas.

How's everyone getting along at home? . . .

Love,

JIM

Frank H. Woltman, of South Bend, enlisted in the Air Corps Dec. 30, 1940, and was commissioned a 2d lieutenant Aug. 15, 1941. He was sent overseas in Jan. 1942, and assigned to the 7th Bombardment Group of the 9th Air Force in India. In June 1942 he was promoted to 1st lieutenant and later was sent to North Africa with the 376th Bombardment Group. There he won the Air Medal, the Silver Star, and the Purple Heart. Lt. Woltman lost his life when his plane was shot down Jan. 31, 1943, over Sicily.

5 January 1943
North Africa

DEAR DAD:

This is in answer to your letter written November 9th, '42. I have taken a long time to answer it but—I'm catching up with the mail I received on and since Christmas Eve. Now—I only have 23 cards and letters. Of course, that includes a bill at the Mitchel Field P.X. which I'll have to write a check for and the Mitchel Officer's Club.

Our V-mail letters get back to the States a bit quicker than the regular mail, I think. However, coming this way they are held up at New York until they are photoed and again at Cairo where they are printed so we can read them. The regular mail has gotten through as soon as 15 days after being mailed. The V-mail *sometimes* gets here that soon but usually takes a week longer. The Limies have charge of the printing and they do their own mail first, letting ours go till they get time. Then, too, as long as the boys at Cairo get their mail, they are satisfied. They sent the Theater Postal Inspector down here to see what I was beefing about so I told him just to read the report I'd sent in. I admitted things were getting a little better—except for the cigarette packages.

I could have sworn I told you about the ME-110 that "WE" got. Well, Halpro went out after a convoy and they took 9 ships, 3 of them with "The famous 9th" men flying them. They gave us the damndest plane, we found out later. Anyhow, we found the ship O.K. and the 3 elements peeled off to take separate runs and our bomb racks didn't work. Toomey called his wing man (9th) and told him he wanted fighter protection as his bombs "hung" and he was going around. In that first run we hit an ME-109 and the tail gunners got another plane from the rear. Toomey pulled out and went around, dropping his bombs, with the planes in good formation, fighting another plane off. The Halpro guys were scared silly and were bending their throttles, trying to get away from the new fighters. We tried to catch up and just as we were nearing them, we saw this twin-tailed plane emitting puffs of smoke. It was then that we decided it was an enemy plane—coming right at us. Toomey was still griped about the bombs hanging and when he saw the German coming, he was in a fighting mood. The Liberators only have 3 guns in the nose but Toomey pulled up, with the wing men right with him, and used his nose guns like a pursuit plane. The other planes did the same and our navigator used his flexible gun. The top turret, just in back of us, was banging away and it sounded just like a boiler factory starting to work all of a sudden. The inside of the cockpit filled up with smoke from the guns, empty shell cases were clanking around and it was a noisy moment. It was just a moment but it was all that was needed. The poor guy never had a chance. His left engine was on fire before we passed him and began a dive to the water for a landing before it went out of control. Broadwell had his No. 3 engine shot out so—he feathered the prop and kept on, with Andy (James Anderson who flew with Colonel Wade in Java and Burma) tacking on to his wing to protect him against any other fighters. (They always attack a lagging plane—or one which is partially disabled.)

Toomey was still fighting mad so—he turned in a 180-degree circle and followed the Messerschmitt down till it hit the water. We saw one man and a life raft—or we saw both the pilot and observer in the water. We didn't strafe them—letting them remain to be picked up and let the Germans know how tough we are from the front. (That is our weakest spot, incidentally.) We were worried about Broadwell getting back O.K. (his first raid as pilot), and even after dark we fretted about. We hit the coastline at Gaza and turned north, failing to see the field. It wasn't lit up, though they did light the runway just after we passed over. Everyone was up in front, looking ahead and of course the tail gunner wasn't in the back end. We were the first ones to pass the field. The navigator thought he'd brought us home so—he started closing up for the night. We flew a bit and then decided to try out radio compass. The needle showed us off course so we followed the needle at times, turning it off once in a while to not use up the radio. It was very weak. We could hear the field faintly but they couldn't hear us so well. Every time we switched back to the radio compass, the needle showed us way off course. We leaned out the mixture and cut the r.p.m.'s down and pulled the throttles back. We got lower so we could see through the clouds and suddenly saw a mountain ahead. We increased the r.p.m.'s and throttles and climbed as fast as we could. We got over that O.K. and still fiddled around.

The navigator was trying to take a star-fix but we'd keep turning too much. He was heartbroken to think we were lost—and it wasn't his fault. We decided to follow the radio compass though we thought it was off. They keep telling us to believe the instruments—our own judgment is more liable to be "off." We flew and flew, headed for the station at Jerusalem because it was the only one we could hear. The radio operator got busy, the British filter system was contacted and they'd been tracking us all the time. The close call with the mountain was when we flew over the bay at Haifa "deck-level" according to the British radio system. We narrowly missed some ships and just got over the hills in time. They wanted to turn on the search lights but decided not to because they'd had no instructions—and we might have been a German plane. They didn't open fire because of some secret radio stuff which just isn't mentioned, even in confidence.

Finally, the navigator said we ought to turn about 110 degrees to our right and just then, the radio message came through that we were 100 miles west of Haifa, heading northwest. The radio compass still said we were heading for Jerusalem. (Look it up on the map!) We had an engine run dry just then so we switched tanks, leaned out the mixture to the "emergency" stop and began a long power glide toward Haifa. They had orders to use the searchlights and were signaling the direction of the field we were to use due to gas shortage. We got to the harbor, made a turn and the radio operator took our Aldis lamp and flashed O.K., to which they flicked the lights off and then on, swinging them in an arc pointing to the field. We landed, without making a customary circle. The tail gunner, a cutup, jumped out of the plane when we stopped and rolled on the ground! That's all for now.

FRANK

Thomas A. Lanahan, of Indianapolis, was inducted into the Army Feb. 1, 1941, and was commissioned a 2d lieutenant in the infantry at Ft. Benning, Ga., May 29, 1942. Going overseas in Aug. 1942, Lt. Lanahan served with the 813th Tank Destroyer Battalion as platoon commander, liaison officer and battalion adjutant throughout his 38 months overseas. He took part in six campaigns: North Africa, Sicily, Normandy, Northern France, the Rhineland, and Central Germany. Awarded the Bronze Star, 1st Lt. Lanahan was discharged Dec. 20, 1945, and is now on the staff of the Indianapolis Times.

18 May 1943
North Africa

Dear Dad:

I've just been drinking some wine which we got from a French farmer who said General Rommel was staying there and drinking the same wine some three weeks ago. This farm was some other German general's headquarters, and Rommel had "visited" him. It was at some place near Tebourba, not far from where we are at present. The papers said that Rommel had gone from N. Africa for some time, but this proves otherwise. However, he had the sense (and luck) to get out in time.

We have received permission to relate our "war" experiences now, but mine, I'm afraid, aren't worth mentioning. Although my outfit was right in there pitching ever since February, I, as personnel adjutant, was in the rear echelon and always about 5 miles from the fighting. However, there is no such thing as a rear echelon to a Stuka, and I saw quite a bit of Jerry's Luftwaffe. Fortunately, his attentions were usually directed at some other objective, and except for some stray machine gun bullets, which landed pretty close, I wasn't much bothered. However, one day, in a cactus patch at breakfast time, I had to run like hell for my foxhole when a flight of his planes came over, but my only mishap was loss of part of my mess gear.

We were working with the 34th Division all through the campaign, and if you read about the action around Fondouk and later at Hill 609, you will know that we were definitely among those present. Fondouk is where we saw the most Jerry air activity, and he controlled the hills around us. We were under constant observation and artillery range. However, our camouflage and choice of positions apparently helped us out, as nothing happened. After we had run Jerry out of this place, we picked up lots of his equipment, part of which we found good use for. I am using some of his Teller mine containers for my files. He got out in such a hurry that much of his food remained half eaten and the colonel and some of the officers who got there in time, ate some very good German cheese and other rations.

After we moved north for the last phase of the campaign, we didn't run into so much action, although the first night was amusing. I was in the third truck moving up, and we got crossed up by the M.P.'s and went down a road to the front by mistake and finally stopped about two miles from the front lines. The road was full of mines on both sides, and we were lucky as hell, driving in total black-out and not hitting them. About the time we found we were on the wrong road, some artillery (ours) started shelling over our heads and the whine of the shells was anything but comfortable as we couldn't tell who was shooting and from where. We all turned around on the road and started back, but the major's half-trac hit a couple of Jerry mines and injured about four men. Later, we found out that we had damn near captured Mateur singlehanded. It was quite a joke for some time afterwards.

This Hill 609 was about the toughest nut to crack in the entire campaign, and the old 34th Division really did some grand work. Actually, its fall paved the way for the entire advance of the II Corps (of which we were part). . . . I was up there two days after the Jerries had been run off, and saw two German parachute troops (dead) still unburied. Our artillery was awful deadly and the German prisoners which we captured said that they had never seen anything like it, and most of them had come directly from the Russian front. One poor Jerry told us that he had been promised a "vacation" in Africa after a long period in Russia, and 23 hours after he was flown into Africa he had been wounded by our shell fire. Adolph sent the best he had against our boys, and you know the result. I have never seen so many prisoners as came in, once the ball began rolling. They all seemed to be glad to be out of the war and had had enough.

No more room now. I'll tell you more later.

Love,
TOM

Ralph F. Iula, Jr., of Carmel, enlisted in the Army May 18, 1942 and was assigned to the engineer corps. He was sent to North Africa in Apr. 1943 with the 335th Engineers Regiment, and saw action there and in Corsica, France, and Germany with the 7th Army. He was promoted to technician 4th grade early in 1945 and was selected for schooling at The Sorbonne, Paris. Discharged Oct. 18, 1945, he entered the Latin-American Institute, Chicago.

June 13, 1943
North Africa

DEAR MOM:

As I write this letter, I'm witness to a scene as picturesque as any I've ever seen in the movies or read of in books. I'm sitting in the back end of my truck, which has the canvas sides rolled up on top and the top covering over the driver's seat off altogether.

We are parked in an olive grove, half a mile from a main highway where trucks almost continually pass. Joe Bentley, using the shade of my truck, is sitting on a packing box which serves to carry the chaplain's hymn books as we go from unit to unit in our organization. In front of Joe is the small portable organ, which has ridden many a mile in the back of my truck. He now begins playing the soulful strains of the opening hymn, which resounds through the grove, past the tents, and to the nearby mountains and their scrubby foliage, where a few weeks ago his men attempted to kill other men and protected the would-be killers from other killers, each fighting for the way of life and the country he thought best.

The men, scattered in the skimpy shade of the thin-leaved olive trees, begin singing and far off through the valley the bugler blows out the army's "Church Call." Two men, who have brought trumpets all the way from the States with them and who have practiced long hours to play hymns together, join Joe's organ refrain and stagger along with the organ music to a disquieting but tuneful finish of the hymn.

Tall, lanky, firm-lipped, benevolent Chaplain Ward takes his stand beside the organ and leads the men in singing several more hymns. A Tennessee Baptist, Chaplain Ward is a quiet, reassuring man who is always willing to help his "boys" in any way they may need his help. Never the "shouting Baptist," typical of the Southern churches, the first lieutenant has earned the great respect of all the enlisted men and officers in the regiment.

Sounds of the "working camp," the kitchen, the blacksmith, and those who prefer sleeping or washing to church-going, echo softly in the background as the chaplain gives the opening prayer. There are more songs, a duet solo by the trumpeters, and the sermon for today.

Latecomers rustle to seats in the little shade left, the chaplain clears his throat and his sermon begins. He speaks quietly, firmly, always keeping the attention of his oft-restless audience by raising his voice just enough to accent a point. Occasionally he will play his little trick of stopping abruptly, for two, maybe three seconds, which snaps the listeners' minds into trying to remember word for word his past few phrases.

The chaplain is impressive to the intelligent mind, and slightly profound to the less intelligent mind, which is mainly what his audience consists of. He uses the simple example of a tree and its fruit to represent life and its good deeds to appeal to his usual soldier. Yet he manages to show a deeper parable for those who would become disinterested in "trop simple" examples.

During the short sermon various interferences, such as a squabble between the two puppy mascots or a flight of P-38's swooping low above us, fail to faze the even-speaking preacher as he continues his sermon.

A silent prayer, during which the twittering of the many birds may be heard plus the braying of a donkey bearing an Arab on his back up a hill path, will end the hour's service.

Joe will end up with a hymn on the organ and the men will sing their lusty best. Then Chaplain Ward will say something like this: "I want to thank all of you for coming today. I know there are many other things you could be doing. You work difficult hours and have hard work. Some men went swimming and I can hardly blame them for that. We hope to be back again next week. Maybe not on Sunday, but whenever possible."

So ending, the chaplain will shake hands with several of the men, congratulate several on promotions and the like, and then will dash over and help Joe and me load the organ on the truck, glance at his watch and say something like, "We are to be at [censored] in 20 minutes."

And since I know the type of road, the traffic at the time, and the location, I drive accordingly. This goes on three or four days a week, and I try to always work in doing the carrying of the chaplain with my other duties, because I really enjoy talking to him and working for him. He will sometimes preach as often as four times a day, covering a hundred miles of territory. That is church in North Africa!

Love,
"JERRY"

→ IV ←

ITALY

IN EARLY July 1943 Allied troops landed in Sicily. Though the Germans fought stubbornly, overwhelming air support and negative Italian resistance gave the Allies strength in conquering the island by the first of August. On the third of September the British Eighth Army landed in Calabria, Italy, while the Americans landed near Naples. The opposition to the American Fifth Army was stiff and the forces barely escaped disaster at the Salerno beachhead. On January 22, 1944, a surprise landing at Anzio near Rome by the Fifth Army threatened the German army south of that point; however, German defense of the Gustav Line delayed the occupation of Rome for nearly six months. The Allies by the end of the year had also taken Florence and Pisa in the north. In April 1945, the American and British forces launched their final offensive against the Germans in the Po Valley, and Bologna, their primary objective, fell on the 21st of April. The German army retreated in disorderly fashion before the onslaught of the Allied armies, and their capitulation came on the second of May.

Wymond W. Krieble, of Clay City, was commissioned a 1st lieutenant in the Army Medical Corps July 1, 1942. Going overseas in Oct. 1942, Krieble was attached to the 60th Infantry Regiment as a battalion surgeon, and participated in the invasion of North Africa, the Battle of Tunisia, and the Sicilian campaign, where he was wounded Aug. 7, 1943. Capt. Krieble was returned to the U. S. and assigned to the office of the surgeon general, then was transferred to various camps. Awarded the Silver Star, an Oak Leaf cluster, and the Purple Heart, Capt. Krieble was discharged Dec. 17, 1945. and is now a physician in Terre Haute.

October 3, 1943
Sicily

DEAR MR. STORM:

I received your very interesting letter a few days ago and I need not say how happy I was nor how much I enjoyed it. It is always good for a man to know that his old friends still remember him and think about him occasionally.

It does not seem possible that it has been ten years since I was a student in your classes, or perhaps I should say member of your classes. I look back upon those days with a great deal of pleasure. Life was so simple and uninvolved. We had problems then, of course we did, and at the time they seemed insurmountable; but as I look back, I believe that about the most pressing problem I had was whether or not I would make the first five on the basketball team. With age comes responsibilities and they in turn bring complexities that only time can solve. We can have no conception of what even the immediate future holds in store for us. I certainly would not have thought ten years ago that I would be doing what I am today. However, this will be the most interesting and trying period in our lives and I am happy in being so deeply involved in the course of events. Nothing can take away knowledge, especially that gained by experience.

It is a difficult procedure to write an intelligent letter due to the fact that there are so many restrictions on what we can and cannot say. One must be a master at saying nothing to make a letter the least bit interesting and there is where I fail most miserably.

At the present time I am in Sicily but have been several other places and have seen many peoples in their native habitat. To sum it up, their manner of earning a livelihood is not unlike that of ours, but only more crude, more primitive and less fruitful. All this brings out the fact that it is wonderful to be an American and a distinct privilege to have had all the advantages offered by our United States. We Americans do not realize how much the rest of the world must envy us.

Our armed forces have been doing a tremendous and a superb job. It is an extremely difficult and a particularly unpleasant job so they deserve all of the glory and credit in the world.

I wish I could tell you where I have been and what I have done and seen, but that would be a direct violation of regulations and would most likely be boring. I hope everything is going well with you. Give everyone my regards.

Sincerely yours,
WYMOND KRIEBLE

Harvey W. Hamilton, of Madison, was inducted into the Army in Feb. 1943. He was sent to North Africa in June with the 84th Chemical Mortar Battalion. After this campaign, Pfc. Hamilton participated in the invasion of Italy and the advance northward. He was discharged in Nov. 1945, and returned to work at Madison.

[Jan. 1944]
Italy

You know we soldiers live on rumors and the rumor was that we were going to guard prisoners that were being taken back to the States. Everybody was happy but there was a non-combat meeting called and when they came back the picture was changed completely. Their first words were, "Boys, this is it. We are going on an invasion." Everybody was quiet, not a word was spoken and you could have heard a pin drop. That was sure a big letdown, but we have learned not to believe a rumor.

Our camp was almost in the same place as when we first came to Africa. The dust was just as bad and the flies in Africa were terrible. We stayed there about a week eating cold C-rations, which consist of three cans of meat unit, meat and beans, meat and vegetable stew, and meat and vegetable hash, that's one day's ration and you know we didn't have an appetite. About that time everybody was guessing where we were going but very few were right. Then the day came for us to leave and we had another long hike to the ship, which was a big British troopship.

We were loaded in just like cattle, every soldier who could be packed in. There weren't nearly enough hammocks so I and many other fellows slept on the deck under the stars. The food was terrible. You know the British (Limies) are tea crazy, they don't know how to make us Americans a good cup of coffee and a soldier is lost without his coffee. They baked fresh buns but they must have had the flour since the beginning of the war for it was full of weevils and white worms about the size of a large maggot. The boys thought the buns were good until they started finding baked weevils and worms. You would see some of the boys picking their buns apart like they were hunting gold and some fellows wouldn't eat them. But I was hungry; whenever I tore a bun open and found a worm I would cover it with jam and butter and eat ahead. I couldn't be watching out for those worms as they had to look out for themselves.

The water was rationed on the ship and we could only get water two hours a day. So we had to stand in line for water, chow, and even to wash our faces in salt water. Since the first day I came in the army I have been standing in line waiting. The old army slogan, "hurry up and wait." We were on the ship almost a week and the morning before the invasion a boy was found dead in bed of a heart attack. So I witnessed a very nice burial at sea. His body was wrapped in Old Glory and as the chaplain was making his last prayer they slid his body off the ship to his watery grave.

The next morning, September 9th, we awoke and all hell was breaking loose. We had arrived at our destination, Salerno, Italy. The big troopship couldn't move in close to shore, it had to stay out of shell range. They gave us pills to keep us from getting seasick, then loaded us on small boats, LCP's (landing craft personnel), and lowered us to the water. There were about twenty-five in each boat. The sea was very rough and it tossed us around like chips while waiting for the signal to come ashore.

Some of the boys were terribly seasick, one boy was vomiting on my feet, another vomiting over the side of the boat and others trying to vomit, so it was pretty much of a mess. One fellow was so sick he tried to jump overboard and we had to hold him in. As we came in, the battleships and destroyers were shelling the mountains trying to knock out the German guns that were shelling the beach. Finally we reached shore and saw boats torn up, turned upside down and helmets floating around in the water and that told us lots of our boys had lost their lives. We waded through water above our knees getting to shore and as we came onto the beach things had quieted down some. We saw lots of fellows sitting by slit trenches but we found out later that they were dead and had been fixed like that so it wouldn't look so bad to the troops coming in.

We were hiking to our assembly area and had stopped to take a breath and smoke a cigarette by some fig trees. We were standing around eating figs when here came a bunch of Jerry planes strafing us. Boy, did we scatter. We finally reached the assembly area which was a cornfield and tomato patch by a nice farmhouse. The tomatoes were ripe and we ate our fill of them. The water in Italy is good and there is plenty of it, much better than Africa.

The first few days at Salerno were pretty rugged. We had about three air raids every day and about that many at night. We had good air cover, but just as soon as our planes left the Jerries would sneak in to bomb and strafe. The antiaircraft gunners were trigger happy and excited and they shot down more of our planes than the Germans.

The Germans were tough with the Italians after Italy got out of the war. One family hung out a white sheet so the Americans would not bother them, but the Germans came along, saw the white flag and killed the whole family, eight of them. They were scattered around the house every place.

I saw three of our boys killed by a tank and one of them had seven .50 calibre bullets through the front of his helmet. It sure is a gruesome sight to see lots of American boys lying in a row dead and covered with blankets. As you know, our weapon is the 4.2 chemical mortar which shoots a shell weighing between twenty-five and thirty pounds. It is good for mountainous terrain and will reach spots the artillery can't touch. The artillery shells go over the hill and into the valley but with our mortars we can shell the reverse side of a hill from top to bottom and also drop shells in ravines that the artillery can't get. It was sure noisy at Salerno. The navy shells whistled over our heads all night.

Our mortars weren't unloaded for three days after we landed. Things were so tough they were going to make Rangers out of us, but our colonel stepped in and saved our hides. We almost had to swim off and let the Germans have it. In fact, some outfits were packed ready to leave and all ships were ordered to stand by and take us off, but our lines held although they were badly dented.

After we got our mortars we moved to another area to move out to a gun position. That night we had a big air raid and they hit a German plane. We could see it when it got hit and also a little ball of fire. In a few seconds the entire plane was burning, then it turned and came straight toward us. I had been standing in my slit trench watching the fireworks and as the plane came toward us I didn't know whether to run or stay. Some of the boys were running around and didn't know what to do or where to go. I was standing with one foot in and one foot out wondering what to do, when suddenly the plane turned and crashed about two miles from us and we breathed a sigh of relief; in fact, we started breathing again.

Our first gun position was in the bed of a dry canal. We were set up in a defensive position just waiting for the Germans to break through. It was here that an 88 landed within six feet of me, but the Lord was with me and it didn't go off.

The photographers were up in trees taking pictures of the big tank battle that was raging just in front of us. The next day we moved to another position in an open field behind a few blackberry briars. We were drinking water out of a stream. We couldn't move out of our holes in the daytime so at night we would fill our canteens and walk around a little. We found a watermelon and cantaloupe patch close by and ate plenty of them. There were many water buffalo around with long horns that looked at us like they would charge any minute but we just kept an eye on them, for a few .30 calibre slugs would stop them.

We stayed there for a few days, then one Sunday morning about four o'clock we started moving cross-country, pulling our carts, one loaded with ammunition and the mortar on the other. That was sure a tough pull over irrigation ditches and through briars and bushes. There were many dead cattle lying around and the fields were full of shell holes. About noon we crossed a blacktop highway torn up with shells and bombs. We stopped in a ditch about one hundred yards from the highway in a clump of wild bushes. We were all so tired we just slid down any place. There was a farmhouse between us and the highway, so my buddy and I took our canteens and started to the house for water.

We heard airplanes when we were about halfway to the house. They were Jerry planes trying to bomb the highway. They dropped two large bombs but missed the highway and came so close to us that the shrapnel and dirt was singing over our heads like a swarm of bees. We were really hugging the ground. They then dropped personnel bombs at the other boys. The personnel bomb weighs about twenty-five pounds. A large chunk of dirt hit one boy on the leg and put him in the hospital. Another one hit a case of rations and splattered meat and beans and stew every place.

We then moved to a very beautiful orchard of oranges, tangerines, lemons, grapes, figs and apples. It was a shame the way our trucks tore the trees down, but this is war. The trees were sure full of fruit but the grapes, apples and figs were all that were ripe.

We were here a few days then moved up by a little town, but now the Germans were moving so fast that we had a hard time keeping up with them. We slept under some apple trees and there were so many apples on the ground that we had to scrape them to one side so we could lie down to sleep. We passed through so many towns I have forgotten the names of most of them but here are a few. Benevento: as we passed through there the people were lined up along the street cheering and clapping their hands. It sounded like the war was over they were so happy. It was over for them. They threw apples and nuts to us and we gave them candy.

We passed through Avellino which was a very nice town until our bombers came over and unloaded. The Italians were warned to get out but they are funny people; they stay in the middle of a battlefield to take care of their stock and will hardly leave their homes, so many of them are killed. They stayed at Avellino and about three thousand were killed. There were so many they couldn't bury them so they poured gasoline on them and burned them in the street. Acerno was the next town and again the Italians stayed and many were killed. There was a nice hospital there but it was torn up completely.

We then kept moving until we reached the Volturno River. We had our gun position on a high mountain and we had to pack the ammunition about a mile. We packed two rounds at a time in a shell carrier made for that purpose, so that was about sixty pounds we were packing. You might have read about the smoke screen that was laid across the Volturno while the engineers built the bridge. Well, we were the ones that laid it. While we were on those mountains we could look down the valley, green with grass or alfalfa and full of shell holes. They were so thick you could almost step from one to the other. On the night of October 13, we crossed the Volturno and stopped by a farmhouse. We again were the first troops there since the infantry had passed.

It was so dark we couldn't see a thing so we just laid down and went to sleep. The next morning we woke up and dead Germans were all around us. They had pulled out in a hurry and left lots of machine guns and ammunition. They had killed a hog but didn't have time to eat it and had hidden it in the house. There was one Jerry that was killed in the garden right by the house. We buried him and hung his dogtag on the cross over his grave. The ditches around were full of dead Germans. We got some pictures from them of Russian scenery so I guess they had been pulled off the Russian front.

One morning we were standing by the house and about forty planes came over. Some of the boys said, "Those are our planes." But when they dove and started strafing us we knew they were on the wrong side. They were trying to bomb the bridge across the Volturno but missed. We were so close we could see the bombs as they left the planes. A few days later we moved to another position but it got too hot for us and we pulled out. There were lots of frozen cherries captured in Naples, also some tomato sauce direct from Germany. We had been told that Jerries didn't have much food but when we saw those frozen cherries we changed our minds.

We passed through many towns and villages, all of them bearing the scars of war. On the night of November 7th we were supposed to meet the infantry and go with them on a mission but it rained just as we started. The roads were all dirt and our trucks lacked about six miles getting us there. We started out pulling the mortars up hill and down hill and so dark we couldn't see a thing and all the time the rain was coming down by bucketfuls. When we got to our destination we were several hours late and the infantry had gone ahead. They told us to lie down and make ourselves comfortable.

We were soaking wet and water was standing all over the ground so you can imagine how comfortable we were. I had a change of clothes in my bedroll so I put them on, got in my bedroll, pulled the end of my shelter half over my head and said, "Let it rain." One boy laid down as soon as we stopped and it started raining harder. He had laid in a low place and a stream of water was running over him. It rained about all night and when I awoke the next morning I was wet again, so we built a fire and dried our clothing. That night we were on the move again and when we stopped the Germans were shelling our area. We found a cistern about ten feet deep and jumped in. Later we moved into a house. Some of us fellows slept downstairs on the rock floor and the family slept upstairs. Before the Germans had retreated they told the family to go with them or the Americans would kill them, so they were suspicious of us for a while. They soon got over that.

The day of November 11th we were issued our winter wearing apparel, consisting of woolen underwear, overcoat and gloves. The next morning we moved out with the infantry and passed through the town of Pozzuoli which was about seven miles north of Venafro. Fires were still burning in the town as we passed through and as we walked along the road we saw lots of signs warning us of mines. We again pulled the carts about four miles. The Germans had the road camouflaged so good it looked as if it ran up to the end of a hollow and stopped. As we moved up the hill we saw a German gun that had been firing on the town but it was destroyed and there were five fresh graves with their helmets hanging on the crosses. They had given their lives for the Fuehrer. The Germans were shelling the hill as we moved up and wounded many of the infantry boys. We were so close to the Germans we couldn't pitch a tent so we just spread our blankets out and went to sleep.

The next morning it started raining and we got wet again. It rained about three days before we could put up our tents and by that time the mud was shoe deep. That was the beginning of the rainy season and it rained almost every day. We got soaking wet almost every day packing ammunition. We had to go to bed so our bodies could dry our clothes by the next morning, then we would start all over again. We went to bed about four o'clock and got up about nine o'clock the next morning if we weren't awakened by shells. We stayed on that hill thirty-eight days and shot four thousand rounds of ammunition. That's sure a lot of war bonds.

The mountain was so steep a mule couldn't climb it, but we packed ammunition up in the mud and rain, sometimes 'til twelve o'clock at night. On steep hills the Italians have made terraces to keep the soil from washing away and walled up with rock. At night we would sit by the wall waiting for the shells to come in before going to bed. They threw a big barrage at us one night and as I ran out of my tent a shell exploded upon the hill in front of me and blinded me for a few seconds. The powder smoke was so thick we could hardly breathe. We stood on the mountain and watched shells explode in the valley below.

One night it was raining and some medicos were sleeping in the ambulance when someone opened the door and said, "Kamerad." It was two Germans giving up. They were sick and wanted treatment. I saw them bring in some prisoners there who still had hand grenades in their pockets.

One Saturday night we got orders to move forward again. So about midnight we started out. As we pulled our carts along the road we saw lots of mines that had just been taken up and also dead Germans lying in the ditches. We had to wait about two hours for the engineers to build a bridge so we just lay down in the road and went to sleep. As soon as the bridge was built we moved on and met the boys using the mine sweepers. A fellow sure steps light when he's traveling a road and doesn't know whether the mines have been taken out or not. We didn't get much sleep that night and the next day we dug our slit trenches.

Late that afternoon the Germans threw over a smoke shell; they were ranging in on the road. That night about nine o'clock they started throwing in the shells. That was the first time I had seen shelling that looked like the picture shows of war. The shells were coming in so fast it looked like the whole hillside was on fire. I had a slit trench that was hardly big enough for me but when the shelling started another boy jumped in with me. How we both got in there I don't know. At times like that a fellow would like to be as small as a mouse.

In a few days we were relieved, after one hundred eighteen days of steady combat. The day of January 6th we moved back for a very short rest, in fact, two weeks. Then I was able to take my underclothing off that I had been wearing since November 11th. I felt like a new man when I took them off and had a hot shower. The Italians didn't have much to eat there. Whenever we ate chow they would stand around with buckets wanting whatever we had left and sometimes we would see an old man digging around in the garbage pit. It was a pitiful sight, little children standing around watching us eat when they hadn't eaten for a couple of days. I couldn't eat with them watching me so sometimes I would just give it to them. Whenever you saw a bunch of soldiers lined up you would know there were some Italian (signorina) girls close. . . .

Marchmont Kovas, of South Bend, was inducted into the Army Mar. 27, 1942, and was commissioned a 2d lieutenant in the infantry May 13, 1943. He was attached to the 82d Airborne, the 101st Airborne, and the 91st Infantry Divisions. He fought in Italy from Rome to the end of the campaign, for which action he was awarded the Silver Star, the Bronze Star, and the Purple Heart. He was promoted 1st lieutenant Sept. 13, 1944, and was discharged Nov. 10, 1945. He returned to South Bend to continue as newspaper reporter with the South Bend Tribune.

[July 1944]
Somewhere in Italy

War certainly has its extremes. After living in slit trenches and ditches with a blanket of ominously whirring artillery shells over our heads as cover, I suddenly find myself in positively luxurious surroundings in a well-appointed apartment house in a city I helped capture. The hysterically happy Italians place everything at our service—what else could they do? So we take the best.

I sit at a mahogany table in a well-upholstered chair and feel like a bull in a china closet. This stationery and ink I found in a convenient drawer. The inhabitants, whoever they may be, have fled from bombings. It's a heaven-sent haven to a warrior just indoctrinated with the hell of war.

For two weeks and more I haven't had my clothes off, not even my shoes; almost three weeks without a shave; K-rations for chow when we got it. Everybody lost weight, got diarrhea from muddy, filthy water. Due to hardships of terrain, heat, no chow, no water, battle strain, the first few days I hardly ate, had no sleep and was so battle weary I really didn't give a damn if artillery shells hit me or not.

There are no atheists in foxholes. I haven't found a man yet who hasn't fervently prayed during a shelling and there are no foxholes until you dig them. Entering battle with tender palms, the first day's digging brought huge blisters, Italian soil being anything but a soft touch. On the second slit trench the blisters broke; the third they bled and they bled, but a guy forgets the pain when Jerry begins raining his abominably accurate artillery fire right on your position. Life is more important. You get calluses eventually on your hands and feet and then your belly from hitting the dirt. It takes a direct hit in a slit trench to get you and they occur. When finally your hole is dug and you lie prone the rest is up to the Lord.

I was fooled about my reactions the first time under fire. I had imagined I'd lay there too scared to even move. (Well, I'll be——Jerry just dropped one next street over, so now I must wear my heavy helmet again.) (There's another one—the civilians are running into their homes, the soldiers, less hurriedly into dwellings.) I found I could crack jokes and not even feel any increased heart action. The second day I began to realize the gravity of shellings when several barrages landed right on our observation post. Then I knew that Jerry knew where we were and it wasn't just promiscuous shelling. Then, too, the sight of mangled bodies, the lifeless forms of buddies, brought a second phase of reaction. It stirred the imagination—"It might have been you. Why wasn't it?" The Lord only knows! Third reaction is callousness to death, a bitter hatred of the Jerries, a burning desire to avenge what they have done to us. This supersedes fear for ourselves.

Many times in moving forward I'm caught without a foxhole. That's bad, but barring ricocheting shrapnel a shell must still fall within a few feet to tag you. Sometimes during severe shellings, when you know people near you are being blown to bits, a man searches his soul and seeks the answer as to who has ordained him to be here in the midst of hell and death while the other four men of a quintet are far behind the lines in noncombatant duty, safe from it all. But the thought passes with new exigencies. After surviving so many shellings I come to the automatic conclusion that I can't be hit. So if I'm in my slit trench I just lay there and wait it out.

A man soon becomes battlewise. By the sound of a shell I can tell whether it's coming or going, whether it will fall near or far, although each one that lands within 100 yards sounds as if it is aimed especially and directly for you. You don't hear the whine of fragments from a burst near you. But fragments from a shell 100 yards away sound like the devil himself is riding it. At first I had the usual tendency to hit the dirt at the sound of any shell, near or far, coming or going. Now it takes one coming right at me to get me in my slit trench.

We laugh at rear echelon men who make occasional visits to the front line and duck from our own shells. On occasion though, it's highly appropriate. I don't believe there's a battery that hasn't at one time shelled its own front line troops. It's wonderful to hear it skim our heads and paste Jerry a couple of hundred yards in front but very disconcerting when they fall short amongst us. The Germans, on the other hand, deliberately shell the area where our troops are at close quarters with the Krauts. Let the chips fall where they may though, the Krauts get the best of it because they are always dug in, and deep.

A few days of fighting and a man is so fatigued he'll sleep through anything. I've slept soundly through some of the most severe shelling the Krauts gave us. During one heavy shelling my G.I. wrist watch stopped. I tried everything to get it started. Two days later another barrage that almost got me started it going again.

I must tell you in detail about this last one. It was July 13, and though not superstitious the circumstances still gave rise to a feeling of impending disaster. All day they missed me by varying margins. Late in the evening I found myself in my OP (observation post) tele (telephone) in hand, in contact with my mortars several hundred yards to the rear. I just told my plat. sergeant that things looked quiet when suddenly one cracked near me. Ascertaining there were no more in flight, I dashed down the rear slope of the hill and started digging furiously in a prechosen spot. With only a start on my slit trench, barrages at regular intervals fell about me. In between each I dug almost frantically and still they fell within a few yards so I couldn't see from smoke and dust. The burnt TNT smell bit my nose. Suddenly the assurance that I just couldn't be hit fled me. I reasoned that if they continued to fall so near the law of averages would get me. There was a farmhouse 100 yards up the hill. I decided instantly to make a dash for it. The shells were coming in salvos, 15 or 20 seconds between each salvo. Not hearing the whine of the next I dashed madly to the safety of the stone farmhouse, helmet in hand as it insisted on falling off. (In combat the chin strap is not fastened.) Just as I bolted through the door one struck nearby and fragments nicked the wall about the door. Later an impending counterattack drove me back to the safety of rifle troops. The next morning when I returned for my equipment at my one-half dug hole, I found it (the hole) had received almost a direct hit. I'm getting more religious each day. But on this particular morning that the sequel came (the 13th was still hounding me), I remembered I was commissioned just 13 months ago on the 13th day of the month.

During the previous evening's shelling my tele wire was cut in four places. At one place I had to crawl out in the open on the hill in plain sight of the Krauts on the next hill. I had just spliced the wire when the terrifying whir of one I knew was headed right for me, hit my ear. I hit flat so hard it knocked the breath out of me. A small bottle of halazone tablets I carry in my shirt pocket seemed to go through me. I found myself in a cloud of dust, smoke and strong smell of powder. Amazing I wasn't hit. No more coming, I leaped into a pit where sat a soldier, stone dead, a fragment as large as my fist having smashed through helmet, skull, brains and all. He was hit the evening before. Another one struck nearby but missed again, then again I dashed madly to the safety of the heavy stone farmhouse 75 yards away where the farmer was gesticulating wildly and shouting "Venite casa!" P.S. I made it.

Close calls become routine and don't even rate conversation anymore. A phenomenon is the callousness a man develops toward death. Men report the loss of buddies and necessary details in simple, casual expressions; no one bats an eye. It is incredible what cruel punishment, mental and physical, a human can take unflinchingly when necessary.

It's "30" for now—only for this letter, I hope. Best regards to all.

"MARCH"

Kathryn L. Snyder, R. N., of Atwood, was commissioned a 2d lieutenant in the Army Nurses' Corps Oct. 15, 1942. Attached to the 16th Evacuation Hospital, Lt. Snyder first served in a prisoner of war hospital near Oran, N. Africa, and later saw duty in Italy, arriving eight days after D-Day. Discharged June 14, 1944, Miss Snyder is nursing at Memorial Hospital, Colorado Springs, Colo.

[1944]
Italy

DEAR FOLKS:

Censorship regulations have let up, so I'll try to tell you a little about it [crossing Atlantic] now. I don't know just how much you read.

We were all having a pretty wonderful time with not a worry or care, and enjoying the luxuries of the boat. None of us had sense enough to be scared. Mills and I were on deck and heard a plane diving. Someone nearby remarked about an aircraft over us, and then we heard a whistle! It landed close by, and we all went below decks for our helmets. I knew for the first time what an awful sound a bomb really makes! We had two more near misses that day.

The next morning around 4:30 I heard another one. I couldn't go back to sleep because I felt so sure they'd be back. About forty-five minutes later I heard the last one. It got louder and louder, then hit. I waited for everything to stop crashing, and expected to be hit any minute by something. Bits of plaster and wood peppered my face. The time from the first whistle of the bomb until everything stopped crashing seemed an eternity. A lifeboat fell through into our quarters (one big room), and that brought about more crashing. When it was over we all hopped out of bed and slipped on our fatigues. I ran up the ramp and saw that the boat was burning, so I went down again and looked around at the wreckage in our ward.

No one screamed or whimpered. They were all as quiet as if nothing had happened, and when they were told to follow in single file, no one pushed or crowded. We went through a narrow galley-way—wading in water up to our ankles with debris and smoke all about. The lifeboat I was in was heavily loaded and one end slipped. The other end was in the water and we had to hang on for dear life to keep from falling into the sea. When they lowered the other end we went down with a bang—and then we started bailing with our helmets! Discovered later that the boat had a big hole knocked in the bottom of it!

By the time we left the ship was burning badly. When we climbed onto the other ship they had tea and chocolate for us, in true English style. We didn't sleep that night, but were all right when we got our feet on dry land. It's much more fun watching an air raid with solid ground under you.

We lived in our fatigues for three days and nights until we got some other clothing, and the assortment we got then was really funny.

About the loss of all our clothing—we have it all back now except the things we had right with us. You see, our luggage was all up on deck ready to be unloaded and the destroyers took it off. How in the world they did it is beyond me. Some of it was a little charred and waterlogged, but mine was all right. We were a tickled bunch of girls when we found it on the beaches. It was just like opening a Christmas package. The last of it was brought in about four days ago, but I got mine two weeks ago. So you don't have to worry about my being properly clothed. With all the new issue and the old I have more than I know what to do with. I do need the slacks, shirts and undies, however. A flannel nightie would be just the thing.

Hope you read of our rainstorm, as it was quite something. It looked as if our hospital had been flattened by bombs the next day and literally everything was covered by mud. All of my clothes, including the ones in my suitcase, were wet. The wind blew my suitcase off the cot and knocked it open. The top blew open and was almost torn off. Between the boat and the storm, it's a sad looking piece of luggage.

Write soon and take good care of yourselves for me.

Love,
KATHRYN

John W. Ely, of Indianapolis, enlisted in the Air Corps in Oct. 1942. He was sent overseas in Sept. 1944 and assigned to the 353d Bomber Squadron, seeing action in Italy. For his service Staff Sergeant Ely won the Air Medal with three Oak Leaf clusters and the Purple Heart. Discharged in 1945, he became a sales engineer in Indianapolis.

November 28, 1944
Italy

DEAR CANDY:

There's nothing like good mail service for the morale. Got your letter of September 18 yesterday. I think you're already aware of everything that has occurred since then, so I'll let your questions go unanswered. I'll try one thing that you suggested though—sending this to the Theta house.

This has been a dull week—no one has flown in the last eight days. Picture this if you can—a fellow's weathered up in a tent about 16' x 20' for days on end. We sit around quibbling and arguing like a bunch of old women about anything and everything. Incidentally, when did the eight-cent air mail postage law go into effect? If you can help me prove it was after June 1st, it will save me $5.00. Also, would you mind settling whose turn it is to get water, who cooked up the last mess of eggs without cleaning the skillet, and who stood "mail call" last night? Then there's an argument with a representative from the next tent as to the relative merits of our stoves.

Last night was another one of those nights. I had to stand guard duty again. The reason we dread it so much is that it means six straight hours of walking back and forth between a couple of planes in the wind and cold without relief. We have a provost sergeant who is a "_____" besides being a sadist at heart, and nothing delights him more than being able to "court martial" someone. Two men in my squadron are up now—one for being caught in a ship and the other for sitting down on duty.

He almost caught me last night. The fellow on the post next to mine had a shack with a stove in it. We were both huddled around it when I happened to glance out the door and saw some lights down the road. I thought surely everyone was in bed by that time, but on they came. I tore off towards my ships, and had just come to a walk in front of one when this jeep pulled up. I halted and challenged it, and sure enough it was the provost sergeant. He wanted to know why I had approached from a direction other than between the two ships I was guarding. He apparently didn't put much stock in my reply that I was just walking to keep warm, but let it go.

It really wasn't so bad last night, though. There was a big full moon and an almost warm breeze blowing. The time passes pretty fast when you meditate on your sins, mistakes, hopes, disappointments, ambitions, etc., in fact, I ran out of time. Even now the war seems remote to me and scarcely enters my mind at all. Before I came I often wondered if I'd be able to sleep the night before a mission, but it soon developed that that was the least of my worries.

I think I've already used up a lot of space for saying absolutely nothing, so am signing off here.

Love,

JOHN

Dwain E. Moore, of Rensselaer, enlisted in the Army Air Corps in Aug. 1942. He was sent to North Africa a year later and served also in Italy and Southern France with the 41st Air Depot Group. In Oct. 1944 he was promoted to corporal. Discharged in Oct. 1945, he is now a teacher.

8 November 1944
Italy

DEAREST MOM:

. . . We planned our trip so we'd have daylight just as we reached the mountains beyond Foggia both for safer driving and so we could see the scenery, since none of us had been there before. The mountains are like those of Pennsylvania or New Mexico with the Tarvia road turning and twisting among them. It rained almost steadily all day making the roads even more dangerous, but we drove carefully and had no trouble. I drove more than half of the way, and Joe Patterson and Don drove the rest. Some of the mountains have orchards and vineyards on the sides, and even there the soil is richer and less rocky than it is down here. The road around Foggia is lined with government farms, each with a similar farmhouse, pair of oxen, and tools. They were made from large estates confiscated by the Fascists and divided up for thirty-year homesteading.

We stopped once and went into a house to get out of the rain (the sides were open and the roof leaked), but kept going most of the time. We ate two boxes of American cookies, some candy, and a tin of little sardines, and decided not to stop anywhere for lunch. We turned north in the outskirts of Naples without going into the city, and took Highway Six to Rome so we could see Cassino and the other towns of contemporary interest up that way. It wasn't a good idea in the rain for reasons I can't divulge, but we wouldn't have missed it. A mile from Cassino, the water rushing down the mountains had made a stream a foot deep across the road; it covered the muffler and our engine sputtered and died. Just then it began to rain harder than I've ever seen. It wasn't a pleasant situation, but the four of us, rain leaking down the backs of our necks, soaking the seats of our pants, kept our spirits up, talked of how we'd tell our kids how we took part in the "naval battle of Cassino." In a half-hour or so the rain let up a little and a G.I. truck pulled us onto high ground, and after several tense minutes we got the engine running on a cylinder or two and finally dried out enough to proceed. It will be an experience to remember. You'll have to imagine what we saw along the roadsides, in fields, how the towns looked, etc. We never lacked for something interesting to look at.

We were pretty wet, cold, and hungry when we reached Rome, picked up a Roman who guided us in the darkness and heavy traffic (there are more civilian cars—Fords, Buicks, Packards, Fiats, etc.—than military vehicles and no traffic regulations, lights, etc.) to the Red Cross club for enlisted men where we got a boy to guide us to a room. All but Don had an extra room in an apartment on the fourth floor of a big apartment house (elevators out because electricity is rationed). We stood by the cooking stove in the people's kitchen until we got a little dry, then the boy took us to a nearby civilian restaurant where we had a small piece of steak, noodle soup, and dark bread for $1.30 each. We were tired enough to go to bed soon afterward, although the rain had stopped. The beds had good mattresses and springs, clean sheets and pillow cases, and seemed the most comfortable I've slept in for over a year. The cost was $1.50 each, but we paid off with eight packs of cigarettes representing 40 cents. We were still cheated, because we found that one could get 80 cents per pack anywhere in town, or $1.00 in a trade for souvenirs.

Second Day: We went to the Air Force Rest Center (Mussolini's Stadium, across the Tiber River from, and out on the edge of, town) to check in. One didn't have to stay there, but had to get two blankets and put them on the as-signed cot. We did that, then crossed the Tiber on one of the many nice bridges to have coffee and rolls at the "Tiber Terrace" club for air force enlisted men. The Tiber is muddy, with man-made banks like a drainage ditch, and only about fifty yards wide. We decided we didn't like the room, got another boy, and found rooms in an apartment hotel at 80 cents a day. . . . The Red Cross club was a nice building at the edge of an extensive (several acres) park right in the city. Car lines run all over the city and there are cabs, but the jeep was very convenient. We could eat at the rest camp, or there were several Italian restaurants around town serving G.I. food for the soldiers at 10 cents to cover cooking, serving and rent. We ate twice at the rest camp, several times at the other cafes, and twice at a civilian restaurant (where prices were very high—50 cents for a fried egg, etc.). We got all settled in the morning, and after lunch we started on a tour with our boy to show us around the city. . . .

Hubert Kress, of Clay City, was inducted into the Army Mar. 6, 1942, and was assigned to the air corps. Upon being sent to North Africa, he was attached to the 1st Fighter Training Squadron, whose purpose it was to give pilots some overseas flying time before being sent into combat. Later he was sent to Italy, where he took care of transit planes and men, and was promoted to sergeant. He was discharged Dec. 1, 1945, and now in civilian life Mr. Kress is a strip miner and farmer in Clay City.

April 6, '45
Somewhere in Italy

DEAR HARRY:

. . . We are very busy here working seven days a week although we all get a day off out of the seven. My day off is Sunday which I chose because I thought it proper. My correspondence has been sadly neglected during the twenty-seven months I have spent overseas, eighteen of which were in North Africa and nine in Italy. Of course, there are two or three to whom I wrote as often as I could find time. A great many of these letters were merely repetitions of those written before.

I need not tell you what kind of outfit I am in as the name of the place should speak for itself. This being the case we are stationed in the country where we can really enjoy the fine weather and fresh air which they do not have in town. All around us are small towns that are very dirty and short of food and clothing. Between these towns, of course, is farm land or mountains. The farm land is broken into small farms of an acre or a little more or less. This is farmed by peasants who get from two to three crops a year. These people all live in town and come out to the field before sunup and remain until after dark. Their only meal so far as I am able to see is a piece of dark bread which they break instead of cut. They wash this down with a little wine, if they are able to get it.

You are no doubt wondering what kind of power they use to farm with. It will be some combination of cows, horses and mules. It makes no difference as to size or color. Sure looks odd to see a horse and a cow pulling a cart or a plow. You see no four-wheel wagons, only two wheels. Their plows and harrows are very primitive, such as your great-grandfather might have used. A great many of the farmers call on the family and their shovels to turn under the sod. You will see one man and any number of women spading or dragging a harrow over the ground. They use wooden mallets to break up the clods—seems as if it would take forever, but they seem to get it done. They use two sizes of hoes, extra large and very small. The large ones are used to do heavy work and the small ones to hoe between wheat rows. Wheat is almost always sowed by hand in rows made by pulling a wooden rake-like implement, only it is much larger and has two handles. Then, too, it has only three or four teeth to mark the rows. The one who pulls this walks backwards and by some miracle makes a very straight row.

Most of this land has trees set out about twenty-five feet apart, with grape vines on each tree. Then they tie wires about twelve feet above the ground between the trees for the vines. These trees are a little like cottonwood and grow pretty fast. The people trim these trees pretty close each fall in order that they might have a little wood for the winter. There is very little if any coal here. Wood is precious to these people. A meal is usually cooked over a little fire which is in a bucket or something they can carry. One family will use it and then another until it goes out. All of the homes are built of stone or cement, usually stone. Often you see a family of ten or more living in one room. In most of the places I have been there seems to have been no way to heat these houses in the winter. It doesn't get too cold, but I slept cold under six army blankets.

From what I can find over here about a fourth of the people live off the church, which is kept up by the other three-fourths. The church seems to be in charge of education here which is very sadly neglected. From my point of view the Catholic Church could open its eyes and do good for the people instead of themselves. Here you see a church worth a million dollars being kept up by people who can't read or write. I might also add that you could buy all a family of this kind has for a very few dollars. Victor Emmanuel's statue in Rome is a very beautiful thing, but a hospital for the sick or some kind of bread line for the hungry would be much better it seems to me. Every town has numerous statues of some king or saint, far too much for such a poor country. I say "poor," as I can't see anything here but population with nothing to earn a decent living. There are a number of Italians who work here on the base, and to tell you the truth I wouldn't give one of them fifty cents a day to work for me. They are not large people, but they are well-built and could if they would do a good day's work.

Among all this I have written about sets our city of tents. There are four of us to a tent. One from South Carolina, one from South Dakota and one from Kansas. You see we are pretty well mixed up. We have a pretty good stove that we made ourselves. There is electricity in all the tents. I might also add that we have running water and for about two feet up the walls are also boarded. Most of us have painted the inside some gay color, others are a little lax and only do what they have to. One tent is completely walled with pin-up gals, must be a thousand or more pictures. We have to prepare our tents for inspection each Saturday. Clothes must be properly placed on the rack and shoes shined and lined up the same under all beds. Mess gear must glisten and is put out for display, same on all beds. One of the fellows has a very good radio so we can have the news right up to the minute. At times we tune in on the German propaganda stations. Their music is mostly our jazz and it is not too bad. When they start talking we sure get a laugh out of them. They can tell some of the most outrageous tales you could possibly think of. Usually they have some woman to try to make us homesick. Oh, we sure get a thrill out of some of their programs.

Our meals are usually pretty good as we have pretty good cooks. Of course, we have our share of the dreaded dehydrated foods, but if the cooks prepare them properly they are not too bad. For breakfast we have cereals, fruits or fruit juices, some kind of eggs (fresh or dehydrated), sausage or bacon, and of course bread and coffee. Dinner usually consists of beans (green and dried), peas, potatoes, C-ration, fruit or pudding, bread, jam, and coffee or tea, or chocolate. Supper is our best meal for which we 'most always have fresh meat, gravy, potatoes, peas, beans (green), often hot buns, pie or cake, and quite often ice cream. We have a nice large baking oven and two good cooks that like to see what they can fix up. All in all I would say that we are fed very well. I am quite sure we are the best fed army in the world. I have seen how the French eat and also the English and Italians. Most of them are using some of our foods. While on the food I almost forgot to mention Spam and corned beef which is served for dinner. I can hardly stand to look at either of them anymore.

The army is having night school at one of the nearby towns. I started but had to quit as I have to work too late in the evening. The school seems to me to be a good thing. Most of the courses were refresher courses in algebra, arithmetic, economics, and many others. I was taking business law, economics, arithmetic and blueprint reading.

I must ask you not to read this too closely and to forgive me for the poor way I have pieced it together. You know I never was a very good writer. Send me if you will the addresses of some of the fellows I would be most likely to know. There are a few here in Italy that I might be able to find. Will try to write again in the near future.

As ever,

KRESS

⇀ V ↽

ENGLAND

ENGLAND passed through its greatest crisis of the war in the summer and fall of 1940, when it held out alone against aerial bombings and the threat of invasion. Supplies from the United States grew in volume all during 1941, and American troops were sent first to Northern Ireland in January 1942. From there they moved into England to prepare airfields and camps for the coming tide of American military might. United States troops were in many instances quartered with the inhabitants, whom they made warm friends. In November a great contingent of the force that invaded North Africa was launched from England. Other U. S. troops arrived for further training and to strengthen the air force. Gen. Dwight D. Eisenhower established Supreme Allied headquarters in London in January 1944 and directed the great invasion of France on June 6. England remained our chief base in Europe until the end of the war.

R. M. Fleischman, of Gary, was inducted into the Army in July 1943 and was attached to the infantry. He was sent overseas in Feb. 1944 to England, and then served in France, Belgium, and Germany attached to headquarters of the adjutant general's personnel office. He advanced to the rank of technician 4th grade in Sept. and received a Certificate of Merit. Discharged in Nov. 1945, T/4 Fleischman returned to a sales position in East Chicago. The following excerpt is from a running account of his adventures kept by him.

Summer 1944
England

So here we were. . . . Bristol. . . . The railroad station and the transportation that was to pick us up at the train (in true army fashion) was nowhere in sight. . . . So we contacted the RTO (Regional Transportation Officer) (one of which is always at a railroad station during time of war) . . . and the RTO, of course, didn't expect us, didn't know where we were supposed to go . . . and cared less. . . . Well, finally after a short delay of two hours, they finally contacted our new bosses and arranged to have a vehicle come to pick us up. . . . It wasn't long until we were pulling up to a modern . . . yes, even futuristic building known as the "bakery." . . . This was to be our working quarters . . . and take it from me, after living eight months in a G.I. tar paper barracks back in the States, tents in the U.K. . . . this concrete courtyard looked like a dream to us. . . . (The name "bakery" was derived from the fact that it was one of several buildings known as the Bristol Co-op Industries . . . bottling works, dairy plant, shoe repair units up the street were already in operation and supplying the populace with their products. . . . This building which was built for use as a modern co-operative bakery was never put into operation because of the war, and consequently they used it for our headquarters . . . and the name of "bakery" stuck to it, even after the Americans used it. . . .) Well, there we stood in the courtyard checking in with the motor dispatcher trying to figure out what our next move was . . . and all the time pinching ourselves that it was a mistake . . . so with the left hand we kept pinching each other and with the right hand saluting all the "brass" that was streaming by us (it was lunch hour and they were coming and going in a steady stream) . . . and we honestly thought we were dreaming and had been brought to the War Department in Washington from the amount of "eagles" and "leaves" that were parading up and down the joint. The payoff came upon reporting to the officer in charge of incoming troops (we finally found him after trying umpteen different officers). The first thing he wanted to know was, "Had we eaten lunch?" . . . and when he found out that we hadn't eaten since five o'clock that morning and it was now about one P.M., he wouldn't transact another bit of business with us until we had something to eat . . . so I had my first ride in an army "sedan," and it felt wonderful to ride in a civilian car again, even if it was painted olive drab. The driver took us to the mess hall, and here again I was in for a surprise . . . (this day was so full of surprises that if I live to be one hundred I'll never forget it). Up until this point every experience I have had with army mess halls had been a matter of parading in front of a bunch of K.P.'s standing in a row "dishing out" portions of food to you as you passed them by with an extended tray. So here came the three new greenies all set for another typical G.I. meal . . . and we almost dropped dead in our tracks when we saw the kettles of food setting there unattended. We were so flabbergasted that we thought we'd better not take anything for fear of incurring the wrath of the entire kitchen crew. "What's the matter, soldier? Aren't you going to eat?" "Sure, but I'm waiting for the K.P.'s to dish out the stuff." "G'wan and eat, this stuff is for you to help yourself . . . you aren't in a replacement depot." So help me, I thought for certain now that it was all a dream, but I didn't wake up, and soon it became a wonderful daily experience to be able to take as much to eat of the types of food you happened to like.

Well, the next procedure turned out to be a "billeting" affair, and instead of the tent or G.I. barracks we knew up till this point, they "allotted" us to private homes, two to the house, and told us, "Now this is where you will live . . . a Mr. and Mrs. Hussey . . . get yourselves located, and take the rest of the day to 'orient' yourselves and acquaint yourselves with the surrounding territory. Chow starts at 5:30 P.M. and you can't miss it . . . just follow the gang of G.I.'s you see all around you going to eat with their mess gears in their hands, and you won't go wrong." Well, our landlords were not home at the moment so a kind neighbor lady allowed us to store our barracks bags and bedding rolls with her until Mrs. Hussey came back, and we took off to "orient" ourselves. I've told you all how the clean houses and little stone fences made every place on the street look exactly alike . . . and how we jokingly said it would be a tough problem to pick out one's house if one ever came home intoxicated . . . (but as the months rolled by we came to know our "home" at 125 Repton Road in the dark as well as the light . . . and I honestly believe that I could pick it out now blindfolded, let alone drunk . . . but I'm getting ahead of my story). Well, we discovered that the entire community was made of civilians and G.I.'s. billeted in the homes. Our P.X. was in a regular store that had been vacant . . . our mess hall in a spot that was about four blocks from our billets and the office about another four or five blocks distant from our housing quarters.

I shan't ever forget that first moment we saw Edna Hussey. She was coming down the street from shopping, and when she saw a couple of soldiers parked on her front stoop, she ran the rest of the way . . . introducing herself, apologizing for not being in when we came, and welcoming us in all the same breath. We were indeed fortunate . . . lucky, for we were by chance billeted with two of the grandest people a guy could want to meet in this or any life . . . folks that made a home of theirs into our home. They were folks of our own age . . . they have a son named Gerald . . . who is today my adopted nephew . . . for I was always known to him as Uncle Bob.

Bristol was my introduction to what aerial bombardment can do to a thriving business district and city. During the early years of the German raids on Bristol and the rest of England, they practically levelled the shopping districts. And each and every person living in Bristol today will never forget those terrible years. I'll never forget my first bus ride downtown with the Hussey's serving as guides. From the "Centre" or downtown district it is possible to see for blocks in any direction. As Bob Hope says in his book, "I Never Left Home," when describing Bristol, " . . . And I'm not Superman. I can't look through buildings." That's the best description: there are no buildings to see through, consequently no supernatural powers are needed to see for a quarter of a mile in any direction from the center of the shopping district. . . .

Our offices were in the "bakery," and it was a swell bit of good fortune for us to be able to work all day, go to the billets at night and relax like a civilian after a day at the "office." As the months rolled by we became part of the family rather than just fellows rooming with the family. We shared our packages from home, their hospitality, went to shows together, had fun together, sang and even shivered together during any one of several night attacks when the Jerries were hovering over England dropping their deadly loads. It was nothing like it was in the early days, but being my first taste of air attack, believe me, I shivered, and there was no denying it.

I could spend pages telling of how we became "English-ized," and became accustomed to tea, fish and chips and all the other traditionally English things, but I'd never be able to tell the rest of my story short of a book if I dwell too much on details. Besides, by now D-Day was a thing of reality . . . American troops had landed on the beaches of Normandy, and our work was buzzing with an ever-increasing tempo. Things began to change fast. People began to look forward with hope and anxiety, and soon we were putting on our leggings and helmets, switching over from the "garrison uniform" to what eventually turned out to be our habitual costume for the coming months and our journey over sea and land to the heart of Germany.

As the days rolled on it was a common sight to see "Adsec" warriors traipsing up and down the streets with full field packs on their backs, steel helmets, rifles, and all the other paraphernalia necessary to an "overseas movement." Then early one morning (and I mean *early*) they came around to every house and woke up the fellows, told them to get dressed and loaded up. THIS WAS IT! Advance Section was "moving out." . . . So we said hurried goodbyes to our friends in Bristol and with lumps in our throats, and forty tons on our backs, we took off for our assembly point. Promptly at 4:30 A.M. we were told that this was a "dry run." They just wanted to see how long it would take them to round up the group for shipment when the day actually arrived! So with swear words on our lips and sleep in our bones we got our poor landlords out of bed again and went to sleep for the remaining hour or so, until breakfast. But the next time was no dry run, and a few days later we were driven down to the railroad station (same one we arrived at so many months ago), and back into the English compartment trains (first class, no less), and halfway across England to the port of embarkation at Southampton. . . .

James O. Chaskel, of Florence, enlisted in the Army July 6, 1942, and was assigned to the 227th Field Artillery, 29th Division. Going overseas in May 1943, Chaskel participated in the Normandy invasion, landing on Omaha Beach with the 116th Infantry, then rejoining his own outfit. He fought through France, Belgium, and Luxembourg. T/5 Chaskel was awarded four bronze stars and the Purple Heart for wounds. He was discharged Nov. 18, 1945, and is now an engineering student at the General Motors Institute, Flint, Mich.

June 7, 1944

To My Family:

THIS IS IT! This letter is made possible to you by and through a merchant seaman who is on this ship which is sailing directly to a beach in France. Purpose—The BIG DAY.

I left Ft. Bragg approximately April 24th, '43, had a rough bus and train ride to Camp Shanango, Pa., arriving April 26th. The camp itself was a hellhole due to the fact that it was a new camp and was even far from finished. The time we got there was a season of rain. It was a mudhole. There was no system to the place. No way of getting into the towns unless you knew someone who could pick you up at the gate. At this camp I had my one and only chance of getting home for a few hours before leaving for embarkation, but my Chaskel luck didn't fail me as all leaves and furloughs were stopped. I celebrated my 22d birthday at this camp. On May 9th we again pulled out and arrived at Camp Kilmer, N. J., on about May 10th, 1943. Kilmer was O.K. We were in good barracks, ate the best of food with very little hard work too. They did keep us busy with the checking of our records, clothes, etc., and were given reveille passes every other night. I took all my passes in New York City and had a swell time every time . . . but it all came to an end May 23d, 1943, when we went to greet the Queen "Lizzy." That was one of the toughest days I have ever had, as we must have carried two barracks bags at least 7 or 8 miles. We boarded the "Lizzy" next to the pier where the "Normandie" lay about halfway up. We lay at anchor for more than 48 hours before pulling out.

The boat itself was indescribably beautiful. She was overloaded with us and we were eating British prepared food, slop. I was picked with several hundred others as part of a gun crew. I was a gunner on a Bofor A.A. 20 mm. We had it pretty rough up there on watch in the wind and spray plus the rain that fell also. We were a happy bunch of fellows when one morning we awoke and found ourselves in a little cove or harbor in Scotland, at a small town or village by the name of Gurek, which is only a few miles north of Glasgow.

From the "Lizzy" we were transported to shore in small ferries, greeted warmly by a Scottish band and people. As we got on the train we were given snacks and coffee by the British Red Cross. . . . I arrived at the town of Oke-hampton at about 8 P.M. The camp was only a short distance to town and we were most glad as we were all so tired we could hardly walk. The camp was on the outskirts of the town and at the edge of the famous Dartmoor Moors. The town of Okehampton was a rather nice village with the regular country people. The camp we ourselves built and made a nice camp of it. The British named it "Show Grounds," and it had been our base until this invasion was under way. We went through a lot of hell insofar as the training and weather goes. There were 29 days of rain, wind and cold and one day of nice weather. The Moors are no nice place to be. We slept, ate and did our work in MUD, wind and rain. Mud up to our knees. Dartmoor Prison is in these same Moors. Let us not forget Sherlock also.

Our battalion was on exercises and problems out in the field more than we were at our garrison camp, "Show Grounds." We have been all over the south-ern and central part of England on these exercises. On the 26th of May, 1944, we left "Show Grounds," Okehampton, in the county of sunny Devon and ar-rived at the seaport of Swansea, Wales. That camp was SEALED and there were no passes of any kind. We boarded this ship, the "Marine Raven," a Victory ship, early Sunday morning, June 4th. Our outfit, 227th F.A., is but very few on this ship as we were and are detached from the rest of our battalion and attached to part of the 2nd Division. There are 48 enlisted men and one officer of us. We are to rejoin our outfit somewhere in the making of the beachhead. We are to hit the Omaha Beach of France. We have seen maps and had all instructions.

We pulled anchor on this ship last night at 7 P.M. just 24 hours ago. At present the beachhead has been made and is going well. My outfit, the 29th, and the 1st Division are the outfits which are making spearheads. When General Eisenhower picks the 29th for the assault troops, well, you just take it from the General and me, *We Have What It Takes and We Will Do It*. Droves of our bombers are coming back from France every minute. . . .

I realize that there will come a day and a minute when my hair will stand on end, BUT now I have no worries as my Mom, Pop, Sis, and Grandpop have given me through their love, confidence, trust and faith in me everything that will see me through in the best way. All that plus my own confidence will get any fellow in and through. DO NOT WORRY and I will see and be with you all in a few months I am sure. We have it going and we will keep it rolling.

I remain

Your loving son,

JIM

Floyd L. Kamp, of Argos, enlisted in the Army on Dec. 8, 1942, and was assigned to the infantry. Being selected for officer candidate school, Kamp was commissioned a 2d lieutenant July 2, 1943. Going overseas in Nov. 1944, he fought with the 66th Infantry Division in France. Promoted to 1st lieutenant in Oct. 1945, Lt. Kamp was discharged March 1946. He now lives in Harbor Beach, Mich.

November 29, 1944
England

DEAR MOTHER AND DAD:

This is the first of my letters from a foreign shore. I am stationed somewhere in England, exactly where I am unable to write because of security reasons. After many trials and tribulations I can tell you that I am feeling very well and things are okay now.

Frankly, there is not much I can write. I hardly know where to begin. I could go on and on for pages describing what I have seen this far and I have only seen a fraction of what there is. In all my life I have seen only a portion of the earth's surface, but I have never seen anything more picturesque than English countryside and small towns and villages. Every bit of land is put to use and the countryside from a distance looks like a checkerboard, only in green. Everything is so quaint here. The homes, the automobiles, and everything else is in miniature of the same things in the United States. There is nothing that you have ever seen which can equal it. The beauty of the country takes your breath away. It is like our large parks, only prettier. Flowers, grazing cattle and sheep, moss-covered fields look like one huge afghan that you could knit, using every color of yarn possible. I am certainly glad and thankful that I can take all of this in for it is really beauty itself.

We are living in one of the many small, quaint villages with its tiny shops and old-fashioned homes. You know the difference as soon as you step out the door. Everything is immaculate. In fact, we feel guilty when we throw away a match stick for it detracts from the beauty. The shops are only a fraction of the size of an average American store, and contain few items. Here each item is taken care of by the individual shop, although they do have multiple stores that are equivalent to our chain stores on a smaller scale. There are drug stores called "chemists" here and bars ("pubs" for public) and many other similar establishments. There are several small movie houses, commonly referred to as the cinemas or flickers and also a restaurant or so. It is pretty difficult to describe these English towns and countryside. You have to see it to believe it.

In America the civilians don't know there is a war on. Here in England the civilians have to bear countless hardships. Everything is rationed. Clothing, food, drink, recreation, and all the other necessities and luxuries of life. The British ride bicycles and walk. It is a rare thing to see an automobile, rare compared to the number of cyclists. You cannot imagine how the war has affected the British civilian. For example, there is only one restaurant in the whole town and there you can order only one dish, fish and chips. That is fish and potatoes. There is absolutely nothing else to be had. If you are lucky you may be able to obtain a glass of tea, although it is rationed also. I sometimes wonder if the Americans I know who complain of too much of this or too little of that and then go on strike could take what these people are taking. I give them credit. They are sacrificing more and have sacrificed more than many men in the war theaters. Wearing old clothes, eating less, giving up everything they hold dear so that England can devote herself entirely to the war effort.

Rationing isn't the only worry here, however, hard as it may be. The constant threat of air raids is here too. I have seen the effects of these air raids many places. Bare walls left standing, and mass destruction. 'Most all is cleared now but it has left its mark. It's hard to conceive. There can be no more courageous group of people. I take my hat off to the British. And the next time someone says he can't buy a candy bar because the United States is sending it to Britain, tell him to go to—. These people are getting nothing for themselves.

There is one more thing. Please don't have any ill-feeling toward the Red Cross, if you do have. For my sake give all you can to this organization. The services they perform are invaluable. There is no more worthy organization in the world; perhaps prisoners of war can tell you even more. When we embarked they were there with coffee and doughnuts and other necessary articles; when we arrived over here they were ready to assist. They are constantly performing priceless services, and believe me each one of us would be lost without it. Next time you contribute remember we are getting the benefits here without having to trouble ourselves more than to take it in our hands or otherwise accept it when it is offered to us.

I am in fine health and have beautiful accommodations here. The men are well housed also, for how long I would not be able to say if I knew. We are all glad that since we were destined to go overseas we were fortunate enough to come to England. I have learned a lot since I arrived here, and believe you me I am going to look up everything I can about this country. . . .

Be good, and keep your health above all, all of you. As they say over this way, "Cheerio!"

Love,
Son, FLOYD

Mary Sinclair, of Indianapolis, joined the Red Cross July 12, 1943, and was named a program director in the Club Department. She was sent to England in Sept. 1943, where she served in a club at Stratford-on-Avon until June, 1944. Then she served with Civilian War Relief in Belgium and Luxembourg the rest of the year. In Jan. 1945, Miss Sinclair was made director of the club at Compiegne, France, and remained there until she returned to this country. Discharged Oct. 13, 1945, she returned to Indianapolis. The following account of her work was written after she reached home.

I have discovered during the past year that even our behind-the-lines civilian life overseas seems to possess in the minds of some of those who were not there an aura almost of heroism. When I was a part of this life, I could scarcely have believed that such a tendency existed. For in the few and minor brushes

I experienced with enemy activity, I was either fatalistically unperturbed and therefore not a bit heroic, or scared to death, and definitely not; and I find that what was then simply taken for granted is apt to be thought of, when one is sitting in comfort, as unbearably uncomfortable, while the things that were hard are the very same things which cause the battle fatigue or nervous breakdowns in regular civilian life.

Some people in Indianapolis might have thought us badly off when we spent a rainy week in leaky tents on Utah Beach in September of '44. But we knew people who went through that area who slept under trucks in their coats while we had blankets and cots. When we had A-rations for dinner we were mighty glad they weren't B's. When we had B's, we could remember how tiresome C's were, and so on. A rather Pollyannaish attitude, but a very sustaining one in such circumstances.

Water was, it is true, an essential and sometimes difficult matter. This aside from the mud it made when it descended liberally in the form of rain or snow. It was a time-consuming essential to health and cleanliness from the time we left New York until affairs settled down after V-E Day. On the boat, fresh water was available about two hours a day for washing, while drinking water was secured each morning by standing in a long queue. In England a drought and the fuel shortage resulted in such signs in hotel bathrooms as, "The 8th Army crossed the desert on a pint a day. Three inches only, please," and in rather intimate squibs in the British papers about the king keeping quite clean with a bath a week in a tub filled only to a line which he had had painted on it.

Bathing in a helmet would be easier if helmets had flat tops, for their dome-like shape results in a tendency to spill. But in spite of this one can make a very small amount of water do for a quite satisfactory bath in a tent. Though it is advisable, if possible, to stand on a board, or the feet become very muddy. After doing this for weeks, the sight of water running out of a faucet is positively thrilling.

Because in all circumstances such as these, everyone around you is in the same boat, you unconsciously and automatically lower your standards so that annoyances come not from uncomfortable beds, inadequacies of food, water, or amusements, but from eternal waiting, from not knowing when you will be moved from one place to another, from exhausting and infuriating red tape and inefficient and petty officials.

In 1943, after a rather lengthy wait for transportation, and a period when we daily received another piece of equipment more unbecoming, more awkward, and heavier than the last, we were told to put it all on one evening and to descend by the freight elevator in the rear of Brooklyn's St. George Hotel, from whence we would make our "secret" departure. A fine, persistent rain was falling, and I am sure that all 175 of us, as we stood in that double line on Pineapple Street for nearly an hour, with drops running off the edges of our helmets, gas masks over one shoulder, musette bags over the other, and pistol belts with first aid kits and canteens of water around our hips, believed that security was gone, and that enemy submarines would certainly meet us on the other side of the Statue of Liberty. For our appearance, in spite of the weather, collected a mixed crowd of citizens, some of whom cheered us, while others were justifiably entertained by our peculiar looks. But without remarkable event, and us on board, the rusty "Aquitania" made another safe, unconvoyed trip to Scotland. From Glasgow to London we traveled at night. It was cold, we couldn't sleep, and we wished that we could look out of the windows, for in the black-out we could hardly tell whether we were going through towns or country. In London we were dispersed to the four corners of England to our assignments.

Guardian angels were hovering close when I was sent to Stratford. Fran, the club director, and Ginny, her assistant, were a rare and delightful combination for anyone's co-workers. Fran was busy in the office with routine affairs of administration most of the day, while Ginny and I were downstairs keeping track of supplies, getting off tours to see the Shakespeare sights, answering questions, and trying generally to be agreeable. Our days were long ones, with one of us always on duty at seven when breakfast began, and all three of us around in the evenings—usually till one or two in the morning.

After a very active day, we usually had a comparatively peaceful lull during the pub and theater hours, but at ten sharp the curtain came down in the theater, all the publicans called "Time please, Gentlemen," and all the soldiers in Stratford ran for the Red Cross. Such hordes descended upon us so quickly that we once had a call from a frantic bobby, who asked us kindly to do something about the queue which extended straight across the way and was blocking traffic on the main road.

While making a valiant effort to maintain some order in this chaos, it also became our self-assumed responsibility to see that as the liberty trucks left to return to camp, each soldier caught the one he was supposed to take. This sounds simple, but you must remember the black-out and the fact that all army trucks look the same when you cannot see the numbers on the bumpers, and imagine the confusion when it was necessary to sort out, among others, the 347th Engineers, the 327th Station Hospital, and the 127th Combat Engineers. We found the only thing to do was to corral a big soldier with a loud voice to announce the departing trucks, then we had to run around and tell all the boys we knew belonged to the departing outfit that they must hurry. There might, too, be someone who obviously could never make it under his own steam, so if no one was already taking care of him we had to find someone from his outfit who would. It was small wonder that with twenty or thirty trucks and all the soldiers they could carry sorting themselves out from eleven to twelve every evening in the market square, the good citizens living round about requested that liberty trucks park somewhere else.

The popularity of sightseeing with G.I.'s was astonishing. The Stratford club was originally organized for a leave club, a quiet spot where the intelligentsia might spend week-end leaves steeped in the lore of literature and quaintness. True, there were many soldiers who did not care a bit whether or not Shakespeare had lived in Stratford, but the numbers who came on tours surprised even the army authorities. The plays too were very popular. Probably the Shakespeare theater had in 1944 its most successful season, with its audiences nearly 75 per cent in American uniforms. We were finally forced that spring to limit the Sunday visitors who wished to go on tours to one truck from each organization. It was necessary to do this because we drew British civilian rations to feed, at the most, about 400 for dinner, and because the buildings on the tour are so small that even twenty soldiers at a time crowded them nearly impossibly.

In France our tours were limited too, because we weren't able to borrow enough trucks from the army. We had tours from Compiegne to Chantilly, Pierrefonds, the Armistice park and several smaller chateaux. Trucks always went off with the boys packed in like cattle. Had the army ever attempted to force them to ride an equal distance in trucks so crowded, they would have been highly and vocally incensed.

Early in December of '43, we started getting ready for Christmas. Every American outfit in England, I think, planned tremendous parties for children. For weeks our soldiers saved their candy and contributed their money to every kind of project for giving the English children a Christmas as pleasant as those they hoped their own families would have at home. Of course, from standards on which the British had been living for years, American soldiers had lots to give, but the G.I.'s seeming delight in spending his spare time in toy making and in hoarding his candy for six weeks to give to children he had never seen, produced in the English an unforgettable impression of American generosity and amazement at the American male's love of little children.

An ordnance company from G-25, the huge depot which was pictured in *Life* as "somewhere in England," sponsored our party. They started after Thanksgiving saving candy and making toys, and on the day before the party brought the results to Stratford in a truck. They had made boats, tanks, and little red carts out of cigar boxes and other scraps, and the 120 men in the outfit had saved two large clothesbasketsful of gum and candy. Our only responsibility for the party was to supply the list of children and the sit-down refreshments.

We held the party in the canteen. Games that are usually played at parties were played at ours, but the boys thought up several others too. One seemed particularly entertaining. The children and the soldiers formed a circle, blind-folding one child. Then two balloons were put into the circle and the child was told to break them with his feet. The resulting hopping and stamping seemed to send the onlookers practically into hysterics. Most entertained was Tommy, a jolly, fat, motorcycle dispatch rider who had stopped on a cold ride for a cup of coffee, and become fascinated with our company. He laughed so hard that he was invited to try to break the balloons too. The children nearly died of joy over this, and Tommy, who stayed all through the party and helped wait on the table when refreshments were served, went back to his outfit to find that the news of the afternoon's events had preceded him, and that he was to be known henceforth as the bubble dancer.

Somehow, from somewhere, that day Fran secured some jello. Not a child present had ever seen it before, and I never saw food disappear so fast. When the cake arrived, the children were so full that they couldn't eat any more, so we had to wrap it up for them to carry home, along with their stockings full of candy, the toys, and the prizes we had managed to have each one win. One little boy burst into tears just as we were distributing the toys, and nothing we could do elicited any information about what was wrong. At last someone got him into a corner where he sobbed out that he needed a "baig" to carry home his "stoof."

It was natural that the soldiers stationed closest to Stratford for the longest time became our best friends, the sort of friends without whom that life would have been much more difficult. The post exchange boys at the 347th Engineers offered to supply us our rations. This meant that we sent out to camp a list of the things we wanted that week, along with the money for them, and the boys brought or sent the rations on the liberty run that evening. They never seemed to mind the extra bother, and even did their best to wangle hairpins and bobby pins and other women's supplies for us.

One day a boy from the 347th Motor Pool ran an errand for us in our little old British truck, which had just returned from a thorough going over in the English garage which did our maintenance. He was utterly horrified by the way it ran; he collected the motor sergeant, and the two of them asked us if we could spare it long enough for them really to fix it for us. They did a wonderful job, but British bolts and nuts don't fit American tools, so they had to make a set which would; they couldn't get at the engine without removing the front fenders, and when they got those off, they found all of the piston rods so burned that they had to send a motorcycle rider to the factory in Coventry for others.

Another time, the boys who drove the mail truck appeared with a tremendous round aluminum army dish which they handed to me with instructions to open it upstairs in private, and the information that it was from the sergeant in the officers' mess, who "wanted to do something for someone who would like something for a change." Upon investigation the dish disclosed a cake the like of which had not been seen for many moons, and which I've certainly not seen since. It was about fifteen inches across and five inches high, and had a chocolate filling which Fran said would make Schrafft's green with envy. Our appreciation was evidently quite satisfactory, for the cake was followed at intervals by others and some pies. . . .

Considering the numbers of exuberant young men who were our customers, it was not too difficult to keep order in our clubs, particularly if you pretended that you were making no effort to do so, but at the same time kept watching for any person who might cause trouble. With all of the unhappy troubled men in Compiegne, France, jamming our little Red Cross so full that sometimes it was hard for us to squeeze inside ourselves when we came back after supper, I called the M.P.'s only once. Soldiers took care of each other, and in general, though always noisy, and sometimes boisterous and profane, they were very agreeable and considerate. Though there was more drinking than one would like, and those who had had too much required a good deal of attention and were no more attractive than they ever are, drinking was not the problem, nor drunks as universal as is sometimes thought.

Early in England I learned a valuable lesson about G.I. drinking. I became very annoyed with a soldier who I thought was behaving very badly. The next day I was told that he had heard the previous morning that his wife and baby had been killed in an automobile accident. Smitty was afterwards one of my best G.I. friends. Over a year later he burst into the club in Compiegne full of news of the men in his outfit, and seemingly very glad to find me there, but I shall never forget waiting that morning in England to apologize to him. Many times later when I could feel the desire rise up within me to tell some poor weaving soul just what I thought, I was restrained and helped by that thought of not knowing what he too might have gone through.

There were many wild raucous youths in the army, but actually I can think of only one who, when treated as though he were a nice person, did not respond by turning out to be one. There were, for instance, six boys in Compiegne who were bored with infantry training and who spent most of their time in the Red Cross nearly driving us mad, and who were, of course, during the daytime absent without leave. Smoky was the leader of this gang, which we finally dubbed the "Dead End Kids." One day in desperation I gave them the simple job of marking some new records which had arrived. Smoky took over as though the outcome of the war depended on him, and ever after that we had no trouble from the kids. They did errands, fixed broken equipment, helped in the checkroom, supervised tours, and were extremely critical of anyone inclined to be disorderly about the club. Of course, in spite of all we could do with them, they stayed A.W.O.L. once too often, were caught and given six months sentences, but later, having served his time, Smoky took nearly a day out of a precious two-day pass to Paris to come clear to Compiegne to see how we were getting along.

I know of no better way to picture the numbers of Americans using Red Cross clubs overseas than by citing the numbers of donuts consumed. The average in our club alone was around 21,000 per day, though one day we used nearly 26,000, with 700 gallons of coffee, a hundred gallons of iced tea, and another hundred of lemonade. For all of the clubs and the clubmobile which operated in our area, we made in the donut kitchen about 40,000 per day. These donuts were produced by a French civilian staff, and were made with hand-operated machines. Although the donut kitchen was only two blocks from our club, we kept a truck and driver busy twelve hours a day, seven days a week, delivering donuts to the club and taking empty trays back to the kitchen.

After nearly a year in the lovely club at Stratford-on-Avon, about fifty of us were collected from various English clubs and sent to the Continent with a branch of the Red Cross—Civilian War Relief. The purpose of this group was to help the army care for the displaced persons liberated as the German army retreated. Their work was much like that of UNRRA. Six months later they were very busy, but in the early part of that fall the Germans methodically removed their foreign slave labor as they retreated, and there was little work to be done. At the same time the great shortage of clubs for the soldiers close to the front concerned us all, so I returned to Paris about the first of December, 1944, to go back into club work. I ended up by being assigned to the opening of a club in Compiegne, where I stayed until I returned to this country in 1945.

With such hordes in clubs, it was difficult to give the personal attention to soldiers that we knew they wanted and deserved. It was hard, too, to provide entertainment. We had no place in France large enough for our dances, nor had we girls who would volunteer as partners. In England this had been no problem. Our volunteers had done a beautiful job wherever we used them, and our dance lists were made up of very attractive and very nice people. In France, we relied instead on USO shows, on bands, on sports, games, and on the soldiers themselves. There was always talent about, there was always music, and the good old songs that everyone knows were sung over and over again.

It was the tremendous appreciation on the part of soldiers for the little things one could do for them which made our life overseas so very satisfying to us. Sometimes we could arrange a meeting for brothers who had not seen each other for two or three years, by calling their commanding officers and arranging for leaves. One evening after the Bulge, a soldier sitting in the office wished out loud that he could see his brother, who was in the 101st Airborne Division. That division, I happened to know, had been moved from Bastogne to a rest area about fifty miles away from us, and the chaplain had visited that particular day at our mess. As we always did, in case we should need them, I had asked what their telephone code name was. So without saying anything, I called the brother's lieutenant, told him who and where I was, and asked if the brother could be given a pass to come to Compiegne. He not only granted the leave, but sent for the brother, and the two boys then and there made arrangements to meet the next day. They came in that evening radiant with joy at seeing each other, and nearly inarticulate with gratitude.

Reunions of relatives and friends were pretty exciting even for onlookers. I shall never forget one unexpected and joyful day when Frank, a big, slow-spoken sergeant, wounded four times (the last time badly enough to warrant his drawing guard duty in Compiegne instead of service with the infantry), burst into the office with his face simply shining. He had with him a fine-looking, much be-medaled young staff sergeant—his brother Johnny. Both had served in the same company of the 4th Infantry Division. Both, platoon leaders, had been hit at St. Lo, and each had, since that July day eight months before, thought the other dead. They had met a few minutes before downstairs in the club when Frank was going into the canteen and Johnny coming out. When, after congratulating them, I curiously asked Frank what he'd said when he saw Johnny, he answered, "There wa'nt nothin' to say—I just kissed him, front of everybody."

There was lots of griping in the army—usually about comparatively unimportant discomforts or things that were unpleasant. But the big things were laughed off. Twenty-five thousand men were shipped off to the front from Compiegne every six weeks. These same boys who had fussed at the club about the length of the donut line, the food at camp, the hikes, the training movies and talks, and the army in general, were apparently happy and gay when we went to the trains to see them off to fight real war. Supposedly, we went down to that siding in the field to cheer their departure; actually we found ourselves being cheered by them instead.

There was in many ways a happy league of Americans overseas. If you were in any kind of difficulty, any other American went out of his way to help you. You always greeted every American who passed you on the street or on the road. The closer we came to the front, the fewer American women there were, and the more exciting seemed our presence. Even truckloads of G.I.'s as they were whisked past would yell, "Hiya, gals! Where ya from?" Often homesick boys would stop us on the street and plead, "Please just say something in American. We haven't heard a woman speak English since D-Day." This sort of treatment spoils people, but it also gives you an enthusiasm for your work and the energy needed to last through perhaps sixteen hours each day for seven days a week.

James K. Cheeseman, of Richmond, enlisted in the Air Corps Apr. 15, 1942. He was sent to England in Oct. 1943 as a bombardier. For the next year and a half he participated in missions over France, Germany, and Central Europe with the 8th Air Force. For several months in 1944, S/Sgt Cheeseman was in charge of his group's operations in supplying the maquis of the French Underground. For this work he was awarded the Bronze Star along with six battle stars. Discharged Sept. 20, 1945, he returned to work at Richmond.

14 May 1945
Harrington, England

Dearest, Darling Ann:

Darling, it seems so endless, just writing and waiting and praying. It seems that someone just doesn't want us to come home. I thought I had learned patience, but I find now that what I thought was far from right. It is just plain hell being so near you and yet so far away. When we do start moving, I will be with you in ten days or two weeks. I'm ready, Government, I'm ready.

Now we shall try to fill your gaps in knowledge concerning the outfit and me. Isn't it wonderful not to have the whole U. S. Army peering over your shoulder as you write? First I am going to sit right down and tell you where I am this instant. I'm at Harrington Air Drome—7 miles from Kettering—18 miles from

North Hampton—and 22 miles from Leicester. Of course you never could have guessed most of that!

Maybe I should tell you about the trip over, dear. I kept a diary but destroyed it soon after landing. You know we left Kilmer in the darkest part of night and proceeded to Staten Island—pier 29 I believe it was. We boarded ship in the morning and were taken below to our bunks. I do not remember how many troops were on the "J. A. McAndrews," but it was too damned many. We were assigned our details and your Jim was given M.P. duty for the full time. We were tailed by subs for three days, and the destroyers raised all kinds of you-know-what during the evenings and early dawn. Ours was the largest convoy ever to cross, I understand. There wasn't a time when you couldn't count at least 50 ships and that was only about one-fourth of them. We had our own aircraft carrier and two battleships, besides being escorted by blimps and navy planes. It was a beautiful picture, darling, and ever so impressive. I didn't like it, knowing what it was leading to, but nevertheless I appreciated the magnificent strength of it. You suddenly realized that any one nation that could send 200 ships across two or three thousand miles of water and not lose a single one would not and could not be beaten—ever. I have never liked the army, dear, and I never will, but I have to respect it for its monstrous proportions.

I could fill up pages on the things that have happened since landing in this silly little country, but I would much rather wait and tell you the things you want to know. There have been a lot of times when I wanted to dig a foxhole and crawl into it for the duration, but on the whole it has been as safe as being at home. We only had a couple of V-2's come in the vicinity of the base here and they only jarred the peace. The worst catastrophe we have had was the strafing of the mess line at Watton (Norwich to you) when we were stationed there. There were fifty-some boys killed and more than a hundred wounded. One other time a bomber crashed into the living site and thirty-five were killed; that one rolled me right out of bed.

Taking it for granted that you want to know all, I will give you a blow by blow description of our London town, as I found it on the second visit. We left here for the train at 8 A.M. and arrived at London about 11:30, after a very nice trip. After visiting Red Cross Hdqtrs., we went to Prunier's for lunch, and after that back to the Red Cross, and as is the English custom, we had tea. About 8 we finally ended up at the Berkeley Hotel for dinner where the atmosphere is as nearly American as a person could expect to find anywhere. The two dinners incidentally came to—seven bucks. The tube system in London is really fascinating, honey. You can certainly get any place you wish to go in a hurry and for only 2d or 4 cents. You can ride all over (I should say under) London. Rainbow Corner provided my night's lodging. I stayed at the Hans Crescent and it was lovely. They have taken over the hotel and charge us 1s (20 cents) a night to stay there. There are three fellows to a room and we have a fireplace (they are very common here), and a private bath and all. It is really nice to have a place such as that to go to, especially the price is nice. There were two infantrymen with me in the room and they gave out with quite an interesting conversation. They told me stacks about Germany and France. Some of it was rather gruesome, too.

Being of the intelligent type, I slept until noon and then toured London for awhile. You could never guess whom we ran into, darling, Anthony Eden of all people. He was very pleasant and exactly the way you would picture him. The only thing better would have been old 54-cigar Churchill himself. He was there, but we didn't have the pleasure of seeing him.

We went to see "Sweet Yesterday." It was a light musical and most enjoyable—and it killed three of the unknown number of hours before we left for home. During the play they serve tea, drinks, and pastries; that is, between acts. You are allowed to smoke in the theaters here so it doesn't seem so long during the plays. They also have a bar or cocktail lounge where you can go between acts or after the play.

How are my twenty-four points, dear? I know they are two of the nicest little girls ever. Just hope your weather is blazing hot so my three girls can get a beautiful tan even if it does make your husband look peaked. It is raining here again today; this is the foulest weather ever. I still can't see why they didn't just cut the barrage balloons and let this island sink.

Until tomorrow, dear

All my love,
JIMMY

→ VI ←

FRANCE

PREINVASION air raids on France and Germany prepared the way for the invasion of Europe, June 6, 1944. Landing on Omaha Beach, the Americans captured Cherbourg while the British took Caen. Following devastating hedgerow fighting, the Americans captured St. Lo on July 18. Gen. Patton's Third Army swept east across France through Tours and Orleans. Paris was entered August 25. British-Canadian troops penetrated the Netherlands and the Americans swung north to Belgium and Luxembourg. Meanwhile, another American force landed in Southern France on August 15. They captured Toulon and Marseilles and pushed up the Rhone Valley. With the aid of the French Underground, the Americans crossed the Vosges Mountains and joined the northern armies on the Rhine. France and Belgium were liberated by the end of October, 1944.

Myron Berkheiser, of Rochester, was inducted into the Army Nov. 1, 1943, and was assigned to the infantry at Camp Wheeler, Ga. Going overseas in June 1944, Pvt. Berkheiser was stationed in England. He fought with the 35th Division in France where he was wounded Aug. 12, 1944. Pvt. Berkheiser was awarded the Purple Heart and was discharged Sept. 23, 1945, as a private first class. Berkheiser is now a grocer in Rochester.

Jan. 1945
England

DEAR FOLKS:

. . . It was about 1:00 o'clock Saturday, July 21, 1944, when I set foot on French soil. We landed on Omaha Beach, which you have read about, and from there walked about two miles in and ate dinner. It was a cold, rainy day. We stayed here until dark and then again boarded trucks and rode in black-out to the depot until about midnight. We were so tired that when we arrived at the depot we spread our blankets out and shelter halves and lay down on the ground to sleep. I went to sleep at once and heard nothing until morning. The other fellows told us that before they were asleep German planes come over and dropped flares but could not see us and then left. I slept through it all. The next day, Sunday, we dug foxholes close to the hedgerows and then pitched our tents and we were warm and had protection that way too. It never got dark until about 10:30 and almost every night as soon as it was dark, here came the German planes. Every field had antiaircraft guns and they would shoot at them. We always called him "Bedcheck Charlie." Nothing ever happened, it was just a patrol to see if he could find us. We could see artillery fire that was about twenty miles away on the front lines. Then came the day when three thousand planes came over; that was a beautiful sight. I never expected to see anything like it. You probably read about this in the papers. This was the break-through at St. Lo. While we were at this depot here in France for two weeks, we took short road marches for an hour every afternoon down along the beach. That was a bad place, pillboxes, barbed wire and lots of German guns and stuff. This had all been captured for several weeks.

Then one Saturday morning at roll call, certain men were called to leave at different times. It was here that we became separated, friends who had become buddies in the past two months. We rode until along in the afternoon. We stayed here until Tuesday evening and again went for another truck ride in the dark. About midnight we stopped and slept until daylight. Then we rode some more. Wednesday night we slept back with the kitchen and moved up again the next morning. Then on Thursday at noon we again moved up to the front lines. This was by truck and then marched up and were assigned to our outfit. It was here on Thursday afternoon, August 10, at about 3:00 o'clock, I joined the 134th Infantry Regiment, Company L, of the 35th Division. Here we were on the front lines, what a funny feeling. It was pretty quiet, no shooting, so we dug in and our officers talked with us. That space in front of us was no man's land. We stood guard for an hour at a time. This wasn't so bad, nothing really exciting here. Here I was making history. The folks back home were reading about the front line and I was on it. We went to bed and slept until 1:00 o'clock and got up for two hours guard duty. It was a beautiful night, the moon was real bright and a person could see plainly. It was cold out as the nights get very cold.

I have always got a laugh when I think back how scared my buddy got that night. He was only a short distance away, and he thought he saw something move on the other side of the fence or hedgerow. It was quite a drop off down to the next field. Everything was real quiet and he called to me in a whisper to come over to where he was, as he thought sure he saw a German crawling on the ground. I went over but could see nothing, so I went back and pretty soon he fired two shots at the object. When our time was up we went back to bed and I forgot about it until along the middle of the morning, so I asked him what he shot and got no answer so I went to look. All it was was a long branch of a tree that in the darkness looked like a man and the longer he watched it the more he thought he could see it move.

Friday morning we shaved and the morning papers came and we read those and everything was quiet. Once in a while a shell would go over, but not often. The cooks brought our dinner to us and then in the afternoon the word came down that we would move out to another location and dig in again. We had been holding this position against the Germans in case they would try to make an escape; this was in the Falaise Gap, which was closed and trapped so many Germans in August. Along about 3:00 o'clock we packed up all our equipment and moved to another position and started to dig in again for the night. After we had dug for an hour or so, the order came down again: pack up everything, we were going to move again. We waited then and ate supper in a sunken road, and also took enough canned rations along with us for at least three meals. It was about 6:30 or 7:00 o'clock when we started out on a road march. We had no opposition for a long time. We marched to the town of Domfront and then turned left or west as we came from the north. We kept marching, and stopping for a long time and then came to a place where several trucks and a farmhouse were burning. Here we left the road and turned south through an orchard past some farm buildings; chickens and rabbits were everywhere and the people had left. From these buildings we went through the fields away from the road toward the hills. It was now getting late in the evening. For awhile we waited in a woods and then about dark we went into a field and stayed for the night. I took guard duty from 11:30 to 1:30 and tried to sleep the rest of the night but it was so cold I couldn't or didn't very much. At these times it seems that morning will never come.

It was now Saturday morning and just getting daylight. It was rather foggy and cold out. Everyone was cold and stiff, but it was better as the sun got higher. The ones that wanted to or felt like it ate breakfast of C-rations. I wasn't hungry so didn't care to eat. In a little while we put on our packs and were all ready to go. Boy, what a load! We were to advance and take the hill which we started up the night before. The command came down and we moved out. We marched up and over hedgerows single file a short distance between each man. We walked and walked and met no opposition. In a little while we met the 137th Infantry Regiment bringing some German prisoners down the hill. They had gotten there ahead of us and had taken it. We went farther up and then dug in to hold our position against a counterattack. After we had dug in, they started shelling us and that lasted for a long time. I ate dinner in this foxhole, and stayed close inside of it too. Then about 2:30 word came that we were to move out. Then we pulled back and went around this hill to the left and down through a lane. There were a lot of companies ahead of us and the moving was slow. We came up beside some buildings and down another lane. The sun was hot, the ground was dry and dusty. The sound up ahead sure wasn't too pleasant and I was pretty certain someone was sure to get hurt. Well, then we pulled back beside the buildings. I felt pretty good, only I hardly knew what to expect next or what to do. Some of the fellows were picked to move around and try to knock out the tanks that were holding up our advance. I was left with our squad, for which I was thankful not to be picked to go on any mission.

We were alongside this French building and the order was given for us to move out and cross the road to our front and turn left and advance up to some buildings and clean snipers out of them. The scouts crossed the road and two mortar shells were dropped at the far corner of the building to our front. I was right behind the squad leader and he said "Wait a minute." While we were waiting two more mortar shells dropped to our right and too close. The next thing I remember I was trying to get to my feet and get inside the building. Everyone else was gone except one and he never knew what happened. I was more or less dazed, but there was a consciousness that someone was at my side, my right side. I was being helped. I looked around, but no one was there. There was help from above. I had a feeling that I had not been forsaken, but we are promised that angels will bear us up. I got into the barn or building and lay down on some hay. There were six or seven men in there wounded and an old French woman, who had been hurt. There were several other soldiers who had not been hit there too. With some help I got my shoes off and took my wound tablets and bandaged my knee and arms. I had very little pain, only my left leg from the knee down was numb and asleep and felt cold. This happened about 4:15 and the medics came about 6:30 and gave me and everyone else a shot of morphine, and about 8:00 or after we were taken to a first aid station. Our squad leader had died in the meantime, sitting in the doorway between the two rooms. He didn't seem to be hurt bad, but the medics said he had died from shock.

At the time we were taken in the jeep to the first aid station they took my name, bandaged me up, put a splint on my leg and gave me a pint of blood plasma, but it seems as if all night I was riding and going in and out of hospitals; we must have stopped at three. I woke up and found that I was so cold, seemed as if I would freeze. I had lots of blankets over me, so the nurse lit a lantern, regular kerosene type, and put it under my cot. This was the 41st Evacuation Hospital. One of the ward boys cut my clothes off and gave me another pint of blood plasma. Then they took some X-ray pictures, and about noon I was taken to the operating room and then given my first ether. I don't know what they did. I was then put in a large tent with lots of men. I ate my first meal, supper, Sunday evening, since Saturday noon. I had no appetite. Every four hours I was given a shot and some pills. Then a pill to go to sleep. I sure had some crazy dreams. I'd chase the Jerries and they would chase me. That kept up for a week or more. We had good care here. The ether never made me sick at all, I guess I didn't have anything to get sick on. I didn't suffer from much pain, only my left leg felt so much as if it were asleep. It was hard to turn over as both arms had bandages on as well as both my legs and back and some on my hips.

I stayed at this evacuation hospital Sunday and Monday. Tuesday afternoon I was taken to another hospital or large tent and left here for an hour or so, ate supper and then moved to the airstrip. The weather was too cloudy and no planes were able to fly so we stayed Tuesday night and until Wednesday evening. About 8:00 o'clock we were loaded again and put in C-47 planes and soon were on our way to England. It was cloudy when we took off, but we were soon at a height above the clouds and the sun was so bright that those clouds looked like big snow banks. I was lucky to be by a window over the left wing and could raise up and look out. A flight nurse and a ward boy kept check on everyone to see that they were all right.

The flight to England had a lesson for me and a beautiful picture to look at, one to compare with life. The ground was dark and cloudy, the sun hidden from us, but as we climbed up the picture also changed. Here we are in life, everything looks so dark and dreary we can't see the sun, but we never look up. If we only look up and see beyond the clouds, God will roll the clouds away and our lives can be full of sunshine. It was a very good comparison of life today.

As soon as we landed in England we were taken to hospitals, and how good beds looked with clean white sheets and white blankets. I could hardly sleep. I stayed here Wednesday night and Thursday. Friday after dinner I was taken to the 192d General Hospital and from there I wrote the second letter since I was wounded. There were twenty-eight of us in a ward and I stayed here for four weeks.

Dr. A. Ebner Blatt, of Indianapolis, enlisted in the Medical Corps of the Army Oct. 29, 1942, and was commissioned a captain. While in the States, he was attached to the 32d General Hospital, the Parachute School, the 502d Parachute Infantry, and upon going overseas in Sept. 1943, he was attached to the 101st Airborne Division. He participated in the parachute invasion of Normandy, the parachute invasion of Holland, and saw action in Alsace, Germany, and Austria. He attained the rank of major in Mar. 1946, and received the Bronze Star, Combat Medical badge, Belgian Fourragere and the Dutch Fourragere. Discharged in Mar. 1946, Major Blatt returned to his medical practice in Indianapolis.

August 6, 1944
France

Dear —:

We went to the marshalling area about a week before we took off. We had been there before and it was fun there. We had briefing for several hours each day (because of the number of men the briefing went on day and night—as soon as one platoon left the tent another one went in), and the rest of the time we read or went to the movies or did whatever we pleased.

Of course, we were inside barbed wire for security reasons—no one could go in or out of the camp. The briefing was so interesting and so exactly like the stuff we had done on maneuvers all spring that no one thought much about the fact that this was the real thing. The afternoon of June 5th was a little cloudy and windy but we knew that we were going that night. After supper we put on all our equipment and were lined up in plane loading order when General Eisenhower inspected us and he spoke to me as he went by.

When we marched out to the hangars to meet our guides all the pilots and crew chiefs were wearing .45's. We went out to the plane, got our chutes on, got in and warmed up and took off. It was just dusk then, and shortly after we were airborne and in formation it got quite dark. Through the door of the plane I could see the lights of other planes in our serial. They were all getting into formation. So far it was just like the ordinary problem, and then the next time I looked out the lights were out—and that meant we were over the Channel.

We flew for what seemed about an hour and just when we got the signal that we were twenty minutes away from the target area, I saw a sudden flame appear behind us, then dive down and disappear. I didn't know whether it was a transport or escort or enemy—and then the coast appeared beneath us in the moonlight and there were sparks and flashes all along us. They were the flak guns. About that time the flak started flying past the door. (I remember hoping to myself that it was not flak but sparks from the engine.) I could see the fields and rivers below in the moonlight and here and there on the ground the flash of the guns. Then we got the red light, and rather quickly (in what seemed two minutes instead of four, ordinarily the four minutes seem like twenty), the green light flashed and I followed Captain Smith out the door. The plane was going fast and the opening shock was terrific. The force of it broke my chin strap and one of the metal fasteners on the helmet and the ground came rushing up so fast I wondered whether or not I should pull my reserve when CRASH—I landed. (The reason the ground came up so fast was because we jumped at about three hundred feet instead of the six hundred feet that we jumped on problems.) I hit the ground so hard that I thought I had broken my back for a few minutes, but I could move my arms and legs O.K., so I started to get out of my harness. I was in a field all by myself, and as I lay struggling in my harness, I could see other planes going over and the flashes of guns all around me (but none in the same field I was in) shooting at them and I saw two sticks jump and I could see the tracers going up at their canopies. I couldn't unfasten the buckles.

Just then I saw a figure coming along the hedgerow. He came out of the gloom holding a rifle. I spoke the password and clicked the recognition signal on the little metal cricket we all carried and got a good hold on my trench knife. (Next time I'm going to carry a .45 come hell or high water.) But, to my profound relief, he answered properly. It was Sergeant Wood of headquarters company. He helped me out of my harness and we went along the hedgerow. Machine guns and ack-ack would splutter in the other fields as some of the planes came back flying low and fast on their way back to England. Once or twice the whole sky would light up momentarily and that meant a plane going down in flames. At the corner of the field about six of our men had gathered. None of us knew where we were and my back hurt so badly that I could not carry all my equipment. J. E. Turner, the dentist, was in the group, and he took one of my bags, Major Ginder another, Corporal Boney another, and I carried the fourth. Altogether in a short time there were about thirty of us and we took off in the direction that someone suggested. Then all of a sudden I was with another group and Turner and Ginder had disappeared. The night was starry and fairly clear where I was and then suddenly I was going down a road with still another group. Every once in a while a machine gun would open up and we would scatter—then a grenade or two would put the machine gun out of action and then suddenly it was starting to get light and visibility was increasing. A machine gun opened up at a crossroad. Dodson, a bazooka man, put it out of action and we crossed the road into a field and there were two dead paratroopers and a dead German. There were only about twelve of us then—three were medics—so we all got in a ditch and put a couple of men out on the snipers who were getting in pot shots at us. My back was hurting pretty bad so I got a grenade I jumped with out of my pocket and waited for the day to break.

Lieutenant Lepsher, a demolitions officer who had taken charge, went off on a reconnaissance to see if he could locate any other paratroopers. The rest of us waited in a ditch and the day grew brighter. There was machine gun and rifle fire in the distance. . . .

When Lieutenant Lepsher came back it was about eight o'clock and bright daylight. We heard the bombers pounding the beach about three miles to our east and we could still hear machine guns and rifle fire, but the snipers around us had either withdrawn or were waiting for us to show ourselves, because no one was firing at us right then. I put on my Red Cross brassard (we had not worn them on the jump because at night the white band is too good a target). Lepsher had contacted some of the first battalion about half a mile away so we sneaked down the ditch and hedgerow back to the road right beside the machine gun that Dodson had knocked out a few hours before and started south.

At another road junction about one-half mile away, we came on about sixty paratroopers coming down the road. It was so wonderful to be back in the fold and not to feel as though one were entirely surrounded by enemies. We joined them and went down the road. We knew where we were at last, just about one mile north of where we wanted to go. As we were walking down the road, one of the flank scouts came back to the road and said there was a man with a broken leg two fields away. I left the column, and with two men to act as protection against snipers, I went over to see him. He had a fractured leg all right, but had already been given morphine. I put a splint on him, and fixed him up generally and noted his position on the map so we could pick him up later. Some sniper fired once but my riflemen scared him away. We then cut down the field to the third battalion assembly area, but there was no one there at all. However, out on the road about three hundred yards away were some Americans, both our division and the 82d, so after taking care of a couple of them, I went on down the road planning to go to the place where regimental headquarters was to be. . . .

When I arrived, Ramey and Colonel Michalis were there. They told me that Colonel Mosely had a broken leg and that they were leaving to go to the regimental objective—a gun position near the coast. Elements from the regiment had cleared the opening of the beach—the sea-borne troops were landed even then, and we had broken up any organized resistance in our area. They had some wounded there, and they turned the two aid stations over to me and two third-battalion medics. All the regiment personnel was going back to the beach. The farm where we were was under enemy fire especially from snipers, but they left about six riflemen as protection. All afternoon we gave plasma and put on splints and dodged the sniper fire. We wanted to clear out the wounded and get back nearer to our own people, but we had no means of evacuating the wounded, no place to send them that we knew was in operation, and besides, the whole yard of the farmhouse was filled with enemy ammunition, both small arms and mortar. It was too heavy for us to carry and we were afraid to leave it, because then the snipers would come in and take it. About four in the afternoon some gliders were towed right over us west toward Ste. Mère Eglise; it sure looked good to see them and to know that we had such air superiority that we could bring them in safely by daylight. About five miles to the west of us the gliders cut loose, and then the planes came right back over us on their way back to England. By that time we had everyone taken care of—the walking wounded were in a barn, the litter wounded in rooms of the farmhouse. Everyone had been fed and we had blacked-out one room for us during the night.

Shortly after that the first of the sea-borne troops came by. They said the road back to the beach was entirely in our hands, although there were still enemy patrols firing here and there. . . .

Charles E. Frohman, of Columbus, was inducted into the Army in May 1943, and was attached to the medical corps. He was made a technician 5th grade and was sent to England in Feb. 1944. There he was assigned to the medical detachment with 3d Army Headquarters and served in France, Luxembourg, and Germany. Discharged in Dec. 1945, T/5 Frohman returned to graduate study in biochemistry.

May 28, 1945
Erlangen, Germany

DEAR FOLKS:

. . . The 4th of July we rolled into Southampton, which had been bombed into shambles. We got to see the old city wall, though, which was still intact. We waited twenty-four hours in the streets, again not sleeping. Someone grumbled, "This is a fine way to spend the 4th of July." It was. No sleep for three days and lousy K-rations. We bought a paper which had a German claim that General Patton was bringing his 3d Army to France, July 5th. That scared us to death.

At 4 A.M. we drove into the open mouth of an LST and at 11 A.M. we saw the Isle of Wight, with its chalk cliffs, fade into nothing. We had left once and for all the homey, friendly shores of England. Our trip across the channel was like a Mediterranean cruise. The Germans had nothing to stop us with. We sailed peacefully over the unusually calm waters with a warm sun beating down on us. It was wonderful.

It was dark when we finally sighted France. It is impossible to describe what that was like. If it's possible to run the whole gamut of human emotions in a few minutes, we did as we leaned against the rail and watched one of the greatest panoramas of all times unfold in front of us. At that time we were still almost in the beachhead stage of fighting. The beautiful dark French coast stood out, littered with tons of wreckage. As it got darker and we drew closer, we could hear the incessant boom of artillery and see the flashes that accompanied it. By the flashes we could see the *entire* German line. That is how small it was. Now and then varicolored signal flares would flash in the air for a brief second. The hum of airplanes came from all directions. The tracer shells going up from our ack-ack and the loud throaty boom and brilliant flash of the 90's showed us that they weren't ours. A brilliant flash, a flaming streak, and an explosion would mark the end of at least one plane now and then. No one wanted to sleep now.

At 12 o'clock the tide had gone out far enough to permit us to leave the ship. The LST again opened its jaws and we drove out. There were other ships doing the same as we and all were beached on dry land like ours, unloading. As we looked back at them, they looked like great steel forts built on the sand.

We unloaded at Omaha Beach two miles from Carentan, and had orders to go immediately to the de-waterproofing area, two miles away. (The vehicles won't run long with waterproofing on them.) And also the beaches had to be cleared quickly in case of strafing and to make way for more troops. Every intersection had an M.P. silently directing traffic in the dark. Never saw so many M.P.'s in my life. We made our way through the blasted concrete beach defenses and onto the roads, where for the first time we saw the famous small fields of Normandy, fenced in by hedgerows and the tall, gawky, twisted poplars that looked so silly and out of place there. Those French poplars were the worst proportioned trees I've ever seen.

All at once our motor started to skip. We talked to it, begged it, prayed to it, even sang to it, but it stopped dead as a doornail. We jumped out, threw up the hood and everyone pulled everything he could find. Miraculously enough after ten minutes we got the damned thing going again. We finally arrived in the de-waterproofing area and started de-waterproofing our trucks immediately. We were through by 10 A.M. and at 10:30, July 6th (the same day), we set off for our final destination. . . .

The front line ran from La Haye du Puits to Carentan to St. Lo to Caen. They were fighting in Cherbourg. We hadn't slept for three days; day was just breaking and we could hear a terrific artillery barrage in the distance when we moved out for our first destination in France. We didn't know where it was yet. We set out with an umbrella of planes protecting us. We soon lost our sleepiness because this was the most interesting trip we had ever taken. The night before it had been too dark to see much, but now we were getting our first glimpse of France. The slim, twisted poplars which looked so weird the night before took on a different aspect. They looked ridiculous instead of frightening. The hedgerows stretched as far as you could see, dividing the land into little patches. Every other field was an orchard and all of them were in bloom. The song, "When It's Apple Blossom Time in Normandy," went whizzing through my brain. It was beautiful. Could this be in the middle of the war? Just then someone sighted a French sign and everything else was forgotten in a series of awed Oh's and Ah's. It was the first distinctly French thing we had ever seen. Then we passed an old farmhouse. I had never seen anything as old before. It looked like something out of a fairy tale book. It just didn't look real.

Then we came to our first French town. It was a little village called Point d'Albe. It's not on the map; it is too small. We went over a small hill and there was the village before us. There was not a whole building in the town; only broken walls and rubble. Everything was covered with a red dust (the stones of the buildings were a red-brown), and the ruins gave the impression that they were made ages ago instead of recently. The town was deserted and silent. Not the silence that you know, but a more profound and depressing silence. It was so quiet it was deafening. There was not a living thing in sight, only ruins. What a gloomy looking place. We had never imagined that war could wreak such destruction.

We then passed through Ste. Mère Eglise and St. Sever, both of which were in the same shape and much larger towns than Point d'Albe. The destruction in St. Sever was beyond description. It was just outside of St. Sever that we stopped and set up. You can find it easily on the map. It's the first flag on the map and the one right by La Haye du Puits. We were three miles from the city and the Germans held La Haye du Puits. All day and night our artillery, which was on the other side of us, kept lobbing shells over our heads into the city. The Germans were shooting back over our heads at the artillery. Although St. Sever was completely destroyed, shells were still falling in the quiet town.

We unloaded our truck in an apple orchard, fenced in by hedgerows, and set up our big tent and our little pup tents. While we were setting up, it began to pour down rain. Ugh! In the midst of it, an old Frenchman came strolling up. He was extremely interesting to us since he was the first real foreigner we had ever seen. The English had the same customs, language, etc., as we, but the French! Well, we attempted to talk but finally he gave up in disgust and went strolling away. By this time we had our tents up and it was dark so we ate supper (another lousy K-ration), crawled into our tents, lay on the wet soggy ground and oblivious to the rain, the shells still whizzing overhead, and what sounded like every airplane in the world, we said, "Come what may," and finally got some much needed sleep. . . .

Love,
CHARLES

Jesse Trinkle Bobbitt, of Paoli, enlisted in the Army Nov. 23, 1942, and was trained as a paratrooper. Leaving this country in Jan. 1943, he was attached to Company E, 501st Parachute Infantry, 1st Battalion, 101st Airborne Division. Sgt. Bobbitt landed in Normandy on D-Day and fought in that area until July, when he returned to England for rest. Then he took part in the invasion of Holland, and was killed in battle at Son, Sept. 18, 1944. Sgt. Bobbitt was awarded four battle stars, two presidential citations, the Purple Heart, and several other decorations.

July 4, 1944
France

DEAR FOLKS:

Sorry I haven't written, but we have been pretty busy on this side of the pond.

I suppose the main questions are where am I, and how am I. I haven't got a scratch and at the present time I am behind a hedgerow in France. That is about all I can tell you as to my present location.

We have had quite a time since I have last written you. We were the first ones here so we got the hornet's nest all stirred up for everyone else. They had quite a nice reception waiting for us when we got here and things were really hot that first night and couple of days. The first day they threw everything but the kitchen sink at us and then they must have had a plumber take the sink out because I think they even threw it at us the second day. On the second night they jumped paratroops behind us and we got to pay them back for the reception they had for us.

One of our main troubles has been snipers. They hide in the trees and shoot at you, and you can't find them for love nor money. It was really tough on them when we did find them. A lot of them dress as French civilians and you don't know whom to shoot.

I think the prettiest sight I have ever seen was on the second day when some tanks came up to help us out. We were really in a touchy spot when they came, and that was the first of the beachhead we had seen and we were beginning to sweat those boys out. When we got the tanks we really went to town.

We were fighting the Czechs and Poles at first but they were really fighting because the Germans had told them that paratroopers would cut their throats if they surrendered so they just kept on fighting. Nice build-up they gave us, wasn't it? Since we left the sector we were fighting in, they say a lot of them are surrendering because the men with "the baggy pants and all the pockets" have left. They were talking about our jump suits; you remember what they look like.

Yes, that was my picture, and the reason I looked so short was because I didn't have any shoes on. I was in the process of changing socks when he wanted to take the picture and I was too tired to put my boots on. Nice looking guy with a week's beard, "ain't" I?

Our regiment got a presidential citation for the work it did. We get a ribbon with a star on it to wear over our right breast pocket. That is in addition to our combat star. Next time you see Paul Stout ask him what his outfit got in the last war. He was all the time telling me about his outfit so tell him I'm laughing now. Also tell him I have some tales that will match his. I have a helmet and some more stuff to send home as soon as I get a chance. I thought Jimmie would get a kick out of the helmet. There are also some German stamps that I thought Grandad would like to see. Tell Dad that there are very few Lugers because they have been replaced with another pistol, but I have him one of those with about 100 rounds of ammunition. No salt and pepper shakers as yet but I'm still looking. I'm beginning to think the French don't use them. . . .

Well, this seems to be all there is to say so I will close. I am O.K. and there is no use to worry. Love to all and God bless you all.

Your son,

J. T.

Ernie Pyle, of Dana, began his newspaper career in La Porte after leaving Indiana University. He worked in New York for the Scripps-Howard Newspapers until 1935, when he became their roving columnist. At the beginning of the war he went to England and subsequently followed the troops in the major campaigns as a war correspondent, writing personal columns about them that were immensely popular. In 1945 he transferred to the Pacific theater to continue his reporting. He was killed at Ie Shima, Apr. 18, 1945. The following piece of correspondence, and another on page 248, were selected as examples of his work that also deal with Hoosiers. They are reprinted by permission.

August 1944

Normandy

Soldiers are made out of the strangest people. I made another friend—just a plain old Hoosier—who was so quiet and humble you would hardly know he was around. Yet in a few weeks of invasion he had learned war's wise little ways of destroying life while preserving one's own. He hadn't become the "killer" type that war makes of some soldiers; he had merely become adjusted to an obligatory new profession.

His name was George Thomas Clayton. Back home he was known as Tommy. In the Army he was sometimes called George, but usually just Clayton. He was from Evansville, Indiana, where he lived with his sister at 862 Covart Avenue. He was a front-line infantryman of a rifle company in the 29th Division. Out of combat for a brief rest, he spent a few days in an "Exhaustion Camp," then was assigned briefly to the camp for correspondents. That's how we got acquainted. Clayton was a private first class. He operated a Browning automatic rifle. He had turned down two chances to become a buck sergeant and squad leader, simply because he preferred keeping his powerful B.A.R. to having stripes and less personal protection.

He landed in Normandy on D-Day, on the toughest of the beaches, and was in the line for thirty-seven days without rest. He had innumerable narrow escapes. Twice, 88s hit within a couple of arm's lengths of him. But both times the funnel of the concussion was away from him and he didn't get a scratch, though the explosions covered him and his rifle with dirt. Then a third one hit about ten feet away, and made him deaf in his right ear. As a child, he had always had trouble with that ear anyway—earaches and things. Even in the Army back in America he had to beg the doctors to waive the ear defect in order to let him go overseas. He was still a little hard of hearing in that ear from the shellburst, but it was gradually coming back.

When Tommy finally left the lines he was pretty well done up and his sergeant wanted to send him to a hospital, but he begged not to go for fear he wouldn't get back to his old company, so they let him go to a rest camp instead. After a couple of weeks with us (provided the correspondents didn't drive him frantic), he was to return to the lines with his old outfit.

Clayton had worked at all kinds of things back in the other world of civilian life. He had been a farm hand, a cook and a bartender. Just before he joined the Army he was a gauge-honer in the Chrysler Ordnance Plant at Evansville. When the war was over he wanted to go into business for himself for the first time in his life. He thought he might set up a small restaurant in Evansville. He said his brother-in-law would back him.

Tommy was shipped overseas after only two months in the Army, and when I met him he had been out of America for eighteen months. He was medium-sized and dark-haired, and had a little mustache and the funniest-looking head of hair I ever saw this side of Buffalo Bill's show. While his division was killing time in the last few days before leaving England, he and three others decided to have their hair cut Indian-fashion. They had their heads clipped down to the skin, all except a two-inch ridge starting at the forehead and running clear to the back of the neck. It made them look more comical than ferocious, as they had intended. Two of the four had been wounded and evacuated to England.

I chatted off and on with Clayton for several days before he told me how old he was. I was amazed; so much so that I asked several other people to guess at his age and they all guessed about the same as I did—about twenty-six. Actually he was thirty-seven, and that's pretty well along in years to be a front-line infantryman. It's harder on a man at that age. As Clayton himself said, "When you pass that thirty mark you begin to slow up a little."

This Tommy Clayton, the mildest of men, had killed four of the enemy for sure, and probably dozens he couldn't account for. He wore an Expert Rifleman's badge and soon would have the proud badge of Combat Infantryman, worn only by those who had been through the mill. Three of his four victims he got in one long blast of his Browning automatic rifle. He was stationed in the bushes at a bend in a gravel road, covering a crossroad about eighty yards ahead of him. Suddenly three German soldiers came out of a side road and foolishly stopped to talk right in the middle of the crossroads. The B.A.R. has twenty bullets in a clip. Clayton held her down for the whole clip. The three Germans went down, never to get up. His fourth one he thought was a Jap when he killed him. In the early days of the invasion lots of soldiers thought they were fighting Japs, scattered in with the German troops. They were actually Mongolian Russians, with strong Oriental features, who resembled Japs to the untraveled Americans. Clayton was covering an infantry squad as it worked forward along a hedgerow. There were snipers in the trees in front. Clayton spotted one, sprayed the tree with his automatic rifle, and out tumbled this man he thought was a Jap.

Do you want to know how Clayton located his sniper? Here's how! When a bullet passes smack overhead it doesn't zing; it pops the same as a rifle when it goes off. That's because the bullet's rapid passage creates a vacuum behind it, and the air rushes back with such force to fill this vacuum that it collides with itself, and makes a resounding "pop." Clayton didn't know what caused this, and I tried to explain. "You know what a vacuum is," I said. "We learned that in high school."

And Tommy said, "Ernie, I never went past third grade."

But Tommy was intelligent. A person doesn't have to know the reasons in war—he only has to know what things indicate when they happen. Well, Clayton had learned that the "pop" of a bullet over his head preceded the actual rifle report by a fraction of a second, because the sound of the rifle explosion had to travel some distance before hitting his ear. So the "pop" became his warning signal to listen for the crack of a sniper's rifle a moment later. Through much practice he had learned to gauge the direction of the sound almost exactly. And so out of this animal-like system of hunting, he had the wits to shoot into the right tree—and out tumbled his "Jap" sniper.

Clayton's weirdest experience would be funny if it weren't so filled with pathos. He was returning with a patrol one moonlit night when the enemy opened up on them. Tommy leaped right through a hedge and, spotting a fox-hole, plunged into it. To his amazement and fright, there was a German in the foxhole, sitting upright holding a machine pistol in his hands. Clayton shot him three times in the chest before you could say scat. The German hardly moved. And then Tommy realized the man had been killed earlier.

All his experiences seemed to have had no effect on this mild soldier, except perhaps to make him even quieter than before. The worst experience of all is just the accumulated blur, and the hurting vagueness of being too long in the lines, the everlasting alertness, the noise and fear, the cell-by-cell exhaustion, the thinning of the surrounding ranks as day follows nameless day. And the constant march into eternity of one's own small quota of chances for survival. Those are the things that hurt and destroy. And soldiers like Tommy Clayton went back to them, because they were good soldiers and they had a duty they could not define. Three weeks after Tommy Clayton returned to the lines, he was killed. It saddened me terribly, for I felt very close to him.*

ERNIE PYLE

Edward R. Pullins, of Rensselaer, was inducted into the Army Sept. 3, 1942, and was assigned to the infantry. Leaving this country in Mar. 1943, Pullins fought in the European theater with Headquarters Company, 2d Battalion, 137th Infantry Regiment, 35th Division. For this action he was awarded five battle stars and the Purple Heart. Sgt. Pullins returned to the U. S. in Aug. 1945, and was discharged Oct. 22. At present he is farming and lives in Rensselaer.

August 21, 1944
Somewhere in France

DEAR EDITOR:

You may have forgotten me for I have been out of circulation for quite some-time. France is quite a place, full of plenty of excitement and adventure. Yes, it's a country where history is being made every minute and it's about the best place for a blow-by-blow description of just what is going on over here. I have been in the thick of things and I must say that it's pretty "warm" over here most of the time. I am not speaking of the weather when I say this, but you can gather what

* From *Brave Men*, by Ernie Pyle. Copyrighted, 1944, by Henry Holt and Company, Inc., pp. 307–9.

I mean. I thought I would give you a few viewpoints on just what goes on from a ringside seat. A good article to go into would be the mass bombing raid carried out over the front around the middle of July. Well, here is how it looked from a front row seat, or I might say front row foxhole, in Normandy:

Our front lines were marked by long strips of colored cloth laid on the ground, and with colored smoke to guide our airmen during the mass bombing that preceded our breakout from the German ring that held us to the Normandy beachhead.

The dive bombers hit just right. We stood in the barnyard of a French farm and watched them barrel nearly straight down out of the sky. They were bombing about half a mile ahead of where we stood. They came in groups, diving from every direction perfectly timed, one right after another. Everywhere you looked separate groups of planes were on the way down or on the way back up or slanting over for fire or circling, circling, circling over our heads waiting for their turn. The air was full of sharp and distinct sounds of cracking bombs and heavy rips of the planes' machine guns and splitting screams of diving wings.

And then a new sound gradually droned into our ears. It was deep and all encompassing, without notes—just a gigantic faraway surge of doom. It was the heavies. They came from directly behind us, and at first they were the merest dots in the sky. You could see clots of them against the far heavens, too tiny to count individually. They came on with terrible slowness. They came in flights of twelve—three flights to a group. And in the groups stretched out across the sky they came in families of about seventy planes each. Maybe these gigantic waves were two miles apart, maybe they were ten miles, I don't know; but I do know they came in constant procession and I thought it would never end. What the Germans must have thought is beyond comprehension. The march across the sky was slow and steady. I've never known a storm or a machine or any resolve of man that had about it the aura of such ghastly relentlessness. You had the feeling that even had God appeared beseechingly before them in the sky with palms outward to persuade them back they would not have had within them the power to turn from their irresistible course.

I stood with a little group of men back of a farmhouse. Slit trenches were all around the edges of the farmyard and a dugout with a tin roof was nearby, but we were so fascinated by the spectacle overhead that it never occurred to us that we might need the foxholes.

The first huge flight passed directly over our farmyard and the others followed. We spread our feet and leaned far back to look straight up until our helmets fell off. We'd cup our fingers around our eyes like field glasses for a clearer view, and then the bombs came.

They began ahead of us as a crackle of popcorn and almost instantly swelled into a monstrous fury of noise that seemed surely to destroy all the world ahead of us. From then on, for an hour and a half that had in it the agonies of centuries, the bombs came down. A wall of smoke and dust erected by them grew high in the sky. It filtered along the ground back through our own orchards. It sifted around us and into our noses. The bright day grew slowly dark with it. By now everything was an indescribable cauldron of sounds. Individual noises did not exist. The thundering of motors in the sky and the roar of the bombs ahead filled all the space for noise on earth. Our own heavy artillery was crashing all around us, yet we could hardly hear it.

The Germans began to shoot heavy, high ack-ack. Great black puffs of it by the score speckled the sky until it was hard to distinguish the smoke puffs from the planes.

And then someone shouted that one of the planes was smoking. Yes, we could all see it. A long faint line of black smoke stretched straight for a mile behind one of them and as we watched there was a gigantic sweep of flame over the plane from nose to tail. It disappeared in flame and it slanted slowly down and banked around the sky in great wide curves, this way and that way, as rhythmically and gracefully as in a slow-motion waltz. Then suddenly it seemed to change its mind and it swept upward steeper and steeper, and ever slower until finally it seemed poised motionless on its own black pillar of smoke. And then just as slowly it turned over and dived for earth—a folded spearhead on the straight black shaft of its own creation—and it disappeared behind the treetops. But before it was down there were more cries of "There's another one smoking, and there's a third one now!"

Chutes came out of some of the planes; out of some came no chutes at all. One of white silk caught on the tail of a plane. The men with binoculars could see him fighting to get loose until flames swept over him and then a tiny dot fell through space all alone. And all that time the great flat ceiling of the sky was roofed by all the others that didn't go down, plowing their way forward as if there was no turmoil in the world. Nothing deviated them by the slightest. They stalked on slowly and with the dreadful pall of sound as though they were seeing only something at a great distance and nothing existed in between.

Yes, that was the greatest and most powerful sight that we infantrymen had ever witnessed since D-Day. We cheered and prayed for we knew what all this meant to us and every foxhole soldier in the front lines. We never knew what devastation was dealt out by the heavies until after our advance and then we viewed a scene which I shall never forget. A scene of tremendous destruction, an unforgettable scene of utter Hell. That raid, carried out by an estimated three thousand bombers, was the spearhead that launched one of the greatest advances since the African campaign. We took prisoners after that raid by the hundreds, some of them stark raving mad, some of them turned into blubbering idiotic creatures by the tremendous concussions. Never in the history of the war will a tabloid of that day be duplicated, nor will the Germans ever question the might of our air force. We in the infantry shall never forget that day, nor will we ever be able to show our appreciation to our brother corps, the United States Air Force. We can only show it by doing our job on the ground, always advancing, always holding, and ever taking advantage of the precision bombings that have made our advances more speedy, with less sacrifice. . . .

Au revoir,
"Buddy" Pullins

Marvin H. Pearson, of Seymour, was inducted into the Army May 17, 1943, and was sent overseas with the 770th Field Artillery Battalion in 1944. He was promoted to corporal Aug. 1943. Corp. Pearson saw action in Normandy, Ardennes, the Rhineland, and Central Europe. He earned the Bronze Star, the Victory Medal, and the Purple Heart. Discharged Dec. 19, 1945, Pearson returned to Seymour to work.

[Sept. 1944]
Somewhere in France

Dear Folks:

Will try to drop you a few lines between showers of German artillery shells. Have had a lot of shelling in the past two or three days. I've had to sleep in a foxhole two nights, but tonight I'm taking a chance and going to sleep by the side of it. Then if it gets too hot I can get into it in a hurry.

We had several boys get hurt, but not more than two or three seriously. The rest were not so bad. I had a close call or two but the worst one, well, I may as well tell you. I had washed some clothes and was laying them out in the field to dry. I heard a shell in the air so I dived for a bank but before I got away the thing went off, and where I dropped my undershirt, a large piece of shrapnel hit and tore a hole as big as my head in it. I was only about three or four feet from it. I took the shrapnel to the C[ommand] P[ost] and we found it was a 170 millimeter gun firing at us. Then we started firing at them and quieted them down.

I was up front on an observation post last night. Had to keep low for about a half a mile, but they saw us and started firing upon us. There were only three of us and no one got hurt, only our feelings, but that doesn't amount to too much over here. After we got up on a hill we looked down and there was a Jerry gun only about 200 yards away. We hit the ground and crawled for the nearest ditch we could find and, of course, the Jerries picked up our radio relays and started in on us but didn't get far, for we soon put them all out of commission.

I can't tell you where I am but I'm in action, but nothing like I'll be in before this is cleaned up over here. We got here before the infantry. Nothing between us and the Jerries for two days. We were afraid to move at night for snipers and patrols, but the infantry moved up this morning, so things are more quiet now than they have been for a few days.

I got two *Banners* yesterday. Sure was glad to get them. Sure like to read the news of the boys. There is always something about some of the boys I knew back home.

Well, I've got to write a few more letters before it gets dark, for I don't move around much after night. It might be dangerous, you know. Well, write often and tell all the rest to write, too. I have a new APO number now so don't forget it. Write soon.

Love,
PETE

James E. Rosenbarger, of Corydon, was inducted into the Army Feb. 20, 1943, and assigned to the 387th Infantry Regiment, 97th Division. In Oct. 1944 he arrived in France and was attached to the 409th Infantry Regiment, 103d Infantry Division. On Nov. 9, 1944, his company participated in a battle near Xainfaing in the Vosges Mountains, and in this battle Pfc. Rosenbarger lost his life, Nov. 16. For gallantry in action he was awarded the Silver Star posthumously.

November 12, 1944
Somewhere in France

DEAR FOLKS:

Please excuse this writing because I am writing from my two-man foxhole here on a mountaintop on the front line. Yes, I am in combat, but don't let it worry you, please.

It is cold and windy here, but no rain now. It's snow. As I sit here I can hear our artillery shells going over, and I love the sound of our guns, which I hear constantly.

As for sending anything, forget all about the food, as we are getting plenty. But send gloves, extra heavy socks to wear under shoepacks, which are rubber shoes and leather hightops combined. This is what we wear, and what a great piece of footwear they are for us. They keep our feet dry as well as warm. Also a wool helmet to fit over my face and neck. As yet I have not received any boxes nor have any of the other fellows, but if you can't get all the named articles, send as fast as possible the gloves and socks, which I know you can get.

I am with a real group of fellows, Dad, because we are in the great outdoors now. No fires except for a squad stove, on which we heat our food. Our holes are in rocks, dug for protection from Jerry and the weather. Every once in a while we talk about what we would be doing if we were home (Heaven to me) but no one ever gripes, because we all know our job is well worth doing, regardless of hardships. The best way to describe this life is to think of how a wolf or fox lives, but still I'll keep my chin up, grit my teeth a little and carry on because the fellows before us did and I know Pepper is, and Cortner did. I doubt if I will get to write Cortner's folks, because of the situation, but if you talk to them say a few words of sympathy for me.

There is just one thing I want you, especially Mother, to do and that is, not to worry about me. I am happy to be well, and hoping and praying that I may continue that way, and will be able to return home safe and sound someday. Remember I still say this job I am helping to do is worth it if I can help keep my home and people from these conditions over here, and we will.

This infantry is really rough, never a job too large for us. There is no question that we will never get all the credit due us, but that is O.K. Don't think there are not real he-men in this outfit or branch of service. My hat is off to the fellows who have gone this far before me.

They tell me today is Sunday, but you can't tell it from any other day. Our faces are dirty, our hands cold, rough and hard, our clothes muddy and dirty, but never a word is said by anyone. As long as our clothes, two blankets and shelter halves will keep us warm, I am contented. Uncle Sam is taking good care of us, especially our food supply. Of course we have to go after it for some distance, but that is just a warm-up hike. Sure can tell that you are high on the mountains as you get winded easily.

There isn't much more I can think of at present except I won't be able to write as often as usual. Please be considerate as your son is thinking about you every minute of the day, and praying God will bring me back to you. . . .

Your son,

Jim

P. S.—The snow on the pine trees is beautiful. Standing in the clouds is something new to me. I also keep my eyes elsewhere, too. My buddy (rifle) and I are never apart, and you might say hand grenades for a pillow. . . .

I heard Mr. Roosevelt won the election, but not the exact figures. I knew he would. I only hope that he can help us to get this war over real soon.

I have not received the Corydon *Democrat* since coming over. "CHINS UP."

This letter leaves here by foot. I wonder when it will reach you?

Robert Baker, of Bloomington, enlisted in the Army in Feb. 1942 and was attached to the signal corps. He was sent to England in July 1943, was moved to France a year later, and saw service there and in Luxembourg and Germany with the 3908th Signal Service Battalion under General Headquarters' Army Pictorial Service. In 1945 he was promoted a sergeant and was discharged in Jan. 1946. He is now secretary to Rep. Ralph Harvey in Washington, D. C.

. . . Before it happened, we talked and laughed among ourselves. In the park ravine, where the light of breaking dawn threw down long shadows, we clumped about in muddy grass.

We had saluted and nodded to the French officers in charge. Now we looked at the riflemen—two rows of seven each. Young fellows, most in their early twenties. And rather nervous—two or three unable to test their weapons without assistance.

Down on the floor of the small natural bowl, we continued to mill about, talking of trivial, unrelated subjects. More French officers, dignified and businesslike, joined our circle which now included a *New York Times* reporter, three cameramen, and half a dozen intelligence officials from headquarters. On the dark bowl rim behind us fifty or so curious G.I.'s stood in knots, audibly speculating on what was about to occur.

Suddenly the condemned man was coming toward us, with a guarding soldier on either side. He carried a stub of a cigarette in one hand, while the other was tied by rope to the wrist of an escort. He was a small, thin fellow, pale and sickly looking, but he walked steadily towards the appointed spot.

When fifty feet from the stake, the prisoner threw away the cigarette butt. He paused to exhale, and for the only time, appeared to falter. Between the two impassive guards he reached the stake and his body reeled slightly as he was pushed down to his knees. An officer stepped from behind him with a black handkerchief, and the little man, looking directly at the men with the rifles, tried to remonstrate against the blinding cloth. But it was too late and his will to resist vanished quickly. Almost as quickly the big handkerchief went around his head, covering all his face, and the rope that had been tied to the guard's arm was slipped around the stake at the prisoner's back.

The riflemen, coached by sign rather than word, cocked, aimed and squeezed all the volley of lead. Blended into the loud flash of their fire was the spraying one of a camera bulb. The half-hooded, kneeling figure lurched into the air, then crumpled to the ground. In another moment—blood welling from the twisted body—a pistol bearer strode forward, and leaning over the man's head administered the *coup de grace.*

In the dim dawn light, two medical officers whispered briefly before signing certificates. Then civilian flunkies lifted the body, and on a makeshift litter carried it from the silent ravine to a waiting cart.

For his aid to the Gestapo, one Frenchman had paid. Hundreds more await the fate of the collaborationist. . . .

Harold Clements, of Lawrenceburg, enlisted in the Navy in Nov. 1940 and was assigned to the U.S.S. "Arkansas" at the end of Dec. He was promoted seaman 1st class in May 1941 and gunner's mate 2d class in June 1943, and turret captain 1st class in Dec. 1943. His ship helped land occupation troops in Iceland in 1941 and participated in the invasions of North Africa, Normandy, and Southern France. After a period of schooling, TC 1/c Clements was assigned to the U.S.S. "Salt Lake City" in Feb. 1945, which participated in the invasions of Okinawa, the Philippines, and the occupation of Japan. He remains in the Navy.

August 22, 1944
U.S.S. "Arkansas"

DEAR MOM AND DAD:

The Allies struck a heavy blow in the invasion of Southern France several days ago and the American warship, as in the Normandy invasion, was present at the initial assault helping to blast a path for the first landings. Not long after we left port the captain spoke to us describing the task which lay ahead. Meanwhile, we were joined by men-of-war of both our own and other nations. As we plowed onward I wondered if the enemy realized when or where we were about to strike and would he be ready to "take it" and "dish it out."

During the night many shapeless, obscure forms of transports and landing craft were overtaken and left behind in the darkness as we moved into our forward and final position. Angry rumblings of bomb bursts and flashes of fire came from the distant area as bombers unloaded their deadly cargo. Swarms of bombers, fighters and troop transport planes droned overhead passing to and from the engaged area.

When the skies began to glow just before dawn, we found ourselves surrounded with ships and landing craft of all descriptions while the shores of France loomed surprisingly near, shrouded with a haze of dust and smoke from the night bombing attack. We were then well within range of enemy coastal batteries and I for one hoped we would not long delay our opening fire. We had not long to wait, however, as the main battery was trained on an enemy installation of casemated guns and the sounding of the firing buzzer announced "standby for opening salvo." With a deafening roar we sent our salutation to Hitler's crowd on the beach. All around us ships of all nations were blasting away as we fired salvo after salvo while hundreds of landing craft moved shorewards.

As you know, the Army took the beach in stride and moved inland in high gear. We had a number of German prisoners aboard for a while. They didn't have the tough superman appearance the German propaganda experts would have us believe. A couple of nights we were sighted by JU-88 snoopers but a lusty barrage of A.A. fire drove them off.

The gun crews really enjoy throwing big stuff over here at the Germans and are getting worried for fear the war will be over for the Navy and we will be left out at the finish. Anticipating this possible situation, the gunners are trying to have the engineers install wheels on our ships so we can catch up with the Army and help chase Heinies through the streets of Berlin. . . .

Yours,
HAROLD

Lester E. (Gene) Hyman, of Logansport, enlisted in the Army Sept. 21, 1942. Leaving the U. S. in May 1944, Hyman was attached to the 596th Airborne Engineer Company, 517th Regimental Combat Team, 82d Airborne Division, fighting in the European theater. Pfc. Hyman was awarded five battle stars, and returned to this country Dec. 14, 1945, where he was discharged Dec. 19. Hyman is employed on the Pontiac Daily Press, Pontiac, Mich.

Sept. 17, 1944
Southern France

DEAR MOTHER:

I am going to try and tell you everything I can about the jump I made on the invasion of Southern France. That is, all that I think will pass the censor.

After we were brought off the front lines in northern Italy, we were sent to a rear area where we trained for a month and a half for an invasion jump. We trained on terrain similar to what it was like where the real thing was to take place. Of course we didn't know where the real invasion was going to be, but we had ideas. When D-Day was near, we left that area which was south of Rome and traveled by truck to the airport, which was nothing but a wheat field. While we were at the airport we had our jump suits and equipment painted for camouflage. There we also had classes where we studied thoroughly maps and sand tables of the area where we were to jump. We also had discussion as to what to do in case certain situations came up.

The day before D-Day we loaded our assigned planes with equipment bundles and were fitted for parachutes. After we got our chutes, we placed them in our assigned seats in the plane. That evening we had a big chow—T-bone steak, mashed potatoes, gravy, green beans, coffee, and pudding. After chow we were told where the invasion was going to be. (I was right about my idea.) Then we smeared our hands and faces with oil paints. When we finished that we went to our planes and lay on the ground. Some of the fellows were joking about what they were going to do the first time they visited Paris. Some were talking about home and others were sleeping. We lay there for about two hours, then we were told to load the planes. We got into the plane without putting on our chutes. The plane took off, circled around, and took up its position in formation. We flew for quite a while. Twenty minutes before we were to jump we put on our chutes. None of us was scared of jumping, but we were worried about what was waiting for us on the ground. After we got our chutes on we sat back down. When the red light came on we stood up and hooked our static lines to the cable in the top of the plane. I was number three man. It was my job to pull the switch which released our equipment bundles from the bottom of the plane. When the green light came on, the number one man pushed out the bundle of equipment in the door and I pulled the switch for the bundles on the bottom of the plane. As soon as the door bundle went out the number one man jumped and we all followed pretty fast. I had a very bad position on the jump. I was completely upside down when my chute opened. I was jerked so badly when my chute opened that my field pack broke loose and fell to the ground. I had all my toilet articles, under-wear and socks in it.

We jumped way above the clouds, thus I couldn't see the ground. I heard a fellow who had jumped from one of the planes in front of us land in water and I thought we were over the ocean. (Later I found out it was only a small creek.) Then a fellow landed in a tree so I knew we were over land. Before I got through the clouds, which were about 150 feet from the ground, the shooting had start-ed. When I came below the clouds I saw that I was going to land in a woods on the side of a mountain. I landed like a feather. By that time I was plenty nervous and scared and I'm not afraid to admit it. It seemed as if I was all thumbs when I tried to unbuckle my chute. I finally got out of it and got my rifle put together and got away from my chute because by that time the enemy was shooting at it and they were coming too close for comfort. I couldn't see where they were shooting from because it was so dark. I started out to find the assembly area and on the way I ran into some of my buddies. We decided to lay low in the woods until daylight so we could see what we were doing and where we were going. When daylight came we ran into some more fellows and finally assembled and got things underway. From then on there were times when things were rough and times when they were pretty easygoing.

We have been on the front line ever since. About three days after we jumped the beach forces had driven as far inland as we had jumped. Well, that is about the whole story "in a nutshell."

I hope enough of this passes the censor so you can get a pretty good idea of what it was like. I hope this thing gets over with pretty soon.

Well, I had better close for now. Write me real soon.

Loads of love,
GENE

Carl J. Procaskey, of Indianapolis, was inducted into the Army Nov. 8, 1942, and was attached to the infantry. Going overseas in Feb. 1943, he saw service in North Africa, Italy, and Southern France. Discharged Nov. 14, 1945, Procaskey is a student in Indianapolis.

Fantasy for Christmas Eve in Wartime

Tonight my world is still and small,
    And o'er the camp lies such an air of peace
That I will think—if of the war at all—
    That for one sacred hour the war shall cease.
One hour—in which again shall live
    The quiet joy, the warmth of Christmases past.
I'll ask no more—no more could heaven give—
    Than lovely memories the heart holds fast.
O'er all the intervening space
    I'll build a bridge of things that we can share—
Of music, stars, the snow, a smiling face,
    A Yule-tree bright, the Christ-child—and a prayer,
Across this span of lightest air
    With eager step my loving soul shall race
To find the old familiar home: and there
    Re-live the joys that war cannot erase.
I'll spend an hour of warmth and light
    At home. I'll know the love of kindest friends,
The mellow glow of Christmas candlelight
    Upon the tree that, package laden, bends
The hushed suspense, the childish glee
    As wonder after wonder is displayed,
The touch of infant hands so dear to me,
    The "Glorias" the Christmas angels said.
And ere my fleeting hour has gone
    And sadly I return across the sea,
I'll grasp enough of strength to carry on
    Another year the task outlined for me.

T/Sgt. Carl J. Procaskey,
Written Christmas, 1944, in France.

Thomas Jackson, of Clay City, was inducted into the Army July 8, 1941, and served with the 3d Ordnance Company, attached to the 3d Division. Going overseas in Nov. 1942, T/5 Jackson served with the 3d Infantry Division in Sicily and with the 3d, 45th, and 36th Infantry Divisions, 5th Army, in Rome and the Arno campaign. He later served in Southern France with the 1st Airborne Task Force. In Central Europe T/4 Jackson was attached to the 7th Army, 4th Division, 55th Ordnance Group. Discharged Oct. 2, 1945, Jackson is now a welder in Terre Haute.

January 25, 1945
France

DEAR HARRY:

I received your letter a couple of days ago and was very happy to hear from you again. I am sorry I never got around to writing you before this, but I guess it's a little like you said, I am just too good for nothing, too lazy, and too busy to do much writing. The honest truth is I have always had to work pretty hard and also long hours since I've been overseas. I am a welder and you know that I am kept busy.

I am sorry I cannot tell you where I am in France, but I can say it is much cleaner, nicer, and in fact, quite beautiful. The people are extremely friendly, in fact they like us so well they only charge us three times what anything is worth. We are used to paying more though. All Americans are rich and you cannot convince Europeans otherwise.

There is positively nothing to buy where I am as it is the gay part of France and all foodstuffs were always imported. The people get their half loaf of bread a day and there are few vegetables to go around. Clothing, I think, is unrationed, but sky high. Meat is what is lacking; they offer soldiers any price for it, but I would hate to write home and say I was sentenced to ten years for selling a can of corned beef. It has happened. Despite the existing hardships the people complain much less and there is less black marketing than in Italy and the Italians were much better off.

The war was quite close here yet. After four years of German domination, when they were driven out the doors flew open and the dancing started. No kidding, you could still hear the guns in the distance. They have stopped dancing for the civilian men now, but women may dance with soldiers. They are a fun-loving race of people, but figure with thousands of their people interned in Germany and the war still unwon that it is wrong for everyone to dance. I, in a way, respect their attitude.

When I first landed here I saw a few women with their heads shaved—I guess you know what for. Quite some time ago some of our boys were watching a dance in a bar. French police entered and picked out a woman and a few days later the paper showed her picture, hanging to a stake—shot for aiding the Germans. I have seen many German prisoners and they are a pretty sad looking bunch too. The soldiers over here are quite peeved as to the way the prisoners are treated in America. Much better than necessary. The same prisoner who is eating our ice cream, drinking our milk, and smoking our cigarettes, probably at one time helped put booby traps on dead American soldiers so that anyone offering help was killed or disabled for life. No German soldier deserves an ounce of respect in any form. Most anyone could sit down and write pages on the crimes of Hitler's soldiers and write true things beyond the realm of human imagination. But I intend to save mine up and someday perhaps they will be interesting to talk about.

When you get this letter I'll have quite a bit over two years overseas. Occasionally someone of the company goes home on the rotation plan. Although many of us are eligible there is no drawing for that. So you have to be lucky and be half dead. Now they have a furlough system worked out and the lucky man's name is drawn from a hat. With my luck it would take about ten years before I get home. There is hope though, but I am always hoping for the unexpected.

That's about all for now. Keep your letters coming even though I don't write too often. Thanks again for your letter. Give my friends my best regards.

Yours,
TOM JACKSON

Elizabeth Richardson, of Mishawaka, joined the American Red Cross in Apr. 1944. Upon arrival in England in July, she was assigned to the clubmobile department. After service with this unit in England, she was sent to France in Feb. 1945 and was placed in charge of clubmobile operations and personnel in the Le Havre redeployment area. Miss Richardson was killed in an airplane accident near Rouen, France, July 25, 1945, while in service.

March 2, 1945
[Le Havre] France

DEAR MOTHER AND DADDY:

We finally left Paris—in a fine cloud of dust and amid much tooting of horn. Reason: a French driver at the wheel of a British ambulance, now an A.R.C. carry-all (including six of us and luggage). Our *homme's* idea of good driving consisted of sitting on the horn and trusting in God—and although at first I felt rather imprisoned in the completely enclosed back of the vehicle, I finally became philosophic and fell asleep, draped artistically over the duffel bags and bed rolls. The roads were horrible, the countryside wet—alongside were the rusted and stripped corpses of vehicles that had met their end in 1940. And destruction such as I have never seen, far surpassing anything in England— destruction, too, that left me feeling not so self-righteous, as it was mostly ours. When we passed the shell of a famous cathedral, I felt pretty small. Our base is on the fringe of similar ruins all more or less recent.

But the setup is ideal. Twelve of us live in a house on a hill overlooking a wonderful view. We run a fleet of four clubmobiles, two jeeps and a sort of enclosed station wagon. We also run our own mess (with rations from the army), seven French servants, a doughnut kitchen and an attached G.I. detail. How we run it, I don't know—it's all a mystery, but it'd better unravel itself quickly as the pioneer group is about to leave us newcomers to the fruits of their labors. Our doughnuts are all cooked for us and we just have to give them out—sounded like a snap to me, but after a day of it, I take it all back.

Our house is really nice—a sort of junior chateau. Right now the Navy is painting the interior and it's rather messy. Because of overflow, Aileen, Margaret, Mary Rea and myself live in a neighboring house in our sleeping bags. But they are very comfortable and all in all we couldn't have better living conditions. Water is always torrid in our house, the Navy has installed a portable shower, and three times a week we have ice cream. We can't drink the local water unless we put pills in it, but we have a liquor ration—one bottle of champagne, one Scotch, one gin, one cognac or benedictine, per month—520 francs. Everybody is very congenial and the Army and Navy, thanks to the pioneering of the first group, take awfully good care of us. They (our predecessors) came in when things were really rough—this house, for instance, had as furniture one baby's crib—now we have everything, including the new paint job. It's especially nice, because we thought, of course, that we were going to be roughing it in the worst way—and it's ten times better than Mrs. Whittle and her bugs!

But I can't describe the destruction—the woods are still full of mines and our kitchen is on top of a temporary graveyard which the French are now rearranging. Thank God most of their rearranging was completed by the time of our arrival. But I gathered that doughnuts and opened graves didn't mix.

We might as well be at the South Pole as far as mail is concerned. It just isn't. However, it gets to us eventually, so don't stop writing. It's supposed to come from Paris via carrier, but this seems to be only theory.

We had a wonderful last night in Paris—three G.I.'s took Margaret, Mary and myself via Metro to the Montmartre region and we enjoyed ourselves with the assistance of much white wine. You can imagine how I felt the next day in the back of that ex-ambulance with our friend Pierre at the wheel.

My love to all of you,
Elizabeth

Alva B. Pace, of North Salem, was inducted into the Army Aug. 25, 1942, and was assigned to the air corps. He was sent to the European theater in Aug. 1943 and was attached to the 42d Depot Repair Squadron, 42d Air Depot Group. Promoted to sergeant, he was awarded two battle stars and was returned to this country and discharged July 29, 1945. Pace is a carpenter in North Salem.

May 4, 1945
Southern France

Dear Sis:

I have just gotten back from a seven-day furlough to southern France down to the U.S.R.R.A. (United States Riviera Recreation Area). It surely is a wonderful place. In peacetimes it is one of the most noted and finest summer resorts in the world and certainly the very best in France. Ordinarily only millionaires can go there. The trip would have cost a couple of thousand bucks easily. As one G.I. wrote who had been there: "A million-dollar vacation on a G.I. salary." And he said a big mouthful. I will write a full detail of it all and you can let all the rest read it. So here goes, though it may sound fishy.

Sgt. Harold Hackenberg and I were the first and only two of our outfit to make the trip. I hope more can go from here also. In other times to stay at the hotel where we stayed would cost $30 a day.

In starting out I might say I got aboard for the first airplane ride of my life. I've had dozens of chances to go up for a ride but just never went. So at 9:00 A.M. about fifteen men from this field boarded an army transport plane and had a fine ride to southern France over the western part of the Alps Mountains, arriving at an airport close to Nice, France, at 12:15. I sure enjoyed my first trip up in the air. One who has never been up cannot realize how beautiful Mother Earth is from the air. At this time of year everything is green and pretty.

The airport was along the blue Mediterranean Ocean. It looked very pretty as we swung over it to make the landing. Red Cross girls served us hot coffee and cookies. We were pretty chilly, as we were up around nine thousand feet to get over the mountains and it's really cold up there. It's no wonder that the boys who fly in the bombers and high altitude fighter planes wear sheep's wool, and electrically heated clothing when they have to go up 25,000 to 35,000 feet. We got on a truck which took us to our hotel where we stayed while we were there.

The route to the hotel from the airport was along the seashore, very beautiful with the Alps on one side and the blue waters of the Mediterranean on the other. When we came to the edge of Nice, there was a large sign reading "No Officers Allowed." We all had a big laugh, but the laugh was on us because there were no officers there, only those in charge, and they bothered no one. So we got to do as we pleased, come and go when we got ready, and no one blew a whistle for us to come running.

Our hotel was located on the main promenade along the beach. It must have cost a cool million to erect such a place. Anyway, we went in and were welcomed by four beautiful civilian girls who were hostesses at the hotel. A bellhop showed us our room and even carried our baggage. Boy, did we get a kick out of that!

"Hack" and I had a room together, with private bath and everything, even a rug on the floor a couple of inches thick. Beds, my gosh, I could hardly climb in! We felt of them and wondered if we could take a week of it. We got washed and went to the dining room for dinner. The headwaiter met us at the door and took us to a table, pulled the chairs back and pushed them up under us when we sat down. Now what do you think of that? I said, "My gosh, they won't let you pull your own chair up."

They had a good orchestra in the large lounge room, so after we ate we listened and took off down the beach to see some of the sights. The beach is only one hundred feet from the hotel door and was lined with bathing beauties— blondes, brunettes, redheads—and of course we were very interested.

We went back to the hotel at 6:30 for supper. We had a good meal, served in three courses as all the meals were. Afterward we went to the Red Cross club to hear Glenn Miller's band play for the dance. I've heard them so much on the radio and was very thrilled to hear and see them in person. The building is enormous in size, built of snow-white marble, and is really hard to look at when the sun is shining. It's a beautiful thing. There was a large and fine theater in it, and we were there three days before we knew it was there. No civilians were allowed except girls. They had to have a Red Cross invitation card or be escorted by a soldier before they could be there. After we got tired of the dance we went to another room called the "Bamboo Room." Only Cokes were sold there and they were brought in by truckloads as there are 65,000 to 75,000 soldiers at the area all the time. We left there and went to the Negreseo Hotel where they were having another dance and floor show. In the show we saw two ping-pong champions give an exhibition. One was national title holder for two years and the other was the French national champion.

The next morning we were up at 8 o'clock and had breakfast. We then took a real honest bath and went out for a walk along the beach. We came to the port where the small fishing boats came in. What they had were small fish, about three to four inches long, called smelts. Some of the fishermen were roasting some fish. They offered us some, but we didn't take any. They really smelled good though. We did a little shopping for some postcards and went to the hotel for dinner. After dinner we went to the Red Cross to get some tickets for the bus tour Saturday morning. The tours are free but we had to have bus reservations and tickets for dinner. We took a long walk over town and saw several places of interest. After supper we heard Miller's band again, took in another floor show and went to bed. We never got in very early.

Saturday morning we were up at 8:15 and had a lovely breakfast. We went for a walk to find some strings for a bass violin one of our boys is making. We found only two, and they were new, but we didn't find any used ones. We went to Red Cross then to go on the bus tour. We loaded into nice busses. Each bus had two hostesses. They were very pretty and spoke good English and were very lively. One of them said for us to laugh and have a good time. The day before she said she had a bunch of sad sacks and she was a nervous wreck trying to entertain them. We made two stops before dinner to look at and take pictures of two very old castles up in the Alps. We had dinner at one of the finest and largest hotels in the world perched up high on a cliff in the mountains. We were there about an hour and a half and left to go to a large perfume factory. A guide there took us through and explained how they pressed the flowers and different processes to make the different blends of perfume. It was a very smelly place.

We were taken to the display room where we could buy any of the products they made. They made face cream, hand lotion, hair tonic, as well as perfume. We were taken back a different route, and stopped to see a castle which was used by Napoleon, arriving at Red Cross at 4:30. Our hostess said she had a very good time and was glad she had a good lively bunch. After supper we went to a large theater taken over for our use. It's a very nice place with a good floor show. We went to a different place each night for the floor shows so we always saw something new.

Sunday was a beautiful and sunny day. After breakfast we took a walk and went to the beach for awhile, then to church. We had a fine baked chicken dinner. After dinner we sat around the lounge room for an hour or so and went for a stroll along the three-and-one-half mile beach. Gosh, I never saw so many beautiful women in my life, mostly dressed in bathing suits which were very scant, all sunbathing. I have a nice tan also. I peeled off in some places where I got too much the first day out.

Monday we went for a boat cruise on the Mediterranean. We were in sight of the Italian coast. We saw the famous Monte Carlo casino and gambling house but it is off limits so we couldn't stop. We got back at noon, so in the afternoon we had some pictures taken on the street. We didn't think they were very good, but they are not so bad, so I'll send one along.

Tuesday the weather was bad and rather cool and there was not much doing. We took in some floor shows and night clubs. Wednesday we did little of interest to write about and Thursday afternoon we boarded the same transport plane back to camp.

Wonderful trip. . . .

Love,
ALVA

→ VII ←

GERMANY

EVEN though the Allied forces were pushing the Germans back from their defenses along the Siegfried Line, the enemy effected a counterattack into Belgium and Luxembourg in December, 1944. Driving through the Ardennes into Belgium, the Germans displayed desperate fighting ability, but heroic resistance by the forces located at Bastogne and troops attacking from the north and south brought the German breakthrough to a halt in the Battle of the Bulge. After this futile counterattack, the Germans were soon in retreat beyond the Rhine. The Americans captured the Remagen bridge and threatened the Ruhr area, the Third Army drove through the Moselle Valley where they trapped Germans east of the Rhine, while others were securing the Saar basin. The Third Army cut off southern Germany, thus forestalling any German move to retire to fight in the mountains of Bavaria. With the Americans, British, and Canadians moving in from the north, south, and west, the Russians converged on Berlin and were allowed the honor of capturing the city, May 2. The end of the Third Reich came on May 23 with complete surrender, and Germany was put under the control of the Allies.

Bruce D. Gribben, of Indianapolis, enlisted in the Army Air Corps Jan. 2, 1942, and after taking flight training was commissioned a flight officer Dec. 12, 1942. Sent overseas in May 1943, F/O Gribben participated in air attacks over North Africa, Italy,

Sicily, Sardinia, Pantelleria, and Lampedusa. He was wounded Aug. 22, 1943, by a 20 mm. explosive from a German fighter off the coast of Salerno, Italy. Bailing out, Gribben was captured by German Air Sea Rescue, spent almost two years in German prison camps, and was liberated on April 29, 1945, from Mooseberg, Germany. Awarded the Air Medal, three Oak Leaf clusters, and the Purple Heart, Gribben was discharged Sept. 18, 1945, and is now a 2d lieutenant in the Officers Reserve Corps. He is living in West Lafayette, Indiana.

Sept. 17, '43

DEAR MOTHER, DAD, AND MARCET:

I became a prisoner of war after being shot down Aug. 22. Only through the grace of God I am alive and not hurt in any way. Thank God for my parachute and "Mae West." My prayers have been answered so far. Go to the Red Cross and find out what you can send me. Things I need: Christian Science Bible, *Science and Health,* and several quarterlies, toothbrush, comb, razor blades (double edge), handkerchiefs, wool gloves and scarf, wool socks, and "Boy Scout" knife. Give to the Red Cross for they are the *only* thing that keeps us going. Write sweet little Fay and tell her that I still love her with all my heart, and that I'll never forget her and I hope she will be waiting for me. Don't worry about me for I am well and warm. Ed is here with me, but none of the others. Ed and I live together. We also need 2 steel mirrors. Don't forget I love you all dearly, and we will be together some day.

All my love,
BRUCE

Charles V. Bailey, of Indianapolis, enlisted in the Army in July, 1941, and was assigned to the infantry. Commissioned a 2d lieutenant in Nov. 1942, he was sent to North Africa in March 1943 with the 39th Regiment, 9th Infantry Division. Lieutenant Bailey also saw service in Sicily, the invasion of France, the Battle of the Bulge, and the crossing of the Rhine. Promoted to 1st lieutenant in July 1943, he was awarded a Bronze Star for valor in Hurtgen Forest and a Silver Star for action at the Remagen bridgehead. After V-E Day, Lieutenant Bailey served with the 10th Armored Division in Austria. Discharged in Feb. 1946, he is employed by the California division of highways.

Nov. 26, 1944
Germany

DEAR FOLKS:

Last year at this time I was enjoying myself in England. As I look back those were pretty good months there, although I didn't particularly think so at the time. I don't believe I ever told you just where I was stationed. It was at a camp not far from Winchester, some 80 miles south of London. Winchester is quite an historic town, as you may have gathered from the booklet I sent, and was one of the earliest capitals of England.

I've certainly seen a lot of country since then—France, Belgium, and now Germany. Belgium, incidentally, seemed least touched of any by the war, and the people appeared the most hospitable of any. It was strange to pass from the enthusiastic welcomes of France and Belgium into the blank stares of the people of Germany. However, one could expect nothing more, I guess.

Last night several of us were discussing Germany and the Germans. While it is not perhaps my place to say, I maintained, and still do, that it is impractical to ever attempt the destruction of either Germany or the German people. In all the war I've seen, I've witnessed the complete destruction of but a few towns, among them Randazzo in Sicily, Montbury in France, and Valone also in France—all of them small towns. In each of these not a thing of any value was left standing. I have no doubt but that in Germany many towns, possibly Berlin itself, have suffered the same fate. I saw also whole blocks of towns in England likewise flattened. All this will naturally require a tremendous amount of labor and material to repair and rebuild. But to destroy a nation of cities and towns and rout its people to the four corners of the earth is a highly improbable if not impossible task.

Frankly, I believe in our lifetime, at least, there will be and continue to be a German people even though we overrun their nation, destroy their armies and industries, and generally take over the land. Then what?

If we take over the running of Germany in conjunction with Russia and Britain, and even France, it must be done completely and with an iron hand and with agreement on all points by the ruling powers. And it must continue until a generation of Germans, educated by the ruling powers, is ready to take over itself.

If, on the other hand, a complete dismemberment of Germany is attempted, *i.e.,* so much to France, so much to Belgium, so much to Russia, etc., there still will be a little group of little German states smoldering with resentment under foreign rule and ready to cause trouble at every turn—a situation that would solve nothing.

Another solution has been advanced whereby the present allied armies chase all Germans, civilians and soldiers, back into the pre-war boundaries of Germany, ring the country with cannon, ships and planes, then say, "All right you . . . , you've had it . . . , what do you propose to do now?" It might bring some interesting, and perhaps even helpful suggestions, but it would take a lot of troops and material, as well as time, all of which is needed against the Japs, whom we cannot overlook in any plans formulated in dealing with the Germans. I believe the only practical plans for the future of Germany will depend largely upon what happens in the next few months both here and in the Pacific. By and large I think the majority of such plans as drawn up by our great planners will go by the boards, as the war goes on.

Frankly, I'd rather listen to the plans proposed by the men actually doing the fighting. Strangely enough, or perhaps not so strange at that, the closer one gets to the front the less talk of "kill the dirty so-and-sos, etc.," one hears. Wounded Germans receive the same attention as do our men who have been wounded and taken prisoner, who say they have received the best of medical care at the hands of the Germans. In short, the fighting man realizes he is fighting other men very much like himself who don't know very much about why they are doing it. Personally, I have no hatred for the individual German unless he be one of those arrogant bastards one runs across occasionally. For the most part they're pretty much like the soldiers of any other army—flushed in triumph, bewildered by defeat. It is one of the greatest misfortunes that the men responsible for wars are not made to fight them.

You may wonder what the A.A.A.-O. "Triple A Bar Zero" is at the top of this stationery. It is some regimental stationery I picked up recently. The A.A.A.-O. stands for "Anything, Anywhere, Anytime, bar Nothing," which is the regimental motto that was used in the fifth War Bond drive. Incidentally, the 39th is the only regiment to have a motto of its own and allowed to wear it painted on the sides of its helmets. Near one of our positions in France one of the men found a German newspaper in which was a cartoon depicting an American soldier with the A.A.A.-O. brand on the side of his helmet, so we concluded the Germans know us pretty well also.

Loads of love to all the family,
Chic

Justin Gail Meyers, of Plymouth, enlisted in the Army in Jan. 1943 and was attached to the infantry. He was sent overseas in Nov. 1944 with the 106th Infantry Division, landing in France. He served in northern France and Germany, participating in the Battle of the Bulge. Awarded four battle stars, T/5 Meyers was discharged in Oct. 1945, and is a salesman in Fort Wayne.

May 29, 1945
Bad Ems, Germany

DEAR JERRY:

I am glad Janette talked to a boy from the 106th. I don't know what he told her, but guess I can tell you a little of what was going on at that time of the Bulge.

You know there is a forward echelon and a rear echelon. Well, the forward echelon is usually about two to three miles behind the lines. I was in the forward with the Major, Condo and Manko. We started in the Ardennes Forest December 8. There had been a small skirmish there two days before but we didn't think anything of that. We (the Division) were replacing the 2d Division which was moving to another sector. We heard gun fire all the time, but it didn't bother us. December 12th we moved to St. Vith and the place wasn't bad. We had a nice dispensary set up and we were dry. It had snowed all the time in the Ardennes and we were wet and cold for four days and nights. We had things fairly nice and quiet for three days.

The morning of the 16th we heard shells getting close. We thought at first our artillery had moved up closer to us as they were in back of us and had been shooting over our heads. Finally the buildings around us started dissolving in thin air. Pieces of shrapnel were bouncing off the building and all hell broke loose. We started to work and stayed right on the main floor. Luckily our building didn't take a direct hit. This kept up until about 2:00 P.M., at which time everything was quiet. The Germans had been using 240 mm. or 8-inch guns on us. That evening our 8-inch guns opened up—also 155 mm. I can't explain how shells sound going through the air if you have never heard them, but it is rather weird.

The morning of the 17th everything started at once. Our infantry was holding off three infantry divisions and two panzer divisions. Our four artillery battalions were firing every gun as fast as possible. The German planes had started to get bothersome. About 2 o'clock this day they told us there were 50

German bombers near us trying to get in. Well, that was the last straw, and I wasn't happy about the whole thing. Everything was starting to get mixed up. Boys from other divisions were coming in shot up and full of shrapnel. The 7th Armored was in the town backing us up. The German planes were driven off by P-47's and P-51's from the 9th Air Force. Some of the pursuits would dive on German armor, but as soon as they did a German plane would hop their tails, then they would nose back up again. About two dozen of our planes stayed in one little group over St. Vith all afternoon.

We lost two infantry regiments and all of our reconnaissance troops that day. They were cut off but still kept fighting. German tanks got within three miles of the town that evening. Most of the forward echelon left, but not the medics—though I was ready to. We were not alone, though, because the 7th Armored medics were there along with a collecting company of our division. That night I couldn't sleep. German patrols kept running through the town and they were firing mortars and 88's in all the time. To top this off the M.P.'s called for Manko and myself to come up to their P[risoner of] W[ar] cage as they had some wounded P.W.'s who were dying and needed help. It was dark as pitch, and I didn't want to go but did. The shell fire made it fairly light, so we struggled down the road about half a mile and took care of them. Personally I didn't care if they all died. What a mess. Next day things got hotter and hotter. Small arms fire started flying around with everything else, and every time a 7th Armored tank would stick its nose out from behind a building the Germans would hit it with mortar fire. This went on all that day (December 18th).

That evening we got orders to get out as there was only one road open. About midnight the three of us got in the back of a truck with a truck load of maps. We left for Vielsalm about three o'clock the next morning and arrived about seven. The German infantry was in one side of town as we left the other side. We lost two and two-thirds artillery battalions here.

Things were comparatively quiet in Vielsalm for a day, then we had troubles again. Buzz bombs started hitting. The motor of a buzz bomb sounds like a Model T Ford. As long as you can hear the motor and see the flame everything is all right, but when it stops you want to start ducking because the bomb is coming down right then.

Again most of the forward moved. By this time we had lost our regiments, all except one and two of our artillery battalions. The 7th Armored was shot to pieces and things were rough. The casualties were streaming in and we were sending them out by ambulance just as fast. Those who were beyond repair were put in a shed next door.

The 82d Airborne showed up about this time and they started digging in right away. Were they cocky—but we were glad to see them—and how! They didn't take any prisoners, so we didn't have to bandage any Germans.

I was at Vielsalm for three days and nights. The place was gradually being knocked to pieces, and every time a German tank would show its nose over a hill or around a corner someone would hit it with a bazooka. We finally got orders to move, so we grabbed an ambulance and took off, but found all the roads were blocked and we were entirely cut off. We went back and in a couple of hours the 82d had blasted one road open so we took off at 3:00 A.M. and got through. Got held up again in a little town about 5:00 A.M., as there were no roads open. German tanks kept getting in behind us. About 8:00 o'clock a flight of P-38's showed up and they kept diving and strafing behind us for about an hour. Then we took off again and got to Ferriers.

This was a clear day and our bombers started flying. Boy! Was that a welcome sight! We were so glad to see them that we actually cried. German antiaircraft was terrific though and they were knocking them off.

We were in Ferriers for two days. Christmas day was bad as we got surrounded again. There were Germans all over. Our air force was out again. The German A.A. was also out. I saw them pick off five bombers in one flight. In another flight they hit one plane that exploded and knocked two more down with it. And that is the way that went, but plenty got through.

I moved Christmas day again in the ambulance along with a couple of corpses that we couldn't get rid of fast enough. From there I went to Lince—up by Liege. Then the Germans tried to knock out Liege with buzz bombs, bombers and fighters. Our A.A. was shooting them down this time.

As always,
GAIL

Richard H. Montgomery, of Seymour, enlisted in the Army Dec. 7, 1942, from college. He was sent overseas Oct. 1944 with the 75th Infantry Division and saw service in England, France, Belgium, Holland, and Germany. He fought through the Battle of the Bulge and was awarded the Purple Heart and the Bronze Star. In Mar. 1945 he was made a staff sergeant. Discharged Jan. 23, 1946, Montgomery returned to Princeton University and then to Harvard Law School. The following excerpt from a longer account of the Battle of the Bulge was written by him while in a hospital after the battle.

The regiment arrived in Hasselt on the night of December 19th. We marched all that night and finally at dawn arrived at our bivouac area in a large farmhouse. We spent all day parking our extra equipment and moving it into a large storage room in Hasselt. The night of the 20th we loaded on trucks and headed in the direction of the barely audible cannon fire. It was a cold all-night ride in which nobody could get any rest, the fourth such night, as the crowded 40 and 8's had been equally as miserable. By this time we heard a rumor from the civilians that the Germans were coming. We laughed, as that was ridiculous and impossible, and everybody knew it.

In the morning we stopped by some 155's which were bellowing interminably and had some heated C-rations prepared by the kitchen. Our last hot chow had been in France some time back. We waited most of the day for orders and finally marched up in front of the 155's about five hundred yards and dug in, not too deeply at first, and soon we could hear a terrific artillery barrage out in front of us and began to get scared, too scared to sleep, although we had arranged for a change of the guard. By morning the holes were pretty deep. Some of the boys had hit water.

It was very cold but we still had all our equipment, shelter halves and blankets, and sleeping bags. That same morning, the morning of the 21st, about 10:00 A.M., a German paratrooper killed a civilian some place in front of our positions. Still there was no military or official information concerning a German offensive. We spent the day digging new foxholes fifty yards in front of the old ones. (Some damned officer thought we didn't have enough to do.) By this time everybody was at the other person's throat. We were all dead tired and the boys were beginning to rebel. The captain arranged for us to get some sleep in a barn with only a skeleton force out in the foxholes to guard the front. I pulled early guard that night, and this was our sixth night without sleep, from 7:00 P.M. to 11:00. We moved out at midnight, back up to the crossroads near the 155's. Here we dropped packs, and hand grenades were issued. There we stood in ranks until daylight, waiting for trucks which apparently were lost. When the trucks did come it started to rain and I was in an open truck. We rode all day in a tremendous convoy which seemed to go through the same town every three hours regularly. We were fooling hell out of somebody. My truck got lost from the outfit but not from the convoy. We were very miserable. Our feet seemed to be part of the steel floor bed of the truck. The cold was unbearable. We had some compensation though—the 1st sergeant was in the back of the truck with us and just as miserable as the rest.

All that night the convoy rolled on. The rain turned to wet snow. Finally at dawn we halted on what appeared to be a logging road. We dismounted and formed a column on both sides of the road with five-yard intervals between men. My squad went off to the right flank looking for snipers. We didn't find them and reformed on the road where the general was passing out hand grenades to the men. I was already carrying a B.A.R. (Browning Automatic Rifle) and all the ammunition my frozen feet could move so I didn't take any. We moved up a mile or so and dug in a perimeter defense around an antiaircraft battery. There wasn't anything between us and the enemy, but nobody told us. About noon our air force started coming over very high and in endless procession. The first group immediately began to draw German A.A. fire and about ten planes came down in flames, apparently disintegrating completely in the air. We didn't see many parachutes. Then the Jerry planes started coming in groups of four and flying low. Some dog fights developed with our fighters. A P-47 came over us about one hundred yards in the air with a Messerschmitt right on his tail. Our A.A. battery swung their machine guns at him—but too late. The P-47 crashed and exploded. The Jerry tried to pull up but he crashed, too. Then a P-38 started down. We could almost feel the pilot trying to turn his plane over so he could bail out, but the controls wouldn't respond. He tried three times and then crashed and exploded.

We got out of our holes to move out and were lined up in the field. A P-47 dived on us as if to strafe but he didn't, thank God! We moved to a new location and dug in, stayed here for two hours or so and moved back to a new place and dug in. About dark we started marching. It was Christmas Eve. We walked to a new position up a long hill. I threw away my gas mask on the way up the hill. We were all very disgusted, tired and cold. The officers halted us at the top of the hill and brought up hot chow and plenty of it—our first hot meal in a long time and our last for a long time, forever for some of us. The colonel came up and gave us a short pep talk. It didn't do much good, at least not as much as the hot meal by a long shot. Lt. Dowler sent me out to the right flank as security with orders to shoot at anything that moved. I did and almost got a second lieutenant. (Most of the boys seemed sorry that I had missed and expressed their regrets.) We stayed there for what seemed like a long time and finally we moved out with as much silence as possible and started a long slow march through the woods. We crept along, for hours it seemed, until the men were going to sleep every time we stopped. I saw General Mickle walk past once. He had on a soft cap which stood out as everyone else had on steel helmets. We had been briefed slightly and knew that we were supposed to move into a town where our reconnaissance had reported there was no opposition. It was a poor job of reconnaissance we found out later. Finally we came to a complete halt and received orders to dig in. Everybody dropped in his tracks and immediately went to sleep despite the intense cold.

We were awakened by a short artillery barrage which was bursting high over a few houses which we could see in front of us. Then our heavy machine guns opened up about one hundred fifty yards to my left and the attack commenced. Nobody could find anybody. The Germans replied to the machine guns with a few rounds of 88's and immediately silenced them. I heard shrapnel flying through the trees for the first time. My squad was together—too much together—and Sanchez, our first scout who had seen action before on Attu, was trying to spread them out. We hit the open field in front of us on the double and in short rushes advanced on the town [Wy]. There was a company in front of us and they had already penetrated into the first street and had pushed on by the time my platoon got there. We reassembled on the street and the officers came up and told us to dig in—in the middle of the street! This was madness and we tried to tell them, but they just became more insistent. The 88's started coming and I ran in the nearest house where I stayed, as my squad was supposed to remain there. Sanchez took off toward the Burp guns which were winging bullets our way. S/Sgt. Uhler, squadron leader, and his assistant, Dodd, were attempting to dig in alongside a small building outside.

I was pretty hungry and with my little knowledge of French talked an old lady into frying some ham and eggs for me and my assistant B.A.R. man, Dawson Jack Brown. They surely tasted good and I began to feel a little better. My feet commenced to thaw a little and pretty soon Jack and I went outside and started to dig in. Lt. Hipp came along and told us to move after we had a good hole started. I had a few words with him and he got pretty mad, so I moved and as soon as he left we went back in the house. The old lady went out to get us some more eggs and was wounded in the foot by an 88. Pretty soon we heard the cry, "Retreat, tanks are coming." This retreat cost us plenty. We ran out of the town and an airplane came down over us and dropped three bombs which to this day I feel were meant personally for me. I looked over my shoulder and saw them coming just in time to dive face down into a little stream.

We were ordered to dig in out in the open field. Jack told the lieutenant he wasn't going to dig his own grave and to hell with it. We retreated back into the woods. Equipment was falling left and right, ammunition, rifles, overcoats, arctics, machine guns, gas masks, and even helmets. Men were running everywhere for their lives. All semblance of organization disappeared. Finally, I heard T/Sgt. Tupper calling in his inimitable voice for the first platoon to reassemble. I threw my overcoat away as did Brown and headed for him. The lieutenant and three others went back into town to carry out some wounded. One was Red Collins, an Indiana boy, and a good friend of mine. Tupper led the rest of us back into the town. There weren't many in the platoon who came.

Then Tupper and I went out to gather up rifles and ammunition for the men who were still in the town. Tupper led me over to where our 3d squad had been ordered to dig in. Two of the boys were still there, blown to Kingdom Come by an 88. I looked at them, but didn't recognize either one. Tupper told me who they were. I still couldn't recognize them. Bloody helmets and rifles were lying in the street and in the yard where they were. Nine men in the third squad had been put out of action by that one 88. Collins died, making three dead out of the nine. Tupper and I took their rifles and ammunition. I remember one rifle which had part of a man's forearm blown into the stock. Tupper wanted me to get it, but I took one look and told him I didn't think the rifle would work! We went down to the town church and put one man up in the steeple as a sniper. Some of the boys had brought in about eight prisoners and we had them lined up in the street. Then Tupper led Sanchez, Brown, Gerstle and me out to the last house in town, that is the house closest to the enemy, and told us to stay there. A mortar section was setting up on the street as we went inside the house. The house was strewn with German equipment, hand grenades, mess kits, camouflage suits, rations, and a large rocket which I had never seen before. It was a Panzerfaust but that was unknown to me at the time. It scared hell out of us just looking at it. There were two civilians in the house, one a boy and the other an old woman, evidently his grandmother, who was obviously out of her mind, probably from the shells.

A few shells came in and we ran for the basement. We were all in it and Gannon came running into the house to tell us that they had retreated again and nobody was left in the town except us. What he said was pretty close to the truth and it scared hell out of us. Just then some one of us detonated a Jerry concussion grenade which had been rigged up as a booby trap in the basement. It paralyzed Brown's left arm and just about put the finishing touches on the rest of us. Our nerves were almost gone. We decided to get out. We opened the door of the house and there was the mortar section spread out all over the street, all wounded, dead or dying. Sanchez stopped to help the wounded and I went with Gannon to look for Tupper. We found him and he reassured us and sent us back to the house, promising to bring help for the wounded and some support for us. We went back then and set up our B.A.R.'s—Gerstle was a B.A.R. man also—on tables looking out of the windows on the ground floor. One side of the house was completely blind; that is, it had no windows and that side faced the enemy. We were expecting a counterattack at any minute, but with the number of shells coming in we were afraid to occupy the top floors of the house and it seemed like suicide to go outside and try to dig in. The ground was frozen solid as a rock and snipers were still firing at us occasionally. A building nearby had served as an ammunition dump for the Jerries and it had been set on fire, and besides all the explosions, the fire was casting light all over the street in front of our house. We talked the little boy into getting us some straw with which we covered the basement floor and after discussing surrender and a few other items among ourselves we decided to let two of us get some sleep.

Brown and I took the first shift on guard from seven to nine. It was one of the most terrifying experiences I have ever had. I was so tired I was almost unable to stay awake in spite of the danger. It was necessary to keep extremely quiet and the floor being covered with glass and grenades, etc., this was very difficult. Brown yelled for me once and told me there were about fifteen men outside and he didn't know whether they were ours or theirs. We didn't shoot and they disappeared. I went back to my window and settled down. A German sniper took off to my right and ran a full clip down a hedgerow in front of me. I swung a B.A.R. on him but it was too late. He had hit the ground. I was afraid to dust the area for fear they would see my muzzle blast and blow our house down *toute de suite*. Then I heard a sound directly beneath my window. I thought they were crawling up to throw a hand grenade in the window. I picked up a grenade and, shaking like a leaf, bent forward to see. It was a large pig which was rubbing his back on the bricks under the window. The pig went a little farther and started munching on a German body, one Sanchez had shot with his grease gun in the afternoon.

The moon had come up and it was pretty clear in the field in front of us. All of a sudden Brown called me and I jumped to see what he wanted. He said there was somebody outside. We waited in silence and with our weapons ready. A civilian came around the corner of the house and Brown covered me while I grabbed him and dragged him inside. I tried to tell him in French that it was dangerous to be on the street. I was so nervous I couldn't think of the words and my attempt was almost useless. Brown tried but we couldn't make him understand. Finally we turned him loose and went back to our vigil. The moonlight made things look human in the fields and I tried to watch carefully for any movement. We knew that if they counterattacked we didn't stand a chance. The quiet settled again and then was broken by three rapid shots and the most terrifying scream I have ever heard. This scream was followed by some soul-tearing moans, and then the poor man cried for his wife two or three times and the gun opened up again. During this I was frozen stiff with fear. We found out later some of the boys had shot a civilian. They had moved up and into the houses near us, but we weren't sure which ones.

By this time it was about 9:00 o'clock and we went down to awaken Sanchez and Gerstle and told them what had happened. They relieved us, and Brown and I went down to get some sleep. The bed in the straw wasn't bad. We had some German blankets and it was warmer in the basement. Brown and I both took off our shoes as we figured we could never leave the house anyway in case of an attack. We were so mad, mostly at our own officers, that we would have surrendered probably at the first opportunity. Brown used to say, "Be the first to see the sunny Rhineland" and go through a pantomime of meeting a German soldier trying to surrender and throwing his rifle down first. It is impossible for anyone to realize the feeling of despair which grips a man when his comrades abandon him. We went to sleep immediately and were awakened by Tupper who told us before we were fully awake that we were going out and dig in in front of the town. I choked back some tears and told him this was suicide, but the officers were back in the town now and they wanted a place to sleep. The basement we were in looked pretty good to them and they started gloating over it before we were out. This only served to make my anger worse. We moved out about twelve and that ended the battle of Wy, Belgium. It was the worst Christmas I ever spent and as far as casualties were concerned, the worst day we ever had. Besides the nine men in my platoon whom I have already mentioned, my squad leader lost his eyesight from concussion and one of the other boys, Littrell, was hit in the buttocks by a machine gun, probably one of our own which the Germans got when we retreated. . . .

Ralph J. Canine, of Terre Haute, graduated from Northwestern University in 1916 and fought in the First World War. Remaining in the Army, he attended field artillery school and command and general staff school. He advanced to rank of brigadier general in 1944. In World War II he served as chief of staff, Twelfth Corps, 3d Army, and holds the Distinguished Service Medal, the Silver Star, the Bronze Star with two Oak Leaf clusters, and several foreign decorations. He maintains his home in Terre Haute but is on duty with the Army in Germany.

Thursday, Dec. 28, 1944

Dear Mother and Dad:

Well, it begins to look as though the Boche was definitely slowed down if not completely stopped. We, of course, think we did our part to change his mind. This corps and army can always look back with pride to our "march to the sound of guns." Things were kinda involved when we got here, but we quickly got it under control. We all worked rather hard and long hours. Last couple of days it's been much better tho, and the general and I have had two good nights of sleep and are back on our toes again. It's been clear and cold for the past four or five days. Down to 15 degrees this morning and forecast is for the same tomorrow. Cold wave hit us just after we landed. Slept in our vans first night and it was snowing when I turned in about 2 A.M. Wet snow at first that covered every branch, etc. Turned cold during night and by next night I had every blanket I owned over my bunk. By next night we had a house—general, his two aides and I. Very wealthy woman and her two maids lived in it. She offered it to us and we moved in and have our mess there. She's traveled all over the world. There's enough beautiful furniture for three houses and enough junk for twenty, but it is certainly comfortable. We had her in for dinner and she certainly hates Germans.

We took time off on Christmas Eve long enough to bathe, change into better clothes and have a fine turkey dinner with all the trimmings, then back to the work. Christmas day was just another day of hard fighting. Only good thing about it was that we killed a good many Boche. This business of the Boche fighting to the bitter end may eventually prove a boomerang to him. We have a hard time making our men really mad enough. Our soldiers just don't hate these Boche the way they should. Somehow they don't realize the only reason we're over here with thousands of good Americans being killed is because of the German people. But slowly it's beginning to dawn on them that the only good German is a dead German—that the whole nation is solidly behind this thing—that if we don't kill them off now they will start another war in twenty-five years. The result is we're killing more and taking fewer prisoners. That's all to the good and if our men will just hate enough, perhaps these boys won't have died in vain. Now if only the people at home would quit talking of reconversion and all that tommyrot and win the war, maybe we could close this thing up over here before next winter. The newspapers we get are full of life as usual, and most of the men here are pretty bitter about the home front. I suppose politics are mixed up in it quite a bit.

I got your cablegram and the letters written after my promotion had been announced. Naturally I am very happy. It's something I'd wanted a long time and had given up hope of getting. Can't say that I feel any different, but I do notice that as I ride around in my jeep with a star on the red, I have to do more saluting than I used to as a colonel. Everyone around here seemed glad I got it or at least said so, and I had many notes from busy people, old friends, that of course made me feel good. One does get a few more privileges as a general officer.

Your letters written after the anniversary didn't mention getting my letter or cable. I thought I'd gotten them off in good time but apparently not. Hope the Merry Christmas cable got there on time. Have had no mail in over two weeks. . . .

Love,
RALPH

George C. Gilland, of Greensburg, was inducted into the Army May 11, 1942, and was assigned to the 820th Tank Destroyer Battalion of the infantry. Going overseas in Oct. 1944, Staff Sergeant Gilland served in France, Belgium, Holland, Luxembourg, Germany, and Czechoslovakia. He fought with the 106th Infantry Division in the Battle of the Bulge. Sgt. Gilland was discharged Oct. 11, 1945, and is now farming near Greensburg. The following letter was written to his wife.

[May 1945]

All we've done since V-E Day is sleep. You asked me what army division I was in. I was in fifteen divisions and in four different armies. I was with the 9th when we first came here, then with the 1st during the Battle of Ardennes and the 15th in the Ruhr pocket and with the 3d on the drive to meet the Russians in Czechoslovakia. I wasn't allowed to tell you and anyway by the time you had received a letter I would have changed. We were used to break through strong points or for some big drive somewhere. We were the boys who would break through the enemy lines and run wild behind them.

Well, now the war is over, I will tell you about the Battle of Ardennes. We got the hell kicked out of us. I never saw my outfit for two days and nights. I had ten men with me and we were cut off behind the lines. I could see we were trapped and I never dreamed we would be living today. The Germans took few prisoners during the battle and usually killed them behind the lines. They threw in their very best troops against us. We made a long stab to get through and with more than brains we made it. One company was wiped out. We were with the 106th Division and there aren't many more, almost all of them were killed.

They threw in reserves from everywhere and they got it the same way. Armored divisions were wiped out like rifle squads. They were rough. There just wasn't any way to stop them for a while. I saw three miles of artillery all firing at once and keeping it up continually. Airplanes bombing, strafing, tanks, tank destroyers, artillery and infantry, everything was in it. I fought with the infantry and engineers any time we could get a group together big enough to fight with. We were shelled for sixteen hours before the attack really started. I thought the next shell would land where I was, but I was lucky. One time I lay among fifty infantrymen and we were shelled and when it was over there were only five of us who weren't wounded. I've had lots of luck.

Then the day came when we went on the offensive and did we ever get revenge. I loved it. These are just a few of the things that happened to us. We have been going so fast since then the rations and mail couldn't keep up with us. We were here and there. . . .

GEORGE

George Burt Ford, of South Bend, joined the Enlisted Reserve Corps at Purdue University in Dec. 1942, and was inducted into active service May 15, 1943. He was assigned to the Army Specialized Training Program from Sept. 1943 to March 1944, when he was transferred to the 94th Infantry Division and sent overseas. Pfc. Ford served as an automatic rifleman from Sept. 1944, fighting in Normandy and Brittany and in the Switch position of the Siegfried Line in Germany. He was wounded in Germany in Jan. 1945. Discharged in June, 1945, Ford is enrolled in the Indiana University School of Law.

January 20, 1945
Germany

DEAR MOTHER AND ANNETTE:

Pulled us back for a couple of days rest, and the Lord only knows how we needed it. I don't know whether you'll ever read about us in the papers, but to us these last seven days and nights are something none of us can ever forget no matter how hard we try. Even if I were able to tell you about it, I doubt if you could believe it. Someone must have been praying for me every minute because I was one of the lucky ones that got out with nothing worse than shattered nerves. I guess I am a poor soldier, but I know I'll never get used to a pounding like that. Either those Germans are crazy fanatics or someone keeps them full of dope, for they made counterattack after counterattack right into the face of what must have been as wonderful support as American artillery ever gave our troops. How we did it I don't know, but we held our own and gave those Huns back triple what they threw at us. Yesterday when it looked like we would be cut to ribbons, the miracle we were all praying for came zooming out of the skies in the form of a bunch of our fighters. I know I have never seen a more welcome sight than those planes thundering down on the German guns, for they shut them up like so many clams. If we hadn't been so nearly frozen and exhausted I think we would have raised up from our holes and cheered in spite of the snipers a stone's throw away from us. Anyway, we got back here this morning in time for chow; believe me, after living on less than one meal a day and what we could find on the bodies of the Germans we had killed, not a man griped about the powdered eggs and greasy sausage for it looked like a feast.

I slept all day today, got up for supper and as soon as I finish this letter am sure I will be able to sleep until chow in the morning. Your letter with the swell picture of you two got here this evening as did your box with the shaving sticks, socks, candy, cookies, raisins and handkerchiefs. Talk about something being welcome and coming at the right time—well this box sure is just that. Will use one of those shaving sticks tomorrow when I go to work on an eight-day's beard, and the food has already been put to good use. You can send me more of the same at any time and also a shaving brush, please. I am all right and will write more tomorrow or the next day.

Love,
BURT

Gene Eckerty, of Princeton, and a member of the Indiana House of Representatives, was inducted into the Army Aug. 4, 1943, and was assigned to the infantry. Going overseas in Nov. 1944, Staff Sergeant Eckerty served in Company L, 10th Infantry Regiment, 5th Division of the Third Army. He fought in France and Germany. In Feb. 1945, S/Sgt. Eckerty was killed in action in Germany. He was awarded the Combat Infantry Badge.

Jan. 8, 1945
Somewhere in ETO

HON. HOBART CREIGHTON,
Speaker of House of Representatives, State House,
Indianapolis, Indiana.

DEAR MR. SPEAKER:

At the present time I am serving as a line sergeant in the 3d Army, 5th Division, on the snow-covered western front. All of the G.I.'s in the infantry, as they march thru the mud, slush, and snow have but one goal in mind—that is, to get the task completed and return home to our families and friends. I wish to assure the members of the House and people of the State of Indiana that our fighting men are making sacrifices of life, limb, and physical and mental discomfort that are beyond the conception of soldier or civilian who has not actually undergone such experiences. They make these sacrifices and take that one step forward when every bone and muscle in their body tells them they cannot go forward—in order that our country might have an everlasting peace.

Many a soldier who has faced enemy machine guns and 88's without the least hesitation will return to Indiana broken in spirit and body, without a suitable civilian job, heavy financial obligations to meet. I take this opportunity to urge the members of the General Assembly to enact legislation to aid the returning combat veteran in obtaining a new start in civilian life.

Before I close I want you to know that the combat infantryman is a God-fearing soldier. He reads his Bible and prays more than all of the people in the States. One of the B.A.R. men in my platoon was miraculously saved from death. The shrapnel from a German 88 entered his breast pocket, but was stopped by the soldier's New Testament. Will you please have the House Chaplain to pray for the thousands of tired, homesick, Hoosier fighting men scattered throughout the world.

I send my very best regards to all the members of the General Assembly. May God bless each and every one of you.

Sincerely yours,
S/Sgt. GENE ECKERTY

William B. Rudy, of Indianapolis, enlisted in the Air Corps in Nov. 1942. He was commissioned a 2d lieutenant in April 1944 and was sent overseas in July. Lt. Rudy participated in bombing raids over the Balkans, southern France, and Rome. Shot down over Yugoslavia in Aug. 1944, he was wounded in the leg after parachuting to the ground and was captured by Bulgarians. Released in the spring of 1945, he was returned to this country and discharged in June, 1946. Lt. Rudy was awarded the Air Medal and the Purple Heart.

Feb. 2, 1945
Stalag XVIII

DEAR FOLKS:

I am very comfortably situated in a prison hospital in Germany and very thankful to be alive. You may as well know that my left foot and part of my leg have been amputated. The doctors don't have much hope of saving my knee which was left stiff as the result of the operation. All amputation cases are eligible for automatic repatriation, so I think the doctors are going to delay a second amputation until the physicians in America have a chance to look at it. But don't get too impatient about this repatriation, because it may take six months to a year. Losing my leg seemed pretty awful to me at first, but I have grown used to it now and realize how lucky I am not to be dead.

Gilbert and Hayden went down with the plane and I got out only a few seconds before it crashed.

I am now up on crutches and enjoying the company of three Englishmen, a New Zealander and a Scot.

Love,
BILL

John N. Davis, of Frankfort, enlisted in the Army Nov. 13, 1942, and was called into active service a year later and assigned to the infantry. He was sent overseas in Oct. 1944, being attached to the Cannon Company, 347th Regiment, 87th Infantry Division, with the Third Army. Davis participated in combat in France, Belgium, Luxembourg, Germany, and Czechoslovakia. Returned to the States in July 1945, and promoted to the rank of sergeant in Dec., Davis was discharged Feb. 20, 1946, and is now an electrical engineer residing in Pittsfield, Mass.

March 24, 1945
Somewhere in Germany

DEAR AUNT ANNA:

It is a nice sunny morning and I've taken my Saturday bath. So now that I am fairly clean, I'll start by writing an answer to your letter which I received yesterday.

The past two weeks have been the nicest that we have had since we first landed in France. The days have been warm and sunny, although the nights are still chilly. We really enjoy it and hope that spring is really here. After last January all of us are allergic to cold weather.

Right now we are in the vicinity of Coblenz, which the division captured a few days ago. The country is very hilly and rugged. I saw a large vineyard on the side of a hill so steep that it is a wonder a man could stand on it, let alone work.

I am getting my copies of *Newsweek* regularly now. By that I mean as regular as any of my mail comes. I really enjoy them, and so do the others as there is a waiting list for each copy. All of us are starved for reading material and we devour anything in print.

One noticeable difference between the French and German villages is the cleanliness of the streets in the German towns. They don't have their manure piled in front of the house. At least they keep it out of sight behind the house.

The Germans have a lot of livestock. Oxen, horses, cattle, sheep, and pigs can be found in every village, along with chickens of all sizes and colors. Of course, they ought to have enough livestock, as parts of France and Belgium were swept bare by the Germans.

It is easy to tell that the Germans had been the conquerors in the early part of the war. They are better dressed than any other European people except the British and they are about even. They also are better fed and their children are fat and chubby in comparison to the French and Belgian kids. You have to give the Germans credit for many scientific advances, but it seems as though they devote themselves to war instead of benefiting humanity. It is curious that a mind adapted to science can also foster some of the most barbaric tortures and killings that the world knows. However, they are now learning the meaning of the war they so enthusiastically sponsored. We are fighting on their soil and it is their villages, towns, and cities, their farms, their livestock, their people that are being destroyed today. And that makes a large difference regardless of what anyone can say.

The inhabitants of the large cities have been bombed many times prior to this spring, but when every small town and village is seeing Allied troops and has been shelled by Allied artillery, they can begin to realize that they are not *Herrenvolk.*

I seem to write on the serious side this morning, but I cannot have or feel any pity for these people. I have no remorse for shelling their homes and killing them. They have sowed the winds of destruction, now they are reaping the tornado that shall destroy them. Perhaps it is hard for many of you to understand this attitude and I don't expect you to understand it. You haven't seen the things we have, you haven't undergone the experiences that engender this attitude. Thank God that you haven't. All that we want is for you to know our feelings, so that you will insist on a firm and just peace. We don't want a peace treaty that will have pity on them. They can be made to realize their crime without our resorting to their level of cruelty and barbarism, but we can be harsh and also firm and just. That is what we ask today and shall ask tomorrow.

Somebody found a pup the other day and the company has adopted him, or him us. We just about exhaust him with our constant petting and playing for someone always has a moment to whistle at him. He is just dog, but very few pedigreed dogs can live better than he has the last few days. . . .

I really appreciate your sending me boxes and volunteering to send me more. They are just a little bit of home to us and I doubt if even I realize fully how much that word holds and has in meaning to me. I do know that I understand and appreciate my home, family, and friends more now than I ever did. I am all right and hope that you are too.

Love,
JOHN

William C. DaVie, of Indianapolis, was inducted into the Army in May 1943 and was attached to the engineer corps. Sent to England in Feb. 1944, he served with the 902d Engineers at the invasion of France and saw service in Germany. Discharged in Oct. 1945, Pfc. DaVie is a commercial art director in New York.

Easter Sunday 1945
E.T.O., Somewhere in France

DEAR MOTHER:

I thought I'd write you an Easter letter at least—in reply to two letters from you that descended in a heap a week or so ago—back February mail that had been eddying around in some backwater. We read that a mail ship had broken down in some out-of-the-way port and finally had limped in some place that had facilities for trans-shipping some millions of pieces of mail. It had broken down four times, probably some vital part like a main drive shaft that can only be fixed in a big dry dock. With shipping as vital as it is, towing a boat is out of the question, besides being very risky business.

The Krauts are dying by inches like a snake, but evidently the U-boat arm is still alive and vicious. Everything they are doing now in their death throes has *only one* redeeming feature, that is to my mind; the fact that they are constantly removing themselves farther and farther from the circle of civilized nations each time they prolong the fighting, and they are smearing themselves and alienating any friends or support they might have by their stupid continuation of a lost struggle. They insist on the last ditch struggle to prove a conclusion which has been foregone ever since they retreated from Moscow and lost the battle of Africa. In this way the only good I can see come out of it is that more and more of them are being destroyed and it is daily coming closer to *my* idea that the entire race should be wiped out. As long as any of them live they will never cease to dream of ruling the world and will stop at nothing to accomplish their aim.

I firmly believe they have a plan for the Third World War—that they anticipated losing this one on paper—but actually statistics show that they have systematically slaughtered enough of the cream of every other smaller nation in Europe that by 1960 Germany will once more have an overwhelming advantage in manpower. This advantage we are helping to accomplish by feeding and caring for hundreds of thousands of strong young German prisoners who are complicating our supply system and burdening our transport system, if only by eating and riding. The only fault in their plan, their only successful rival competitor, enemy, and conqueror, is Russia. They undoubtedly counted on beating Russia and failed. Since this is so, and also since Russia has done the bulk of the fighting—by which I do not mean to underestimate nor belittle what our own boys have done, but when you compare the Russian front of 2,500 miles with our own front and remember how many years the Russians have been absorbing the heaviest punishment the Germans could deal out and the tremendous destruction that has been wreaked on Russian soil and citizens— you realize how incalculably more difficult our own fighting would have been without them. I am in favor of giving the major part of Germany to Russia, who certainly has earned it and who can be counted upon to see to it that Germany will never again threaten the world with slavery.

I know you have never agreed with my deep hatred for the Germans and everything they admire and stand for. When I realize how much you personally have suffered, I am at a loss to understand your attitude. I don't doubt that in your case it is a miscarriage of a Christian virtue. I find it not only blind but positively dangerous to try to deal with these animals on any such basis. One might just as well read the Ten Commandments to a spotted leopard, walk into the cage and not expect to be eaten. The only reason I consider it important that you and everyone like you, who has no active opinion against these sub-humans, should listen to me is that *we have not won the war even after the fighting ceases.* This is definitely only one step in their thousand-year plan to dominate the world. They are stubborn and absolutely unchanging in their ideas. They live forever and breed like rabbits and everywhere they emigrate they remain a hard, foreign, unassimilated element whose sole desire and ambition is to Germanize and brutalize the world into an exact replica of Germany. Each time they are allowed to proceed with the next step in their plan, it takes more and more blood, sweat, and tears to stop them, and the next war they have planned may very well destroy the entire world, *if they are allowed to proceed with it. It is possible.* Destruction of men, materials, wealth, resources and *brains,* which are the race's rarest and most precious possession, can reach such a rate that the world will revert to an uninhabited jungle. You have only to notice how difficult it is to operate the United States today with only 13,000,000 men missing to see it would not take too much more to wreck the place.

This is a strange kind of an Easter letter, I will admit, but in another way it is the best and only kind I feel will guarantee a more peaceful Easter in years to come—in fact the only kind that will guarantee that there will be any kind of an Easter when you remember the Nazi sacrileges against the Christian churches in Germany. You need no imagination to see the horrible little paperhanger enshrined in your own church this Easter, if his plan had not failed. I write this because the peace conference and the San Francisco meeting are the payoff on the tremendous debt the nation owes the dead and wounded. *This time there must be no slip up.* The world cannot afford to fail, and civilians like you are the only ones who now have a voice to raise and see that justice is done and the sacrifices of millions are not in vain.

This does not in any way affect my love for you, but I have given you my reasons for what I think and I hope I have convinced you that these next few months in America are the most important months in the history of the world. We may not have another chance to find the right answer. I won't try to suggest what you can do, but if you do no more than talk to people, which I know you do constantly at the University, you can do a great deal of good with the *thinking* people if only helping to convince them that whatever else is done the Germans must not be allowed the slightest possible chance to make war on the world again. There is no way to punish them justly for the misery, torture, pain, death and destruction they have deliberately unleashed on helpless peoples, but *they must be stopped from doing it again in twenty years, as they have five times in the last one hundred years.* I will leave the means to you, ways will certainly present themselves.

I send you my best love, and hope that this finds you, as it leaves me, in good health and suffering only from the natural results of this German-inspired world tragedy. Once more my love to you.

BILL

James F. McKillen, of Angola, enlisted in the Army April 4, 1942, and was stationed with the 9th Armored Division, Ft. Riley, Kans., until transferred to the Anti-Aircraft Artillery O.C.S. He was graduated Feb. 3, 1943, as a 2d lieutenant. Before going overseas Lt. McKillen was attached to the 589th A.A. Automatic Weapons Battalion as battery commander, Camp Stewart, Ga., and with the 291st Infantry, 75th Division, as rifle platoon leader and company commander. Overseas in Jan. 1945, Lt. McKillen participated in the Battle of the Bulge, the Rhineland campaign, and the central European campaign. Promoted to captain in Sept. 1945, McKillen was awarded the Bronze Star. He was discharged Oct. 15, 1945, and is now a manager for the B. F. Goodrich Company in Indianapolis.

DEAR FOLKS:

When I joined the 75th division, my regiment was on the Maas River just across from Roermond, Holland. We were on line at the time and were on line continuously from then until shortly before V-E Day, when we were pulled back into a rest area.

While we were on the Maas, we were making preparations for the river crossing and the capture of Roermond and so we were doing a lot of night patrolling across the river, and that is one thing about the infantry that I dread the most because those night patrols into enemy territory always scare me, particularly when there is a river between you and your friendly troops.

We made the river crossing in force one morning and captured Roermond and held it while the engineers built some bridges to bring armor across. After that we started fighting with an armored division. We were with the 5th Armored for a while and the 8th Armored for a while. We were chasing the Krauts toward the Rhine and they were running pretty fast, so the fighting wasn't very heavy and aside from the fact that we were moving all the time it wasn't such a bad deal.

We reached the Rhine at the city of Rheinberg, Germany, and there the Krauts had their backs against the river with the bridges out and they fought like cornered rats and that was pretty tough. We fought for around two or three days to take Rheinberg, and that is the first place you came close to collecting $10,000 insurance.

I was on reconnaissance one morning in the edge of Rheinberg and had just stopped to get out of the jeep and go into a building so I could get upstairs to get a better view of the situation. There was a German self-propelled 88 mm. gun setting down the street which I hadn't seen, and just as I got out of the jeep they fired on it and scored a direct hit and blew the jeep all to pieces. Jeeps are hard to get, too, so that made me mad. However, one of our tanks was coming into town at the time and got the German gun before they could pull out.

After we captured Rheinberg, we set up defensive positions along the Rhine south of Rheinberg, and that is where I was in the farmhouse that I sent the picture of. Things were pretty hot the first few days we were there, and we couldn't step out of the house in the daytime as we were right on the bank of the river and the Krauts could see every move we made. However, they must have decided to save their ammunition to use against us when we started to cross the river, because they quit firing after a few days and we could move around fairly well.

While we were there we were continuously making night patrols across the river to get information that would help in the river crossing, and I can tell you that regardless of what you read in the newspapers, the 9th Armored Division wasn't the first one to cross the Rhine. By that time I had begun to think I was in the Navy instead of the Army, I had been on so many boat rides. However, later our regiment received a commendation from General Montgomery for the work we had done in getting information about the enemy's positions across the Rhine.

Just before the Rhine crossing was made, I was transferred to the weapons platoon and had to have my mortars set up to fire across the river while the crossing was being made, so I had a foxhole right on the bank for observation and really had a seat on the fifty-yard line. Tell the folks that is what I meant when I said I had a front seat at a million dollar show with no tickets to sell.

That Rhine crossing is something I wouldn't have missed for the world. All that you read in the newspapers about the Navy and engineers copping the show is true, but they didn't give them half enough credit. Those sailors and engineers carried boat load after boat load of doughboys across that river, and did it under terrific artillery fire.

Two of the 9th Army's "Varsity Infantry Division" plus "Old Hell on Wheels" (the 2d Armored Division) were to push through us and make the crossing, and the preparation they had was something. The air corps was out in force all day long the day before the attack was made and they dropped everything on those Krauts but the kitchen sink. At midnight, and H-hour was to be at two in the morning, our artillery preparation fire started and I've never heard anything like it. I don't see how any Krauts could have been alive on the other side of that river, as that artillery barrage lasted for two solid hours right along the river banks.

There was an artillery observer with me at my forward observation post and he told me that we had over ninety battalions of field artillery behind us in that barrage, and there I was trying to see where the shells from my 60 mm. mortars were landing. I finally gave up and told my gunmen to fire up all their ammunition as fast as they could and I settled back to watch the show.

About five in the morning I decided that I'd like to see what was going on on the other side, so I hitched a ride across on a LCVP, and got the surprise of my life. Here it was only three hours after H-Hour and those darn engineers were already on the other side building a road and the leadway to a bridge to start bringing armor across.

The Rhine crossing had been a lot easier than anyone had thought it would be and a lot less costly. Of the division that made the crossing through my area, one regiment had only eight casualties and another only five.

After that we pushed off across the Rhine and started following the 5th Armored Division again, cleaning out the pockets they had by-passed. We fought through a lot of woods and took several small towns and also a rubber plant which was supposed to be the largest synthetic rubber plant in the world. That was where we stayed in the beautiful apartment buildings that formerly housed Gestapo guards. A little later we captured a large aluminum plant where I got the hot shower, the first in several weeks. That was as far forward as we went in the direction of Berlin, and the next day we were pulled back and started fighting to clean out the Ruhr pocket.

That Ruhr pocket was the roughest fighting we ran into as far as I'm concerned. In the first place, it wasn't considered as important as the drive to Berlin so we didn't get very high priority on air and artillery support. They told us that they estimated there were only 80,000 Krauts in the pocket, mostly A.A. and service troops, but when we had the pocket cleaned out we had taken over 300,000 prisoners, including two divisions of paratroopers, the crack armored division, Panzer Lehn, and a lot of SS troops, and they were really fanatics. There were a lot of A.A. guns in that pocket, though, and they used them against us, and believe me, those A.A. guns are really mean when they're used against ground troops.

In cleaning out the pocket, we captured the city of Dortmund and had some pretty heavy fighting there, as there were a lot of SS men and paratroopers there, who were making the Volkstrum and Wehrmacht men fight; they didn't surrender very easy. . . .

Our last attack was made Friday, April the 13th, and there were several times that day when I thought it was going to be my last attack for good. The minute we jumped off we were caught under a terrific artillery barrage from A.A. guns and I lost one whole machine gun squad, and I had a pretty close call myself. A piece of shrapnel cut a hole clear through the toe of my boot, but never even touched my foot, except to slightly scratch it and bruise it a little. Lucky my boots were too big for me.

However, we finally got through that barrage and managed to keep out ahead of it all day long, fighting through the woods, and that day our company fought as I never saw them fight before. That day every man in the company, including the newest replacement, fought like a veteran and they really had blood in their eyes. We were on foot and going through heavy woods all the way, and still reached and captured our final objective on the Ruhr River nearly three hours before the company on our left, which was mounted on tanks, came up beside us.

That closed off the Ruhr pocket and so two days later we were pulled back into a rest area and then came into this place and are now doing a little police work. We have rounded up a few Gestapo and SS men and several German soldiers who ditched their uniforms for civilian clothes, but all in all it hasn't been too exciting.

Loads of love,
JIM

Myron G. Burkenpas, of Lafayette, was inducted into the Army in Nov. 1943 and was assigned to the infantry. He was sent overseas in June 1944 and served with the 7th Corps Artillery in France, Belgium, Luxembourg, and Germany. Pfc. Burkenpas was discharged in Nov. 1945 and is a department manager in a retail store at Lafayette.

April 12, 1945
Somewhere in Germany

DEAR DAD:

Sometime ago I wrote you folks a letter telling you about the pillboxes in the Siegfried line, and you passed it around to a number of the fellows at the factory to read. I didn't write that letter with the intention of having others read it but I am this one. I only wish I could handle words cleverly enough so that all the papers in the nation would publish this letter.

Dad, I have been pretty close to the front lines since last summer. I have seen quite a number of men lying dead on the field of battle, men who had died from violence in various forms, but they were strong, healthy young men who died while fighting and had had in some degree a fighting chance. After seeing death close at hand quite often a fellow gets over his first shock, and although death never becomes commonplace a fellow becomes used to seeing it. I should really say, he thinks he does. Again I've seen death but in such a form that would shock the hardest of men.

I have visited a German concentration camp for Russian and Polish prisoners of war. From a distance the prison camp looks like any army camp, low flat barracks buildings placed in rows and not a tree around. Upon closer inspection you see the double barbed wire fence, nine feet high, with the rolled loose wire in between. We passed through the gate with the guard box on either side. There was the usual military equipment lying around that we always find where there has been a skirmish or prisoners have been taken. At the gate we saw our first dead man. He was said to be a German who had administered the beatings to the prisoners of the camp. The prisoners had gotten hold of him before he could get away when the Americans appeared and had made short work of him. We passed on through the gate and walked down the main camp street.

Dad, you have read of the atrocities of the Germans and thought how terrible they were. I have heard and read of them, but they have always happened someplace else and I'm afraid I was guilty of saying to myself, "I'll take all of this talk about atrocities with a grain of salt." Today I walked down that prison camp street and saw with my own eyes some of the horrible things these Nazis have done. We turned the corner at the end of the main street and there in an open space between the barracks lay the bodies of twenty-eight men and boys. I walked up to within a few feet of them and looked down on their shaven heads, their sunken stomachs, their ribs standing out like rails on a fence. One little fellow about fifteen lay naked on his stomach; half of his buttocks was solid black from being kicked. Another older man was still on his knees and forearms, braced in such a way he couldn't fall over. I saw all of this in one quick glance and then the real horror of the thing struck me; every one of those twenty-eight men had a bullet hole through the back of his head. The Germans had a reason for this mass slaughter. The Americans were coming, they had to march their Russian and Polish prisoners on back far behind the lines so they would not be freed and could still be used as slave laborers. There were those who were too starved and weak to make the march, so the easiest way to get rid of them was a bullet in the back of the head.

We soon walked away from this spot of horror only to be confronted with a sight still more terrible. A short distance farther on down the street was a small brown building about the size of a single car garage. We walked on down to within a short distance of this building. On the broadside of the building there were double doors that were standing wide open. In the building, stacked up like cordwood, were the bodies of sixty to seventy-five men and boys. It would have been hard to guess their ages, their bodies were so shrunken from starvation, and seemed so small lying there in that horrible pile. The bodies had been sprinkled with some sort of powder to keep the odor of decaying flesh down, but the stench of death was everywhere. That smell, Dad, is something that I will not forget soon. We passed on down the street and saw the brick building with the big steel oven where the bodies were cremated. I saw all this with my own eyes and I'm not exaggerating this horrible thing no matter how hard I might try.

I don't like army life, but for the first time I can wholeheartedly and honestly say that I'm glad I'm here doing a little bit to help stop these horrible atrocities. I don't tell you folks everything and I debated in my own mind for some time about telling you this, and then decided if every grown American could realize what has really been happening here we could not help winning the right kind of peace as well as the war.

There is a story that when the Americans first arrived and found this camp they got the mayor of the nearby city, took him out to the camp and showed him the scenes I have just described. The mayor said that he knew nothing of that sort had been going on. He was then returned to his home in the city where, a short time later, he committed suicide. Maybe the individual German doesn't know the horror that exists in his country, but he is indirectly responsible and should be shown the suffering he has caused. If all Germans and all Americans could see and realize what I've seen today, the American individual would understand why the government is demanding unconditional surrender and the Germans would realize why unconditional surrender is demanded of them. Dad, it is for you to decide whether you want Mother and Dorothy to read this, but tell the boys at the shop what it is all about.

All my love,
MYRON

Morris E. Layton, of Indianapolis, was inducted into the Army in Dec. 1942 and was attached to the engineer corps. He trained and served with the 665th Engineers and became a technician 5th grade. T/5 Layton was sent overseas in Jan. 1944 and was with the invasion forces that struck France in June. Thereafter he moved with Gen. Patton's 3d Army, except that he was also in the Battle of the Bulge. Discharged in Nov. 1945, he is a mail carrier in Indianapolis.

April 14 [1945]
Germany

Dear —:

I have seen so many things in recent days that I would like to tell you about if I can. I would like to tell you about what I have seen in a way that you might realize what has been going on and is still going on inside Germany. But I know that is impossible, for you must be here to see it and to smell it. Since landing in France, more than nine months ago, I've seen many things, much destruction and torture, and death, but never have I seen a sight like I saw yesterday.

You may have read in the paper about this place and again it may not have ever been in the paper. I've read about these places but I didn't believe it too strongly, until I saw it yesterday with my own eyes.

I've seen everything I'm writing about and have taken pictures of it and it is the truth. If you can believe, you know it is true.

I'm talking about a German prisoner of war camp and the hundreds of people I saw almost starved to death and lying around dead in the streets where the Nazis had murdered them before leaving. I'm talking about the hill a little piece farther on where there are also rows of dead soldiers who had been prisoners and who the Nazis either starved to death or murdered. They are all skin and bones. A little farther on is where they had them dig their graves, then they burnt them. There is a metal rack for holding the wood and bodies. But they didn't quite get to finish the last batch for the fire is out and there are the partly burnt bodies of many people still lying there looking at you.

I could tell you about the scaffold in the courtyard used for hanging, in case they didn't want to shoot or burn a person. There is one place where they take off your clothes, put you in a place that is very hot and opens up your pores, then they lay you in a room that has lye all over it. Just another way to kill a man.

I've heard there were prisoners here from most of the countries fighting Germany. Some were Americans. But I believe most of them were Russians, Poles, and Yugoslavians.

One of the big German SS guards came back to the camp yesterday. He still believed they were pigs and he was the superman and could still beat them around. He could not get used to the idea that Germany is lost. So he came back. But things were different now. A big Russian hit him in the head with a shovel. Another one grabbed a bayonet and stabbed him to death. He'd stick the bayonet in then take his foot and shove it all the way in. They even cut his eyes out. He's lying off to the side away from the other dead. I suppose all the emotion of many months finally expressed itself in these two Russians.

I can look out my window up the hill and see the camp and on farther up the hill where they are burying them as fast as they can. They went down into town and rounded up a bunch of civilians to dig graves. Some look like bankers and lawyers and have never felt a shovel before. But they are getting the feel of one damned quick now. They are not digging one big grave, but a separate grave for each body. And the digging is in almost solid rock. But there is an American soldier with rifle ready, and every grave goes down six feet. And everybody is out on a mattress cover.

The German civilians say they are innocent, that they had no idea what had been going on up the hill behind that double, ten-foot high, barbed wire fence all this time. But the Americans say you are all guilty of this crime of your country. You are Germans and this is your country and it is your duty to find out what is going on and to run your country as it should be. It was quite a sight to see. The many rows of bodies, the Germans all digging graves and sweating, and the soldiers all standing around swearing and taking pictures of them. The Germans would hardly look up.

Down in the prison camp it is terrible. I saw many bodies lying where they'd been shot with pools of blood around them. One fellow didn't fall over, but just sort of huddled down in a bunch. Before the Germans left they killed all the men they couldn't take with them except a very few who managed to hide. In the place where the men stayed it looks like a stable. There is a passageway through the middle; on both sides there are straw mattresses side by side, two rows deep. If you slept in the back row you must climb over the ones in front for there were no aisles except the one in the middle. The smell was terrible. There was blood, vomit, and others could only relieve themselves in bed for they were too sick to move. Many little brown pans were scattered about that they had eaten from. They were just starved to death.

Some of the prisoners have come back and are just hanging around. They don't know what to do. They are the palest and skinniest men I've ever seen; they can hardly walk. The army has little time or food to give them. They are fighting a war and have no time for anything else. You see them along all the highways, some riding but most walking, all going home after so long. One boy was riding a kiddie car. He'd carry it up the hill and then could ride down the other side. Two boys had their legs off and were hobbling along on crutches. It's quite a trip from here into Belgium on crutches. But they are all happy for they are going home. And I guess to 'most every man, regardless of what happens to him or what is the matter with him, his thoughts and every wish in his heart is to be home—everything else is of little importance. For they've seen too many who will never return and they believe a leg is a very cheap price to pay to be home.

One of our boys went into a camp. He was the first American soldier to go there. The men were starving. They had nothing at all to eat and no place to get anything. Many of the men cried when they saw him. Some were too weak to move. We have no food to give them. We are getting very little for ourselves now. We have come so far and fast that the food isn't catching up. I've seen people along the highways picking up little pieces of food soldiers have thrown away.

These prison camps are around every town I've seen. This is the only one I've been in. I don't know what the conditions are in the others. These camps held slave workers from other countries, and they did all the hardest and dirtiest work for the Germans. The Germans believed they were the greatest people on earth and everyone else was pigs and animals to be worked and treated as such. I can see more clearly than ever just why I came over here. . . .

Love,
MORRIS

Victor Muller, of Ferdinand, was inducted into the Army in Oct. 1943 and was assigned to the 12th Engineer Combat Battalion, 8th Infantry Division. He was sent overseas in Feb. 1945 and saw action in Germany. Wounded, he was awarded the Purple Heart. Pvt. Muller was discharged in Feb. 1946 and entered medical school.

June 10, 1945

GREETINGS:

Just received a letter from Pop dated June 4th. Boy, that's as good as I did at Camp Gordon. Sure wish they were all like that. There isn't much news to tell you. . . .

Glad to hear my [Purple] Heart arrived. Don't worry, I'm not looking for any clusters for it. Sometimes you don't have much choice though. Tomorrow we have a ten-mile hike, so maybe I'll see a little of the surrounding country. You'd think we had lost the war if you could see us now. We're restricted to the company area when not training and have to be in at 2200 even though it is still light outside. At the same time we can look out and see the German P.W.'s who have been released doing as they jolly well please. But then that's the army.

. . . The drive across the Cologne plains was a classic in screwiness. It was so fast that we moved every day and often more than once a day. We worked almost solely at night, for the plains are so flat you can see for miles; and every road, bridge site, road block or what-have-you was zeroed in by Jerry artillery. I can't begin to remember the order in which things happened, but I'll try to tell you a few of the jobs we did and how we lived. . . .

Every curve and every street was defended by a road block, a hollow log barrier thrown across the road and filled with sand or stone. They were invariably mined or covered by machine gun fire, but only once were we caught. A bouncing betty was set off one night and five of the men were hit, although only one died. Another fellow and myself were working on one side of the block while the five were on the other side. Shrapnel cut the bill off the other fellow's cap and one piece went through the sleeve of my jacket, but neither of us was hurt. Of course a machine gun opened up immediately and we departed *tout de suite* until a tank came up and blasted the machine gun. Let me tell you that a Jerry machine gun is one thing that never failed to stand my hair up. I'm as used to artillery as the next man (indeed, Easter week the only sleep we had was during an artillery barrage which would force us to stop work) and rifle fire doesn't bother me too much for it is easy to take cover, but the sound of the machine gun would play hell with me. They are not really too dangerous unless they hit you with the first burst, because they are hard to swing around fast, and a ditch or a plowed furrow is as good as a pill box against them. But the Jerry machine gun fires some 1,200 shots per minute, over twice as fast as ours. I don't mean that it's better than ours, it isn't; but the sound is most disconcerting. No rattlesnake can match its buzz and the snap-snap-snap over your head isn't exactly comforting. I'm glad the Japs don't have one like it.

Mother asked if it wasn't cold swimming in the Rhine in March. Believe me it was the coldest water I was ever in, but I don't think it was just the cold I was shivering from when I got out.

About a week after we had taken Cologne we were called on to make a reconnaissance patrol of the east side of the Rhine and to bring back a few prisoners for questioning. There were fifteen of us, five engineers to handle the boat and ten infantrymen. We started right after dark. The river was about 300 yards wide and unluckily there was a strong current close to the far shore. Well, we carried the boat down to the water trying to be as quiet as possible, but armed as we were someone was always bumping a gun against the side of the boat.

Anyhow, the first time we tried it we saw several Jerry boats trying to get behind us and cut us off so we had to turn back and hightail it out of there. After we reached shore we decided to try it a little farther downstream so we carried the boat (wt. 850 lbs.) about one-half mile downstream and tried again.

During this time our artillery was laying down a slight barrage along the bank to cover us, but it unexpectedly backfired, for we hit this channel or whatever it was and were carried right down into our own artillery. 'Tis not an easy matter for five men to handle a couple of tons in a swift current and we broke our backs trying to get out of there. Well, by this time we were all pretty jumpy. I could see Jerries all along the bank and so could everyone else, but the major who was on the bank with the radio (we had a walkie talkie along for contact) said it was absolutely necessary, so we carried the boat, which weighed 1,850 pounds by now, upstream again and tried once more.

This time we ran into an underwater cable about three-fourths of the way across and made what seemed to be enough noise to be heard in Berlin. I would conservatively estimate my pulse at 220 just then but nothing happened, and we made it back O.K. We were all ready to call it quits but the major said "once more," so once more we dragged the boat upstream about half a mile and tried it from there. Things happened fast after that and I can't remember everything. We were a little over halfway when the first flare went up. For a second we froze and I kissed everyone goodbye, and then the second flare came down and opened not more than ten feet from the boat. Hell broke loose and we all started to bail out. I can remember one man screaming and fumbling with my life belt to get it off. Then I swam as far as I could under water and when I couldn't stay under any more I swam like h—— on top. By now they were lobbing 120 mortar shells all along our bank so I cooled off a little and drifted downstream until I was out of range and then made for shore.

Well, we got hot coffee at the C.P. and they put a couple of blankets around us and that was that. Two of the infantrymen we never saw again and my squad leader was hit twice in the hip, but he hung on the boat and later they got him in. So that's how I went swimming in the Rhine. I didn't enjoy it nearly as much as the Riviera.

So long,
BUD

Norbert Wagner, of Waterloo, was inducted into the Army in Oct. 1942. Assigned to the 11th Armored Division, he was sent overseas in Sept. 1944 and fought in France, Belgium, Luxembourg, Germany, and Austria. He was promoted to corporal in June 1943 and was discharged in Dec. 1945. Wagner is now working in Adrian, Mich.

[May 1945]

Today I saw the most hideous sights in my whole life. At noon-time today a truck left our bivouac on an excursion tour of a nearby concentration camp. When we approached the area we saw what resembled a modern penitentiary with its gray cold walls. We parked our truck outside the main gate because we were not permitted to enter due to the filthy condition within the area.

To our left and down the hill we saw a huge barbed wire enclosure with about twenty wooden barracks. Around the barracks wandered many refugees with little or no clothing. This enclosure was outside the main gate. So we walked over to it for a close look. It will be difficult for me to find words which will ably describe the sights I saw. There was a double fence of barbed wire with a guard's path between the two. This whole section was isolated from the other refugees because they all had typhus. Since we were immune to typhus we felt safe to approach the area. A walking skeleton with a tight skin stretched over it is the nearest description that I can find. Some of the refugees had no clothing on and walked around nude so they could get the full benefit of the sunlight.

Our medics are doing as much as is humanly possible, but starvation and lack of resistance against disease will cause many more deaths. As we walked along the inmates begged us for cigarettes. We were warned by a guard not to give them any because they have been deprived of things for so long that they fight like wild animals if one gets something and another one doesn't. Many of the inmates were ghostlike in appearance with high cheek bones, scrawny legs, bulging pelvic bones, a hollow place where their stomachs should be.

Huge red sores were on their bodies in several places, mostly on their legs where we could easily see them. Their eyes, beady in appearance, were deep-set in the eye sockets. Throughout this whole area we were aware of a sickly odor of filth, disease and gangrene. We wandered up to a side gate of the concentration camp and found that some Hungarian and Polish refugees had set up a guide system. They spoke English very well and asked if they could take us in groups of six through the whole camp. These guides had withstood the hardships of confinement much better than many others.

Before telling you about the trip through the camp, I'll tell you something about the guide. He was very impressive because he was relating to us his and others' hardships from firsthand knowledge. He said, "What I tell I know for a fact. This is no story. You Americans with your democracy cannot fully realize such hardships and cruelty did exist." He showed us how this camp was used as a reception station where the new refugees were stripped of their clothes, given a shower and allowed to wear their underwear.

We were shown the jail in which were many SS troopers. Some of them were in bad shape. They had been beaten up by the refugees when the Americans captured the camp six days ago. A modern kitchen served good food to the Hitlerites but the refugees were given only coffee at each meal and one slice of bread at dinner and supper. The coffee was black and no good. These people were in agony with the lack of food. For five years they survived without sugar or solid food.

I saw the gas chamber in which the people thought they were going to get a warm water shower but instead a deadly gas would come out of the pipes. Forty persons would be packed in a small room at a time. Some of the walls were niched from bullets that SS troops had fired at victims who refused to enter the gas chamber. I saw what had been an iron beam where other victims were hung up and tortured. In another room was a small blast furnace in which a sliding table carried the unconscious victim so he could be consumed by the heat in twenty minutes.

We noticed in a side room a stone table which was a strange contraption. The top was almost flat but it was sloped towards the middle with a drain leading from one end to a pipe to the floor. Above the table was a water faucet. We asked our guide what this was for. He explained that if the victim was too fat to go into the furnace he was put on the table and cut up in small enough pieces so he would fit into the furnace. The water washed the blood down the drain.

We passed a hospital and the guide told us that it was known as the House of the Optimist. Many refugees upon entering it would hope that they would never come out of it so they could be relieved of their misery. One of the other clerks who was with another guide went into the hospital and watched a doctor operate on an unfortunate cripple. It seems that the skin had grown over the bandage on his leg and the doctor (French) was trying to remove it. The agony of the patient was unbearable and so the clerk left the place before he lost his dinner or fainted.

Going a little further we went through a gate and found more barracks in which were more starved inmates. One of the fellows (our soldier) thought he would be generous and give two inmates cigarettes. Immediately he was swamped with others wanting cigarettes. When his supply ran out the inmates argued and fought each other for the precious gifts.

Our guide told us that 800 to 1,000 men were held in the barracks during the winter. They were so crowded that they couldn't lie down to sleep but had to alternate in a standing or squatting position. The size of the barracks was only 25 feet by 75 feet at the most. When I looked in the barracks there were about 60 to 70 men lying comfortably on blankets on the floor. The place is quite clean now that our army has taken over.

Forest E. Collins, of Clay City, was inducted into the Army July 21, 1943, and was assigned to the air corps. Going overseas on Aug. 20, 1943, Collins was attached to the maintenance division, Base Air Depot No. 1 in England. Later he served in France, and was stationed with the 45th Air Depot in Germany. Returning to the States in Mar. 1946, T/3 Collins was discharged Mar. 17, 1946, and is now the owner of an electric appliance company in Clay City.

Sept. 26, 1945
Frankfurt on the Rhine

Dear Folks:

I'm in Hitler's Germany. Yes, what there is left of it. It is a terrible devastated mess. At no place have I seen anything of any value. I don't believe I can describe this country so that you can get a mental picture of how it actually looks. It is awe-bewildering. You cannot grasp it from any picture, photograph or group of pictures. You cannot grasp what it means to look up a street and see, as far as you can see, nothing but empty, roofless, floorless hulls of buildings with the entire space between hulls either a muddy, water-filled bomb crater or a mound of twisted sandy debris; and pivoting around, see overturned, rusted, some blackened skeletons of railway coaches and engines scattered about pell-mell to either side of the railway tracks, whole trains still standing helpless, worthless and immovable alongside the wrecked station platforms where they stood months ago at the hour they received their death blow; signal towers swaying dizzily, advertising a last dying signal unlike anything to be found in the code books; towering walls of brick, impossible yet still standing, to stretch the imagination of a master mason; tall smokeless chimneys standing as a tombstone above masses of rumpled twisted steel girders that mock and defy any attempt to molest the once priceless precision machinery lying buried beneath; an occasional lamppost patiently trailing its wires from a windowless, globeless socket; empty roofless church spires overlooking a congregation of uncountable empty stores and apartment houses; railroad bridges making intricate openings for the fish's playhouse in the river below; landscapes of worthless, silent, motionless hulls. And going from one point to another and one city to another, every town, village, and city and seeing only an exact repetition of all these pictures every direction you look as far as you can see, in vain you hunt and search for something whole, something untouched by war, as you travel for hours, miles and miles and days by improvised rails and detours. Only until you have experienced this feeling of complete, total devastation can you grasp the meaning of these pictures.

This is all that remains of the once proud and beautiful Germany. The wages of war! Where are all the people who lived in these homes and worked the factories? I could not guess. Many, no doubt, are still resting there, victims of disillusionment.

The world is a small garden and this is a spot where the elephant stepped and dragged his foot. Though crumpled, bruised, and lifeless now, it will grow back again in time.

And so ends a chapter in this world we call modern and civilized.

Love,
FOREST

Ansley Gordon Friend, of Dunkirk, was inducted into the Army May 11, 1943. Sent to the European theater in June 1944, he was attached to the 160th Engineer Combat Battalion, with a technician 5th grade rating, then was transferred to Company G, 375th Regiment, 95th Infantry Division and promoted to rank of sergeant. For his combat duty, Sgt. Friend was awarded five battle stars, the Bronze Star, and the Purple Heart. Returning to this country in July 1945, he was discharged Oct. 1 and is an accountant for a furniture store in Dunkirk.

[1945]

DEAR MOTHER:

. . . Golly, here I have rambled on for five pages and haven't even started to answer your letter yet. I'm so full of joy that I'm just "epervessin" all over as B. Lee used to say. Ha.

You wanted to know all the facts and figures on how, when, and where I got hurt. I guess I could tell you but if I were to tell you all that I and the other seven men who were with me did and all the things that happened to us you would think that I had been reading too many comic books. Ha. The only thing that I have to say, and all the rest of the fellows that I took on the patrol agree with me, is that we are about the luckiest bunch of guys in the U. S. Army. The eight of us worked behind enemy lines about two miles for six hours and every one of us got back without a scratch on us. All this was done in broad daylight, too. I'm not bragging a bit on what I did that afternoon. I'm just thanking the good Lord that He was on our side. He had to be or we would never have got back. I got hurt when we first started out. We had just started across an open field towards a church about a hundred yards away when Jerry opened up with a couple of burp guns. The rest of the fellows dove in a ditch but I was too far out in the field to go back, so I set a new record for the hundred yard dash all the time Jerry cutting patterns around me with his little pop gun. When I nearly reached the church I ran into a six-foot hedge fence which I tried to jump; I nearly made it. I lit on top of it on a sharp pole and hung up. I was wondering how I was going to get loose when the son of a so-and-so solved my problem for me: he cut the pole in two with his bullets and I lit very nicely on my head on the other side. I guess my hip jumped partially out of place but I hit it with a hand grenade and it popped back in again and yours truly took off again and got inside the church.

I sorta settled a little score I had with them when I got inside. I went up in the top of the steeple and spotted twenty of the dirty—down below me. I had a field day, it was just like shooting ducks in a pond. I let my M1 do my talking for me and when I got done the rest of the fellows walked up to the church without a bit of argument from the Krauts. I finished the patrol out all right but the next morning I couldn't walk on my right leg so I got to take a vacation.

I guess that about winds me up for now so I'll say so long and good luck. I hope this finds you in the best of health. Tell everyone I said Hi.

Lots of love,
GORDON

Margaret Spencer, of Waveland, joined the American Red Cross in Nov. 1943 and became a hospital staff aide. After work in this country, she was attached to the 185th General Hospital and sent to England in April 1944. In Feb. 1945, she was sent to

France and assigned to the 51st Evacuation Hospital of the 7th Army, which moved into Germany. Miss Spencer returned to this country in Nov. 1945 and continued to serve with the Red Cross on the disaster reserve staff.

August 10, 1945
Welzheim, Germany

DEAR DOROTHY:

It's too late tonight to write many of the things I want to tell you. I expected to get an earlier start, but there were a few interruptions. . . .

This is the fourth day of continuous rain and swishing wind. It's sent me snuggling back into (instead of on top of!) my sleeping bag, in addition to my regular four thicknesses of blankets. But the slap and slash of the rain and the billowing, flapping canvas make our pot-belly oil burner a never-to-be-forgotten cozy comfort.

We weren't griping much more than enough to keep in practice—until to-night. The four of us—Helen Kelly, a red-haired Irish nurse from New York; Mike, a restless perpetual dynamo of nervous energy; and Lucille and I—came over from mess. Lucille was getting ready to go to a party Mike had talked her into somewhat against her will. I planned to go back to the Recreation Tent and see that everything was O.K. until movie time, then come back and write you. (We have no patients now, but the personnel keeps us busy, as we're fifteen miles from the nearest "Sinker Station," and thirty or forty, I expect, from the nearest Club.)

But as we were lingering around our stove the wind came with a vicious sweep from the northwest, and with a rending "pop" one of the sloping side seams of the tent ripped into a gaping 2 or 3 foot "window." We grabbed the edges in a frantic tug of war, but the wind won and our snug little home was laid open clear to the top of the center pole!

A detachment squad started over "on the double." There was a quick council as to whether we would have to crowd, bag and baggage, into the other tents. Lucille, feeling very much in the public eye, so to speak, was finishing dressing as it was time for transportation to arrive to take the group to the party. The rest of us were trying frantically to "anchor" and cover our clothes and the papers, letters, toilet articles and knick-knacks on our packing box bedside tables.

As a calming influence in our confusion the C.O. descended on us (in true C.O. style) with the news that the Red Cross tent was momentarily on the verge of taking off, and that I'd better dash over—but quick. As our detachment "ready squad" had by this time dug up a tent for us and was starting to collapse the remains of our old one, I couldn't just leave. (Anyway, I hadn't any idea in the world what I'd do about it; it was always a source of wonder to me that our huge turtle-back affair sat up straight in *any* weather.)

I had retrieved my camera and tried for a couple of shots of the "action." Wouldn't you know that in the confusion I'd forget to turn up the roll and take double exposures!

In less time actually than it's taken to tell about it, the damage was done and repaired, and I took off from our clover patch through the strip of wheat toward the hospital area with vague ideas of pursuing a vanishing R.C. tent. But the fellows had that situation under control, to my very real relief.

I was ready to sit down and just relax for a minute, but—the storm was still on the war path; now it had caused the movie to be cancelled. (I never did know whether it was because the power was off, or that the tent seemed too wobbly.) So there I was with a tent full of restless G.I.'s, disappointed at not having a movie, and hating to go back to their tents, cold and wet as it was. (We've been fortunate in having a movie almost every night these last few months.) They were anxious, too, to hang around the radio to catch the latest peace rumors.

I had come across some popcorn in our supplies (must have been donated to us somewhere along the way), and this seemed the perfect time and place for it. But how to pop it! I wouldn't say we found a *workable* solution to that question— we just used it anyway. The fellows lugged one of the gas field stove units over from the mess, along with one of the huge aluminum containers of the kind we used to have with coffee for the parties in England, remember? There just wasn't anything smaller.

First, the stove wouldn't work, and it took quite a crowd to give suggestions, while one of the fellows from the mess who happened to be around repaired it. Then the container got hot so quick that when I put in the butter (precious contribution from the mess sergeant) it flared up and burned! (Consequently, the "delicious buttery kernels" were slightly sooty!) You can imagine a couple husky G.I.'s trying to "jiggle" the corn around in one of those cans—the volunteers were quickly exhausted; the onlookers greatly interested. In the meantime, I was trying to mix up a pitcher of hot chocolate on the "pot belly," which was also surrounded by an attentive audience. A chess game was in progress nearby, and the ping-pong tables were doing their usual rushing business.

And so, far into the night. It's the kind of evening, though, to give you real satisfaction in your job!

It's considerably after midnight now, and it's raining furiously again. The wind whisks odd drops under the stove pipe cone and they plop down with a steamy sizzle on the hot, rusty metal. It's dripping, too, through a pin-prick hole, to make a raised dark puddle about two-thirds of the way down on my bed. It will never soak through all those thicknesses of blanket before morning, though, so I can regard it with practically an unconcerned eye. But not for long; at this point my eyes simply refuse to regard anything, period!

Affectionately,
MARGARET

Marion H. Rimmel, of Brimfield, was inducted into the Army in July 1943 and was assigned to the coast artillery. He was sent overseas in Sept. 1944 and fought with the 11th Armored Division, 3d Army, in France, Belgium, Luxembourg, Germany, and Austria. He was promoted to staff sergeant in Sept. 1945. Discharged in April 1946, Sgt. Rimmel returned to study at Indiana State Teachers College.

[1945]

HI MATT:

Now that it is all over on this side of the world, I guess that I will take time out to write a few lines. We were really on the move until the last minute, so did very little writing, even to my parents. (Much to their dismay.) Perhaps you have read numerous items concerning the actions of the 11th Armored Division, so I won't bother you with any of our division history and so forth. You can rest assured that the 101st Airborne Division will never forget us in and around Bastogne though.

After that we penetrated the Siegfried line, on into Germany proper, and then into Austria. No doubt we would have been in Czechoslovakia in a matter of days if the war hadn't ended when it did. Oh well, it is all over now, so all we have to do is wait until the C.B.I. calls us or the W.D. makes up its mind that we can go home. Here is hoping that it is the latter.

First of all, I wish to thank you for getting the *American* to me so regularly, Matt. I will venture to say that I haven't missed one edition since getting in the service. You can rest assured that you are doing your part if not a lot more, as the paper is certainly a great morale booster to me and all the other fellows in the service that I have talked to.

Now to tell you about a few sights that I have seen in the past few days, Matt. As a rule, I don't relate many sights that I have seen, but as all newspaper men are eager to hear of unusual sights, I just can't resist trying to describe a German concentration camp to you. Our division overran it the day before hostilities ceased, and I was able to witness the sights the next morning. The first section of the camp had barracks divided into small rooms about the size of a small office. The Germans had three-decked bunks across the room and normally about thirty men could live in the place if they crowded up. At the time I got there, the Heinies had put two and three men in each bunk making it hold about ninety men. You wonder how it is possible to get three men in one bunk, I suppose? Well, it was comparatively easy after looking at the poor devils in the place. They were barely alive and so skinny that the bones stuck through the skin on many a man. The slaves had two young Germans carrying the men out when I got there and what a sight the sick men were. All men had diarrhea very bad and had passed blood for a long time from the looks of them. They were unconscious and on the verge of death. There was nothing that anyone could do, because they were past the healing stage. I saw one fellow die as they were washing him up. He just couldn't stand the shock of the water, I guess, as it had been better than a month since any of them had washed according to one French slave that I talked to. He wasn't the first one to die that way, though, as there was a whole wagon load of dead men just outside the gate that were awaiting burial.

The next block over from this line of barracks there was a place to cremate the bodies. There was still a leg and arm in it which hadn't completely burned up at the time I looked it over. The slaves had one consolation there, though, as one of the SS troopers got sick and couldn't leave when the rest of the SS troops took off in face of the oncoming American and Russian forces. The slaves captured him and then made him live in the same room as the dead and deathly ill were put. At the time I saw him he hadn't been fed for five days; that along with the constant stench of the room made him look pretty sad. The Russian who toured the place with us fellows said that they were going to make him live just as he had made so many of them live and die. I wouldn't be surprised if there isn't one SS man short in the German Army by this time. Ha!

By this time we had begun to think that we had never seen anything so terrible. But even worse sights were to be seen in a very short while. Our group then proceeded to the other sections of the camp, and there, in the main section, we saw no less than two hundred corpses that had just been dug up by the German civilians. The Germans had buried them in large pits and laid them in on top of each other. The G.I. in charge of the detail said that it was just a start as the bodies in view represented only one small pit that had just been dug open. There were still twelve more long pits to exhume, so you can imagine the slaughter that has been going on there. That is just a small portion, as all bodies have been burned and quicklimed up until a month ago. It was not hard to see how death came to the individuals either, as some had large gaping holes in their heads from beatings, others were starved to a mere nothing, and the rest had pieces of their bodies cut away for grafting purposes on the German soldiers. The Russian in our group explained that many of the strong slaves were cut up for grafting purposes and then strapped to a table and drained of their blood. Yes, they did things methodically there.

Just above the burying pits there was another section of the camp that held the gas chambers. It was a very small room, yet they crowded two hundred men into it at a time when the executions were held. It is a bare looking room except for small holes on the sides and top of the thing. They generally left the slaves in for about an hour and then began the process of disposing of the bodies in the ovens. The room directly across the hall was used to hang and shoot others. I could see where the blood had been and tried to be washed off by the Germans, but it just couldn't be done. I suppose that just too much blood had been spilled on it. There was also a guillotine in that room. The guillotine execution was always held in front of the entire mass of slaves in the place. The slave that was showing us around stated that he had witnessed three such exhibitions, the last one being in December. Just a short ways from there, a small opening appeared in the wall. I inquired about it and the fellow stated that people slated for death were told that they were going to have their picture taken and had to look in there. While they were looking in the little opening, an SS trooper would shoot them in the back of the head. Then in another room they had the assorted weapons of torture, such as clubs, guns, and so forth. Just to show you how thorough the place was, they even had a room refrigerated where they could store bodies awaiting disposal.

The women didn't even escape from the ordeals either. Naturally they were in separate sections of the camp from the men, but occasionally they did get together. As soon as the woman had her child, it was flung at the wall in front of the mother's eyes. It wasn't unusual for them to kill the woman then, from the stories that have been told me. Even in the work camps they were treated very badly. I toured one such place and the women were just as starved and ill-fed as the men. It was hard to recognize them as women except for the longer hair on the head.

This is poorly written, I have left out a lot, and I probably didn't see everything in that hate camp, but I think that you will agree that what I have mentioned is even too horrible for words. The smallness of the camp is the worst of all, though I can still imagine I smell that odor at times. Death isn't a pleasant smell after a few days and that is all there was to look forward to after getting in that place before it was liberated. I would hate to attempt to guess the number of persons killed in the place, but I'm certain that it ran into thousands. The turnover was about five thousand per month, so in five or six years that adds up pretty fast. This camp that I saw was inspected by Hitler two years ago and he commended the officer in charge. There is a little story connected with the head officer of the camp also. At the time Hitler came to power in Germany, this fellow was serving a prison term in a Berlin prison for killing a wealthy Berlin resident. As fantastic as it seems, Hitler studied his case and released him from prison to oversee the camp. He was really a maniac at the time of the Berlin murder. The story is told that he killed the fellow just for pleasure. It is certain that he did enough killing while in this camp. . . .

MARION H. RIMMEL

Bryson Wells, of Fairmount, was inducted into the Army in Jan. 1943 and was attached to the ordnance department. He was sent overseas in December and was stationed in Ireland and England until the invasion of France in June 1944. He saw service there and in Belgium, Luxembourg, and Germany, and was promoted a technician 4th grade in April 1944. Discharged in Dec. 1945, T/4 Wells is assistant city engineer at Benton Harbor, Mich.

April 20, 1945
Germany

DEAR MOTHER AND DAD:

This is one letter that won't be the ordinary "How are you? I am well" kind. I have seen and been through one of Germany's most famous institutions—the concentration camp—and I don't feel like writing a letter about the weather and the neighbor's babies, if you get what I mean. It took a strong stomach and a mind used to similar sights to view the results of the "New Order" and its "Kultur."

To begin with, this place had been captured or freed by the Americans only a few days when I visited the place, and so I was able to see the camp at near firsthand. The first thing we saw as we came up the driveway was a ten-foot high electrified fence, with about every hundred yards, a guard tower mounting a searchlight and machine guns (now dismounted).

We passed through a nice looking entrance into a stone-paved court filled with about thirty or forty buildings one story high, and about one hundred feet long by twenty-five wide. These buildings at one time held upwards of fifty thousand men and boys—no women. More about the women later. At the present time there are about ten thousand left in it.

As we walked along we were followed by a crowd of hobbling wretches that had once been men. Now their whole effort is to remain alive, to get a bite to eat, a cigarette to smoke, to catch a glimpse of these American soldiers—soldiers who don't beat and curse them but who feed them and give medical care to those who require it. I say "hobbled after us" literally. They were so thin their legs looked like my arms. They were emaciated by starvation, slavish labor and dysentery.

Here and there one of them would have the cunning, bestial glare of a madman, a monomaniac whose single thought was for food, food and more food! Most of them had sores where the points of bones, shoulder blades, etc., had lost their normal covering of flesh and had rubbed raw on their clothing, or rags, I should say, or their straw pile beds. I watched one poor fellow take about three minutes to get to an outdoor toilet seat, from a door about thirty feet away. There were signs on his clothing of failure at previous attempts to reach the seat. Yet, such signs of filth were not common here—the Germans made them wash everything. But all they had was water—no soap at all.

We went on walking, and once, looking back, I saw several of them in a feeble imitation of a fight. They were fighting over a cigarette butt one of us had thrown away. Some of the boys had chocolate with them—D-rations or Hershey Tropical that we get as part of our candy rations. They threw them over the fence around one of the huts, being careful to make sure that one person got it all, and not a disputed half. They thanked us in broken English or their own language, whatever it happened to be. I saw the flags of several nations flying, denoting the "residence" there of Russian, Polish, French, Belgian, Czech, and Dutch, but not English or American flags for the same reason. There were American flags flying alongside the others, but as in a place of honor and respect only.

I didn't have anything but a cellophane bag of C-ration bouillon powder to give them, but if I had had candy I would have been afraid to give it to them, as their stomachs are not used to much food, and it is too concentrated. They told us later that the American medics were feeding very lightly, but even then it was hard to keep it down, and what stayed down was passed through their bowels by dysentery too quickly to help them very much. But they are on the road to recovery, and that's what matters.

By the time we had walked around and seen all these things, it was getting on toward time for us to leave. So we headed for the thing we had mainly come to see. This was the torture room, the crematory and the place where bodies were kept before disposal. We had been told beforehand what to expect, and so we purposefully went to see it last. Even the pitiful things we had seen would have been anticlimax to this one overbearingly evil thing.

The building was a low, brick structure, with a squat brick smokestack on one side of it. It was surrounded by a seven-foot high board fence, so as to permit no one to see the things that went on behind it, I suppose. As we went through the gate, the first thing that met my eyes was a pile of about forty or fifty dead men, piled four or five deep, like cordwood. They were for the most part naked, and thus exposed the most hideous cuts, bruises and broken limbs that sub-human minds could inflict on them. They were even thinner than the live ex-prisoners. All these were the result of the Nazi delight in torture and, so a Jew told us, a few were cremated alive for the same reason. Their guards and torturers were the infamous SS troops, who are the elite Nazis.

This pile of bodies was by no means normal, the Jew told us. They killed more than they could burn because the Americans were coming, and they exceeded their quotas because of that. The day before the medics had taken away about the same amount as we saw for burial and the same amount the morning of the day we were there. Normally the output of the killers was about the same as the capacity of the crematory ovens. I took two pictures of this pile of bodies and then followed the rest of the bunch inside.

The building inside reminded me of a small, neat, old-fashioned bakery. There were two furnaces of brick and steel, with three doors each for the placing of the body and the removal of ashes, if any. When we saw the place there were bodies in various stages of cremation in the ovens, and I took a picture of the most recognizable of these. In the rest of the oven were things that couldn't be recognized as bodies. In the end of this room was an elevator entrance. It was of the type and size used in hospitals for the removal of patients from ward to surgery, etc. Only in this case, it was used to bring in the dead "patients" from the cellar room in which they had been tortured and killed.

We went down there next to view the instruments of torture and death that had silenced so many men. They were few—only a row of stout pegs about eight feet off the floor, a rubber hose, a hose connected to a water faucet, a rope, and last but not least, an oversized potato masher-like club. There was a stuffed suit of clothes hanging by the neck from one peg and beside it the club. It was rather splintered, as if it had been stirring concrete instead of mashing potatoes, and of a peculiar dark color, a sort of brownish red. Needless to say, this was the main means of the torture and death of hundreds if not thousands of men. The hose was only an extra tool; it wouldn't break bones or fracture skulls, it would only bruise and cut. The water hose was used to wash the bloodstains from the whitewashed walls and to revive the fainting. It was further used to torture by the forced introduction of water, under pressure, into the mouth or other openings of the person, being used to rupture internal organs. At one side of this room was the elevator to the crematory.

After seeing and passing through this mass-production disassembly line of human beings, we were all rather speechless with horror. We were thankful, too, that such things had been confined in a military sense of the word, to the European side of the Atlantic. This, then, was the "New Order" which was to breed a new "civilization"—to last for a thousand years and which was to be as superior to Christianity as Christianity is to the ancient paganism. This was Germany. Yet, to give the devil his due, there had been German army officers and men in this camp, and they received no better treatment than the Jews from the Ghetto of Warsaw. A Jew told us that, and he said that he had been there for seven years, so he should have known the truth of things.

Oh, yes, I promised to tell more about the women's side of the camp. I said that there were no women in the camp. There were more actually on the inside with the men, but the best looking of the women taken captive in the foreign countries were kept as prostitutes by the SS guards, until pregnancy resulted. After that they followed the same course as those whose bodies we saw in the pile and the crematories. The only crime of these women was that they happened to be better looking than ordinary, or happened to catch the eye of some lustful SS trooper.

The people of the surrounding towns, when questioned, said that they knew something was here, but they were afraid to try to find out what it was. So they were "surprised" to see such things when they were taken through. Some women fainted, some cried, and the mayor of one town hanged himself when shown what they had been living with since Hitler came to power.

As a bit of Teutonic irony (unconscious, of course), as we left I happened to look through a lane in the surrounding forest and down a little hill. Over the crest of the next hill, about a third of a mile from the camp fence, was the steeple and cross of a little village church.

Maybe some more people would like to read this firsthand account of what a concentration camp looks like. If they want to see this letter and think they can stand it, let them see it. Maybe if enough people understand what totalitarianism is, they will guard against it at home.

I'll try to write a normal letter soon.

Love,
BRYSON

→ VIII ←

V-E DAY AND AFTER

AFTER the collapse and surrender of Germany, May 4–7, 1945 (Italy had given up on April 29), the Allies arranged their zones of occupation and military government. Germany was divided into four areas, and the United States took control of the southern part. Berlin, which lay within the Russian zone, was administered by the Four Powers jointly. Reparations in kind were so divided as to give the largest share to Russia. American troops were withdrawn from Czechoslovakia, and Hungary and the eastern half of Austria went under Russian control. Special tribunals were created to try the Nazi leaders as war criminals. The victors organized the United Nations after the adoption of a charter at a conference in San Francisco in June.

Ernest R. Lee, a reserve officer of Indianapolis, was called to active duty in Aug. 1940 as a 1st lieutenant of infantry. Promoted a captain in Feb. 1942, he was assigned as aide to Gen. Dwight D. Eisenhower and followed him to England in June. He served also at the headquarters of Allied forces in North Africa, Sicily, Italy, France, and Germany. He achieved the rank of colonel in June 1945. Col. Lee received the Legion of Merit from Gen. Eisenhower and decorations from Great Britain, France, French Morocco, Russia, Belgium, and Luxembourg. Discharged in Dec. 1945, he remains a reserve officer commanding the 329th Infantry Regiment, 83d Division, and is a business executive in Indianapolis.

DEAR MOTHER:

We left our CP (Rheims)—flew to a field near Berlin where we were met by Field Marshal Keitel of the German Army, and an escort of Russian fighter planes escorted us into Templehof airdrome in Berlin.

As we approached the Reich capital it was covered by a thick haze, mostly smoke from the fires that were still smoldering. The first glance made one believe that there was little damage, but as our plane dropped lower we could see that the buildings that we thought were undamaged were merely hollow shells and the interiors had been completely gutted by fire and bomb blast. Those that had not burned were leveled either by bomb or artillery fire, and few people were moving about. Templehof was a huge field and while the landing strips were O.K., the huge buildings and repair shops were completely gutted. A guard of honor was drawn up to meet us, complete with flags of Russia, Great Britain, and the U. S. After inspecting the guard and having it pass in review, we entered cars and drove through the city to a former German Army engineering school located at Karlshorst, a suburb of Berlin.

On our trip through the city we were guided by Russian WACs, who are armed and form a part of the Russian forces. The route was lined with troops and civilians were barred. The roads had been fairly well cleared of rubble, and the suburb, except for blast damage, was relatively undamaged. However, the rest of the city was a sight—I did not see a house that was still standing that did not have some type of damage either by fire, bomb or shell. Life in Berlin had practically ceased to exist.

Upon arriving at Marshal of the Soviet Union Zhukov's, we were met by a number of officers, fine appearing and quite correct—never did so much saluting in my life. In the middle of the afternoon we went to his office for a meeting, at which time Jim Gault and I presented him with the flag of the Allied Expeditionary Force, as a gift from General Eisenhower. Before going over we had a short snack of red and black caviar, radishes, a salad. Returned to the meeting in the evening to make final preparations for the signing and to make arrangements for differences in certain words—for instance, the word "equipment" means things in English that it does not mean in Russian. This finally was accomplished and we went into the large room for the formal signing.

The table at the front of the room was occupied by Marshal Zhukov, Tedder, Spaatz and other ranking officers of our delegation. The table down the center of the room was occupied by other officers in our party and opposite us were Russian officers from Zhukov's staff, ranking from major generals up. Behind us was a table for the German officers. They came in after we were all seated—Keitel giving us a salute with his Marshal's baton—a typical Junker type, arrogant even in defeat, turned out within an inch of his life and with all his decorations (even wearing the gold Nazi badge, which was a bit unusual, since it might mean that he was there not only as an army officer but also as a member of the Nazis)—Stumpff of the Air Force, in a beautifully turned out uniform, but otherwise more like his name than anything else—Von Friedeburg of the Navy was next and he looked like the wrath of God—dark circles under his eyes and very nervous—their aides standing behind them, very properly dressed, full uniforms, gray gloves and each with nothing but arrogance—these people have no conception of the suffering they have wrought, and even if they have they feel that it was a part of their mission.

The full details of the signing have previously been reported, so there is no need for me to repeat. They were asked to leave the room after the signing took place and then it was turned into a banquet hall. The tables actually groaned under the load of food and drink and each place had at least four different glasses for vodka, brandy, champagne and beer. Marshal Zhukov got up and made a speech telling of his admiration for the Boss and the A.E.F. and what they had meant to the Russians, etc. He then proposed a toast to the Boss and the force he commands—they filled the glasses with vodka and the band broke out into their drinking song, which is played every time they drink a toast. The glass contained about four or five fingers of this dynamite. You are supposed to down it at one drink and then prepare for the next one. I knew it would be impossible for me to try and keep up with them, so had advice from a Russian friend to take a lot of butter and oily salmon they serve, to help form a coating on the stomach and keep the fumes from going to my head. So each time we had a drink, we did this. The Russian lieutenant general across from me, who had downed his with me in the toast, saw what I was doing and grinned and took a piece of his salmon off his plate and put it on mine and grinned and winked at me and made motions for me to eat the fish. The next time we had a toast and I picked up my vodka glass, he shook his head and motioned to my wine glass, then we took the toast in wine. It was most decent of him, as they never drink water. Then Air Chief Marshal Tedder responded and again we had a toast. This went on for 29 times by actual count and did not include the small toasts the boys across the table or a few seats down would propose in the meantime. What a banquet! The first course consisted of red and black caviar, Russian sausage, ham, sardines, smoked salmon, salad. Next came a soup made of cabbage which tasted somewhat like sauerkraut made with cream—this followed by a meat course with potatoes and peas and strawberries and mixed cherries and plums to finish up. We sat down about one A.M. and finally left the table about 5:30. I admit I was tired. We took off at 6:30 for Rheims and so drove back to Templehof, but made a tour of the city on the way.

It is impossible to describe Berlin—the easiest thing is to say that it is a dead city. When one looks at it at close hand it appears exactly like a city that you expected to see destroyed, but it is difficult to adjust one's mental reflexes to its complete destruction. After leaving Karlshorst, we drove to the Alexanderplatz, which was supposed to have been the head of the Gestapo. This was completely burned out and nothing was left but a broken, stinking, charred mass—and amongst the ruins were the remnants of tanks, guns, trucks, cars, bodies of horses and humans. All through the city we saw bodies being removed and taken away for disposal. Smoke still hovered over and it was impossible to imagine what this city of 4,000,000 looked like before it became this pile of broken masonry. Next we drove through rubble-filled streets, where both Russian troops and a few civilians were trying to clear the remains of the Kaiser's palace—this likewise was almost completely destroyed and what was still standing was damaged beyond repair.

All the bridges over the River Spree, which flows through the city, are destroyed and hulks of boats are sunk at the piers and bodies of horses and, I imagine, humans float among the ruined bridges. Drove down the Unter den Linden to the once famous Adlon Hotel, again just an empty shell looking out on the scarred boulevard and the remnants of tanks and guns still there—the building across the street from the Adlon still smoking and, while we watched, one of the upper floors caved in adding more rubble and dust to that which thickly coated the street. Then through the Brandenburg Tor (or gate) which is almost intact, except for the bases which are covered with rubble. On top of the Tor one of the horses that pulls the chariot has been smashed and has fallen to the ground—the chariot likewise is smashed and only one horse remains. The statue "Victory" itself is a mass of smashed masonry and huge blocks of granite. Two Russian soldiers at the door barred entrance as Berlin has not been cleared of mines and one walks gingerly and looks but does not touch. On the Wilhelmstrasse, facing the Chancellory, is all that is left of a Russian tank that had met with a German antitank gun, firing from the front of the building, a mass of burned out twisted metal, but its gun still pointed toward all that remains of Hitler's once proud palace.

It is difficult to get around as many streets are still blocked with barricades, and it may be weeks or months before they are removed and all the minefields cleared. The Reichstag is another hollow shell and probably more completely gutted than the fire that Hitler tried to blame on the communists. Russian soldiers are looking at it and while we are there a wagon full of Cossacks passes and two of the men are playing accordions—music, death, dust and destruction—quite a picture. The trees in the Tiergarten look as if a hurricane had hit them—torn, twisted, blasted by bomb and shell fire—hardly a bit of foliage left—and among them lies the remnants of the battle—again all types of equipment blown to bits, some looking like nothing one could possibly identify. A parachute dangled from one leafless tree and under the trunk of another was all that was left of a six-barreled mortar. In the center of the Grosser Stern a statue of the "Victory Amazon" still stands. Surrounding the base are German A.A. guns, some smashed, some in their last positions, barrels pointing toward the sky or down one of the avenues, looking for tanks that they never had a chance to stop. A Red soldier has been buried here and his grave is surrounded with Red flags and a Red barricade to hallow the ground.

The Russians are everywhere, some walking, some on horseback, others in jeeps and American-made trucks—all going about their work. Workmen are putting up arches and getting ready for the Victory parade, which the Soviets will have moving down the Unter den Linden. A troop of Cossacks moves by, pulling guns and guarding some prisoners who are helping to clean up the place. One passes a building that is more badly smashed than some and it gives off the sweet, sickening odor of human flesh that is rotting and has not been cleared away. A hollow, mangy dog picks his way over what is left of the Opera, and that is Berlin as I saw it—a city that defies description—a city that could have been truly great if men had devoted their energies as enthusiastically to the efforts of peace as they did to war.

We heard that Hitler's body had been found; whether it has or not makes little difference. The huge buildings from which he and his henchmen tried to conquer the world lay smashed and broken—their records stream over the streets and drift about with the wind—and above all the rubble dust, a fitting ash to be worn with the sackcloth which should be worn. Whether Berlin will be rebuilt or not is a question I cannot answer—if it is, the entire city, what is left, will have to be torn down and begun again—how long will it take? How long will it take us to educate these people to the Brotherhood of Nations? That is about the length of time needed to rebuild Berlin.

The peace is almost anticlimatical after all these years—a sort of letdown feeling and still continuing with our work. The job at hand will be almost as tough as the fighting, but we can all thank God that it is over and no more of these fine boys of ours will be killed here. We must bend every effort to finish the Pacific job so we can all return and take up the life we left so many years ago—it seems that I have known nothing but war for so long that nothing else exists, but a few days at home will change all of that.

Meredith J. Rogers, of Dupont, enlisted in the Army in June 1940. He was sent to the European theater in Oct. 1943, where he served with the 2d Engineer Combat Battalion, 2d Division, and participated in the Battle of the Bulge. He was awarded a presidential citation for gallantry and was promoted to sergeant. Sgt. Rogers remained in the Army, and is now stationed at Fort Lewis, Wash.

May 18, 1945
Czechoslovakia

Dear Dad and All:

It has been sometime since I last wrote you but I am still O.K. and have been getting the letters and packages that you have sent O.K.

Everything seems strangely quiet around here now—no more planes strafing and bombing. No more tanks ploughing across the fields, no more grim-faced, tired doughboys moving forward. But V-E Day didn't call for much of a celebration here—there were too many things to think about—too many buddies sleeping forever in France and Belgium, Luxembourg, and Holland, and in Germany and Czechoslovakia and Austria. We have crossed 24 major rivers and many minor ones, and each one has become a memorial to the dead Americans who fought for the bridgehead. As a combat engineer battalion, our casualties have been heavy.

Very often at night nowadays I go to bed only to lie there sleepless while the vivid memories of the past year parade through my head. I recall the bitter inch by inch struggle for a toehold on the coast of Normandy—the landing craft heading for shore and the wreckage of material and human bodies being hurled high into the air and then coming down to spread a red stain upon the

water, when a Hun artillery shell made a hit. Long hours of helplessly standing by while German dive bombers strafed and bombed. Memories go on and
on—many things one would like to forget—but forgetting will be impossible.
Is it any wonder that we sometimes wonder if the things we are fighting for,
and that many have died for, really mean enough to make the victory worth the
price that has been and must still be paid? But after seeing the result of tyranny
and intolerance all over the face of starving Europe, I personally, and thousands
like me, am well convinced that the end justifies the means. So we will continue
the fight until the last foe has been conquered—but while we can win the war
the problem of winning the peace rests mostly in the hands of those on the
home front.

Naturally there is much discussion and speculation these days and a favorite
sport is the counting of points toward discharge. It is pretty sure that this is
one of the crack outfits scheduled for the C.B.I. theater, yet so many of the men
feel that they have done their share and want out as soon as possible. I can thoroughly understand and agree with that viewpoint; however, for myself, I feel
that the cause is just as important now as it was a year ago. So, although I had
the highest number of points in the company and could have left here two days
ago with the first quota to return to the States, I waived my priority and signed
a certificate certifying that I elected to remain on active duty in a combat unit
until after the defeat of Japan. I can assure you, however, that it was pretty hard
to turn down the chance to return to the U.S.A. after nearly two years overseas,
but for one thing, quite a few of my own experienced men are leaving, and I feel
that I will be needed to train and weld the new men that will be coming to us
into an efficient, smooth running, dependable crew, if I am to have the privilege
of training and leading in the war against the Japs as good a crew as I had here
in the E.T.O. . . .

June 7

As I write this I am sitting in my room in a large lakeside, summer resort
hotel—that is, it was once a summer resort for the Czechs, then the Germans
took over and it became a holiday spot for German officers on leave, and finally
when things got tight for them they turned it into a hospital for the German
wounded, but now it is an American army camp, and a very nice one. It is located in the hills, several miles from town; the hills are covered with pines and are
very pretty at this time of year. They look pretty from a distance, but if you take
a walk into the hill and through the woods you find too many things to remind

you of the war; foxholes and trenches, camouflaged gun positions, remnants of barbed wire entanglements, mine fields and tank traps, here and there large areas of blown-down trees, blasted by artillery, and the wood's roads are still choked and made impassable by abatis road blocks, which are long stretches of road with trees felled across it from either side so that the branches are interlocked with a trip wire leading to buried land mines tied to the branches here and there. On the way from Normandy we had to clear hundreds of road blocks of this type; it's a rather dangerous process. They are usually covered by hostile artillery or machine gun fire as well as being mined and booby trapped. Of course, that's all over now, but many things still remain as a reminder that the war once passed this way.

The Pilsen radio station came on the air again a couple of weeks ago. The city held a ceremony and dedicated the station to the 2d Infantry Division and V Corps as the liberators of the city, and decreed that as long as we are in the area the station will present practically all American programs for the entertainment of the troops.

On Memorial Day, May 30, we held a battalion review and parade, the first in a year and a half, followed by an impressive memorial service conducted by the division chaplain in honor of our dead buddies. Everyone felt the solemnity and dignity of the occasion and as the colonel called the roll of honor, the names of those no longer with us, heads were held high with pride but there was a tear in nearly every eye; as each name was called you could tell that all the older men in the outfit were recalling the time and place, reconstructing each battle and skirmish, remembering. I only wish that the families of our own dead comrades could have been present to see for themselves that their boys are not forgotten.

There is not much to do here now. The barest minimum of military duty, rest and recreation are the order of the day with swimming holding first place. Everyone is getting brown as an Indian and fit as a fiddle. Just the right amount of exercise, plenty of sunshine, plenty of rest, and a regular diet.

We know we are going to the Pacific, likely we will spearhead the invasion of Japan, but we also know that we are scheduled to sail for the U.S.A. soon and get a furlough. So we don't think about Japan now, plenty of time for that later. We just kill time, waiting for transportation home, and think about the States. It's been a long time and I, like all the rest, am very impatient to be home again, even though I know it will be for only a short time.

Not much more to say, so will close for now.

MEREDITH

Ernest H. Ellett, of Coatesville, was inducted into the Army in Feb. 1943 and was trained at Fort Knox. Going overseas in Jan. 1944, he was attached to the 24th Tank Battalion, 13th Armored Division, 3d Army in the European theater. He fought through France and Germany and was promoted to technician 5th grade. Returning to the U. S. in July 1945, T/5 Ellett was discharged Dec. 1946 and is now a sheet metal worker in Hammond.

May 29, 1945
Bavaria, Germany

DEAREST MOTHER AND DAD:

Received my birthday cards from both you and Mary Lou today. Thought them very nice and was surprised for I had forgotten I had one coming up. . . .

The situation over here seems funny, but if the United States was invaded there would be a hell of a lot more resistance after the bulk gave up than there has been here. These P.W.'s have to be released and these 12- to 14-year-old boys don't like to see their country beaten. Being at the age when there is not much fear, they try to make a show. The SS is very dangerous for they are killers and know they will have to stand trial for the many crimes they have committed. There is no way for them to escape, for once picked up they are stripped and each one has an SS tattooed on the fleshy part of his left arm. After seeing what even I have, one can kill and it does not wear on your mind. I was once afraid that it would. The noise and excitement stay with you longer, or seeing a G.I. tank burning with all the hatches closed.

It is a big temptation when you see Germans going home to just start shooting regardless of what they do to you, for now it is a crime to kill one. I stood my first review in Germany today. They had lots of bronze stars to give so had a ceremony for them. We had five in my company. It seems like a lot to lose for a piece of metal but it is funny what a man will do even for a total stranger in battle. The band played the old 7th Cavalry march—"Carry On"—I think is the name of it. You will remember it from the movie of Custer's Last Stand and I think that was his outfit. Might be either an Irish or a Scottish march. Anyway it made you feel good. We have our flags all over this country now and hope they keep lots of them here. I would rather not stay here but would sure like to help set some up in Japan. I think I will get that chance soon but hope to get home for a while first.

We all have our new battle jackets so we may be going home in not too long. Most of our chow is flown in by plane and that isn't much but C-ration cheese and rice. We do get some meat; in fact, we had pork chops today and steak yesterday, so you can see we still fare pretty good with Uncle Sam to back us up. I wish people there could see some things that exist here. I know they were defeated, but they put all they had into it. I see in the paper where people bitch about things that if they would only think they would know didn't mean much in comparison to what lots of men gave up over here. Soldiers in the States bitched because we get 20 per cent more money and the chance to get Lugers. I am sure there are lots that would swap places. We got seven packages of cigarettes and seven pieces of candy a week free, yet there were 20 rations they were not able to get to us, and I know of three days I went on one package of cigarettes and no rations except what we could find, and the Krauts were in about the same shape. They carry sardines, and your stomach at times like that doesn't take to them very well. None of this could be helped for the trains were having a big time, too. I guess Chick thinks he was cheated, but I doubt if he realizes what it is like to have 88's coming in so fast that you think the ground is going to come apart and smoke is so thick you can't see. Then they have screaming meanies that make chills run up your spine even if they don't come close. These come from a 6-barreled gun. They usually fire one and then let five follow close. They sound like a woman when badly scared. They are a form of rocket.

I have been getting the paper fairly regularly, and the packages arrived the 25th and 26th. Was very glad to get them both. Packages don't last long in a tank's 5-man crew. A crew gets pretty close in combat so share 'most everything. We were lucky in a way for we were together almost all the way. The gunner and I are still together. He is from Chicago and a good fellow. I have turned down lots of chances to make good to stay with them and to do what I felt I wanted to do. I was a sergeant at Fort Knox for a while but turned it in to get in a combat outfit. I had trouble with my feet and legs, but went to General Scott at Knox and he said a man with my record should know what he wanted and would see that I got it, so was sent to the 13th Armored Division. They tried to put me in the ordnance. I wanted the armored infantry, but they put me in tanks and I have liked it better than I thought I would. I tested them for quite a while so thought I had had all of them I wanted. They are a hot and noisy piece of equipment but can raise a lot of hell. They aren't, as a lot of people think, safe against anything. They do all right against near misses and small arms, but draw lots of fire because the Krauts fear them. This outfit is what might be called a regular army outfit by the way they work. Most of the men have two years and over service and act like soldiers under fire. They follow orders and never lag, as do some outfits with less training. We are said by higher-ups to be the best in the division and our record shows it. We have above-average officers, which is something in this war.

Had better close for now. Hope Dad is feeling better. I have got back my weight I lost (20 lbs.) in combat. I weigh 175 now.

Lots of love,
ERNEST

Karl Price, of Indianapolis, was inducted into the Army on Oct. 6, 1942, and was assigned to the 355th Engineers, where he remained for his entire army service. Going overseas in Oct. 1943, Pfc. Price received battle stars for the following campaigns: Normandy, Northern France, Rhineland, Central Europe, and the Ardennes. Discharged Oct. 30, 1945, Pfc. Price is now a law student at Stanford University, Calif.

June 29, 1945
Somewhere in France

DEAR DR. EFROYMSON:

Your letter of June 13 has just come to me in the northern French plain about thirty miles from Rheims. Coming back to France feels something like a homecoming but we already miss the good leisurely life we knew in Germany. Whenever we found a building that was still intact (which was rare), we just moved right in and made ourselves at home. Often Germans were made to move from their homes to make room for our billets. Now we are in tents in the middle of a great dusty clearing under a hot sun. There are other advantages of Germany that we no longer have. Everyone there tried to please us, especially the girls, and I'll admit it felt good to be saluted and otherwise readily accepted. Although there were rigid laws of nonfraternization no one seemed unduly concerned with them, and one could find officers as well as enlisted men speaking to German civilians in downtown Bremen on obviously non status. I learned a little German myself, while I was there.

There is another reason why many of us are not too happy in our present area. Our purpose here is to be redeployed to the Pacific theatre. The men with enough points for discharge will leave us here and the rest of us will soon be on our way direct to the Pacific without even a 30-day furlough to the States. I have been among the very few fortunate enough to have had an emergency furlough to England and even at that I don't think it is quite just or necessary for us to go direct to the Pacific because we have established such a fine record here in the E.T.O. We were in all five campaigns here in this theatre and thereby I have five battle stars each worth five points. These twenty-five points plus my time in the service and time overseas gives me a total of seventy-five points toward discharge. I imagine this score will be just a few points short of the critical score so I am trying to accustom myself to the idea of two more years away from home, this time in the Pacific. Frankly, I am looking forward to the new lands, people, and experiences for I realize the great value of my stay in Europe. However, I also realize that I have been extremely lucky here and I have absolutely no assurance that my luck will continue in the Pacific.

I have been out of civilian life for almost three years and this has affected me in some ways but I know that if I am away for two or three more years, this period will leave a deep mark of some kind in my young life and I think the possibility is great that it may not be a favorable mark. Young as I may be, five years is a long time, especially since my state of preparation for a secure life is so poorly developed. I still have no very definite plans for my future although I think I would enjoy some phases of law and government and I know these fields require many years of formal preparation. I hope you don't interpret this as requiring from you those services normally performed by a chaplain. I just thought you may be interested in a soldier's attitude toward going to the Pacific with seventy-five points and five campaign stars from the European theatre. . . .

Since we are not too far from Paris, we are allowed eighteen-hour passes to the French capital. I had a pass last week that I enjoyed more than I expected, but at the same time I think I have come to know the real Paris, and this realization is not something to enjoy. I visited a friend of mine there who is one of the very small minority that does not work on the black market. She still works at the same job she has had and now she is even more disgusted with Paris than I am. I will admit that no city can compare to Paris in the beauty of its structure or its gay life, but she also holds honors when it comes to immorality. Not only are the sex morals below anything an American could imagine, but the standard of all morals is low. I thought America was supposed to be money mad but a glance at any black market operation, which only requires a quick glance in any direction when in Paris, shows that we are, at best, second raters. Paris is without food, yet the people will commit any crime for attractive clothes. I saw a very fine show at Casino de Paris and I thought it was typical. The dancing and music were artistic, the costuming and settings very expensive, and the staging better than anything I have seen, but there was always a superfluity of nudes whose sole purpose seemed to be a reminder that you are in Paris. . . .

My work in this camp has been entirely musical. My only duties are to play with our dance band and military band. We play for formations, parades, concerts, and for dances in the nearby towns. Whenever we leave camp to go to Rheims, Charleville, or Mezieres, we pass through the old fixed battlegrounds of the last war. Many of the old trenches and dugouts are left as they were dug in the hard white clay. The cemeteries dot the hills and stand out as dumb reminders of the futileness of war. Whenever I pass these rusty wire entanglements or those smooth-edged trenches, my thoughts become a congested mess.

Please give my regards to Mrs. Efroymson.

Sincerely yours,
KARL PRICE

Robert E. Stine, of Edinburg, was inducted into the Army Aug. 15, 1942, and was attached to the signal corps. Going overseas in March 1943, Stine participated in the Tunisian, Southern France, the Rhineland, and Central European campaigns. He was awarded four battle stars, and the Meritorious Service Plaque, which was presented to his outfit, the 207th Signal Depot Company, by Gen. Patch, commander of the 7th Army. Discharged Oct. 15, 1945, T/4 Stine is co-owner of a food market in Edinburg.

[1945]

DEAR MOTHER SCHALLER AND LARRY:

I am back from Paris and I had a most wonderful time. It was my first three-day pass in the army but I don't see how it could have been better if it wasn't in the States. I was pretty lucky, too. Instead of having three days and nights in Paris we had four days and three nights. Then, too, I won a small bottle of Chanel No. 5 perfume in a drawing at the Red Cross. In addition to that, when I got back to our outfit last Saturday night we learned that during our absence our company was notified that we were entitled to the Bronze Star award for the Tunisian campaign so my points jumped from 73 to 78. Now if the critical score falls enough I will be O.K. However, even if it falls that low it will most likely be several months before I get home. In the event it does fall to around 76, our whole outfit, excluding replacements, would be eligible for discharge. I'll just have to sweat it out, I guess.

Well, here it is—a detailed account of my trip. We left our company here in Mannheim Monday noon, July 2, by truck for Strasbourg, France, where we boarded the 7th Army leave train for Paris. We stopped at the Nancy station about a half hour where we obtained donuts and coffee from the canteen in the station. We arrived at the station (East side) in Paris the next morning about 8 o'clock. The train ride was pretty rough as about 30 men were crowded into each car which is very small. Most fellows slept sitting up, what sleeping they did. I climbed up into a baggage rack and got a few hours of fairly good sleep.

When we got to the Paris station we had breakfast at a special mess which serves all men coming in or going away on passes. After chow we were loaded into busses and taken to our living quarters. We were stationed at "Rainbow Corner," a section where five or six hotels are within a few blocks of each other where men are stationed on pass. The Hotel de Paris is used by the Red Cross for feeding and furnishing entertainment for all men stationed in "Rainbow Corner" or this particular area. This hotel was one of the largest hotels in Paris in peacetimes. Short orders such as coffee and donuts, and Coca Cola and donuts also are served here all day long. Also check rooms, reading and writing rooms, ping-pong tables and other games are to be found here in this hotel. We were each given a map of Paris and a map of the metro (subway system) so we could find our way around. The hotel we fellows had our living quarters in was very nice and each man had a nice-sized individual room for 60 francs or $1.20 for all four days and three nights.

Well, when we got located we cleaned up and went over to the special P.X. for all American personnel on leave to get our weekly rations we were entitled to. Then we walked around a little, stopping at a sidewalk cafe for a couple beers and back to our room. We then went over to chow. After chow, we spent the afternoon walking around window-shopping and making reservations for the Follies. That night we attended the Follies, which were pretty good—a little raw—but that is Paris. We used the subway for the first time and how they packed those cars full of people. After the Follies we went to the Opera Night Club, one of the better Paris night clubs. The floor show was good. About 2:30 we got back to our rooms tired and sleepy.

We were up about 8 o'clock next morning, bathed and had fresh eggs for breakfast. Then we went on a tour of the highlights and historical points of Paris. We traveled in regular busses and a lecturer was assigned to each bus to point out the various places of interest. Several places we got off the busses and went inside or around the particular place while the lecturer gave a brief history of the place. Some of these places were: American Embassy, Arch of

Triumph, Tomb of the Unknown Soldier, Eiffel Tower, Notre Dame Cathedral, Royal Palace, Avenues des Champs Elysees, Chamber of Deputies, Seine River, building in which Madame Curie discovered radium, building in which the great composer Schubert lived and died, and many other places including the statue of Joan of Arc and the tomb of Napoleon.

This trip was about two hours long and was very interesting and helped acquaint us with how to get around the city. We got back just in time for chow. Following chow we walked around taking pictures, stopping for a beer or wine. We again visited the Eiffel Tower and went up in it on an elevator. Boy, we were sure up in the clouds where we could see all over Paris and the people and cars on the ground looked like ants. Oh, yes, during the morning tour we went through the Notre Dame Cathedral which is really beautiful. A lieutenant and a nurse were being married at the time we were going through the Cathedral and a large choir was present. The stained glass in the building's windows is very beautiful.

That night while in the chow line, everyone in the line participated in the drawing and I was one of the lucky ones to win the perfume. I was indeed lucky as Chanel perfume, which is supposed to be the best, isn't on the market at present. Production of it was halted during the war but will probably begin again soon. Girls in the perfume shops go crazy from soldiers wanting Chanel perfume and they don't have it. I could have sold my bottle for $45.00 to a WAC who was in the line behind me but I laughed and told her I was going to send it to my girl back home.

That night we took the subway to Pigalle, one of the lower sections of town. Here a small amusement park was strung out along the streets. We walked around here a few minutes then took the subway over to the "Coliseum Night Club," better known as "G.I. Paradise." This night club is operated for American military personnel and their guests. A girl can get in only as the guest of some service man or service woman. We each took a French girl with us. We drank about five bottles of champagne at $8.00 per bottle. They had a good floor show. At 1:30 they close up so we escorted the girls by subway to their homes and returned to our hotel and hit the hay.

The next day we bought a few gifts and souvenirs and continued walking around seeing the sights. We even got to go through the American Embassy. We visited one of Paris' largest department stores also.

That night we went to the train station to catch the train back. About 9 o'clock they started loading the train. After a while the train was filled and pulled out with several units, including ours, still on the platform to be loaded. We expected another train to pull onto our track for us but none came. Soon a voice boomed through the loud-speaking system notifying all unit commanders to bring their men back in the station, gather up their passes and take them up to the RTO officer, have them stamped and return to this station the same time tomorrow night to catch the train. Well, we were happy to get an extra day in Paris. We caught busses back to our quarters and then from there we proceeded to the night club we visited the night before. We got a table, had champagne, and took part in the singing of popular songs led by the orchestra. We got back to our rooms about 2:30 and to bed we went.

Next morning we bathed and got ready for our last day in Paris. We spent the day sight-seeing and saw Madeleine Carroll in the Red Cross that afternoon. That night we caught our train back. We got into Strasbourg, France, about noon the next day and called our outfit to send a truck to pick us up. We had three or four hours to wait so we walked around seeing the town and visiting an old beautiful cathedral in the east part of the city. We had a good dinner at a French restaurant. We had potatoes, peas and carrots, bread, beer, soup, and a basket of fresh plums and peaches. We had everything but meat which we couldn't get because of the rationing. However, it was a good meal. Our truck came about 4 o'clock and we got back to our company about eight, tired, dirty, sleepy, but happy. I took a shower and fell in bed and immediately went to sleep. We didn't get over four hours sleep any night in Paris as we wanted to see all we could with what time we had. Now I have to catch up on my sleep.

All in all I had a most wonderful time in Paris. I have read and heard about Paris for years and it is all and even more than I expected it to be. It is really gay Paree. True enough, the women in Paris are beautiful and they and the men all dress very well. The first few hours in Paris we almost got drunk from the perfume the women wear. The air scented with perfume really smells good and in the subways it smells like a perfume shop. The streets of Paris are all paved and on the most part run on an angle. At many corners as many as six or seven streets come to a point. The buildings are made of stone and are fairly tall. The stores and shops are very attractive. We saw where most of the famed Paris styles of clothes originate. There is one section of town which is made up almost completely of dressmaking houses and firms. The weather was nice, warm, and sunny during our stay.

Someday I hope to return to Paris on a vacation or trip if I can ever afford it. Paris is a grand old town and so much better than any I have seen since coming overseas.

Well, it is now 10:15 and I am going to bed. Please excuse this poor writing as this is the third long letter I have written since coming back. Tomorrow night I think I will type a letter and make several carbon copies. Hope this finds you all well. Write when you can. I have some pictures of Paris I will send you. I am having a wooden box made and will send the things to Mother and mark them for her to give out.

Oh, yes, I spent about $100.00 on my trip, but if it had been double that I wouldn't complain. I enjoyed every minute of it and it isn't everyone who gets to visit Paris sometime during his lifetime.

So long for this time,
BUD

→ IX ←

ALASKA AND THE ALEUTIANS

THE AMERICAN counteroffensive in the Pacific began with air raids on Japanese-held islands in the early months of 1942, culminating in the surprise attack on Tokyo on April 18. This was followed by two stinging defeats for the Japanese navy in the battles of the Coral Sea and Midway in May and June, which checked Japan's advance in the Pacific. The enemy, however, occupied Attu and Kiska Islands in the Aleutian chain, thus threatening to press the war home on the American continent and making Alaska a frontline theater of operations. The danger was met by the building of the Alcan Highway, intensive air attacks, and finally, the reconquest of Attu in May 1943.

John A. Frump, of Clay City, was inducted into the Army and attached to the medical corps in July 1942. His first overseas service was at Attu, Aleutian Islands, and after returning to the United States, he was sent to New Guinea. He also saw service in the Philippines, where he was attached to the 24th and 31st Divisions, and in Japan. He attained the rank of sergeant in June 1944, and received the Bronze Star. He was discharged Dec. 4, 1945, and is a student at Indiana University.

November 27, 1943
Somewhere in the Aleutians

DEAR HARRY:

Here it is immediately after Thanksgiving and winter is here to the fullest extent. You probably remember several weeks ago I said that the snow was on the mountains all around us and was gradually growing colder as the snow crept toward us. Well, we have been invaded by it now for the last few days and have found it difficult to get around in such great quantities of snow and snowbanks. Of course, snow here is no different from our Indiana snow, but the ever-blowing wind seems to put most of it in places where there isn't any sort of obstacle that can stop a little snow. It isn't odd for anyone to get snowed under. You see, we live in tents (have for eight months) and the snow seems to have a habit of collecting right in the doorway.

Would you like to know just what kind of living conditions we have? I don't think I'll reveal any military secrets in explaining, I hope. Most people probably think, "Oh, how horrible, living in tents in that terrible Aleutian weather." It is far from the bedroom or dining room at home, but still it's surprising just how comfortable one can fix a little tent up. The tents aren't so large (16x16), 3 to 5 men to a tent is average. So you see we aren't too crowded, and have a little privacy, which isn't expected in the army. For our own comfort we have managed to scrape up enough lumber to lay a crude floor and a door that still stands even in the most damaging williwaw (wind storm). A few days ago we got electricity, which is rationed to a certain extent, but we have lights when they are most needed. The electricity is a great luxury to us (try living without lights or using candles for seven months), and to the few who had radios it is the best thing that ever happened to them. Our mess is practically the same as our living quarters, all tentage. Since the Japs have been chased out there isn't much for us to do, only try to improve our living quarters, but as yet we are still living as a field unit.

Do you remember what Uncle Sam said? "Every man shall have turkey for Thanksgiving dinner." As far as I'm concerned he kept that promise. We had turkey that was almost as good as if Mom had fixed it. We had a variety of foods that not many civilians could sit down to for a Thanksgiving dinner. It was by far the most outstanding meal we have had since we left the States. We had ice cream, which was the first we have seen for eight months, and pumpkin pie, the old favorite for Thanksgiving dinner, and like the ice cream the first in eight months. Now everything wasn't on the sunny side though, the mess kit with food on top of food isn't like chinaware, nor is the tent like the dining room at home, but I guess we shouldn't complain.

Thanksgiving was a regular duty day, but they weren't so strict on us so we went skiing that afternoon. We were using a fairly large hill and I think I made it to the bottom standing up one time out of approximately 50 attempts. I had never been on skis before, but I had a wonderful time learning—pretty rough, too.

When the sun shines, which isn't very often, this is one of the most beautiful places I have ever seen. Just like the movies. As the sun comes up, it shines on the mountains before it gets high enough to shine down on the lower parts where we are located. Can't you just picture the sun shining on the snow-covered mountains and in the other direction water just as far as you can see? Seriously speaking, it is beautiful; but confidentially, I want to get out of here.

I can't understand why the people at home won't cooperate with you to the fullest extent in your wonderful idea of getting the home town boys together when it is possible. If they only knew how much I enjoyed meeting Robert Deeters out here I'm sure they would change their minds and notify you of any change of APO numbers. To me, letters from home, or meeting a home town boy, are much more welcome than "pay call."

You said you thought that there never would be any action between Japan and the United States through the Aleutian chain. Should Russia declare war on Japan, don't you think this would become a four-lane highway to Japan? It's true the weather is terrible and the seas are rough, but it is also the shortest route.

I agree with you that the war isn't about over. There is no advantage in kidding ourselves into thinking that it is. It seems to me that we had two strikes on us when we went to bat and have come out of the hole by getting a hit, but the winning run hasn't scored yet.

I can't begin to tell you how much I enjoy your letters. You write a letter that is tops with me—local news, current events, and all that a soldier wants to know about, even his family. I don't just read it once and give it a heave, but read it over and over and absorb everything. I want you to know that your time isn't wasted by any means when you send me a letter.

I would like to do you a favor without asking one of you, but the one I have in mind is impossible. I can't get films here, but if you would like to have some scenery pictures of the Aleutians, just send me a roll of film (size 620) and I'll do all in my power to get you some good pictures. If you are interested send it at once.

Thanks for your letter.

Yours,

JOHN

Meyer Maierson, of Indianapolis, was inducted into the Army Oct. 21, 1941. He was attached to the 477th Quartermaster Regiment, North West Service Command, and to the 51st Quartermaster Depot in Hawaii. Commissioned a 2d lieutenant, he served in the American and Asiatic-Pacific theaters. Discharged Feb. 15, 1946, 1st Lt. Maierson is a wholesale meat dealer in Indianapolis.

June 3, 1944
Yukon Territory

EDITORS: *SPEAKING OF HOME,* INDIANAPOLIS,
GENTLEMEN:

I was very pleased to be placed on the mailing list of your paper and it is a very good publication.

I have been up here in the Yukon Territory of Canada and Alaska since January of '43 and, although now it is an inactive spot, when we originally came up the Alaska Highway it was a different story. We arrived in Dawson Creek in January and the temperature was around 50° below zero. We were very fortunate in having such mild weather as three days before it had been 76° below zero. The men were driven up the road in the back end of army trucks in weather ranging from 30° to 60° below zero and our first camp was on Steamboat Mountain, 50 miles north of Fort Nelson. Due to the depth of the snow along the side of the highway we had to haul water for 17 miles. It was usually about half frozen when it got back to camp and I can assure you that no baths were taken for a good while.

My outfit moved to Watson Lake where we stayed for seven months. Our work was diversified, and we not only built a camp for 300 men, but we cut the trees, sawed them into boards on our own sawmill, cleared telephone right-of-way, cut 150 tons of ice and built an icehouse to store it besides our regular trucking and housekeeping activities.

Last year for three months the road was closed and we ate reserve rations as no one could travel on the road during the thaw. The menu became somewhat monotonous, but no one was hurt. In fact, all the men gained weight. They worked very hard, too, and I can assure you that cutting trees with snow up to your waist is no picnic. The temperature was usually always below 20° below zero.

At the present time I am in charge of all police activities on the highway from the Alaskan border to Mundio Lake, a distance of 850 miles. I also patrol the Norman Wells road, 550 miles, and the Haines cutoff, 200 miles. It sounds like a lot of territory, but no matter where you travel you are still in the middle of the woods. The Haines cutoff goes through one of the passes in the Rockies where many people died during the gold rush of '98. The pass is a desolate place approximately 10 miles wide and 20 miles long. The snow drifts 30 and 40 feet, and a good deal of the time the road was impassable.

There is a lot of good hunting and fishing up here and most of the camps along the road had bears for pets.

I am now located in Whitehorse and, due to a sensible rationing program by the Canadian government, at no time was there any shortage of meat, butter or any other food products. Whitehorse normally has a population of 300, but with all the influx there were approximately 20,000 people within a 10-mile radius, and at any time you could go in a restaurant and buy a steak and get all the extra butter that you wanted. Many of the men who went back to the States on leave came back with a very sour opinion of American efficiency after being up here. In Fairbanks, Alaska, and all the other towns, we could always buy a good meal and with a good selection to choose from. I often wondered myself what was the cause of all the shortage and confusion.

In addition to my highway patrol activities, I am in charge of the guarding of the controversial Canol refinery, and with all the questions and all the scandal, they are producing gasoline and petroleum products.

MEYER MAIERSON

⇥ X ⇤

SOUTHWEST PACIFIC

Even before the tide of Japanese aggression in the Pacific area had reached its fullest flow, American troops were being sent to New Zealand, Australia, New Caledonia, and other islands still in the possession of Allied powers in preparation for the eventual counteroffensive. This began on August 7, 1942, when U. S. Marines established footholds on Guadalcanal and Tulagi Islands in the Solomon Archipelago. From that first precarious landing, Allied forces moved steadily up the island chain, fighting heavily on New Georgia and Bougainville, mauling the Japanese Navy and bombing Japanese bases. In the meantime, Gen. MacArthur had started his counteroffensive in New Guinea, pushing across the Owen Stanley mountain range to Buna and sending landing forces to Milne Bay, Lae, and Salamaua. Under MacArthur's overall command, Allied land, sea, and air forces completed the discomfiture of Japan in the South Pacific by establishing bases on New Britain, the Admiralty Islands, and at various points along the northern coast of New Guinea, leaving enemy forces cut off from effective participation in the war.

Robert M. Renneisen, of Jasper, enlisted in the Army Air Corps in Sept. 1940, and was commissioned a 2d lieutenant on April 30, 1942. He saw service in Australia and New Guinea in 1942 and 1943 with the 38th Bomb Group of the 5th Air Force. In 1944–45 he was in public relations work with Air Materiel Command at Wright Field, Ohio, and since 1946 Capt. Renneisen has been stationed with the Public

Relations Division, Air Defense Command, Mitchel Field, N. Y. He was promoted to the rank of major, U. S. A. F. Reserve, May 1947. He received the Air Medal and three Oak Leaf clusters, the Distinguished Unit Citation badge, and the Meritorious Unit Citation badge.

March 5, 1943
New Guinea

DEAR MOM AND ALL:

Revision of censorship regulations permits us to say quite a bit more now than was formerly allowed. And at an opportune time, too. I'll try to give you a picture of the big show that just ended. . . .

By this time the composition of the Jap convoy was three cruisers, four destroyers and seven large ships, either transports or cargo carriers. Six others had been hit previously, either sunk or so disabled as to force separation from the main force.

But the worst was yet to come. How terrific and thorough that initial tide of co-ordinated destruction turned out to be was revealed in part when we arrived for our attack.

We had what amounted to almost a new crew. Following our return from a well-earned leave, our co-pilot was promoted and given his own crew. Our veteran turret gunner, who had one Zero to his credit which he had shot down over an earlier convoy, was in the hospital and so we had a new boy here too, likewise uninitiated. Rounding out the newcomers was the navigator, borrowed from another crew. Still, as usual, we were to lead the flight. And the colonel, always on hand whenever anything big is brewing, elected to ride along as an observer to see the show. (The colonel is our group commander, Lt. Col. Bryan O'Neil of New Jersey.)

The rendezvous was accomplished and we were on our way. Mac (Lt. McMillan, the navigator) gave us a heading that would enable us to intercept the enemy somewhere between its last sighting and its destination, all too apparent because of the military situation in this theater. But a compass course was unnecessary. The sky was literally filled with airplanes of all descriptions. All one had to do was to fall in line and keep out of his neighbors' path.

Everyone was on the keen edge of anticipation now. Although our bombers hadn't been "jumped," according to reports from the first wave, everyone knew the Zeros were up there somewhere. There had been plenty of dogfighting between the top cover and the convoy's escort this morning, even though the fighters hadn't broken through to get at the bombers.

As lead bombardier it was going to be up to me to pick up the target and decide on the course which would govern the pattern of our bombs, so I was scanning the cloud-flecked sea anxiously, striving to pick out the long white pencil lines in the water that would denote the telltale wakes of our foes. But it was a touch and go proposition. Just halfway between our line of flight and the sea itself rested a blanket of tiny, fragmentary cumulus clouds, polka dotting the sea's surface with puffs of white. Right now this was a handicap, but it held its element of satisfaction too. Nothing looks better to a bomber's crew than a nice handy fleecy cloud, into which one can duck when the Zeros strike.

Still no sign of the expected shipping. But the weather ahead looks heavier. Two huge white clouds, many times the size of the others, loom along the horizon ahead and to the right of our course. Possibly our targets are hiding in here, so we bear slightly to the left, starting to flank them.

But wait! What's that right at the base of the cloud? "Pilot from bombardier. Pilot from bombardier. Ship at base of smoke cloud. Go ahead."

"Bombardier from pilot. O.K. I see it. Let's take a look at the other one." And it's the same story here. Both are transports, about eight or ten thousand tonners. And both are aflame from stem to stern, billowing forth huge columns of dirty grey smoke which has piled up in the sky for thousands of feet. We are still about thirty miles away, but the towering inverted cones seem alive as each writhing billow adds to the already mile-wide umbrella that the ships trail to the southeast.

Now two more come into view, like their mates, both dead in the water. These too are afire, one by the bow and the other amid-ships, but neither to the extent of the first pair sighted. Both are partially screened, making identification difficult, but one apparently is a destroyer while the other is a small auxiliary, a transport or cargo vessel.

But where is the convoy? Surely more than this remains. Fourteen ships don't just disappear. And air attack is ineffectual against sea power. Or is it? Maybe the books are being rewritten today.

Here's a target now. About five miles off to our right sits a destroyer. But there is no wake. What's wrong? It must be dead in the water too. Over we go.

"Zeros at 2 o'clock." It's the voice of the co-pilot, Jim Hungerpiller of Atlanta, Georgia. Cpl. Frank Nino, our new turret gunner, is next, "Zeros at 10 o'clock upstairs." Our eyes flash up instinctively and there they sit. Eight of them. The ones on the right have crossed over, so now there are six of them in a sloppy echelon about two thousand feet above us and a half mile ahead. The other pair are riding wing to wing and a little closer. But heading our way now.

I duck back on the bombsight. We have swung over toward the destroyer and are about to start our bombing run. A glance has assured me that Mac, our navigator, is kneeling just behind me with two fists full of machine gun, thumbs on the trigger, ready to go. The destroyer is in view now in the sight, but I take another glance around.

It's a white ribbon farther off to our right disappearing into a cloud of smoke that catches my eye. The streak emerges from the far side as the boiling wake of another destroyer. This one is under full steam and heading for home. "Which one, Ez?" I yelled at Capt. Best, our pilot. Apparently he has had eyes for something more than the Zeros and has spotted the new target too, for the plane dips farther to the right and we roll into a sharper bank.

"Give 'em a burst up there. Keep 'em away." It's Hungerpiller again. He is having his first look at Tojo's top toy and doesn't care for too close a view. Mac's answer is the stuttering chatter of his machine gun, the tracers lacing a red-streaked pattern in a wide, ragged fan toward the greenish bellies of the too far distant enemy birds.

"Pick out something. Let's get out of here. They're all over us." The colonel is coaching now, having a complete view of the proceedings from his vantage point in the plexiglass navigation dome amidships.

Best sizes up the situation instantaneously and rolls the plane back to the left. The cruising destroyer is still a good distance off and apparently the low altitude boys are after it, as they had led the formation and broken off in that direction. And the sitting duck is just ahead now, an ideal target for horizontal bombing from medium altitude, which is our assignment today.

We're roaring downward now—our standard practice in order to gain additional speed and hamper the sightings and aimings of enemy antiaircraft fire. We're due for that any minute now. But no, the sitting duck is even deader than we had ever hoped it might be. The usual curtain of red-ribboned hail and the spotty black puffs of ack-ack bursts fail to appear.

Level now and the bomb bays open. Just ahead lies the Jap warship, fully broadside to our run. Five times the tiny yellow light flickers on the panel and twenty-five hundred pounds of destruction are shrinking away into the distance as they arc their way toward the water. "Bombs away." The nose drops back down and again we're racing downward. Another look around but Mac's big grin tells me that our share of the sky—that in front and to the sides of the nose—are clear of opposition, so back to follow the bombs my eyes go.

It's time now. There they are. One, two. Wham! Number three of the five hits square on the bow. A perfect bracket for the string—two and four framing the nose in a sandwich of destruction around the bullseye blast. A bombardier's dream come true. Two more bombs hit home on the deck as the strings from the wingmen on the right of the formation crash into the stricken can. Only the left wingman's strings fall harmlessly into the water. We had led the ship a bit to ensure a hit in case the ship got underway at the last instant.

Down, down and now we're nearing the water. That's the safest place for medium bombers when Zeros are in the sky. There's one direction from which they can't attack you then. Looking back we see the first puff of smoke from our victim. He's catching fire by the bow. But it's immediately enveloped in two huge geysers. That must be thousand-pounders from the Flying Fortresses way upstairs. The boat is listing badly now.

Off in the distance the other destroyer has run into trouble, too. Smoke is rolling off it as other medium bombers race back and forth belching and spitting deathly streams of strafing machine gun fire. Scattered throughout the area, covering fifteen to twenty miles, is wreckage galore. Now we can realize where the convoy is. Or rather was. Rafts and lifeboats, rubbish and cargo, all mixed with floating bodies and debris. It is a panorama of utter destruction.

Back on the ground we check over our ships, and compare stories. Only one of our formation has been hit, but the damage wasn't serious and everyone is safe and whole. It seems that the pair of Zeros dove directly onto the formation and then pulled out for a second attack from the bottom. The other six passed by the formation, then cut back in for repeated attacks from four and eight o'clock. None pressed home their passes in the manner which we had faced before. None made frontal attacks either, for which I give many thanks, as I, being lead bombardier, am expected to concentrate on perfecting the bombing run for the entire formation, leaving the wingmen to bear the brunt of the defense against attacks aimed at the nose.

Recapitulation at home revealed the completeness and overall perfection of the victory. The very enormity of it was scaring. For the lack of evidence remaining gave rise to suspicion that perhaps a major portion of the enemy had escaped.

But reconnaissance proved without a doubt that the triumph was even greater than anything but the wildest sort of dreams. It wasn't a rout, but was exactly as

General MacArthur expressed in his congratulatory message to the Air Force: the most complete annihilation in the history of combat. . . .

Paul E. Taylor, of Indianapolis, was inducted into the Army in Dec. 1941 and was attached to the 126th Infantry Regiment, 32d Division. He was sent to Australia in April 1942. In September he was moved to New Guinea and marched over the Owen Stanley Mountains. Pvt. Taylor was killed in action Dec. 6, 1943, and was awarded the Purple Heart posthumously. The following letter was the last he wrote to his parents.

October 1, 1943
New Guinea

DEAR MOTHER AND DAD:

Here is that past due communique from your wandering son. We've covered a lot of interesting territory since the last writing and have seen plenty of sights. About all I can do, though, is to arouse your curiosity along this line because of the censorship, but as I told Mimi, read the papers and you will probably know more than I of the important information.

As for the less dramatic, a few notes here and there will serve to bring it all back to mind when the time comes that it can be told. I imagine the mail will be irregular for some time now, so just keep writing as often as possible, and eventually they will catch up. I'll turn them out from this end whenever possible.

Every so often the question comes up as to what we are fighting for, and the usual points of profiteers, democracy and their substitutes, but even the large question seems clearer now. If there is hope for a peaceful settlement, if there is hope for a steady advance for mankind, certainly that hope will be found in a nation and government whose responsibility and aim is education for all, and where the responsibility for decision is the people's. What could come closer to the recognition of the value of the individual? What hope of fair treatment of conquered nations can be found in any other philosophy? Or, perhaps it is better said in this way: what form can offer more respect for the rights of advancement of these people?

Of course, our interests are not entirely unselfish. Many interests seek wealth and commercial strength from the struggle, but what nation would be more apt to be unselfish than the one which already possesses nearly all of the essentials. We are fighting for what appears to be the strongest hope for advancing the status of the individual man the world over.

Knowledge is an immense force. Even God's judgment is according to knowledge. To really know a man, a country, or a people, is to be more sympathetic, more tolerant toward them. Someone said, "If you really know a man, you cannot hate him."

Why this long drawn out discourse? Well, it was partly due to a Boake Carter article sometime back which either Mimi or one of you sent me, in which he attempted to prove an eye-for-an-eye, tooth-for-a-tooth philosophy by Biblical quotations. Much as I generally like him, he couldn't push that one down my throat. Christ was pretty definite on that subject, and retaliated with, "But I say unto you"—in short, we fight not because we hate.

Tell the folks who sent their regards, thanks.

Loads of love to all,
PAUL

Walter M. Goldsberry, Jr., of Greencastle, enlisted in the Marine Corps in 1940. He trained at San Diego and was sent to officer candidate school at Quantico, Va., being commissioned a 2d lieutenant on March 31, 1942. Sent to New Zealand in Feb. 1943, he served with the 3d Marine Division in the New Georgia and Bougainville campaigns. He was promoted to captain in May 1943. Returned to the United States in May 1945, Capt. Goldsberry served as instructor at Quantico, Va., until November. He was sent overseas again in April 1946 to China, where he served until returning to the States in April 1948. Capt. Goldsberry is stationed at Treasure Island, Calif.

December 29, 1943

DEAR FOLKS:

Censorship regulations have been relaxed to the extent that we may mention our participation in the recent Empress Augusta Bay campaign on Bougainville Island. Certain facts, pertinent to the operation, still must be withheld. I'll give you what I can.

As is 'most always the case in these amphibious operations, our jumping off point was an advance training base located on another of the Solomon Islands. We boarded the transports and got "squared away," "shook ourselves down," with as little confusion as is possible. Marines are past masters at this art.

We knew our destination, and yet tension among the troops was at a minimum. Most of us had already had battle experience. The Japs and their ways were known to us, but still we were eager for battle. We possessed our share of

Marine spirit—pure cockiness. We knew that we were good, but we had already learned that most heroes are dead heroes. We had no illusions of grandeur. We would whip the Japs but it would cost us, for we respected their ability.

These were the things that we weighed in our minds as we moved toward Bougainville. Our landing time was to be at dawn. Approximately two hours before that time the convoy was attacked by enemy torpedo planes. With one exception—ours—no ships were hit. It was a converted destroyer. The torpedo caught her aft, on the starboard side—in the fantail. The boilers went up almost immediately, followed by the explosions of the depth charges which we were carrying. It sounded like all hell had broken loose. Within a very short time, all that remained above the water was the bow. It was standing unnaturally high and protruding at a peculiar angle. Sailors and marines were hurriedly yet calmly helping the wounded over the side and then jumping or climbing into the oily water below. Personnel aft didn't have a chance. The oil on the water was catching fire and the ship was sinking rapidly, consequently there were anxious moments until we were all clear of the ship and the burning oil. Only two small rafts had been thrown clear of the ship. The wounded and those without life jackets were crowded onto these and shoved clear of the burning oil. With one booming, final explosion—probably more depth charges—she settled, with the flaming water closing over her.

Now followed two and one-half hours of floating aimlessly around, searching for comrades lost in the hurried departure from the ship, and waiting to be picked up. For the first time in months we were thankful that we were in the tropics. We were perfectly comfortable and mentally at ease; the thought of sharks didn't worry us. They seldom bother man. At daylight we were picked up by a destroyer. The rest of the convoy, which had been lucky enough to escape the misfortune which had befallen us, had been successful in their landing. We, who were uninjured, were set ashore—stark naked and more oily than the proverbial greased pig. Our less fortunate comrades were returned to a base in the rear.

We were definitely in a predicament. There we were—without clothes, weapons, or anything—almost on the front lines. With the customary Marine knack of getting the situation well in hand, however, we set about re-equipping ourselves. With a pair of shoes from one guy, trousers from another, shirt from still another and a weapon from a casualty, we had the bare necessities for battle. It was a far cry from our original neatly camouflaged uniform and tediously packed pack—with all of our toilet articles and the many little items which go to make living easier, under front line conditions. Yet we soon took our positions at the front, and were angry enough by this time to be more than anxious to get a crack at the Nips.

Admiral Halsey was entirely correct when he said that the terrain at Empress Augusta Bay was the worst yet encountered in this war. The jungles were extra dense and the swamps, which covered most of the area, were in many places simply impassable. With no Jap resistance, it would have been impossible for even light infantry troops to push forward more than a few hundred yards a day. Amphibious tractors were our only means of supply. Wading waist deep in water, scrambling over submerged logs, hacking through dense growths and bamboo, slapping at mosquitoes and having your clothes and skin ripped by "wait-a-minute" vines in itself isn't exactly a picnic. Add to all of this the necessity for keeping your weapon dry, the demoralizing uncertainty of sniper fire and your own physical weakness from dysentery and you'll know what we sometimes go through.

I probably sound as though I think we're going through more than should be expected of us. If I have, I've given you an erroneous impression. We are suffering a lot at times but we are consoled by the fact that we know that everyone is doing all in their power for us. We received our turkey, both on Thanksgiving and Christmas—right in the midst of the fighting on the front lines. It was a treat. And the Seabees—they're miracle men. In a remarkably short time they've transformed the jungles and swamps into roads and airfields. Their engineering marvels have transfigured the whole area. No more do we say— "Don't let the name Empress Augusta Bay fool you." Instead of the "hole" that it was, it is fast becoming a place as beautiful as its name seems to indicate.

The campaign has progressed very smoothly. Though it isn't over, we all feel that it has been a good job well done. The Japs still own most of the real estate and are willing to die to hold it—and so they will. They're completely cut off. We admire the Japs for their tenacious fighting spirit, but we despise them for their resemblance to human beings.

For fear that I've painted too terrible a picture of things out here I'll say again that I know we're not forgotten. We can all keep going as long as we know what we're fighting for is still back there. Our lives may mean less to us as we get further into this thing, but the lives of those around us become more and more dear. It balances us.

This has been a very impersonal letter so far, and since I've developed quite a case of writer's cramp from writing on my knee, I'll close. I hope that you've all had the merriest of holidays and I still hope to see you—sometime.

Love,
WALTER

Doan Helms, Jr., of Attica, enlisted in the Marine Corps Dec. 12, 1941, and served with the 3d Marine Division in New Zealand, Guadalcanal, and New Hebrides. He landed on Bougainville with the initial invasion and participated in three battles and numerous skirmishes. Returned to the United States after contracting a tropical disease in Samoa, Cpl. Helms was discharged Oct. 4, 1945, and returned to study at Indiana University.

December 19, 1943

DEAREST FOLKS:

It's very warm today, not a cloud in the sky. Seems more like the Fourth of July than the holiday season. I went to church this morning—quite a large crowd of sailors and Marines and Navy nurses. The Navy has built a large building which contains a library, post exchange, chapel, etc. It strikes me funny how they (the Navy) call this Mobile Hospital a "ship" (we're on dry land, of course, just an ordinary camp of barracks). Anyway, the sailors walk around with their "port and starboard" lingo, and we Marines have had more time at sea than ninety per cent of them. I've spent over two months at sea myself, and you wouldn't believe how many thousands of miles I've covered.

I wish I could tell you just why I'm hospitalized, but I can't. Many of us are here for the same thing, but reference to South Sea or tropical ailments reveals the location of particular places where they could have been contracted, so I guess that's the reason for the necessary noncommittance.

Action was, in some ways, just as I thought it would be, and in many other ways, quite the opposite. I thought I would be nervous during the hours prior to the day of attack. But I wasn't, nor were hardly any of the others in the outfit. That's what all these months in the tropics, under intensive training, have done for us. Our minds have become, should I say, "calloused?" We sat up half the night before "D-Day," and sang old songs, new songs, ribald, and religious. Then everyone hit the sack, slept like logs, and got up the next morning for a lousy breakfast. (Ordinarily this is a feast, sort of a "last meal" attitude and which it was for a lot of guys.)

Before going over the side, I counted eleven card games going on about the decks; guys hunched over in tight little groups, with their combat equipment on, heedless of what lay ahead and entirely interested in the cards in their hands. We landed under fire, as you probably know, and from then on one was quite busy with the perplexing little problem of trying his best to keep alive and prevent the Nip from doing likewise. We did a very artistic job of spreading his guts hither and thither about the landscape, and he in turn, by bombing and strafing and shelling and machine gunning and sniping and knifing, proved to us that he is very tough, very brave and very worthy of respect, as far as his fighting ability is concerned; but he just couldn't seem to pull enough of those qualities out of his bag of tricks to stop the boys from the U. S. When our officers finally managed to calm us down and talked a little sense into our heads, they convinced us that it would be advantageous to take a few prisoners (prior to then the only Nip worth while was a dead one—anybody who looked as though he might have a spark of life in him was "done over"). Anyway, the few prisoners, when assured that they really weren't going to meet their honorable ancestors, "talked," and it seems as though the U. S. Marine is a bogey man in their nightmares.

It's impossible to guess how any one individual will react when under fire. The guy you thought was tough folds up, and the green-acting kid turns out to be a one-man wave of destruction, and so forth. Here's an example of sheer courage: A young Marine attempted to throw a grenade into a Nip pillbox, where an Arisaka .31 machine gun was chattering away. His grenade struck a tree trunk and bounced back right in front of him. Five of his buddies were on either side. For anyone to attempt to run would have meant being mowed down by the Arisaka. He considered for a second, and dived squarely on top of the grenade and was blown to bits, exactly like the scene in the "Fighting 69th" movie, only this was the real McCoy. None of the other boys was injured. Another guy I know walked right into a Nip machine gun, it was so effectively camouflaged. He got a burst of about twenty rounds in the stomach and fell out of range. His buddy crawled to him, and started dragging him out. The Nips managed to get the machine gun jacked up into position and cut both Marines to bits. Three other fellows and myself buried them the next day right where they fell, with their helmets for markers. Both were Catholics, so one Marine who helped and was also a Catholic, said a few prayers, and that's all there was to it. Life is cheap down here, isn't it? Still, I heard over the radio last night where 350,000 railroad men intend to "strike." Things don't balance up. All over the world guys are digging through snow and ice and mud and volcanic soil with their little entrenching shovels and burying their buddies in shallow, hasty little graves, with just a helmet or canteen with his name scratched on it to mark the spot, and back home a politician dies from overeating and gets a $50,000 funeral. It's rather difficult to swallow.

I had a whole sack full of souvenirs—had a sniper's .25 rifle, ammunition belt, canteen, etc., but lost the whole works while being evacuated to the hospital. On top of that, they stripped me of my carbine, knives, ammunition, and everything, so I'm quite denuded. I still have a Nip shirt—that's about all.

The Nip is quite shrewd. He likes to sit up high and dry in the top of a huge banyan tree with a light Nambu machine gun and shoot while someone else is firing also. When things are quiet he'll sit there for hours. You can walk all around below and never know he's up there. But just let some machine gun in the distance open up, and ping, he's got you and no one knows where the shot came from. He straps himself in with an enormous leather harness, and seldom falls out, even when dead. Johnny Colihan and I put thirty slugs in one and he never fell—just flopped out in an upside down position and hung by his harness—ready for the buzzards.

I'd like to tell you about fear and how it hit me. I'd been under bombings, strafings, gunfire, etc., and could honestly say I was not actually scared—not in the ultimate sense of the word. Naturally I had the jitters plenty, but as for really experiencing what news correspondents call fear—I hadn't discovered that yet. It came all at once. The Nips opened up one day with heavy artillery. I wasn't even near a foxhole when I heard their 90 millimeter mortars and 75 millimeter field guns open up three or four miles away. First a dull "thunk," then came the shrill, unearthly, persistent whistle of the shell—like a police siren, in a way. Each shell sounded as though it was made especially for you, and all at once it contacted the earth and let go with a great big WHAM! and you bounded off the deck like a ping-pong ball. After about ten minutes of this, Old Man Fear began to creep into me, and into everyone else lying in the same area. A cold hand seemed to reach in and clasp me by the brain, squeezing out all sense of reason. All my training and ability of concentration left me. I was just one big lump of quivering flesh trying to burrow my way into the earth. Guys on either side were being blown to pieces and some would jump up and run about in circles yelling, "Stop the guns!" This was shellshock in its worst form. I wanted to get up and run, anything. I needed help, mental help, and I found it. I prayed. I don't even remember what I said. I just asked for help for the ability to get hold of myself, and I was answered. No, I didn't hear an ethereal voice, or feel a guiding hand on my shoulder; nothing fanatical, just calmness which settled over me, which permitted me to concentrate, and study the situation. I found that the enemy was firing at specific intervals with short lulls between. During a lull I lifted my head and looked for some sort of protection, and spotted a foxhole about twenty yards away. I made a dash and dived headlong on top of a dead Jap, but was safe nevertheless. Twice I prayed like that, and both times

I was answered. For the first time in my life I discovered genuine Divine help, and so did every single other Marine who got in a tight spot.

I wish I could be with you this Christmas. I'll miss not being home even more than last Christmas, but think how much luckier I am than the guys who will never be home again. When I compare myself to them I realize that when you have life alone, you have everything.

I guess I've overelaborated in this letter. Hope you receive it all. Have not gotten the packages yet, but will eventually, I'm sure. Don't worry about me, I'll be perfectly O.K. when I see you again.

All my love,
DOAN, JR.

Henry E. Wahl, of Bloomington, enlisted in the Navy Reserve on Jan. 19, 1942, as storekeeper 3/c and was commissioned an ensign Feb. 17, 1943. He participated in the battle of Treasury Island, Oct. 1943, as fighter director (Argus 6), and the battle of Admiralty Islands, March to June 1944, with Sopac liaison party. Promoted to lieutenant (j.g.) in 1944 and advanced to lieutenant in 1945, Wahl was discharged Nov. 30, 1947, and has returned to Bloomington where he is a salesman. The following excerpts were taken from letters to his wife.

January 13, 1944

... Last night I was again on the watch. A beautiful night. A lovely full moon in a cloudless sky. What a beautiful night! What a horrible night! The watch was strictly routine until a strange flight was picked up in an unusual location many miles away. I was on watch and considered it probably some of ours. The flight closed steadily. Repeated attempts at communication were fruitless. Finally I decided the time to act was at hand, and the sirens wailed. These tremendously bright tropical nights can also work as a disadvantage—the planes had enough visibility to fly in formation. Very soon the guns were in action and hell broke loose. With a chill I was told we were being hit by dive bombers! One of the types of raids I had always hoped to avoid. Naturally I'm breaking some rules of censorship; but I'm purposely keeping out any military matters.

Soon the crashing of bombs was heard through the tremendous din. Then a cheering report, an enemy shot down; but there were lots of them. After many trying minutes we were once more relaxed. Now for some sleep. The casualties: two killed, five injured. Suddenly another report of enemy aircraft, close! Again the din, the slamming, the roaring and we had some close ones. The men started nervously, sweat bands standing on their heads. Once again the utter relaxation from strong nervous strain. Five killed, five wounded.

Nine hours of nerve-wracking work, and the worst yet to come, the particulars of which I cannot divulge. But knowing bombers are diving and not a shot can be fired in defense. Dirt falls in our faces, our dugout groans and strains. Finally, all clear. Eight killed, twenty-five wounded. It was a rough night. Men are still missing, and various parts of anatomy are still being assembled for identification. Our worst raid.

The reactions of green men, their first duty under fire, were interesting. They did a commendable job, though one got sick from nervousness. And so after thirteen hours, I dragged my weary bones to my bunk. The moon is full tonight. Ho hum. It's all part of the game. But it's bloody, and rough.

January 18

A little self-analysis proves interesting at times. First, all of us are a bit highstrung. With the sound of a motor at night everyone tenses, grabs his helmet and gets set to run. We always expect to be bombed or strafed. It gives one a sad, weeping feeling when I can see in other faces what surely must reflect in mine. How long will it take us to revert to normal? It all hangs over us day and night. Sudden noises, people yelling. I start—why the noise, didn't the sirens work? It's a reflex.

When night comes there is the sensation, I suppose, of a wild animal. Make it coal-black dark. The eyes and ears become alert, searching. When we go to bed shoes and helmet are near so we can dive into them and be gone. The feeling of the hunted, I assume. Now, assuming the Japs are human—or a reasonable facsimile—I wonder how they react and feel. For they really catch the stuff. It all adds up to this desire to be where it's so very quiet, away from everything.

We have a phrase "sweating it out." When I get back I'll tell you what that is. If anything is taken from my life that phrase represents the reason. The responsibility that sometimes arises is shocking, not only in our case, but in others. I saw an officer give an order which resulted in a nerve-wracking ordeal. We were bombed, and the situation was such that we were not able, for reasons not to be divulged, to raise a literal finger of defense. To hear a plane wind up in a howling crescendo! Now this may sound pretty rough. Strange, it doesn't affect us so much. Only when the mood hits us; when things have gone pretty badly "upstairs." The fellows come in, silently pack gear to be sent back to the States. Never a word, walking in a daze. Truly war is for the souls who bounce back quickly. But never fear, I can take it. Just don't like to.

January 23

. . . I've been quite interested in the results on people as a whole of their reactions to a couple of heavy bombings. It certainly brings everyone right smack dab into the war. McGarry lost a great deal of his arrogance and has become rather subdued. Just let a plane be overhead and right away helmets are put in the open, lights go out and everyone gets set. Last night some damned fool dove on our camp. I don't know who he was or what he had in mind, but the results were comical in this tent. We heard him wind up. McPherson and Osborne left so fast that only a slight movement of the tent flaps proved they were inside in the first place. I took time out to turn out the lights, and went out the back way and on to my belly. I figure running is the worst thing possible. In a matter of a very few seconds one would have thought the spot was deserted. I couldn't resist seeing the humor of the situation. Did you ever see a bunch of little pigs startled? Some fall flat, others scoot like a streak for twenty feet and skid to a freezing stop. Others hightail it till a physical obstruction halts them. That's just what we did! I fell flat. Ossie hit for the foxhole, and Bill went about halfway from anywhere and came to a full stop. People must think me queer when I get tickled over such things. Perhaps I am; but I still contend it was funny.

Nothing much ever happened while we shock troops were holding this island. But when the gold braid came in and they take a plastering, well—things are going to be changed! The island is not properly defended, this should . . . that should not. Sure, and I'll tell even a general, things are not such and so! But surely people in command down the line knew our limitations and capacities. Why didn't they send up whatever was needed? Of course that question is better left unanswered. But I'll give you the answer. (Not you, general; I mean my wife.) Initial landings are strictly up to the parties involved. Either we do or don't. But when the "precious ones" move in they expect to find a fortress, and can't figure out why we didn't build it from our combat packs. These Army boys are plenty defense-minded. And jittery as all heck. Makes me feel pretty seasoned.

Charles D. Putnam, Jr., of New Haven, was inducted into the Army Sept. 28, 1942. He was sent to the Pacific theater in Jan. 1943 and was attached to the 37th Division, 6th Army. Pvt. Putnam received the Purple Heart for wounds he sustained and was returned to the United States and discharged in Dec. 1945. He is now a tank wagon driver in New Haven.

May 21, 1944
South Pacific

DEAR MOTHER AND DAD:

Hello there. How are you by this time? All right, I hope. I received two letters from you this week. On May 17th I got one written May 4th and on the 18th I got one written April 20th. That's the way the mail has been coming ever since we landed here. I'm glad to get letters, though, however mixed up they come. This has been a pretty rough week. At least the first half of it was. Monday morning we got up early and went up past the front lines as far as they have a road built and there we each got a case of C-rations. Strapped them on a pack-board and started out to carry them up to an outpost in the mountains. It was a pretty rough grind getting up there as it had rained Sunday and everything was mud. The trail followed a river which cuts the only pass between the ranges of mountains. These jungle trails are just wide enough for a man to walk in a lot of places. Then there are roots, logs, fallen trees, etc., across it, which makes it a super obstacle course. Up steep rises and down. Some places were so steep we had to dig footholds in the roots and rocks to get up. We carried these forty-pound cases of rations up over about seven miles of that. We crossed that river 16 times on the trip up and back. It was swift but not deep. In places it was a little over waist high. It was just as clear as glass and cool and very refreshing. The mountains reared up high on each side and they were covered with dense jungle which made it very scenic. It sort of reminded me of the Smokies in Tennessee. All we carried back was our pack boards. I was so tired I was about to drop. My feet were sore from walking over those stones with everything wet that I had on and I was miserable. We all griped around and thought it was terrible that we had to do that. Tuesday they didn't get much out of anyone. Everyone was so tired they just wouldn't work. I fooled around, carried a little dirt and filled in a few low spots on the ball diamond. In the afternoon we went out in an altogether different direction. Followed the beach up a long way by truck and then we went in the jungle quite a ways. Followed another river and established an observation post where we could observe our fire on a target which we were to fire our howitzers on for practice. I found eight Jap hand grenades while I was up there. I didn't even bother to carry them back, although I wish I had for we can take any kind of souvenirs like that down here to the C.B.'s and trade for a lot of things, such as light bulbs, or plastic glass which the boys make link bracelets and watch bands, etc., out of. Light bulbs are very hard to get. We were without a light in our tent for several nights because we couldn't get a bulb.

Well I was sure tired again that night. I soaked my feet in hot water each night and that helped a lot. On Wednesday we had to carry another load of rations up to that outpost. It didn't seem far at all going up as compared to what it seemed the first trip. We got along in better time. We had more breaks and didn't walk as fast but made better time. It hadn't rained since Monday afternoon and the trail wasn't nearly as muddy. We got up there about 11 o'clock. The patrol that had gone out that morning from the outpost ran into some trouble and we had to wait until about 1 o'clock till they carried back a few wounded from where they had the trouble. We carried them back from the outpost then. I had thought Monday's trip rough but it wasn't anything compared to Wednesday's trip back. The trail was too narrow to carry a stretcher on, so we had to follow the river all the way. It was sure a rocky trip back but we were glad to do it. There's something about carrying a wounded man that makes you overlook the work part of it. There were six of us on each stretcher at a time. The fellow that I helped with was a lieutenant who weighed 215 pounds. He was certainly grateful to us. He said many times that he would sure owe a lot to a lot of people when he got back. He had been doped up just enough that he was in good humor in spite of his wounds. We called him "Shavetail" to his face and kidded and joked with him all the way. We could only carry him about 50 to 100 yards most of the time without putting him down to rest. I don't believe the others talked so much and weren't in as good spirits. We got back to the end of the road and loaded them in an ambulance about six o'clock. We ate supper and I soaked my feet and lay down to rest for a few minutes. I had my clothes all on and no net over me, but I felt much better. I undressed and went back and slept for a couple of hours until breakfast. That Wednesday was quite an experience. We were very lucky in coming back. We had to travel right out in that open river bed and we'd have been easy picking for a Jap patrol on the slopes above. We had a chaplain along for which I was glad. They say that the chaplains don't carry any weapons. This one did. He has learned that the Japs have no more respect for a chaplain than they have for anyone else. While we were up there Monday, one of the boys got so tired that he wouldn't carry his .45 back, so I bought it from him. They are not issued but the boys have gotten hold of a few and they are very nice for patrols and things that way. I imagine it will come in handy in a foxhole on many a night before I get home, although I hope I never have occasion to use it.

You may be surprised to receive a letter like this. I hope I can write many more like it. They relaxed the censorship regulations to a great extent last Thursday. There are a lot of things we're not permitted to say yet, but they're relaxed enough that a fellow can write a halfway decent letter now. It was a problem before. I nearly tore the few hairs I have left out every time I sat down to write. It was a problem when you couldn't write anything at all except, "Hello, I'm fine, Goodbye." It helps a fellow's morale when he can say a little about what he thinks would be interesting to you.

Thursday morning we went out on sort of a jungle combat range. It was a very good course. I wish we'd have gone through it before we went up to run the outpost the week I was up there. We were out there a week. It's near the beach and this river where we established the O.P. the other day. We went out on patrols every day we were up there. It's the outpost on this very left end of our sector. We didn't see any indications of enemy activity during the week we were up there. Saw a lot of dead Japs and their equipment. We're getting a lot of this sort of training. I guess the colonel wants us to get all the experience we can. We were sort of rookies of this division. We were pretty green when we landed here. During the big counterattack they had a while back, we got a few Japs right down here in our area and we had a very hot night here one night. They opened up on one of our lieutenants and the bullets just hit the dirt about six inches apart behind him as he ran for cover. We were up for several days with almost no rest. We did our share of firing and I guess we got our share of the Japs on this island. We fired harassing fire almost every night during the attack. It was quite an experience, especially the night they came into our area. We knew they were right at the edge of the clearing and we had to get out there and fire our howitzers. We had brought Fijians in and they went in and ran them out. They had machine guns and everything. Those boys from Fiji are professional soldiers. They may be black and natives but they sure have my respect. They go in the jungle barefooted and if there are any Japs in there they will get them or drive them out. They claim they can smell a Jap. They are big, husky-looking fellows who are all man. We had to go out on a patrol while those Japs were out there and those Fijians were out there too. Well, we got on the wrong side of the river and the Fijians had orders to kill any white person there. They ran onto us. I thought I heard something and I got up out of the weeds and looked around but couldn't see a thing. I took a drink from my canteen while still standing on my knees. They had been stalking us for an hour and had a bunch of us surrounded. They had five British tommy guns trained on us. Well, my light hair and that American canteen were all that saved us. That is the only time that I have ever been thankful for my light hair. It sure saved many of us that time. I'd say these Fijians are the best soldiers the Allies have. I guess Fiji is the nicest South Pacific island. They say it is just like the stories you read about the South Sea Islands. They say they have the beautiful native girls there and the palm trees and a beautiful sea. It is more civilized and built up than the other islands. This island would be very nice if it were cleared and a few cities built on it. The climate isn't bad at all. It is a lot better than Guadalcanal where we landed after we left New Caledonia. We weren't there but a few days and I'm sure the place we have here is a lot nicer than we'd have ever been able to make it down there. The mosquitoes are terrible down there. There are a few of them here but they hold down malaria pretty well. There have only been a few cases on this island. They give us Atabrine to keep us from getting it, and we sleep under nets at night and that helps a lot.

It is getting late so I will close. Say hello to everyone and write when you can.

Your loving son,
CHARLIE

John H. Compton, of Indianapolis, was inducted into the Army in April 1942 and was assigned to the medical corps as a 1st lieutenant. He was promoted a captain in 1943 and was sent to New Guinea with the 29th Medical Depot Company in March 1944. In 1945 Capt. Compton was transferred to Manila and then sent to Japan. He was discharged in January 1946 and returned to work in a pharmaceutical firm at Indianapolis.

July 3, 1944
New Guinea

DEAR MR. BROWN:

When you got me into this war did you realize I might get shot? I just found that out the other day. Three officers, including myself and a platoon of men, were sent up to establish a medical depot at a new base. I am now the commanding officer of the Medical Depot at Base G. The only catch is the Japs haven't all left yet and they are taking pot shots at the men here. The Japs are up in the hills and come out at night looking for food and a few throats to cut. When we first set up our area here, we put up our tent about 200 yards from the men. For three nights I didn't sleep any. We have two armed guards on all night and every time they went by the tent I knew it was a Jap sneaking up on me. All I have for protection is a hunting knife and a machete and I had those two weapons close by.

None of our men ever had guns before. I had most of them issued carbines, so every night after work they try a little shooting. It sounds like a small scale war going on. If a Jap ever comes in this area I'm going to hide in a foxhole. This trigger-happy bunch would shoot at anything or anybody.

We are a depot platoon but have no depot yet. I found out after we got here we were supposed to build our own depot. A major and a lieutenant from the engineers came out and in a brief time explained how to build the warehouses, then left a sergeant and a few men here to supervise and we are doing the rest. In another week I'll be a construction engineer. I can almost run a survey line now.

We didn't bring any vehicles with us and all we've got for transportation here is a broken-down small truck. You have to park it on a hill to get it started by running it downhill. Our area is on the side of a hill or small rut. It rained hard the other night and we almost got washed down the hill. We had a small trench around the tent but that just slowed up the water for a while.

A lot of Jap medical supplies were captured here and some of their microscopes and other equipment are really something to see. We are being issued Jap cigarettes and if I smoke many more I'll have T.B.

The Japs have the right idea about war and how to carry it on. There were quite a number of Geisha girls captured here. Bringing your girls right along with you is a great idea. I saw some of the gals in the stockade and can't say much for them.

We have one celebrity here. Lew Ayres is the chaplain's assistant in a hospital not far from us. I saw him the other day and he doesn't look much like the Lew Ayres from pictures.

This being C.O. in an outfit just getting started is a pain in the neck. I don't know anything about army regulations or rules and nobody in the outfit seems to. I sure am learning the hard way. I'll end up by being court-martialed yet.

At the other place, it was snakes that bothered us; here it is spiders. I saw one today that was big enough to saddle and ride. He could bite off your arm and not half try.

As this place gets bigger we won't be able to handle it and I guess we never will go back to the other outfit—just keep going on ahead. This is too damned close right now for me. So far there have been no air raids but they claim there are about 70,000 Japs back in the hills starving to death. I hope they go ahead and starve and don't come down here.

The climate here isn't bad. It is hot in the daytime but it cools off at night and you need a blanket. Army cots aren't quite long enough for me. By the time I get back and we all have dinner together I'll be so used to eating out of a mess kit, I'll just bring it along. You can sure pile a lot of food in one of them. We are eating pretty good. We aren't busy so we have four cooks and a mess sergeant. All the mess sergeant does is scare up food. So far he is doing a good job.

Must stop and try to figure out some army regulations in regard to reports.

Your brave and fighting C.O.
JOHN

P. S.—Washington was never like this.

Clifford R. Leap, of Speed, enlisted in the Navy April 10, 1943, and was commissioned a lieutenant (j.g.) in the Civil Engineering Corps (Seabees). Leaving the United States in March 1944, he served as assistant construction officer with the 24th and 12th Naval Construction Regiment and as 105th Naval Construction Battalion Engineer Officer and company commander. He was stationed at Milne Bay, New Guinea. Lieutenant Leap was discharged Feb. 16, 1946, returned to Speed and is a civil engineer. He is also commanding officer of Volunteer CB Unit 9-64 at Louisville, Ky.

[Sept. 1944]
New Guinea

DEAR MR. DORSEY:

I am still fighting the battle of mud and rain in New Guinea. I've been kept pretty busy; but after all I guess I could do a lot more if I had to, as the fellows at the front are doing. Last night I saw a picture at the main theater ("Guadalcanal Diary") that made me realize how little we are actually doing in comparison to others.

This base sure has changed a lot since I arrived here some six months ago. We are almost civilized now. As the commander said yesterday, "We are roughing it out here now, with modern plumbing (not quite a true statement) and electric lights." The roads are beginning to look less like hog pens or swamps and the buildings are chasing the jungle back all the time. No! We haven't gotten traffic lights as yet; but anything can happen here.

There is little I can tell about our work out here so a lot of this letter will be repetition of things I've written to others, so I hope I won't tire you too greatly.

The base now has seven outdoor theaters (so we have quite a choice of pictures provided you have transportation to get to them) and seven chapels. For some reason the chapels do not have as great a seating capacity as do the outdoor theaters, two of which each have a seating capacity of 1,800. However, our church attendance has been excellent. In one three-week series of meetings at our main chapel there were 85 consecrations, 215 rededications and 85 baptisms. Sunday we had our eighth successive Sunday afternoon baptism service at the foot of the mountain in a clear, cold and swift little mountain stream. The pool is just below some rapids. With the green jungle closing in on both sides, and almost closing in overhead also, with the sparkling water flowing over and between the big boulders lining the banks of the little stream, it makes a beautiful Temple of God for such a service. War and battle seemed far remote. There were eight sailors baptized last Sunday and it was an inspiring sight, seeing those fine young men accepting Christ. God surely had been working in our midst out here. You may notice I said the mountain stream looked cold. You see, Jesse, I am not a very good Baptist. In fact I've taken my raincoat with me to all of the baptism services except the last two and haven't needed it on any of these occasions. That's certainly unusual for New Guinea. So we too, like California, have unusual weather only in the reverse order. Well, anyway it isn't all rain, even if it is almost all the time.

I have a new jeep all my own to run around in. I've had it about six weeks and have put about 1,500 miles on it. Some of my traveling has to be by motor launch. There is, however, one very pretty jungle road you would enjoy. There are eleven mountain streams to ford, and at some places the road has been cut out of the sides of the mountain with pull-in spots for passing. The steep slope of the mountain is on one side of the car and down below on the other side is the sea. One could almost spit into the jungle on one side or into the bay on the other side without getting out of the car. Poinsettias grow wild on bushes and make a very pretty picture. The red leaves of the poinsettias against the background of the blue-green sea and the purple mountains in the distance across the bay (quite a distance) all framed with tall slender palm trees and the green jungle. That, with an occasional beautiful sunrise or sunset, is the beautiful side of New Guinea. There is, of course, another picture which includes mud, rain, land crabs (which look pretty wicked, but are harmless; I killed one with my bath slipper last night on the floor of our hut), bats (one was killed the other day that measured six feet wing spread and had a body the size of a fox terrier; a fellow took a picture of it and I have hopes of getting a print of the picture), flying squirrels, wild boar (saw three of them on the jungle road one day), rats (caught three or four rats in our hut last week), snakes of all kinds (I don't like snakes; one killed in one of our tents last week was four feet long, slender, about as big around as your thumb and green all over; the medical department classified it as deadly poison, but could not name it), sharks (don't think I like them either; there is no swimming in the bay because of these sharks), and an occasional mosquito. The malaria control boys do a good job. They have a very difficult job (with all the jungle and swamps to contend with) and a thankless tiresome job at that.

The food is excellent and the nights cool enough to sleep well. Getting back to the thought of food I might say I haven't as yet acquired a taste for such things as dehydrated potatoes and eggs. I am old-fashioned. I like my eggs to come with the shell on and my potatoes not to look and taste like the kitchen floor had been scrubbed with them before serving (they are very dark, almost black in color and I don't mean the skins). The fellow or company that developed dehydrated food should be shot as a saboteur for wasting so much food. Nobody eats them if they can help it and I honestly think about 90 percent of it is wasted. It also does unpleasant things to our temperament.

I have attempted to paint you a picture of both sides of life out here and, as is the case here as well as in the States, one sees whatever he looks for. So it's better to look and think about the pretty side.

Too many of us are living today by looking back and not forward. Someone has said, "I hear so many boys say I am living or looking forward to going back home" (well and good if not carried too far), but it's better rather to look forward towards living today so that when we go back home we will be better qualified to enjoy our homes. I pray that our leaders may look to God for guidance at the peace table that we may truly win the peace as well as the war. Surely God in all His wisdom made the world big enough for all of His children. We only have to learn how to live together. Well, now that I've preached a sermon I'll stop.

Your friend,
CLIFFORD

Kenneth N. Rider, Jr., of Franklin, enlisted June 30, 1942, in the Army Air Corps and was called for training in Jan. 1943. Receiving his wings in Waco, Tex., Nov. 1943, and after training further, Lt. Rider flew to Australia in June 1944. He served with the 307th Group, 424th Squadron, of the 13th A.A.F., known as MacArthur's Long Rangers. Lt. Rider was killed on his ninth mission over Balikpapan, Borneo, Oct. 3, 1944. He received the Purple Heart posthumously. The following excerpts were taken from letters to his wife.

August 7, 1944
Admiralty Islands

. . . I have to close now as tomorrow is the big day. Brady all dressed up in his flak suit (armor to cover the front of his body from flak), flak helmet, .45, canteen, etc., goes out on his first strike. Even though it's not a real "hot" target I am thrilled, scared, full of wonderment, and oh, a lot of things. Here's hoping we really paste them.

August 9

Well, my first strike is over . . . forty-nine more to go. It was a lot of fun and I learned a lot. I rode with one of the old crews as co-pilot. The pilot was from Idaho and really a swell fellow. They all were and did everything they could for me. Still, all in all, I would just as soon have had my own crew with me. I just don't feel like I am at home without all the fellows. The target wasn't hot at all, had a free ride. I will admit that I tightened up a little on the run. My arms felt tremendously large sticking out of that flak suit. Here's hoping we can get through the rest as easily as that one. . . . We went over to the quartermaster's to buy some more clothes today. Every time we move with A.T.C. [Air Transport Command] we have to throw away about half our stuff. First time I have ever seen native women, and I hope the last. Gad, what a sight!

August 30

Strike three now and not a very particularly eventful trip. We did have one exciting two or three minutes when we went through a thunderhead. Honestly, that B-24 jumped around like a piece of paper in the wind. Japs, O.K. Thunderheads, well, I hope that is the last one (but it won't be).

Our food here is getting quite lowdown. We have had canned Vienna sausages every evening for the last three nights. For a break in our diet we will probably have some canned bully beef. It's a shame how they waste the cans on some of this stuff. Oh, well, we do have lots of vitamin pills. Over here one's whole life comes down to two points; first, getting home and hearing from home while you are away; and secondly, killing, destroying, harassing, hounding, burning, doing all in your power to wipe out the Japanese army, navy, their entire empire if that is necessary. . . .

August 31

At the present moment the formation is taking off on course and really looks swell. The B-24 is a beautiful ship in the air, isn't it? Man, there's nothing more comforting over the target than to look into the cockpit of the lead ship and see some more Americans, watch those turrets track around the sky. Sibley gives out with "Bombs away," and then the usual "Let's get the hell out of here." And get we do. I guess there is little glamour left. When we came in yesterday we really had a tight formation and I don't mean maybe. The squadron C.O. was in the leadship and had a grin from ear to ear.

Every fellow on the crew is really swell and they all behave like veterans. My only hope is that I can always do my job as well as they do. You can always know that I'm putting every effort in it and trying my very best, which is all anyone can ask.

As far as the crew goes, we got along swell on our first strike. I envy Lindsey and Salmon more than anyone else. Being in the Sperry ball and tail respectively they can see those bombs hit and everything else on the ground. Leon and I can't see a darned thing from our position. Lindsey says that maybe we are lucky in not seeing too much.

Vernon Clayton Buchanan, of Indianapolis, enlisted in the Army Air Corps on Feb. 9, 1943. Upon graduating from bombardier school he was commissioned 2d lieutenant and left the United States July 28, 1944. He saw action in New Guinea, the Netherlands East Indies, and the Philippines, where he was killed in action over Angeles, Central Luzon, on Jan. 9, 1945 while giving air support to the Lingayen Gulf invasion. He was awarded the Bronze Star, the Purple Heart when wounded Nov. 11, 1944, an Oak Leaf cluster to the Purple Heart, and the Air Medal, the last two posthumously.

[1944]
Somewhere in the South Pacific

DEAR MOTHER AND DAD:

This is a letter that I hope need never be delivered, for that would mean that I am considered missing or killed in action.

I need not tell you how I feel about you. I realize now that I could have done much more for you and proved myself a good son. As it is, I hope that you don't feel that these years you have spent in raising me have been wasted.

I want to thank you for your love, your cares, the life and opportunities you have given me. I am sorry that now I will no longer be able to justify your belief in me. I may as well tell you now what I had planned had I come through this conflict whole. I would have returned to the States and asked Virginia—I have told her this in a similar letter—to become engaged to me. I am just conceited enough to imagine that there was a chance that she might say "yes." Next, to finish college and find a decent job. Settled, next would come marriage and, I hope, two children at least, a boy and a girl . . . just like their mother. Those were my plans and dreams.

Please don't think that you have lost everything in losing your son. Remember, I volunteered for this and knew what it might lead to. I have spent some of my happiest moments in the A.A.F. I feel I have done something to be proud of, something perhaps that will aid America to remain "the land of the free, the home of the brave." If my death helps end this war one minute sooner, I consider it worthwhile.

Millions all over the world are fighting for what they believe in and for those they love, and thousands are dying. It is not in vain!

I hope you will continue to love Virginia. Help her if you can; she may need your sympathy as you may need hers. I have told Virginia that I hope that she can find someone she can love as much as I love her. Please believe me, I mean it. I want her to be happy.

Mother and Dad, thanks for everything.

Frances, keep up the good work. And be an individualist if you desire. A person's choice is his right.

Alyce, I think that if you really want it, you can become one of Indiana's best doctors. Or if you should choose to follow another field, I'm sure you will succeed.

Jeane, think that you can make something of yourself if you concentrate. Try, try! And don't mind criticism.

Loretta, you know yourself. You are really sharp and can do anything you set your heart on. You have initiative. Your poetry is good, too.

Rosemary, you follow Lorry. You are the good, dependable type upon which our country is based. I predict that you will make some man an excellent and loving wife.

Dorothy, you mischievous scamp. You are just naturally cheerful. Always try to be.

I know that this will be a painful subject—my money and assets. Use them as you see fit. You know better what you need than I do. Some may go to give my sisters an education—as much as they want. I believe that my bank account, with interest accumulated, would be sufficient to send Alyce through medical school, if she wants. Please feel free to use it in your own way.

That's about all, folks. Don't feel too bad. As Tennyson says, "'Tis better to have loved and lost than never to have loved at all." Keep your chin up.

Goodbye. I love you with every ounce of me.

Take care of yourselves.

Eternally your son,
VERNON

Stanley N. Brothers, of Clay City, was inducted Nov. 23, 1943, into the Army and was assigned as instructor in the air corps at Seymour Johnson Field, Goldsboro, N. C. In the spring of 1944 he was transferred to Keesler Field, Miss., as an instructor in the air corps, and in Nov. Pvt. Brothers was assigned to the 83d Mobile Training Unit in Denver. On Dec. 21, 1944, he was transferred to the 3716th A.A.F. Base Unit, North American Aviation Corp. in Englewood, Calif. In Jan. 1945 Pfc. Brothers arrived in Hawaii and subsequently participated in the air offensives of the Bismarck Archipelago, China, Luzon, Southern Philippine liberation, the Ryukyus, and Japan, earning the Asiatic-Pacific theater ribbon with six battle stars and the Philippine Liberation ribbon with one star. While overseas Brothers was attached to the 342d Fighter Group, the 348th Fighter Group, and headquarters of the 35th Fighter Group. Discharged Oct. 11, 1945, as a corporal, Brothers took a teaching position in the public schools of Terre Haute.

Feb. 26, 1945
Somewhere in New Guinea

DEAR MR. STORM:

Somewhere in New Guinea there is an outpost; a base where pilots and air crews are taking their last training and last bit of instruction before moving up. They move up there where life is more exciting and its price goes down by the shillings.

We have our school and headquarters close by the line and I can throw a stone into the jungle from the door, causing a greater disturbance than we used to throw after winning a tourney.

These fellows are very young and every morning you wonder if all the faces you looked into the day before will be present tomorrow. I might add that several mornings the roll has not been complete, because someone tangled with the sea, river, or peaks. Sometimes a cross wind on the strip causes him to miscalculate and it is the last breeze he will feel against his face. Inexperience on a run causes them to come in too close and they are knocked out by Jap dynamite set off from the tree tops. The white crosses beyond my tent describe it better than I can here.

This is a move-up place. This is where it begins and by the sight of the scrap heaps a large portion of it also ends. This morning on the way to my class I saw five Jap prisoners and to see them makes your blood boil, as you realize but for them you could be home enjoying life and going ahead with your plans.

This evening a few fellows that I have learned to know very well invited me over to a party. We slipped into the mess hall, or "'Tomaine Tavern," and slipped out coffee, cream, sugar, Spam and bread; which we cooked over a helmet filled with 100-octane gas, no stamps needed. While we were gathered around the fire a few natives came through the area on their way to a village down the river to attend a native festival. They were painted up and dressed in feathers that reminded you of the women back in the States; which is also a probable hangover from barbarism. These natives had with them an oversupply of jungle juice, which is brewed from anything you can imagine—berries, garbage, and river water. A pint of it will make you go elephant hunting with switches. One of the fellows who has been over two years and who is handy at trading with the natives bargained for a liberal amount and then the evening proceeded with the air of an American Legion convention. Before long Red, who owns three native drums that he intends to send home, had these natives in action about our fire. It was a sight to see and one I'll never forget as I watched them leap and prance. They chanted various songs, or better, just noise; with their feathers and grass skirts swaying in the breeze. By the time this ended the fellows were feeling their jungle juice and the community sing began, with all the old familiar songs that everyone knows.

Van, a long-legged Texan, who is a graduate of Texas A. & M., and who used to sing there in a glee club stole the show; full of jungle juice and on his knees in the center of the ring and with a nice tenor, he sang "On The Road To Mandalay," until actual tears dripped from the fellows' eyes. Mine were full and my heart heavy, as I pictured my wife sitting at her piano and playing the same song as she has so many times. Then you think that just a little way across a sea there is a land where the dawn comes up like thunder, and you realize that before long you will fly there and carry on.

We are about ready to take off again; where I cannot tell you. One thing sure we are leaving behind a swell outfit of men; young men, gray of hair and with deep lines running over a young face. It is always like this, leaving them and going on to more men in a like predicament; all with the one thought, how to get home again.

Yesterday four of us took a forty-five mile ride down a river to the sea; never have I seen jungles so thick or been on a river with worse rapids. We passed two native villages and the natives lined the banks by the hundreds; some of the children swam out in the river to touch and look over our raft, that I lifted from a cracked-up plane. We saw many strange birds, also white parrots with orange topknots. It was a real trip and we got many pictures that will be interesting to look at, after the carnage is over. This is about all I can think of and I whipped this up in a hurry; there is much more here that should be said.

Yours truly,
STANLEY

→ XI ←

CENTRAL PACIFIC
AND THE PHILIPPINES

THE American drive across the Central Pacific to Japan started in the Gilbert Islands in Nov. 1943 and extended by the summer of 1944 through the Marshalls to the Marianas, within range of Japan itself. Saipan was taken, Guam was recaptured, and the Palau group invaded, thus clearing the way for the invasion of the Philippines. United States troops under Gen. MacArthur landed on Leyte Oct. 17, 1944, and the United States Navy delivered a decisive defeat to the Japanese fleet in the Second Battle of the Philippine Sea. With the occupation of Mindoro, the American forces swept down on Luzon, where resistance was surprisingly light, and Manila was entered Feb. 6, 1945. Gen. MacArthur restored civil government in the Philippines on Feb. 27.

A sketch of the late William R. Evans, Jr., will be found on page 8.

April 1942
U.S.S. "Hornet"

DEAR FRIEND:

You will pardon, I hope, the presumption which allows me to write thusly after a silence of so many months. Or is it years? By this time I have learned that no matter how others may, for the sake of convenience, reckon the length and breadth of this world, its true unit of measurement is in terms of happy memories, and although censorship prohibits much that I should like to say, allow me, by right of those bright memories of your gracious hospitality, to wish you one and all a bounty of health and good cheer.

The fates have been kind to me. In a war where any semblance of pleasure is, to say the least, bad taste, I find many that would please you. When you hear others saying harsh things about American youth, know how wrong they all are. So many times now that it has become commonplace, I've seen incidents that make me know that we were not soft nor bitter; perhaps stupid at first, but never weak. The boys who brought nothing but contempt and indifference to college, who showed an apparent lack of responsibility, carry now the load with a pride no Spartan ever bettered.

Many of my friends are now dead. To a man, each died with a nonchalance that each would have denied was courage. They simply called it lack of fear, and forgot the triumph. If anything great or good is born of this war, it should not be valued in the colonies we may win nor in the pages historians will attempt to write, but rather in the youth of our country, who never trained for war, rather almost who never believed in war, but who have, from some hidden source, brought forth a gallantry which is homespun it is so real.

I say these things because I know you liked and understood boys, because I wanted you to know that they have not let you down. That out here, between a spaceless sea and sky, American youth has found itself and given itself so that at home the spark may catch, burst into flame and burn high. If the country takes these sacrifices with indifference, it will be the cruelest ingratitude the world has ever known.

There is much that I cannot say, which should be said before it is too late. It is my fear that national inertia will cancel the gains won at such a price. You will, I know, do all in your power to help others keep faith—as I know you do—with these few who gave so much.

It was not my intention to wax patriotic or poetic; I hope you will see the sincerity intended. Remembering the countless, happy hours spent with all of you has been a constant source of contentment. Thoughts of Connecticut laurel are perhaps incongruous as I become accustomed to the business of death, but they serve as a balance wheel.

My luck can't last much longer, but the flame goes on and on—that is important. Please give all my best wishes to all of the family, and may all you do find favor in God's grace.

BILL

John H. Horton, of Clay City, was inducted into the Army Sept. 2, 1942, and was assigned to the infantry. Going overseas in April 1943, T/5 Horton was attached to the 48th Field Artillery Battalion, 7th Infantry Division, 10th Army, participating in the engagements of the Asiatic-Pacific theater. Awarded the Philippine Liberation ribbon and six bronze stars, T/4 Horton was discharged Nov. 27, 1945, and is now employed in Indianapolis.

New Year's Eve, 1943
Hawaiian Isles

DEAR MR. STORM:

Your Christmas greeting found me in good health and spirits.

I know the majority of the folks back home are sacrificing luxuries for us and are working hard and buying bonds to end this war. The thing that makes us boys over here both sad and angry are those selfish cowardly quitters that dare call themselves Americans and then go on strike in essential industries such as coal mines, steel mills, and railroads. We want to get this war won and come home and the sooner our weapons reach us the sooner we will win. We often hear and read, "Put labor leaders [censored] and all other strikers in the army." That makes us mad. A striker in a vital industry today is a traitor. He is not a good American. I wouldn't, and I know a lot of other soldiers wouldn't, want a quitter in my outfit. He would be a liability, not an asset. We hope the only way we will see the word "strike" used in a newspaper is when we strike *at* the enemy and not *for* them.

I feel better now that I have this off my chest.

Yours very sincerely,
JOHN

John A. McNeal, of Tipton, enlisted in the Seabees on Nov. 27, 1942, as storekeeper 2/c. In 1944 he participated in the invasion of the Marshall Islands with the 109th Seabees, for which action he received a battle star when he was injured in the bombing on Roi-Namur Islands, Feb. 12, 1944. He received the rank of disbursing storekeeper 1/c in June. Discharged Jan. 11, 1946, McNeal is now a field examiner for the Indiana State Board of Accounts.

1944

Marshall Islands

An LST is a boat, long, not so wide, which pushes up to the beach, lets down the front end so equipment can be driven out onto the beach. You have probably seen pictures of them. Living quarters are on the side between the part where the equipment is stored and the hull of the ship. The deck is also covered with equipment, loaded by an elevator. The LST's are notorious for their rough riding. As we pulled out of Pearl Harbor into the ocean it rolled so violently it seemed it would roll completely over.

Attached to the sides were pontoons weighing 70 tons, so we were told. They were to be used as a bridge in event we could not reach the shore. As the ship rolled the pontoons would come down on the water or waves with a resounding smack. Water would shoot up several feet between the sections of the pontoons and the wind would carry it across the deck, drenching everyone. To release the pontoons the ship was to be listed 15 degrees and then they would be cut loose.

Since there were bunks for only half of us, the rest slept on deck in hammocks, slung under gun turrets and from the railing to anything else they could be tied to, such as equipment on the deck. We also slept in trucks, on trucks and under trucks. Some slept down among the heavy equipment in the hold. We also ate on deck wherever we could find a place. I felt elated as we were out of sight of land and in spite of the rolling I was not seasick as several others were. We had been one of the last to leave the harbor and as we joined the other ships waiting outside we proceeded on our way about 1600. As the fellows ate I decided I had better get something, probably something light. I ate two or three bites and gave it up. I was really sick that night and reverted to form. I also had to sleep on the floor, and as it was above the engine room and by the exhaust, the floor got so hot it was unbearable without something to lie on to take up some of the heat. After that night and the next day I had a pretty good trip. . . .

We first sighted land on the morning we came in, although we knew we had been near Jap-held islands during the night as we came right through the Marshalls to Kwajalein Atoll. We came on around and into the harbor surrounded by the islands of the atoll. The attack had been launched there rather than from the sea as they said the Japs expected. They evidently did not think we would start here as they were apparently caught completely by surprise. When looking at a map it seems almost fantastic that we went right through the Marshalls to Kwajalein Atoll, and for weeks while there on a few dots of land we were surrounded by Jap-held islands.

As we lay in the harbor from that morning, Feb. 2, until noon Feb. 4th, we could hear the guns going off. Some we could see firing and it would seem minutes until we would see the shell land probably two miles away. Marines would come out for water and would show us souvenirs. But there we sat doing nothing and really seeing and hearing nothing most of the time. One said, when he got home and was asked about his part in the war, he would just get a pained expression and say he would rather not talk about it. However, he now has plenty to talk about. The harbor was busy with amphibious tanks and landing barges scuttling here and there. As far as one could see in any direction there were dozens of cargo and battleships of every description. . . .

About 1230, Feb. 12th, we had an alarm. No M.A.A. whistles tooted and many did not hear the alert siren. The ones who did took it lightly. A few minutes later the lights came on and the guns started firing. We could hear planes in the distance, but thought they were our own from the carriers. One fellow said, "It would do us good if a bomb would drop in some unidentified spot." About that time, with a great WHOOSH-BOOM! and a mountain of fire, a bomb exploded. I asked if that was what he considered an unidentified spot. But no one seemed to appreciate my humor. About twenty of us were in a large foxhole. I was near a corner. The man in the corner pulled a sack of sand over himself and he was whimpering and shaking violently.

Another bomb dropped with a terrifying WHOOSH and the whole island seemed to erupt into a volcano of flame, debris, shrapnel and flares. Shells and bombs were going off everywhere. We lay there until it seemed an eternity would pass before the shrapnel, etc., would cease raining down on us. Something hit me in the side and from then on I kept my side covered as best I could with my arm. Later on I found it was a piece of shrapnel and I had a bruised and burned side. Just before this a man came tearing over the side with nothing on but his shorts. Blood was streaming from his head.

We looked up and could see the concussion had leveled our tents and fire was racing through them toward us. We had to make a run for the beach. Everything was lit up by the fire, flares were arching into the sky, shells were going off like firecrackers at a big 4th of July celebration, bombs were going off making a fantastic Hades of the island. Men were running everywhere frantically like wild animals before a forest fire only faster and without reason. They ran out on the beach in front of the guns of those few who were ready to repulse an invasion, and had to be herded back. Many went on out on the reef and were caught by the tide. I heard one or two were killed by our men as they came back in when they did not stop when challenged. There was no way to know if they were our men or part of an invasion force. Everything about the raid was terrifying, yet for me it was hard to believe that flying all about me were death-dealing shells and shrapnel. It was real because I could see the evidence, yet I had to keep telling myself it was real and convince myself I could not walk right into it all and not be hurt.

I later found out several bombs were dropped, one hit an ammunition dump of shells which kept going off for a long time. Another landed on the edge of an ammunition dump. The result was shrapnel set off two other ammunition dumps, covering the entire island with shells and bombs and left a crater 100 feet across and 30 feet deep. Our shells and bombs from the dumps were doing more damage than their bombs. The strong wind swept most of the island with fire, setting off the shells and bombs strewn all over the island.

The concussion heaved one man out of his foxhole. In a tent clear across the island four men were sleeping. The two with their feet or heads toward the blast did not feel it. The two lying sideways to it were thrown out of bed into the middle of the tent. The explosions continued for about three hours. We continued to go from foxhole to foxhole along the beach working down to the end of the island out of the path of the fire. Someone got the idea we were receiving a barrage from Jap ships and they were working it towards the beach, so we were ordered to move on. It was the fire moving towards us, setting off the bombs and shells. Destroyers laid down a smoke screen around the island and some thought it was gas.

The Marine corpsmen were doing a wonderful job. They were working back and forth. They dressed one man across from me and another beside me as he held on to me trying to keep from crying out. . . . Seeing the men running around wildly, hitting the deck, whimpering and cowering, it did not seem possible they could be the same men back home we went to church with, fellow lodge or club members, men we deal with in stores, etc. In other words, any and all acquaintances back home could be these same men. Unless you have seen it and experienced it, it is beyond imagination to picture what it looks like or the feeling that will so change a man. One man jumped into a trench, these extended around the island, and landed among some Negroes. One next to him was beginning to get hysterical. Another across the trench was very calm and noticing the agitation of the other said, "If you had been living with your God like I've been living with mine, you wouldn't be so scared." The man from Texas said as he told about it, "You know, it made me think a little about myself."

Several men were killed, many were never found, evidently blown to bits or washed away. Veterans of many raids (Marines) said it was the worst they had ever seen, worse than all the others combined. Men in ships that were anchored out in the water said that it looked as if it were impossible for anyone to remain alive on the island. It was equal to a three-hour bombardment. . . .

William S. Thorne, of Bedford, enlisted in the Marine Corps on June 15, 1942, and was assigned to the infantry. He left the United States in July 1943 and participated in the engagements on Tarawa, Saipan, and Tinian, with L Company, 3d Battalion, 8th Marine Regiment, 2d Marine Division, returning to the States in Aug. 1944. Cpl. Thorne received the Pacific theater ribbon with three battle stars and the Purple Heart with a gold star in lieu of a second one. Cpl. Thorne was discharged Oct. 10, 1945, and became a student at the Fort Wayne Art School, Fort Wayne, Ind.

July 13, 1944
Saipan Island

DARLING MOTHER AND DAD:

Well, sweets, I'm still here even though the place is declared secured and don't know how long I will remain here at this spot; not too long I hope, for the insects drive you crazy and we are half that now. Ha!

The morning following that I last wrote you, we were again rushed to the front lines for the final push to the sea, so we landed first and also finished the fight, and our squad celebrated it by capturing three Jap prisoners who only had the sea to their backs and had but two choices, to swim or surrender. The rest of the company killed and captured several more, so we really had a field day. The island was declared secured on Sunday, July 9th, but we still fought for two more days after that. We were withdrawn again yesterday, but today we went out on another patrol for "Nips," for there are still plenty of them in the mountains as they have hundreds of caves in which to hide.

Last Sunday, July 9, was a happy yet sad day, for they held services by our chaplain in a battle-torn field to which hundreds of us went, carrying helmets and rifles, for we were still on our toes as the enemy was near. It was the most beautiful sermon I ever heard and I honestly felt like crying, as did the rest of the fellows, for every night and day we prayed that the fighting would end, and when the chaplain told us that the American flag had been raised and that the island was secured, our emotions were great. I was looking around at the boys who were all bearded, dirty, and hollow-eyed, as all were dead tired, when the chaplain said this, and the look that came over everyone's face was a sight I'll always remember. Those few words brightened our hearts and spirits more than any words in the world.

After the services we expected peace and quiet for the first time in 24 days and nights, but we were disappointed, for the few (?) Japs who were left alive apparently didn't know the island was lost to them. That same night they tried to break through our lines but failed. We ran into some more the next day when we went after those who were hidden in caves, and that night we still got more; then we were relieved. There'll still be some hidden in these blasted mountains for months, for you'll never get them all, but they are isolated; the main force is utterly broken, and the island now belongs to the U. S. Gosh, what I wouldn't do for a night of rest, for sleep there has been none. Ever since I hit this place I've averaged only four hours sleep a night, if that much, and now that the place is secured, they still make you stand guard at night. I don't know how much they can expect a guy to stand.

I really lost a lot of weight this time for you can see it in my face. Remember how fat and round my face used to be? You ought to see it now. My cheeks are flat and my eyes look sunk. My physical condition is still in good shape, though, so I'm not as bad off as I might sound to you. I got dysentery twice, my only ailment, but it's more a nuisance than anything and caused by food and infected flies. When eating you have to brush flies from your food continually, for if left alone for a second it is black with them. I've never seen so many in my life and they help drive you nuts. Don't be surprised to see me go into the backyard when I get home and dig me a foxhole to sleep in that night, for that's all I'll be used to. Ha! And rain, gosh, that's all it does, especially at night when you are uncomfortable anyway; nothing like a muddy foxhole. Ha! Out of the 28 days I've been here it rained 25 of them and I'm not kidding, and of the 24 days to take the island, our company was on the front lines for 19 of them not counting the two days after, so we did more than our share in its capture. Our 8th Regiment did more front line duty than any other, so *maybe* we'll get a much deserved rest. The boys need it anyway, they ought to see that. . . .

Sometime you might read an article about the patrol of a squad of men who ran into a Jap ambush on the highest peak of the mountain. If you do read about it, I was there. I lost a year's growth on that patrol; I'll never forget it. You'll never know how lucky I've been. We were in on the capture of the town, too, as well as taking about three large mountains and the lowlands. In fact, we were all over the place. By looking on a map you would think this to be a small island, but it isn't; it's a darn big place. I was lucky yesterday, for they actually gave me a helmet full of water to wash with after so long a time, and today I got to wash in the rain. Oh, yes, I got a chance to shave, too, the first shave I've had for a month; never again do I want a beard. I'm afraid to comb my hair for fear it will all come out, as I wear my helmet day and night and my hair's so matted it's pitiful. I won't know how to act when I get back home to normal again. Ha! . . .

Your ever-loving son,
"BUD"

William L. Madigan, of Indianapolis, was inducted into the Army and was assigned to the air corps in May 1942. He was commissioned a 2d lieutenant in June 1943 and was sent to Hawaii in May 1944. He was assigned to the 11th Bomb Group of the 7th Air Force as public relations officer and served on Kwajalein, Makin, Saipan, Guam, Okinawa, and Japan. He participated in the invasions of Saipan and Iwo Jima. Capt. Madigan was discharged in Dec. 1945 and returned to newspaper work with the Associated Press in Indianapolis.

February 25, 1945

Finally, without violating security regulations I can pass on some observations on our D-Day mission to Iwo Jima. We had a couple of civilian correspondents who wanted stories on the preinvasion bombardment by the heavies and the assignment went to me. . . .

Back at the briefing tent, it was pure routine. It wasn't basically different from the first mission against Iwo last August. And for the seventy-third consecutive day there wasn't much new information to give the battle-wise crews who were to fly this last mission. There was, though, a highly electric tension.

A midnight lunch—the *piece de resistance,* that delicacy Spam—and the truck ride through the tropic night to the flight line. The crews seemed preoccupied, thinking, I suppose, about a thousand little personal things. The truck jerked to a stop in front of the big bomber perched on her hard stand, a snub-nosed silhouette of power against the gleaming white coral.

A few crisp last-minute instructions, reminiscent of the tense moments in the dressing room just before the team gallops onto the playing field; a check to determine that no one had in his possession any papers which might serve to identify his outfit in the event of capture. The ground crew pulling through the propellers; the familiar send-off from the crew chief: "She's a damn good ship in tiptop shape. She'll get you there and back. Good luck!" Then we climbed aboard. . . .

There are those minutes when the silence is broken by the methodic chug, chug of the little electric motor used to start the engines, a few hesitant, uncertain coughs before the 1,000 horses in each of the big power plants really take the bit in their teeth. A struggle to hook up the Mae West in the dark. Then we're moving down the taxiway to the strip, jerking, bouncing, scraping. . . .

Symbolic of every take-off is the moment of uncertainty, accentuated this mission because of the extra heavy load of gasoline and bombs. Strange how even the veterans "sweat" those take-offs. Your mind keeps spinning at 100 miles an hour and, like the animated General Motors sign above Times Square, the question, "How much runway left?" runs monotonously through your head. Down the runway she rolls, rocking a little, picking up momentum. Above the drone of the engines, the flight engineer chants as a litany—"95, 100, 105" (miles an hour). The warship strains, leans forward it seems, and lumbers off into the black unknown of the Pacific night.

For hours we flew through a heavy overcast—the kind of somber cloud formations that only the regular flashing of the taillight of the lead airplane penetrates. The engines have settled down to a steady, almost deafening roar, interrupted occasionally as the pilot throttles back to jockey into position. But still inside the fuselage the human tension persists. It's too cold in the waist of the plane to sleep, too crowded in the pilot's compartment. So desperately you just hunch over behind the radio operator and nod, awakening fitfully when the plane lurches through a downdraft. . . .

The stars are visible again—after aeons, it seems—growing dimmer by the minute. And now you're out of the overcast. Far to the east is the pink, warm glow that precedes another sunrise. About 30 miles south of Iwo—at acorn-like Minami rock—the formation begins to reassemble. The bombers wheel into position—rugged, formidable, slugging airplanes that pack a Sunday punch!

The welcome sunlight is bright against the interminable blue of the ocean and the silver wings emit blinding flashes of reflected light. As the bombers approach the target we can see the Navy's surface vessels—assembled in one of the largest battle fleets of the Western Pacific war—lying fanshaped in the water—battleships, PT boats, landing craft, destroyers—all of the best—and behind them a tail-like wake. Your first reaction is one of additional security! Slowly the battleships circle the volcanic island pouring salvo after salvo into the scarred defenses. Almost to the horizon are yellow bursts of flame. And dust is beginning to rise from the Japanese island bastion!

Now the waist gunners, clad in their flak suits and helmets, are test firing their fifties with jarring repercussion. The wind whips a high gale through the plane from the tail gunner's compartment to the heavy-laden bomb bays. Eyes are straining to glimpse that dark speck in the sky that may mean enemy fighters. The formation is drawing tighter, wing under wing. . . . We're over Suribachi Yama—the ominous volcanic crater which forms the southern tip of the ham-shaped island.

Below, the red volcanic ash of the beaches transforms the sunlight into a dull, almost subdued pastel of haze. Smoke and dust cover the island like a shroud. Sharply the formation swings across the bit of land in evasive action to avoid the innocent-looking black puffs that are antiaircraft bursts. . . . We're down to 5,000 feet now, unusually low for this target, and on the bomb run. Over the intercommunication system comes the clear call: "Bombs away." The 30-ton plane wobbles slightly as the string of high explosives falls. And on the beach below—where in 60 short minutes the first assault wave will smash— the impact throws up coils of billowing, dirty smoke, punctuated by orange spurts. The formation wheels away intact leaving a pockmarked strip of land— only five miles long and two miles wide—where death once again has fallen from the skies. But none of us is fooled, for underground, dug in, still awaits the enemy, thousands of Japanese, full of fanaticism and fury, still determined to die for the Emperor as they did at Tarawa, Kwajalein and Saipan. . . .

Off the target now and abruptly the tension is gone. The crew is "working for the wife and kids" now; they figure they've done the job for Uncle Sam. The pilot, a husky Colorado rancher, puts the plane on automatic pilot, relaxes and reaches for a cup of coffee. The ball turret gunner pulls out a picture of his best gal in Mississippi. The boys are heading back home again. Four easier hours later they're going into the traffic pattern. . . . The crew is climbing stiffly out of the plane and into the trucks that will carry them to the mess hall. It's all in a day's work out here—just another mission—the last, incidentally, to Iwo, battered southern gateway to Japan!

Harold A. Losey, of Tipton, enlisted in the Navy as an apprentice seaman on Dec. 29, 1941. He went to radio school in Pearl Harbor, and served aboard the U.S.S. "Antares," the U.S.S. "Medusa," and the U.S.S. "Enterprise." He attained the rating of radioman 1/c in July 1945, and participated in the first and second Battles of the Philippine Sea, the Battle of the Solomons, the invasion of the Gilbert Islands, Okinawa, and the bombing of Tokyo. He was awarded the Asiatic-Pacific Campaign medal with seven battle stars and the Philippine Liberation ribbon with two stars. Discharged Oct. 1, 1945, Losey is a lineman for the telephone company in Nashville, Tenn.

Dear Mom and Pop:

To start off, I'll say this will be one of very few of this type of letter you will ever get from me. I will try to tell you what has been going on. I haven't written for some time—to anyone—because we have been in more scrapes than ever before. Right now we are heading for our base. We should be there in two days.

Last week we left Island X and headed back. I saw the island very well. We could see our bombs explode and could see the battleships shelling the beach. It was a wonderful sight.

Since leaving our last port we have been in the Central Pacific most of the time and have been in everything that has been making the news. Awhile back we sighted the Jap fleet. We tried our best to sink them all, but they ran too fast.

One evening, just at dusk, we were attacked by Jap torpedo planes. They came in low over the water and every one of them went past every ship with us, just to get at our ship. They know this ship and the record it has, so that explains why they tried for us.

I was up on the signal bridge and could see everything. I'll tell you, it was the most wonderful sight I ever saw. The tracer bullets showed up like red hot coals and it seemed impossible for any plane to get through it. The planes were twin-engined ones and came in at us at 300 miles an hour. One caught fire and sailed right over the bow blazing like a torch, not more than 75 feet from me. It hit the water and strung out like the guts of a rabbit, blazing, as the gasoline caught fire.

We knocked every one of them down and only one or two, who did not attack, returned to some base from where they had come. We did lose a few men from strafing, but there was no other damage. The next day, after their fleet had been spotted, several hundred carrier-based Jap planes attacked us. Before the aftermath was over, we had shot down over 300 planes. I was scared as h——, but I don't care who knows it.

When they started coming in, I lay down on the deck with my steel helmet on and my face covered with flash-proof clothing. I could look at the overhead and just imagine a bomb coming through it. It's the waiting that gets you. First they tell you to stand by to repel air attack—then silence, then the guns open up and it sounds like all h—— has broken loose. Then, when the firing slows down and you are still alive and haven't felt the ship shake like an angry dog, then and only then does your heart start beating, and you feel warm and happy to know you are still alive. You can't imagine what a bomb can do. Just the flash of it can burn a hundred men as crisp as a meat loaf in a split second. That's why we wear flash-proof clothing. I've thanked God so many times since I last saw you. He's probably getting tired hearing me!

The evening of the big air battle, a Jap plane came back and tried to land on our flight deck with our own planes. They waved him off because he didn't have his tail hook down. He didn't want to die—not that Jap. He made one more circle and ran out of gas and dropped into the sea. Too bad we had to miss him; that would have been one for the books.

Another day we picked up a bunch of Japs floating on rafts. They were glad to be picked up and all of them were wounded. One was only eleven years old. He had been on a cargo ship we had sunk.

Since I left you last, here is what the ship is credited with doing. She shot down 194 Jap planes, 204 destroyed on the ground; sank 68 ships, including a Jap carrier; dropped 1,180 tons of bombs on ships and enemy installations. And a few other things I can't remember now.

We have been away from our base about six months and it has been a long, old grind. It will be good to see shore again, see what a girl looks like and how people live. Ever try going without seeing a man for six months, Mom? Or you Pop, ever try not seeing a girl for that long? Might not mean so much to you now, but at my age—well, it's different. I think you know what I mean. Oh, I'm not kicking. I've done it before and I can do it time and time again if I have to, only I sure wish those d—— Japs would fight it out like men, so we could whip the h—— out of them and go home.

They haven't a chance and they know it. Just stand by and watch us hit the Philippines and go on up to Tokyo. It's coming—we can see that from out here. Don't know just how long it will be, but it will be soon. We are returning to base for a two-week yard period and then we are to go back to the Central Pacific. These orders may be changed any minute. I wish we would go up north for awhile. It was so hot down there you almost die all the time.

It's getting cooler now that we are nearing base. We can already pick up U. S. radiograms on the radio. Just think, folks, your son has been within 700 miles of Tokyo! Might make it someday.

By the way, we still have a bunch of Jap prisoners in the brig and are taking them to base. I see them pretty often. Little dirty devils. I could take on three of them at once.

Everyone says we will be back in the States before this year is over. I hope so.

I could go on for hours telling you these things and still not even be started. So much has happened that I can't even remember all. Someday, if you want, I can tell you anything you want to hear about this old Pacific. And just remember what that book said that I sent you—wherever there is anything doing, our ship will be there fighting. We haven't missed out on anything; we have a record behind us that no other ship has ever come close to equaling. We have to keep up that record by fighting all the time.

She is a good ship, but she is getting kinda old and worn from too much work and too many bomb hits. We haven't been hit since I last saw you, but have had a couple of misses and a torpedo went right past our bow on the evening of the air battle, then it jumped out of the water, dived again and exploded back aft of us—churned the water like an egg beater for hundreds of feet around.

When we reach base there will be several transfers for the gang. I don't know who will get them. I figure I might get in on the next bunch, maybe three or four months from now. That is only a guess. I would kinda hate to leave the ship. She has brought me and many others through a lot of danger, safe and sound. But I guess I would take a transfer if I could get one because that would mean a few months in the States and that is what we all want out here.

I'll write again as soon as we reach base. Give my love to all and most of all, remember, both of you, your son thinks you are wonderful parents.

Your son,
HAROLD

A sketch of the late Ernie Pyle will be found on page 108.

A sketch of the late Ernie Pyle will be found on page 108.

1945
Marianas

Before starting out on my long tours with the Navy, I decided to visit the famous B-29 Superfortress boys who were bombing Japan from the Marianas. I had "kinfolk" flying on the B-29s, and I thought I'd kill two birds, visiting and writing at the same time. So there I was sitting on a screened porch in my underwear, comfortable as a cat, with the surf beating on the shore and a lot of bomber pilots swimming out front. The B-29 boys, from commandant down to enlisted men of lowest rank, lived well. They were all appreciative of their good fortune. Of course, they all would rather have been home, but who wouldn't?

The man I went to visit was Lieutenant Jack Bales, another farm boy from near Dana, Indiana. Jack is a sort of nephew of mine. He isn't exactly a nephew, but it's too complicated to explain; I used to hold him on my knee and all that sort of thing. But now he was twenty-six, and starting to get bald like his "uncle." Jack's folks still live just a mile down the road from our farm. Jack left the farm and went to the University of Illinois and got a good education. He was just ready to become a famous lawyer when the war came along and he enlisted. He spent a year as a private, then got a commission and flew over from Nebraska with the B-29s in October of 1944.

When I telephoned Jack and said I'd be out in about an hour to stay a few days, he said he would put up an extra cot in his hut for me. When I got there the cot was up, with blankets and mattress covers laid out on it. Jack had told the boys he was having a visitor, and on the assumption it was a woman six eager volunteers had been helping him put up the cot. When I showed up, skinny and bald, it was an awful letdown, but they were all decent about it.

Jack lived in a steel Quonset hut with ten other fliers. Most of them were pilots, but Jack was a radioman; he and another fellow had charge of all his squadron's radio. He didn't have to go on missions except now and then to check up. But I learned, to my astonishment and pride, that he had been on more missions than anybody else in his squadron. In fact, he had been on so many that his squadron commander had forbidden him to go for a while. Not that he enjoyed it; nobody but a freak likes to go on combat missions. He went because he had things to learn, and because he could contribute something by being there. But he seemed to show no strain from the ordeal; he said that sitting around camp got so monotonous he sort of welcomed a mission just for a change. Another time or two and he would have his quota authorizing him to go back to rest camp for a while.

During flight Jack sat in a little compartment in the rear of the plane, unable to see out. In all his missions over Japan he had seen only one Jap fighter. Not that they didn't have plenty around, but he was so busy he seldom got to a window for a peek. The one time he did, a Jap came slamming under the plane so close it almost took the skin off.

Like all combat crewmen, Jack spent the night and at least half of each day lying on his cot. He held the record in his hut for "sack time," which means just lying on a cot doing nothing. He had his work so organized that it didn't take much of his time between missions, and since there's nothing else to do, you just lie around. Jack said he had got so lazy he wouldn't be able to face a job after the war, so he thought he'd work into civilian life gradually by going back to school again.

The B-29 fliers slept on folding canvas cots, with rough white sheets. Sleeping is wonderful in the islands, and along toward morning you usually pull a blanket over you. Each flier had a dresser of wooden shelves he'd made for himself, and there were several homemade tables scattered around. The walls were plastered with maps, snapshots, and pin-up girls—but I noticed that real pin-up girls (wives and mothers) dominated the movie beauties. Eight of the ten men in the hut were married.

Although the food was good, most of the boys got packages from home. One kid wrote and told his folks to slow up a little, that he was snowed under with packages. Jack had had two jars of Indiana fried chicken from my Aunt Mary. She cans it and seals it in Mason jars, and it's wonderful. She sent me some in France, but I'd left before it got there. Jack took some of his fried chicken in his lunch over Tokyo one day. We Hoosiers sure do get around, even the chickens.*

Ernie Pyle

John W. Crawford, of Terre Haute, was inducted into the Army April 19, 1943, and joined the medical corps as a technician. Leaving the United States in July 1944, he participated in the action on Leyte and Okinawa, where he was killed while in the First Aid Station, April 12, 1945. Pvt. Crawford was awarded the Purple Heart posthumously.

January 25, 1945
Philippine Islands

Dear Miss Ray:

When I was a student in your classes at Wiley [High School], when we were rocked from complacency by the wreckage of Pearl Harbor, and when the fall of the Philippines caused us to offer prayers for those caught on Bataan, little did I dream that I would see an even mightier Pearl Harbor, great invasion fleets, and take part in the liberation of the Philippines.

I was steaming north toward the Philippines and Imperial Japan in the month of October. In all directions as far as the eye could see were ships of every conceivable form and function carrying assault and support troops into the "mouth of the unknown." What awaits us in the Philippines? This question was in the mind of the lowest private and the highest general. What kind of reception did the Japanese have planned?

* From *Last Chapter*, by Ernie Pyle. Copyright, 1946, by Henry Holt and Company, Inc., pp. 28–30.

As I progressed farther north and nearer to participation in one of the greatest amphibious operations of history, the suspense increased. Recreation and physical training continued as usual on the crowded ship, but both G.I.'s and "swabbies" lined the rails with eyes seaward. When would the Japs try to stop us?

On October 19 last minute preparations took place. Weapons were cleaned and checked, equipment was put in perfect order, and the debarkation nets were ready. That night I didn't sleep much. I expected to be attacked by enemy aircraft and vessels at any moment. As usual I spread my blankets under the stars and wondered what war is really like to the tune of salt wash. From the port side of the ship came strains of old religious songs rendered by a group of riflemen.

At 3 A.M. on October 20 the ship went into exceedingly dangerous waters with paravanes lowered. I sprang to the rail expecting to see the whole Japanese navy, but I was reassured at the sight of our accompanying destroyers and aircraft carriers. Where was the Jap navy and air force? The answer, of course, was our own navy and air force. To them, I salute! I had sailed for over a month on the Pacific ocean without a sign of the "Rising Sun."

The convoy broke battle formation, and the ships took their positions for debarking assault troops. The bay was crowded with hundreds of ships and thousands of invasion craft of all kinds. The war and flash of naval gunfire heralded one of the most spectacular shows on earth. Columns of black smoke rose from the shoreline, as the battleships and cruisers steamed back and forth relentlessly shelling Japanese positions.

Out of the clouds which hovered above the rugged mountains flew swarms of U. S. naval airplanes. The first enemy resistance was ten bursts of antiaircraft which exploded harmlessly. One of the planes dived toward the source of the ack-ack and no more bursts occurred. On and on they came—those airmen—leaving in their wake wrecked Jap supply dumps, motor convoys, and field pieces which I later saw along the roads and in the wrecked villages.

The assault waves debarked into LCVP's and LCM's. These were men from American towns and hamlets equipped with the best and latest tools of war, everything from waterproof matchboxes, pocket stoves, and insect repellant to bazookas. These were the riflemen, the B.A.R. men, the bazooka men, the flame throwers, and the machine gunners. These were the former students, the former businessmen, ex-farmers and former civilians. Now they grimly faced a task for which each had been trained and equipped: General MacArthur's return to the Philippines.

The ships rendezvoused while the bombardment continued. Each bore two numbers, that of wave and that of ship in wave. Each found its proper place and circled there awaiting the signal to proceed shoreward. Shortly before 10 A.M. the first wave of infantry transferred to amphibious tractors which headed for the shore with the roar of a thousand powerful motors. The men made last minute adjustments on equipment. Safety catches clicked on MI's and carbines. Prayers were earnestly muttered, prayers which remembered wives and kids and mothers. At 10 A.M. the "iron monsters" emerged from the ocean onto Orange Beach, the ramps went down, and the Yanks had returned to the Philippines.

My first shock of the war was the mutilated body of one of my comrades which I passed upon going ashore. Not many hours before he had laughed as heartily as anyone. My soul, if I have a soul, turned very sick.

My second shock was the family of Filipinos which I saw in a heavily bombed area, their home and lives destroyed.

My third shock was the tracers I saw going over my foxhole the first night, as I hugged Mother Earth. I couldn't quite believe that anyone could want to kill me!

As company aid man I accompanied my platoon through swamps and rice paddies, into jungle and into the hills, with my morphine and battle dressings. Back in your classes I hated war because of the experiences of others. Now I know how it feels to lie in a water-filled hole, hear a Jap mortar "poop," and grit my teeth and pray, wondering where the shell will land. There is no other feeling like it. It is hope and despair, hate and love, faith and doubt, past and future, dirt and filth, cowardice and courage, and life and death rolled into one.

The Japanese soldiers I have seen reeked of death and decay, whether they were corpses or prisoners of war. A pile of glistening bones, a maggot-infested, stinking body, or a cringing, starved creature who gave up after months of existence on roots and corn was the Jap I saw. Those who put up the active resistance were too cleverly concealed to be seen at all.

One Jap, however, went out with U. S. patrols in order to convince others to give up. One day another outfit captured him. When asked his rank he answered, "I was formerly a superior private in the 16th Division of the Japanese Imperial Army, but now I am a sergeant in the 381st Infantry, U. S. Army." He was returned!

The Filipinos are generally very friendly people. Many speak English, but the extent of most native vocabularies is, "Good morning, shir!" or "Any dirty clothes to wash, shir?" Natives are doing a huge laundry business.

The cities and towns are hardly that at all. The majority are composed of a group of thatched huts set on stilts. There is much to be desired in sanitation, of course, in such an area.

Filipino girls like to wear bright colored silks and large straw hats. A few are faintly attractive, but compare in no respect with American girls to my appreciative eye. I was surprised one day when on patrol I looked through a wrecked schoolhouse and found the memoirs of a high school senior. Was my face red! But I shouldn't have been so nosy in the first place. In many respects girls are girls the world over, insofar as they grow up to love peaceful homes, husbands, and families.

So much for the return to the Philippines. What I have experienced makes me hate war ten-fold times as much as I did back in school. What I have seen makes me love my country and its ways of freedom infinitely. I will certainly appreciate the old U. S. A. when that great day of peace comes—and there are millions like me!

I plan to obtain my A.B. at Washington University and to return to the University of Chicago for graduate work. At the present I am carrying correspondence work with the University of Chicago and A.F.L. . . .

With best wishes I remain your friend and former student.

BILL

Russell L. Woolsey, of Clay City, was inducted into the Army Nov. 28, 1942, and was first assigned to the 924th Engineer Battalion and later was attached to Company B, 1913th Engineers. Leaving the United States in Nov. 1943, T/4 Woolsey was engaged in action in Oro Bay, Cape Gloucester, Hollandia, New Guinea, and the liberation of the Southern Philippines, for which action he was awarded the Asiatic-Pacific ribbon with four battle stars and the Philippine Liberation ribbon with one battle star. Discharged Oct. 11, 1945, Woolsey is now a printer in Clay City.

Jan. 28, 1945
Philippines

DEAR HARRY:

Have a little time this morning and will write you a few lines, or at least start them.

Thanks to you, Harry, I got to see a home town boy. George Long's outfit is just up the road a few miles from me, or at least it was. I got to go over there Wednesday, and he said he looked to move in a few days. We had a good visit together and it was good to talk to someone from home. I understand Paul Gilbert's outfit is now here. I'm going to try and find out.

We have a fairly nice camp area here, but the Filipinos are pretty numerous. Had to put local M.P.'s to keep them out. We always have a large number around mealtime. I feel sorry for them, but we can't feed them all. Some of them will even take what's left in a fellow's mess kit.

We haven't had any mail for several weeks and I don't know what's going on around Clay City. Have any more of the boys got home on rotation? We will soon be overseas eighteen months and it is rumored that our rotation will start in a couple of months, but I'm pretty sure it won't start until after this campaign is over.

Our camp area is in the city park of this town, or at least what is left of it. I imagine at one time it was a very beautiful one. There is a water fountain in each corner with many flower gardens systematically arranged, and a large concrete band pavilion in the center. A Filipino band gave a concert there last night. They played several popular numbers, and these Filipinos aren't far behind the Americans as some of them did some jitterbugging. One of the girls sang "Blue Moon," dedicated to the boys of Company B. In my travels here I noticed that most towns of any size have such parks. The municipal buildings are generally pretty nice and attractive.

The people here are very friendly. Went out and visited the homes of two families I got acquainted with. Took some pictures of the two families. They served us with lemonade and cakes that resembled doughnuts. Both were very good. They live in bamboo huts and the inside just sparkles, especially the floors. However, that's not the case in all the homes, but the people do well with what they have. These two families are former residents of Manila, and just came from there in December. Had to get out as prices were very high. For instance, a cup of coffee cost twenty-five pesos in Japanese money, and a set of false teeth a thousand. Wages are low and, you see, the poorer class has it pretty hard. Am sending you a ten-peso note.

It's getting close to bedtime so will close for this time. Forgive me this time for not answering sooner. We were getting ready to move when I received your last letter and have been on the move since. Am trying to catch up on some of my back mail.

As ever,
R. Woolsey

Theodore L. Sendak, of Gary, was inducted into the Army April 14, 1941, and was commissioned a 2d lieutenant on March 29, 1942. After attending the civil affairs school and the Joint Army-Navy Far Eastern Planning Board, Capt. Sendak was sent to the Pacific, serving briefly in New Guinea and then being attached to the Philippine Civil Affairs units from Nov. 1944 to Nov. 1945. Capt. Sendak participated in engagements on New Guinea, Leyte, and Southern Philippines. Discharged as a major on the staff of the administration reserve, Sendak is now a public relations director for veteran affairs for the State of Indiana. In the following letter to his wife, names were added later.

Jan. 1945
Ormoc, Philippines

For the uninitiated, my life may seem like bedlam. I'm convinced of it. The titles, Detachment Commander and Labor Recruitment Officer, may not mean much to you, but they spell much of the bedlam for me. Not to mention the war that's going on all 'round.

Up at the crack of dawn, not for reveille. No, it's too early for that. But a fellow just can't sleep through the noise of our artillery barrages designed, methinks, to rouse us almost as much as our Japanese foe.

Somewhere in the dawn's early light we grab breakfast; and we're on the job by 7:30 A.M. I select this hour not because I want to but because by that time there's already half a hundred Filipinos at the headquarters steps with half a hundred heartaches, complaints, pleas, requests. The place soon resembles the main entrance to a department store back home just before opening time when 1,000 pairs of nylon hosiery are to go on sale. [The headquarters was a well-battered and shot-up house on the beach at Ipil, where one division landed and which was the line beyond which civilians could not go. Troops were deployed from there on out towards the mountains to the east and through razed Ormoc to the north.]

But the destruction in the wake of any war is what provides the work for civil affairs officers. Theirs is the job of trying to stabilize conditions among the civilian populace back of the fighting lines. It runs the gamut of public relations, human emotions, and just plain effort. There's no praise meant; that's just the overwhelming picture which hits the officer in the face every day.

Early each morning, the mayor [of Ormoc, Mr. Catalino Hermosilla, now deceased] comes in to discuss his latest problems. The fact that he has led thousands of Filipino refugees through the Jap lines is a wonder to me. He lost his own mother one trip.

The mayor is a big help. In the course of our daily talk, we both see that the vehicles of the Army units employing native labor which we hire get off to the proper *barrios* to pick up their crews. This the mayor has arranged the night before when I give him the following day's requirements. Before we're through talking, we make a quick trip to the nearest air raid shelter (foxhole to you) for the duration of a short alert.

With the all clear signal, we're back to work. The mayor leaves. A dozen different persons come in to seek travel passes in order to return to their destroyed homes long enough to dig up buried heirlooms, money, and family goods. One woman with three toddling infants wants to go to a distant town to see her husband who's a wounded guerrilla. [She is refused, of course, because for one thing her husband is in a combat area beyond Ormoc; so Mayor Hermosilla finds shelter and food for her in the resettlement area south of Ipil.]

The military police [of the 7th Division] bring in an aged Filipino couple found adrift on a raft for 24 hours, their faces drawn and sickly. They tell of having paddled with their hands to escape from a nearby Jap-held island [Camotes Island, across Ormoc Bay, where a naval battle occurred]. They, too, are sent to a nearby refugee collecting center [Mayor Hermosilla's].

I finally get down to the paperwork part of this job. Official letters have to be signed, records perused, new mimeographed forms approved.

Then there's lunch. And every mealtime finds a variety of guests—"visiting firemen" from higher headquarters and the War Department itself, guerrilla chieftains, occasional G.I.'s separated from their own outfits and in need of food. Come one, come all. But we're hardly finished eating before an urgent request comes in by field phone for a special labor detail to help unload supply ships. And I dispatch a truck to pick up a reserve crew of native workers and race over hill and dale to the appointed spot.

A few minutes later, I find some old army prayer books and hymnals, and present them to the parish priest to replace some of those which the Japanese had destroyed. He invites me to mass on Sunday. I promise to try to make it. The clerk comes in with a written message from a farmer forwarded to us by the *teniente* (village headman) of another community. It reads: "I am looking for my horse. Half Arabian, half Filipino. Four-foot tall. Brown. With white spot on forehead. I am Francisco Tan."

I check that. Then I dispatch another labor detail with one of our medics to assist in the burial of several natives killed by booby traps of some sort. Meantime I sign certificates on several payrolls for our finance officer, and okay a travel pass or two for the civilians.

Our finance officer brings in an ordinance concerning bona fide currency for us to have mimeographed. The transportation sergeant requests a special detail to salvage a small diesel-powered Japanese craft, long derelict on our shore. The welfare officer informs us he's established several civilian laundries in nearby villages, and asks that we hurry up the production of the ceiling price lists to distribute. Our supply officer wants to know "Where-the-hell-are-those-trucks-and-labor-gangs" he requested 30 minutes before to haul in five or six tons of rice before it rains. I patiently say "Yes" to them all, and am tempted to call out, "Next case, please."

At about 3:00 P.M., the mail orderly stacks a bundle of personal letters on my desk for censoring. Yes, I'm stuck with that unhappy job, too. With that done, I get a welcome change. I go with the messenger by jeep to meet the plane. We get there all right, swap yarns with the pilot a few minutes, and start back, only to find one of the bridges out. Apparently our engineers had blown it and decided to build a new and better one. The stream is too deep to ford, and there's no other way home. I look anxiously towards the officer in charge. He replies aloud to my mental telepathy. "Don't get your intestines in an uproar, Captain. We'll have a new bridge all rigged up in about an hour." We doubt his one-hour promise, but can only sit and chew the fat.

At this point I should offer both an apology and a tribute to the Corps of Engineers. Each man knew his job. Huge logs rolled into place; reinforced steel rails fell into position; crossbars took shape; finally, floor boarding covered its entirety. And, one hour and ten minutes later these hardworking engineers all lined up and made a comic business of ushering our jeep across the new double-lane bridge they had erected before our very eyes.

So we arrived back at PCAU (Philippine Civil Affairs Unit) headquarters later than expected, but never too late for another experience. I had just stepped in the door when our guards brought in five Chinese brothers named Ik Yim whom they had accompanied to dig up their buried treasure in a neighboring *barrio*. To my untrained ear, at least three different languages and dialects seemed to be going on simultaneously. The oldest Ik Yim suddenly dumped two moulded gunny sacks on the floor in the middle of the room.

The scene which followed found the five leading Oriental characters on their haunches sorting heirlooms, while we stood in audience. First they rolled out hundreds of thousands of pesos in now-worthless Japanese occupation currency. They grinned, and I wondered how hard they were finding that to take. They jabbered among themselves. Then an old fruit jar (Ball Brothers, Muncie, Indiana, no less) spewed forth gold and silver jewelry, uncultured pearls, and a variety of other precious tidbits. The oldest brother stood up at that moment to show me his official papers and identification, among which was a deposit book on a leading bank in China, with a prewar balance of one million dollars. Next he dropped down to begin the tedious job of counting, piece-by-piece, 650,000 pesos in valid Filipino money ($325,000).

With that chore done and the requisite records made, we remained standing while the brothers Ik Yim gathered their recovered wealth into the gunny sacks, smiled at one another and exchanged felicitations in Chinese, bowed and scraped and smiled to us while thanking us in English, and finally went through the same rigmarole in a Filipino dialect for the benefit of several of our Filipino G.I.'s near the door as they made their exit.

Supper is cold on "My Day." But I finish it in time to join the other officers for our evening conference on the day's work. We sit around and smoke, discuss our problems, tell the latest latrine rumors, and plan things for the next day and beyond. In a while we adjourn.

Now, if there aren't too many air raid alerts tonight, maybe I can get some letters written. So I crowd, in my turn, into the outfit's black-out room, to write with one hand while swatting mosquitoes with the other. Out of one of those late sessions comes this. And when I come to the end of one of these days, I stumble in the dark to the edge of my quarters, crawl under a mosquito net, clear it of mosquitoes, put my .45 beside me inside the net, and retire for the night. At least the mosquitoes won't bother me; and I trust I won't dream about war and civil affairs.

A sketch of Stanley N. Brothers will be found on page 231.

1945
Philippines

DEAR MR. STORM:

This war over the bananas is progressing favorably for the natives. With each purchase, good American-backed money becomes distributed throughout these damned ancient, crawling islands. How one could while away three years here is a miracle. It taxes my potent imagination.

The slant-eyes are holed up here, starving like rats on an abandoned ship. The average one now weighs about ninety pounds and has shrunken to about four feet and nine inches in height. You would think they would come in, surrender and enjoy good American hospitality. That is far above their mechanized brain. They are caused to move by someone pulling strings. They hole up in caves. No reorganization and no retreat to live to fight another day. There in the caves and holes they are forgotten by their emperor and we toy with them like a kitten does a morbid mouse. Even the air corps passes its time and days off bringing them in, in various styles and models. The last and closest one I saw yielded up a Japanese American dollar bill to be used in the invasion of the States. There, my friend, is confidence for you; the confidence that is hard to shake and one in which danger hides. That American invasion dollar is snugly attached to my short snorter, which is growing up with every leap and bound we make into new territory. I have already been offered twenty pesos for that one bill. The short snorter is over sixteen feet long now. Last Thursday I added a bill from Formosa, several Chinese, French Indo-China and a Jap Australian invasion note. It must be somewhere around three hundred dollars in value now.

It is amazing how well death and stench go with war, and danger becomes its business. Without that danger, that excitement, the war lulls and the price of bananas sinks to a new bottom. Therefore, we who are supposed to be of average mind continue to stick out our necks, to wonder and to find out what it's like across the ridge, no matter what type the ridge may be. For our last stupid act our lieutenant has confined us to school teaching without leaving, unless by special permission. It is good to have officers, if for nothing more than to stabilize your living. Ours goes so far as to plead and beg us to use judgment, the same as a father does a child, or a teacher a student. It has been my experience that judgment gets in my way over here. I realize judgment's pink and rosy state of health, but that same judgment offered a barricade to my seeing, my knowing and my own mental health; not mentioning the surrender to a dull and nebulous life.

Last Thursday we borrowed a jeep; anyway we contracted for it, G.I. method, and proceeded on a trip to the outposts along the perimeter. This perimeter to the north of our base is one of rugged hills, steep cliffs and peaks. You can get an idea as to the condition of the terrain by the fact that several times we stopped and pondered whether or not the universal jeep could make it. No lesser car, without four-wheel drive, could even start the journey. We stationed ourselves with carbines, assigning each to a particular side, front and rear, to watch for the straggling sons of Nippon, who come out to search for food and to loot the grain fields. Each time we passed an outpost, someone was always busy giving a few Nips the last rite Mother Earth has to offer those weary of the war. Far and few between are those who surrender. These outposts, which consist of left-behind infantrymen, are wonderful. You might think they would have a bad taste for us more fortunate ones, who have many times more comforts than they. Never have I found the slightest trace of ill will, or contempt among them. In all cases they have been friendly, glad to see someone else from different organizations and willing to talk your head off. They even are so polite as to point out a holed-up Nip, remarking that "once again the air corps will steal our bread" and maybe a humorous remark, "there go the infantrymen's souvenirs." This day one of the members of the second patrol we ran across decided to go with us. I shall never forget him. He hailed from Kentucky, and played the part, talkative, friendly, tall and built like a race horse. He was no air-mattress-dwelling noncombatant. Without much observation you could see that war and fighting were a part of his very make-up. He was rugged in appearance, nimble, alert, and you felt confidence in his deep, piercing and searching eyes. Here was a man that preserved our bananas. The bananas of this war. Time and again as he talked, always asking about our planes, their speed, and what kind are they that sweep down sowing antipersonnel bombs and raking the Japs, barely a few yards ahead of us, I could picture him stalking a squirrel high in some Kentucky hill. I imagined him to be the type who knows every inch of his neighborhood, where the best hunting can be had, fishing, even where the best blackberries grow.

Occasionally we stopped to explore a cave, or some Jap hideout. Every now and then we traded rifles to shoot at ration cans, or natural targets. He marveled at our carbines but didn't know exactly where it would fit into his part of this game. Once I slipped and rolled down the side of a cliff; he was there to help me to my feet and smilingly he pointed out a land mine that I missed rolling over by a few feet. This stopped my breathing and shook my dwindling ambition. He asked if we ever saw a land mine go off. Naturally that instrument is always demobilized before we come on the scene. To satisfy our whims, he tied a piece of communication wire to the propeller or wheel-like affair that barely struck through the ground. We climbed upon the cliff carrying the wire very gently with us into an old foxhole, from which point of safety we gave it a yank. There was a long whoom-m, a cloud of dust, and flying fragments. They smacked into the side of the cliff, knocking dust and dirt down our necks. With the sound of the thunder, I cleared the foxhole; leaving my shoes behind fully laced and intact.

It was no trouble to locate the scenes of the battle; you merely looked across from one hill to another to spot a scorched, burnt and brownish clump of trees, piles of rocks and always the smashed equipment. As you walked over the ridges to get to these scenes you were amazed at the shell and shrapnel pieces covering the hills and lying in the grass; thicker than any ground covered by hail, thicker than any Hoosier ever saw. As far as you could see were ration cans and packages, indicating that the men who took the strong point had been pinned down and were forced to eat at least one meal of cold detestable food. Our friend always took the lead, pointing out hidden mines, which seemed far too close together and numerous. This trail always led through the scorched rocks and burned trees to the caves and the graves of the enemy. The cave is their last stand, their last act of war; when the cave becomes untenable the jig is up; the emperor is minus more blood for the empire.

We crossed several of these various spots, which covered some twenty or more miles and finally parked our jeep, locking the steering wheel with a chain and lock to keep some wandering G.I. or Nip from taking it and pressing it into service. In the valley ran a swift, clear stream, tumbling over rocks worn smooth and round. It reminded me of the mountain streams of upstate New York, the ones my wife and I used to visit in the summer, she to drink in the scenes and try her hand at painting, and I to lose myself with the rod and reel.

All along the creek banks, which were steep, were more holes and caves once used by the enemy. Each cave held its share of torn clothing, papers, canteens, shell crates and a deathly smell. One of the queer things about this enemy is that you never see a Jap ration package of food, never a cook stove, never a portable kitchen, or never a trace of heavy equipment, like we use to chase him back with. What manner of an enemy is this? What manner of war did they hope to fight? How successful did they hope to be? Their war here doesn't take on the appearance of organized warfare. I have never seen a Jap heavy truck, a Jap bulldozer, and how can you fight a war or maintain a supply line without the immortal bulldozer? They have been on Luzon for three years. At our present base, which is the largest and was the largest on the island, they had only one air strip and a road to take off planes from. How can you fight our air force without strips? Nowhere have I seen where they built up anything stable or solid, such as roads, buildings and fortifications. Always it's a cave, a hole; they are undoubtedly the diggingest race I have ever seen. They even dig their own graves, making it ever so handy.

We slipped from stone to stone down the creek; our Kentucky friend always in the lead; and we never disputed his right to lead. He tested each cave for traps and mines; we entered last, for that was part of his business, to lead. You had to marvel at this fellow's art, his confidence and his training. Whoever thinks this army isn't trained should spend a day with this man. . . .

This war is crowded with thousands of these happenings, thousands of impossible and peculiar odds and ends. I think you might be interested in some I have seen and some I have heard. Anyway that is about all I can write of since I am so far from any other type of material.

One is of a chaplain who followed this fighter group all the way through for two years. He received a telegram on Friday night calling him back to Australia, at once. He got permission to wait over until Sunday, as he wanted to deliver his last sermon. He never delivered it; he fell full of bomb splinters in a raid on Saturday night.

The other day a pilot landed a P-47 on the strip with the canopy open. Some freak current of air opened his parachute and it was pulling him from the plane, when he finally cut the shrouds with his knife and continued down the runway to a nice stop.

One of the finest majors I ever met was playing football out here in the lot yesterday afternoon. He was active, healthy and having the time of his life. They are burying him in a few days. His jeep was hit by a plane and he was burned by the gas. In the orderly room today were orders releasing him from the service and sending him back to the States and home. He missed it by one day.

Not long ago a Nip fighter plane was strafing the area. Fellows were lying in foxholes watching him dive and circle as he sprayed the tents and equipment. All of a sudden his plane blew apart into a hundred or more pieces. He had been hit by a bomb from a Nip bomber from about thirty thousand feet up. It was a mistimed affair. The bomber continued to lay five-hundred-pound eggs across the area.

Four fellows occupying a tent in one of the squadrons here dug a foxhole. Three didn't want to add a roof to it. The fourth decided to build himself one about ten feet away with a roof. The next night the three were killed from splinters from a near miss. The fourth received only a few shake-ups.

In a raid not long ago a Jap bomb fell on the edge of a trench. It was a dud and failed to explode. One of the G.I.'s reached out carefully as far as he could and patted the bomb's nose saying, "You gold-bricking son-of-a——."

An Aussie pilot was going down the runway to take off, when a cross wind caused him to crash into a bank. He nonchalantly pulled back the canopy, took up his form and wrote in the trouble, while the plane blazed and smoked. Most people would have run to clear a possible explosion. Another Aussie was trying for a take-off when his plane got out of control; he was heading directly for the engineering shack. He tried the brakes but they burned out and his plane came to rest in the end of the shack, after the prop had chopped about a fourth of the building down. He crawled out and drawled, "The bloody so-and-so, is anyone hurt?"

These are only a few of the things that go on beside the killing of the enemy. I just talked to a staff sergeant who had been in the army three years before Pearl Harbor. He was a graduate of an engine mechanic school, but for months while in camp in the States preparing to come overseas, his job was feeding and watering four ducks for an officer of the camp. There is the tale here of a master sergeant who has fifteen years' service. His job at one time was cleaning the officers' quarters. One day he walked into the room of a newly commissioned captain to sweep the floor. The captain, noticing the stripes and hash marks, told him to sit on the bed and watch a recruit sweep for once. . . .

What is the latest on the Russians and Allies in Central Europe and the Balkans? We don't get much on that here. Do I smell trouble or is my sense of smell bad? Tell everyone hello that might be interested and give my regards to all.

> I remain your friend,
> STAN

Henry Edmonson, of Clay City, was inducted into the Army on Oct. 8, 1941, and was assigned to the field artillery. He went overseas in July 1943 and served with the 122d Field Artillery Battalion, 33d Division, in Hawaii, New Guinea, the Philippine Islands, and Japan. During June 1945, Sgt. Edmonson served in support of the Filipino Army in Northern Luzon. Discharged Nov. 29, 1945, Sgt. Edmonson is working as a mail clerk in Louisville, Ky.

> February 28, 1945
> Philippine Islands

DEAR HARRY:

Going through my old files this morning I found a letter I had written you back in December and forgot to mail. How's everything back there? I imagine it's as usual. I used to get disgusted back there, nothing ever happened, but I'd sure like to be there now. A fellow never realizes until it's too late how nice he did have it, but I'd bet 10 pesos right now that there is someone griping to you, or has been sometime today about not being able to buy some little something or other. Every day here the people come in from the hills carrying all they own with them.

Wednesday afternoon: Just as I expected, some outgoing mail came in and then a couple guys came in and started a bull session, and then I tied up the outgoing and took it to the APO and picked up the incoming. We didn't do so good today, only eight bunches for the Bn. We've still got quite a few Xmas packages out yet. Harry, it would make you sick to see the condition some of those Xmas packages were in. You can tell people and tell them, but it doesn't seem to do any good. Don't accept any packages containing candy of any kind, hard, soft, homemade, etc., for shipment over to this side of the world. The heat melts it into just a gooey mess. The worst of all were these overseas mailing boxes. Nine out of ten were busted; you know, the kind that has printed in big letters on the side "For Overseas Mailing Only." The company that manufactured that box ought to be run out of business. As long as the bags don't get wet they aren't in too bad a shape, but we got in one shipment of around 100 bags that had been soaked. I had to haul away wheelbarrow after wheelbarrow load of soggy packages that had no names on them. My pet peeve is these packages from home with the address either torn off or soaked off and yet still in pretty good shape. I tear it apart real carefully, looking for the address and find nothing but a Xmas card, signed with love, Ann, Mary, etc., nothing else. It's so easy to write the name and address on the card.

I did find out to whom one package like that belonged. The card was signed Alice, Jean, and Harry, and inside the package was a newspaper from a little town in Oklahoma. I checked the home addresses and found a fellow from there, called him on the phone and asked him if he knew Alice, Jean, and Harry and he said, "Hell yes! How did you know?" If I can make out the last four numbers of the serial number, I can find the guy. Another time I had a package come in and all I could make out of the address was the first name Frank, and inside was a nice pocketbook, with a picture of a baby in it. The fourth Frank I showed it to recognized the baby.

I wish the people at home could see the expressions on the boys' faces when they get a letter from home. You can be pretty disgusted with life and it's surprising how much better a letter will make you feel. I remember one night when the mail clerk for headquarters battery here blew the whistle for mail call at the same time the mess sergeant blew mess. Not a soul came in to eat until all the mail was distributed. The mail clerk's watch was 15 minutes fast and did the mess sergeant blow his top! Even some of the fellows that were eating early chow got up and left their supper to get their mail. When a fellow doesn't get mail for a couple of weeks he is sorta hard to get along with.

Harry, the Philippines to us are quite a place. Just like coming back to civilization again. Seems odd to see houses, good roads; we are living beside a concrete highway. Boy, what a difference from those mud roads in Guinea. A few civilian cars go by once in a while. Mostly army vehicles, though. I never knew the army had so much equipment. I think the Japs are beginning to realize that too, now. You know it makes one realize you folks back home are really going to town. Makes you proud to be an American.

It sure didn't take the natives here long to cash in. When we first came they wanted one bar of soap for an egg, but now they want five bars. Their biggest shortage seems to be clothing. They are all small, but they seem to have plenty of food. They are very polite and dress in clean clothes, but their homes—the flies sound like bees, swarming around. Most of their houses are pretty well shot and they just don't have any furniture. The poorer class use water buffaloes for transportation with sleds, but the little richer or more fortunate ones, maybe fortunate in that they have been able to save their ponies, ride around in two-wheeled carts, with a woven top. Reminds me of the old covered wagon. I've seen only two horses since I've been here. It must not be compulsory for the kids to go to school as I see several of them herding their buffaloes around. They ride one and lead one. They are perfectly at home on the buffalo's back. I was wondering how in the world they mounted the things until I saw one little fellow grab one by the tail, put his foot on the crook of the buffalo's hind legs and crawl right on up. There are more Japs here than there were in New Guinea where we were, but here you can see what you are shooting at, down there you couldn't. It seems as hot here as it was down there but there isn't much mud. I was going to say not as many bugs, but since I lighted the gas lantern I'm beginning to wonder. Bugs all over the place.

Thanks for your Xmas poem, Harry, it was very good. I got a copy of the Clay City *News* the other day dated November 15, and I see the boys are all doing a much better job of writing than I am. I can see now why it's taking so long to clean the Japs out; they are past masters at the art of digging in. It's going to take a long time yet to finish them off. At least I'm thankful we are out of the jungle. If you write me again I'll answer quicker next time, and thanks for that letter you sent just after I got the news about Paul. It sure helped.

Sincerely,
HENRY

Stewart William Hartfelter, of Sullivan, was commissioned a 1st lieutenant in the Army Chaplains' Corps in May 1942. He was sent to Hawaii in June 1943 and was attached to the 130th Infantry Regiment. Lt. Hartfelter saw service in New Guinea, Morotai, the Philippines, and Japan with the 33d Division as assistant chaplain and as chaplain, winning the Bronze Star. Promoted to the rank of major in May 1945, he remains in the Chaplains' Reserve Corps. Discharged in April 1946, Maj. Hartfelter is now minister of the Presbyterian Church, El Paso, Texas.

March 14, 1945
Philippines

DEAR AUNT KITTIE:

I have owed you a letter for quite some time now and I thought perhaps you would appreciate a letter which you can read to the Women's Association of the church. I have been terribly busy these last several weeks, as my division is in action against the enemy here in the Philippines. We are four Protestant chaplains short in our division; at full strength we have ten but have only six now, and this has placed an extra burden of work on all of us. So I hope you will forgive me for not writing oftener.

Perhaps I can relate some experiences and incidents which will give all of you a clearer picture of what has taken place over here and what is taking place now.

Newspapers report that our troops who landed in these Philippines met very little, if any, opposition from the enemy. Such reports also tell of how our troops are sweeping through certain sectors and up certain valleys and past certain cities and towns at a rapid rate of speed. Such reports, though very true in a general sense, sometimes leave the impression that we are defeating the Japs with practically no difficulty, and a general feeling is left that our forces are suffering such light casualties that they are almost negligible. It would appear that our victory is just a matter of days.

But the picture as we see it over here is quite different from the impressions held by many folks back in the States. No one should sell the Jap soldier short. In the two previous campaigns in which our division participated, the Japs we met were poorly fed, were suffering from disease and jungle rot, were poorly equipped and had low morale. The latter we learned from the prisoners we captured. But here in the Philippines the Jap is a different soldier. He is nasty and rugged; he is a savage fighter; he is well equipped; he is efficient in the use of arms; he is in excellent physical condition; he is very much a formidable foe. Our liberation of these islands is not an easy task and simply because Manila has been turned over to the Filipino government does not mean that these is-lands have now been completely liberated. True, the Japs have withdrawn from the valleys, but they have gone to the mountains where, for the past three years, they have dug elaborate caves and tunnels in which to store their supplies, am-munition, and weapons. These also serve as entrenchments for themselves where they are fairly safe from our air power and much of our artillery. If you will look at a map and study it, you will notice that hundreds of square miles of these Philippines are made up of mountainous regions. These mountains rise sometimes to a height of 4,000 feet and are steep, rugged, and have very little foliage which our men can use for cover as they scale the mountain. The infan-trymen have to move forward in the open in the face of fierce Jap machine gun, sniper, and mortar fire. So when you read that our casualties are light, it simply means that they are light in comparison with those suffered by the Nips. We are losing a goodly number of men, but we are getting more than ten Japs for every one of ours which they get.

Though the infantryman is the one who has to take the final inches of ground, and much of it has to be won in vicious hand-to-hand fighting with bay-onets, yet too much cannot be said for our American artillery. Their accuracy is phenomenal and is far superior to the Jap artillery. The Jap 77 mm. gun is their best artillery weapon. The American infantryman could never move forward if he did not have the artillery covering him. The American superior air power is of inestimable value, for our ground forces can now fight without fear of attacks from the air. The Japs bomb us occasionally at night, but their attacks are small and do very little damage.

It all adds up to this: the American soldier over here is not optimistic about an early end to this war. He knows too well that he has many square miles of hard fighting before him and he rightfully expects the fighting to be even hard-er the nearer we move to Japan.

Let me now give you a word picture of the civilians here in the Philippines and the kind of an existence they have had during the past three years. I choose the word "existence" with care, for life under the rule of the Japanese militarists is not a way of life; it is just a way of existence—and there are many cases where it was not even that.

Three years ago when the Philippines fell into the hands of the savages from the "land of the rising sun," the Japs inaugurated two policies toward the people here. In the urban areas they treated the people with reasonable consideration. They did not ravage the women, nor did they pillage their property. All this was for a specific reason, that reason being propaganda. Their policy was to win the

Filipino-Americans, that is the title the civilians wish to be identified by, over to sympathy with Japan. They tried to convince these folks that they would be better off under the rule of Japan than under the influence of America, even after they would receive their independence in 1946.

But to show you the deceitfulness of this policy, when our forces landed and eventually pushed on to Manila, as you have read in the papers, the Japs refused to allow the civilians to evacuate and kept them there as prisoners to shield themselves. As these islands were gradually liberated from their grasp, the atrocities of the Japs increased in the same degree.

The other policy which the Japs employed when they took control of these islands was practiced in the rural areas. Here they confiscated food and livestock, stole clothing and especially blankets, raped the women and especially the young girls of 14 and 15 years of age, and forced the men to labor for them without paying them even so much as a starvation wage. These are the people I have met and seen. All of these Philippine Islands are primarily rural areas. Most of the children I have seen are suffering from extreme cases of malnutrition, tuberculosis, and malaria run rampant; people are pleading for blankets to keep them from suffering from the cold, chilly nights. I have seen tiny children who have been orphaned when the Japs slew their parents for objecting to their taking food, clothing and stock. No American living in our native land can ever understand what these people in occupied lands have gone through and suffered.

Naturally, in these past few minutes while you have been listening to my description, you have been asking yourself, "Well, I wonder what the United States is doing now to help these destitute people?" That is an excellent question and I am proud of my country for the answer I can give.

A few days ago one of our patrols came back from the mountains. The men were tired, tattered and torn, unshaven and dirty. There is nothing about that which is unusual. But tenderly cuddled in the arms of one of these men was a nine-months-old baby girl. Her mother and daddy had been slain by the Japs and she had been left lying in the brush. She was suffering from severe exposure and hunger, having been there for about three days. Our public relations officer here at headquarters immediately contacted nearby civilian families and found a home that could adopt her.

What about the needed medical care of the civilians in general? Our army doctors are doing the best they can to take care of the most needy cases. This means an extra burden on our doctors, as they are kept exceedingly busy taking care of our wounded, but they still find time for this clinical work. Just a couple of evenings ago a young mother carrying her baby stopped in my tent and asked if we had a doctor near. Her baby was running a temperature. Our medical officer lives in the next tent to mine, and hearing what she said, he came over and took the mother and baby to our dispensary and gave the baby the best of medical attention. I have seen old men and women, young children and older children, receiving care in our army hospitals for sickness and sometimes for wounds received from the Japs. You would be proud of the American soldier if you could see the way he opens his heart to those in distress.

How are these civilians able to earn a living? The American Armed Forces are now employing hundreds of civilian workers to labor in our camps and build installations. For example, at our headquarters in the rear fifty men were employed for three weeks to build a chapel of bamboo. They were paid a standard wage as skilled carpenters, and the chapel is beautiful in its quaintness. There are several hundred others employed around the area. All these are paid in American-Filipino currency and they have commissaries stocked with American goods where they can buy some of the necessities of life. These people are rightfully proud. They are industrious. They do not ask for charity. They do not want someone else to keep them. They want to work and earn what they eat and wear.

The last picture I want to paint in words is a hasty sketch of what my ministry has been like here in the Philippines. I have five services on Sundays. My first is at 8:30 here in our lovely chapel at headquarters. From here I go to the portable hospital which is attached to our division. My third service is with our engineer battalion and the fourth and fifth are with our quartermaster and ordnance units. During the week I have held as many as nine services. These have been with the combat troops. In addition to this I visit the hospitals at least five times a week and there I spend worthwhile hours talking to my wounded men. It is a great source of satisfaction to see that these men receive such splendid and expert care. None of us will ever know the great number of lives which have been saved by blood plasma, the sulfa drugs, and penicillin. Then, too, I have my sad work at the cemetery and keeping the records of the burials of my men. Our United States cemeteries are hallowed ground, and when I look on the row on row of white crosses they represent more than the markings of a number of graves. As I look at each one I think of the Cross of Christ and I remember that it too is a symbol of sacrifice, the sacrifice made out of God's love for us.

Perhaps you have been wondering more about what kind of services I hold for our combat troops and the conditions under which these services are held. A description of one Friday afternoon will give you some idea.

For three days several of our rifle and heavy weapons companies had been fighting inch by inch up the steep side of a mountain ridge. The Japs were well dug in and were entrenched in their caves and tunnels. They rained machine gun and mortar fire down on our men. The sun beat down with vengeance and for thirty-six hours our men had to fight without water. But as casualties fell they still moved forward and near the crest of the range they engaged the Japs in hand-to-hand fighting. Early in the morning the crest was reached and secured. First the men buried our dead in temporary graves, then lay down to rest. A few days later these men buried on the mountain were removed to one of our United States Armed Force's cemeteries. No man is ever left in an isolated grave.

That afternoon Father Rogers and I climbed to the top of the range to see our men and hold services for them. From the crest we could look down across the opposite valley and see the enemy there in their dug-in positions. On the crest one was within range of enemy machine gun and sniper fire.

My Protestant men kept watch from our secured positions while the Catholic men dropped back below the crest and attended mass. Then the Catholic men held the positions as my men dropped back to attend my service and receive communion. That was an unforgettable moment. Every man on that mountain that day attended either the Catholic mass or my Protestant service.

No words can hope to describe what I felt in my heart as I looked into the faces of those men, faces that had been unshaven for days, faces into which had been ground the grime and dust and sweat from hours and days of desperate fighting, faces that were drawn from exhaustion and fatigue, eyes that were bloodshot from the tortures of battle, lips that were cracked from those thirty-six long hours without water, and clothes that were torn by death that passed by. . . .

As evening hastened on and the men began preparing to dig in their foxholes, Father Rogers and I started down the mountainside. At the foot of the mountain we stopped in our battalion aid station to see the wounded that had been brought down from a nearby mountain. There we found six civilians also waiting for treatment. They were refugees from the mountains. One was a woman, thin and pale. Two were men, weakened from long hours of forced labor. The other three were children. Their big, brown eyes were filled with fear and terror. To them strangers had come to mean suffering and pain. One little five-year-old girl had a compound fracture of the right arm, the five-year-old boy had an infected foot, and the other, a little six-year-old girl, had been shot through the right shoulder twenty-five days before by a Jap sniper. As I started to leave and passed by a stretcher where one of our wounded men lay, he took me by the hand and said, "Chappie, if we have to go through all this hell to prevent all this suffering by tiny, innocent children, then it is worth it."

Surely somewhere across the horizon lies a better day. It will not come tomorrow; another month will not bring it here, but one day God will lead us to it.

With love and affection to all,
STEWART

Lloyd H. Wilkins, of Indianapolis, was inducted into the Army, May 13, 1942. He was first assigned to the Air Corps, and later to the Counter-Intelligence Corps. Going overseas in March 1944, he saw duty in Australia, New Guinea, New Britain, Dutch New Guinea, the Philippines, and Japan. For this service he was awarded the Bronze Star. He was discharged Nov. 20, 1945, as special agent in the Counter-Intelligence Corps and is now doing newspaper work in San Diego, Calif.

March 17, 1945
Philippines

DEAR MR. STUART:

A man within reach of a typewriter in this spot couldn't be reasonably expected not to use it for trying to describe to someone else what has happened to one of the most beautiful cities in the Far East. And while I know those telegraph machines have probably been unwinding complete accounts of just that for some time—well, I'm still in reach of a typewriter and it's difficult, believe me, to keep its cover on.

We pulled in here by air a couple of days ago from the Netherlands East Indies, circled the city twice and then settled down on an airfield still littered with the shattered airplanes of the Rising Sun. From the plane we had seen our first glimpse of a destroyed city—blocks and blocks of shattered buildings, great governmental structures blasted and burned until only parts of walls were left, hotels, theaters and department stores converted to rubble.

Then we drove through the downtown area. There is no way to describe the total destruction here. It is almost unbelievable, although we see it every day, that any section could have been so thoroughly demolished. Not damaged, or partially damaged, but demolished from the ground up. No more thorough job could have been done. Streets littered with debris now are gradually being opened, but it is a tremendous job.

Perhaps I can better picture it this way: If this were Indianapolis—actually it is a city more than twice as large—you could see something like this from the roof of the Star building: the Scottish Rite Cathedral razed by fire, every inch of wood in it burned in a heat so terrific that every metal fixture and steel window curled and twisted, the steel girders sticking through the gaping walls still standing.

The War Memorial, American Legion building, the churches and buildings and apartments as far north as Sixteenth Street are totally destroyed—down to the ground. The Central Library's pillars are hanging by strands of steel cables, the stone ripped away. The outside steps are cratered; the building itself is only a thin stone shell, roofless and blackened.

To the west there is nothing but rubble from you to at least as far as White River. The Chamber of Commerce building, the Indianapolis Athletic Club, Illinois Street, the Capitol, filling stations, small hotels and business places are wrecked. There is nothing but emptiness.

Downtown, as far south as South Street and farther, not more than five or six buildings still stand. Ayres', Wasson's, Block's, the entire Circle, every establishment, hotel, restaurant and business place is burned to the ground, burned until only stone and steel remain. Here and there a building shows that once Indianapolis was a modern and progressive city—but that building has no roof, there are no floors left in it and it may lean precariously, with tons of concrete threatening to break loose at any moment and crash into the street.

We are at present located in one of the very few buildings still inhabitable in this city. How it stood we cannot understand, for the structures on all four sides have been entirely destroyed, and from the roof we can see only five or six in the entire downtown which still appear to be usable despite shattered windows. Even now the dust from all this rubble hangs thick in the air, and heavy trucks rolling through the city stir up more.

But there is a hammering and clattering all through these miles of destruction—hundreds of Filipinos are trying to make the city take some shape, to clean the streets and sidewalks and to open small shops. They trot through the streets carrying heavy woven baskets, suspended from a stout wooden pole, carting away the few nails, bits of metal and fixtures they find in the rubble. A half-dozen small restaurants and even a tiny bar or two have been opened amid the debris, with these entrepreneurs tacking up bright painted signs to lure their first customers.

There are two or three newspapers of five-column tabloid size, one of four pages, the others of a single sheet. Their columns reflect the struggle the city is having to get back into operation—electricity may not be available for two months, the water system only recently has been reopened on a small scale and of course there are no transportation facilities whatever. There are classified advertisements seeking information as to friends and relatives and others, from such as utility companies, calling for their employees to report back to work.

Some of the residential and smaller business sections still are standing, and there are enough beautiful Spanish homes and gardens remaining to make one realize how beautiful this city was at one time. There are small shops in Mexican-like districts—areas about like business sections of Indiana Avenue—but they have little for sale. Vegetable markets gradually are being reopened and sanitary measures are being taken. . . .

At night the city is entirely black except for dots of light, miles apart, where army units have set up their own portable generator units. Streets are deserted, and in the early morning hours there is still the rumble of artillery firing from where fighting continues outside the city itself.

The people appear to be in pretty fair shape for the most part, although they have suffered terribly and will continue to suffer for many months until the city recovers. The food shortage, critical for a time, is being bettered and the necessities of life appear to be reaching the bulk of the population. . . .

There isn't much on the lighter side. As you walk down the street, the dark-haired, bright-eyed Filipino youngsters shout "Hello Joe," grin a mile wide, and want to walk hand in hand with you for half a block or so. There are profiteers already well established to overcharge the Americans, but there are also many, both rich and poor, who want to give things away because that's the way they feel. Which is about the same way it is any place.

I'm enclosing a few bills, of which you may already have quite a collection. If so, perhaps some of the boys around the office might like a souvenir.

Best regards to you and all the rest of the staff.

LLOYD

Alex Kovachevich, of South Bend, was inducted into the Army April 18, 1942, serving first in a military police battalion and later in the engineer corps. He participated in the action on Luzon Island and returned to the United States in Sept. 1945. He was discharged Jan. 19, 1946, with the rank of sergeant and is now a welder in South Bend.

May 9, 1945
Philippines

MY DEAR WIFE:

I am just fine and I'd like to tell you what I do here, but I must remember the censor. At least I'm not in any danger. I went to the big city of Manila. Boy, I'm telling you Manila sure is torn up. Most of the people are homeless. The Japs burned their homes, and the city itself is a total wreck. . . .

I am going to get started to writing this letter now. You see, I sleep close to a busy road and the G.I. trucks go back and forth, and gosh, do they ever make the noise; so I can't think, listen and write at the same time. I can hardly wait to come home again.

I saw Manila again. It's plenty large but everything is torn up so badly that it looks like a junk yard all over. The Japs made the people go into their homes and then set fire to the homes with people in them. Some tried to escape from the fire, but the Japs shot them in their effort.

I have a fair place to sleep and eat—of course, it isn't like being home with you and Larry, but I can take it for a while. I should be used to this rough life by now. I live in an open air hut as it is so very hot here. The sun really burns the heck out of us. Everybody that was white is sure tan now. Right now are the rainy months for rice growing.

I haven't received the wrist watch yet. Don't worry about it, it'll get here someday. I've talked to some of the boys who have been here for some time and they tell me they still haven't received their Christmas packages yet, so it takes time to get here.

I'm going to try and get some sleep tonight and go to church tomorrow, so until tomorrow night I will say so long, with all my love to you and Larry.

Your husband,
ALEX

Dota Claudius Brown, of Hudson, enlisted in the Seabees on March 4, 1942, and was rated a second class petty officer. On March 2, 1943, he was commissioned an ensign and was made commanding officer of an armed guard crew aboard the merchant ship "Lucretia Mott," which sailed to Africa, Sicily, and Italy. Returned to the States, he was made naval gunfire liaison officer and attached to the First Marine Division for their landing and occupation of Peleliu Island, where he won the Silver Star. He was then released from this duty and was placed aboard a destroyer escort, the U.S.S. "Jack Miller," DE 410, as torpedo and gunnery officer. In May 1944, Brown was promoted to lieutenant (j.g.) and in Nov. 1945 to lieutenant. He was released from active duty Dec. 25, 1945. Lt. Brown returned to Hudson and is an entertainer.

June 9, 1945
San Francisco, Calif.

DEAR MOM:

I have been so rushed and busy with all sorts of little things I just haven't had time to write to anyone since we arrived in port. I will do these few lines before I retire to let you know the latest good news in the life of your sailor son.

Day before yesterday they started getting the ship shined and ready. Early yesterday morning everyone was up bright and early to clean and swab down the ship from stem to stern. There is no admiral present so our skipper arranged for a navy captain to come aboard for the ceremony. Then as the sun grew higher and hotter the men all changed to the uniform of the day and the officers all wore greys. I put on my tropical worsted uniform for the first time since I was in the States a year ago. One of the colored boys shined my shoes to a polish like a mirror and I wore a pair of the socks you sent me. There were side boys dressed in white at the gangway.

At 10 A.M. all of our crew came to attention on the forecastle, lined two rows on each side of the ship with the officers in the center. Men on the ships tied along both sides of us were there to watch from their ships. The speaker system was rigged. Then the navy chaplain was piped aboard. I was called front and center. After reading the citation, congratulatory letters and forwarding endorsements, the captain pinned on your son a SILVER STAR medal for a certain episode which happened at Peleliu nearly nine months ago. Such a high award came as a complete surprise and it is needless to say that I was overwhelmed.

There were several pictures taken during and after the presentation. They are being developed and printed this week end so I will have some soon. I hope they turn out well. In the wardroom later there was a special dinner and I had liberty all afternoon. The medal has a beautiful red, white and blue ribbon with a bronze star suspended which in turn has a small silver star inside a wreath done in relief. I shall make copies of the citation which was read over the speaker system to all hands. I will send the original papers and the medal to Lillian with instructions for her to forward them to you as soon as she has seen them. You can see them and keep them for me.

This is about the most exciting thing that has happened to me since I received my commission as an ensign back in Boston. We received 34 bags of mail so the checkbook and several letters came from you. I will answer them as soon as I can, but I did want to dash off this bit of news first. We can now tell that we were working at Okinawa until May first so I'll write a little about that next time. I'm still in there pitching.

Love from your son,
CLAUDIUS

The citation is a temporary one and the real one will reach me later printed on parchment. My name was engraved on reverse side of the medal.

Edward Wiles, of Rensselaer, was inducted into the Army on July 7, 1942. Attached to the 99th Field Artillery Battalion, 1st Cavalry Division, Wiles fought in the Southwest Pacific. Promoted to staff sergeant, he was discharged Oct. 27, 1945, and is a coach at the Fair Oaks High School, Fair Oaks, Ind.

June 10, 1945
Camp "Mabuhay," Rest Camp
First Cavalry Div., P. I.

DEAR FOLKS:

To begin with, the rest camp is just what the name implies. It is not a hospital or "recuperation," but simply a nice, comfortable place where First Cavalry Division soldiers, fresh off the fighting line, can spend a few days enjoying life. Each outfit is allowed periodic quotas.

The camp is located on an estate owned by a wealthy Filipino planter. Before the war it was frequently visited by General MacArthur and the late Philippine President, Manuel Quezon. Our name for it—"Mabuhay"—means "long live" in the native Tagalog language.

We have a large swimming pool with diving boards and all the trimmings, just like those in the States. Our reading room has the latest magazines and books, writing paper and tables, and best of all, large soft chairs. In our recreation room there are ping-pong tables, dart games, checkerboards, and plenty of cards and tables.

The post exchange here is as well supplied as any on the island. We have plenty of fruit juices, candy, cookies, chewing gum, one can of beer a day, and ice-cold drinks. And the food is a real treat, especially for soldiers who have been living on field rations.

On the entertainment side, we have a movie every night, except dance nights, which are every fourth night. The girls from a nearby town have formed a local version of the "USO" and make fine dancing partners. In addition we have band concerts by our own band.

Best of all, a soldier here has no "details"—which means no work. If he just wants to sit around and do nothing all day but relax, that's O.K. with the people who run the camp.

We have two Red Cross girls here who are doing a fine job. They organize the dances, serve snacks at odd hours during the day, join us in our games and generally make the place a lot brighter just by mingling with the fellows and talking to them. The commanding officer of the camp, who really got the whole thing organized and keeps it running, is our Division Special Service Officer, Major John Anderson, Tucson, Arizona.

This may sound like a "soft war" from all I have told you, but there was plenty of tough fighting before the Japs were whipped and there will probably be plenty more. As I said, this is just a "relaxing point" for combat soldiers, but next to being home, it's about as nice a place as I could ask for.

Ed

⇢ XII ⇠

CHINA-BURMA-INDIA

SHORTLY after the attack on Pearl Harbor, the Japanese entered Malaya, and the British troops stationed there retreated toward Singapore, which fell Feb. 17, 1942. Java was occupied three weeks later, and the American-Dutch fleet was destroyed in the Java Sea battle. With the Dutch East Indies in their hands, the Japanese turned toward Burma. They occupied this country and successfully cut the Burma Road (Stilwell Road), supply line to China, which was opened in Jan. 1939, running from Lashio in Burma to Chungking. The Japanese had cut China in two, and in order to get supplies to China, the Americans constructed the Ledo Road in 1943–1944 from Ledo in northeast India to a junction with the Burma Road near the Chinese border. The American Air Force also flew supplies to China over the "Hump," a route from India over the Himalaya Mountains. In March 1945 the British entered Mandalay, and at the same time Chinese troops captured Lashio, the old terminus of the Burma Road. The British recaptured Rangoon on May 4, completing their conquest of Burma and reopened the road, which allowed supplies to flow into China again.

William R. Wangelin, of Indianapolis, enlisted in the Army Sept. 30, 1942, and was assigned to the band at the pilots' Basic Training Field, Gunter Field, Ala. In June 1944 he was sent to radio operator's school (ATC) at Reno, Nev. In Jan. 1945 Pfc. Wangelin was sent to Myitkyina, Central Burma, where he flew the "Hump," for which service he was awarded the Air Medal and the Distinguished Flying Cross. Discharged Feb. 6, 1946, Wangelin is now residing in Indianapolis.

Sunday, 22 April 1945
China

DEAR FOLKS:

After raining all last night it was warm again today. I had just the kind of flight I like—two hours this afternoon. The clouds were beautiful, but we were busy dodging them. We had no deicer boats so didn't go out again.

That's the way it is here—safe. An American chute is just like an American grenade. They're made that way. I've talked to lots of Marines and guys who said they had never heard of a grenade failing to go off. It's the same with our chutes, God bless 'em.

I'll try to tell you more about my jump. To begin with, we were hopelessly lost but didn't know it at the time. We were getting near the end of our gas supply. One engine cut out. We were in a storm which got very rough. We'd picked up a load of ice and were losing altitude fast. I'd known all along we were going to have to go, and put my chute on and went up front. I saw the altimeter spinning like crazy and said, "The hell with it—let's go." I opened the back door. Couldn't throw out any cargo because of the extreme turbulence. I carried the pilot's and co-pilot's chutes up and one would hold the plane while the other put his on. I was back at the door when they put on the auto-pilot and came back. It was all black out, with snow going past about 120 m.p.h. and frost and ice all over the plane and door. I saw them coming back and motioned to go and the pilot nodded his head so I went—but fast. I took a little hop, feet first and facing the tail. I didn't even see it go by and must have missed it by a mile. The roar stopped immediately and was replaced by a steady hiss of air. Very pleasant sensation, like floating. I tried to remember to keep my feet together. I had my jacket on and had pulled my pistol from its belt and put it in a pocket of the jungle vest. I had no intention of messing with the jungle vest (they contain a little of everything) or with the pistol belt, which had a canteen, two extra loaded magazines, knife, and first aid kit on it. I took the vest out looped over my left arm. I figured if I dropped it—the hell with it. If not—O.K.

Well, I could tell I'd turned on my back by the direction of the air rush in a few seconds. So I found the cord and pulled. Then I waited about two weeks for the chute to open. On my back was a good position because of the chute being on my chest. I had intended to wait a little longer.

Well, I expected to be made a eunuch when the chute opened, or at least be paralysed for a few hours. Leg straps, you know. The jolt was so light I thought it wasn't open. I could only see the pack above me so I pulled it down (very hard, I should have known) or maybe pulled myself up. That was why I let the ring drop. I was yelling and cussing and praying and everything. I felt around on top of the pack to see if it was fouled. About that time the lightning flashed and I saw the canopy above me—which made me happy more than somewhat. Then I relaxed and began to enjoy the ride. It was so nice and quiet and occasionally I could see I was drifting down through clouds. It was raining. I realized my hands were very cold so I worked them and soon got down where it was warmer. I heard the plane coming back and was kind of worried. The air had been so rough I wouldn't have been surprised at any direction the plane took—despite the auto-pilot. I heard a whoof which I took to be a puff of air. A big orange light came up through the clouds over my left shoulder. At first I thought we were over a field and they had turned a searchlight on. Then I saw the plane burning till I drifted over a mountain. My chute only had two risers instead of four so I couldn't turn or control myself very well. I thought I had a few minutes to go yet when all of a sudden I sat down—in the mud. It was a steep hill or mountainside field with little rivulets running down through the red mud.

Me and my chute were a mess. I hung my vest on a little pine tree and struggled with my chute making a kind of shelter in the pines. I looked around and yelled but could see or hear nothing. Being very happy I sang, prayed, and whistled. I don't remember what—whatever came to my head. I fished my pipe and glasses out of my pocket. I figured out what time it was at home and wondered if I would have to stand in the mud all night under that chute. Boy, was I ever happy. Then I saw a light coming up the hill and yelled. It finally turned out to be a little Chinese gal with a bunch of grass for a torch. Not knowing who it was I held up my hands to show I was friendly. It was a long while before I figured out what age, sex, or race she was. I gathered up my chute and vest and followed her, slipping and sliding down the hill. She kept me hopping and she pulled another bunch of grass for a new torch. Her shack was only about 50 yards away, but I couldn't see it 'til we were almost there. It was very small—made of mud, sticks and grass. There were two little kids, a boy and girl, who wore only little vests. No men around. I sat on the floor and dried out by a little fire which we all blew on and fed little sticks. I took a chocolate bar out of my vest and divided up—which made quite a hit. I sang some blues for them. I don't know how that went over. I showed them my signal mirror and compass and fishing kit and other stuff that was in my pockets and jungle kit. I don't know whether I made her understand where I came from or not. There was a little bamboo platform overhead (I couldn't stand up straight), and she made motions for me to go up and sleep with them. I thought otherwise so I lay down on the dirt floor by the fire and she got me a grass mat. She got a small chunk of wood to glowing and put it back in a sort of mud fireplace—to save the fire, I expect. She used a pair of iron tongs which was the only implement I noticed. They went up to bed.

I don't think any of us slept much. I shivered quite a bit, being still damp. There were little things crawling around on me, but I know lice don't crawl so I figured them for fleas. There was a little goat sleeping at my feet and a puppy at my head. There were a smelly bunch of pigs over in one corner. When I'd get up to go out the little goat would cry till I came back. About dawn the girl went out but I was half dozing so didn't pay much attention. I heard someone call "hello" and went out. I didn't know whether it was a missionary, soldier, or what. It was the co-pilot. He was a mess and had spent a miserable night out—as had the pilot. The gal went away again and soon came back with some Chinese men. I started to cut my chute in half to take along for a tent, but since they offered to carry it I took the whole thing—also they got the co-pilot's. We must have been pretty high as we got worn out running around the rice paddies on that mountain. We came to several larger, better houses. The whole population gathered around; there was much jabbering on both sides. They watched us clean our guns and open our jungle kits. They made washing motions and gave us hot water to wash. They showed us some eggs and we had them boil them—in the same little teapot. Then they made us rice and tea. We thought it best to eat nothing unboiled. Soon some other men came with the pilot. I passed out little things such as Life Savers and little bits of tinfoil.

After hanging around awhile we left with our chutes and four men. We thought they made railroad motions but weren't sure. We got on a little mountain road and soon saw a road in the distance following a river. We spent four or five hours walking downhill. A train was sitting in the station and we went across the river in a ferry like a bateau and through the same town and to the train. A G.I. was standing on the back platform. I said, "Hey, Joe, where are we?" He said, "My God don't you know?" We got on the train with them and went to their small camp. They treated us swell. The next day we rode the same train back (all day) to an air base we knew.

The next day we made an accident report and a report to the intelligence department—a lot of red tape—and we finally got a plane back to our home base that night. There are other details that might interest you. Is there anything else you want to know? I'll be able to tell you how the Chinese live, dress, etc., when I get home.

Love,
BILL

Donald G. Pribble, of Rockport, enlisted in the Air Corps, Feb. 12, 1943. He was sent to China in March 1945 as a radio operator in the 14th Air Force, first with the 317th Fighter Control Squadron, then with the 81st Fighter Group. Pfc. Pribble was also stationed in India. Discharged March 16, 1946, he returned to college.

June 28, 1945
Somewhere in China

DEAR MOTHER AND DAD:

Yesterday I went to town and visited the university again. While there I picked out a nice jade ring for you. The best jade is found at the university. It is light green and very translucent. Dark green jade is more expensive but it isn't as translucent as the light green, and I think that's what makes it so pretty. I visited the radio station at the university. They have a big transmitter that sends code to the States and another smaller one that is a regular broadcasting transmitter. The chief engineer could speak just enough English to explain the setup to me. But instead of transmitter, he said, "broadcasting engine."

While at the university I met an American music teacher and, of course, the first thing I asked her was if there was an organ any place in China. To my surprise she told me there was one right in this very town and it's the *only one* in Free China! She wrote me a letter of introduction to a Chinese friend of hers who is a member of the church, which is Catholic, where the organ is. This man was a doctor of philosophy and got his schooling in the States. He was very interesting to talk to. He was easy to find so I showed him the note and he took me to the church this afternoon. All the priests there are French, including the organist. The organ is a two-manual job that has to be pumped by a long pole at the back. I was surprised that it had such good tone despite the fact that it needed some work done on it. It was about 25 years old and was made in Paris. I played on it for a while, then asked the priest to play for me. His technique wasn't so good, but he was very good at improvising. He has been in China for ten years, but his home is in Paris. He didn't look over 30 years old.

After we finished playing, he took me out into the courtyard and introduced me to about half a dozen other priests and the bishop of the church—all from France. It was very pleasant to listen to their English with the strong French accent and also to their pure French. It just seems to roll out—so different from the Chinese tongue. Next Sunday the bishop, who has a long white beard down to his belt, is celebrating his 50th year in China. It's to be quite an occasion. The new priests are to be ordained at that time.

All the priests are very hospitable. They asked me how long I had been in China, all about America, etc. The organist asked about the organs in the States and asked whose music was the most frequently played. I told him Bach was first, but that the composers of France ran a close second. He seemed quite pleased at that. While we were sitting there one of the priests brought out two bottles of beer. He asked me if I would like a glass and I told him "no." He seemed very much surprised that I didn't like beer. So he offered me whiskey, wine, gin and brandy. Well, I felt that I should drink something with them, just to be polite, and since I had never tasted brandy I told him I'd have a glass of that. That was the first and the *last* brandy that I'll ever drink. Gosh, it was strong!

Well, we chatted for about an hour and then I thanked them kindly for their hospitality and left with an invitation to come back whenever I could. They were very interesting and I do intend to go back again someday.

All for this time.

With love,
DONALD

Leslie J. Van Steenberg, of Fort Wayne, enlisted in the Army Air Corps in Jan. 1942. Commissioned a 2d lieutenant in Feb. 1943, he was sent to the C.B.I. theater where he flew the "Hump" from Nov. 1943 to Dec. 1944, completing 102 round trips. Lt. Van Steenberg was awarded two battle stars for the Burma and China campaigns, the Air Medal with one cluster, and the Distinguished Flying Cross with one cluster. Promoted to captain in Sept. 1946, he was discharged in October and is a store manager in Fort Wayne.

DEAR—:

We were on a night flight to China and lost one engine and were forced to bail out. We didn't know exactly where we were, but not very far out from our base. We couldn't maintain altitude and being in the overcast were afraid we might run into a mountain, so there was nothing else to do but jump. I couldn't get one leg strap of my chute fastened, so was delayed slightly, making me the last one to leave the ship. I waited as long as I could, trying to fasten the leg strap, but met with no success, so I dove out and pulled the rip cord—I still have it, too. I was afraid the jerk would hurt me, but it didn't even strain me. I did lose my right shoe and flying boot when the chute opened.

When the chute first opened I was in the clouds and couldn't see anything, could just barely make out the chute over my head. Shortly afterwards I got below the clouds and the ship crashed underneath me and burned, lighting up the whole sky. I watched very closely to get and keep my bearings as to direction and terrain, as I knew when I hit I wouldn't be able to tell anything. I could see a river below me and another large river quite some distance away; also I was surrounded on three sides by jungle-covered mountains. It seemed like it took me an awfully long time to get down. I started swinging several times and stopped that by pulling the risers, also I tried to guide the chute towards the river by pulling the risers, and I think I met with some success. I wasn't a bit scared and remember thinking very clearly what to do. I got down below the mountains and knew I was going to light in a valley very soon. It was a very dark night and I couldn't see very much, but just before I hit it looked like I was going to fall into what I thought was a tree so I grabbed the risers and the next thing I knew I was on the ground.

I hit into some low jungle undergrowth right next to a banyan tree. The undergrowth broke my fall and I didn't hit hard at all. I lit near the bottom of a small mountain in a valley near a small stream as I could hear water running. The ground was on an angle of about forty-five degrees, and it was hard to keep from sliding on down. I pulled my chute on down from the trees and crawled to a slightly more level place and propped my feet against two banyan trees, wrapping myself up in the chute to wait for morning. It was too dark to see anything and I knew there was no sense trying to do anything until morning. There were no signs of the rest of the crew and not much noise, except the stream and some peculiar jungle sounds the trees and things make which is pretty weird and hard to describe. I had just about got set for the night when it started to rain, more fun! At first not much got through the trees, but I realized it would, so I made sort of a tent out of part of the chute by throwing it over some bushes at my head and wrapped up in the rest of it. Boy, you have never heard such a noise as rain in the jungle. I wasn't exactly scared, but sort of nervous. I tried to sleep, but every time I would just about get to sleep, one of the louder noises would wake me up with a start and I would swear someone or something was coming. After a while I got used to the noises and didn't pay any attention to them, and I guess I fell asleep for a little while.

First Day: At dawn I opened my jungle kit in the chute and made a pack out of the rest of the chute, folding up the silk, and started down the little stream as it was running in the right direction, I thought, to lead me to the river. The stream had a rock bed, but the jungle grew almost over it and it was still pretty tough going. I stopped and cut my chute in half and tore everything else off it and left enough to make a lighter pack, as it was harder than h—— to carry anything and I had too much with me. Shortly after that the stream disappeared into a swamp so I started off in the right direction. Soon after that I ran into a water buffalo trail and followed that for about an hour, and it led me right to the river around noon. At this point it wasn't much of a river, it did have a pretty good rock bed but there wasn't much water running and you could cross it almost any place by jumping or stepping on rocks.

It was a lot easier walking along the river than in the jungle, but there wasn't anything but rocks, no sand, so it wasn't easy. I had put my left flying boot on my right foot so I had a left oxford and left flying boot and the rocks weren't too easy on my feet. The jungle kit has two packages of D-rations in it, a very nourishing chocolate, and is supposed to keep you going for around ten days. But you sure get tired of it. . . .

Third Day: Broke camp around 7 o'clock again, decided to try and get around the cliff once more, but slipped and fell into the river, so went back to the camp and dried out. Was just about to start out again when the rest of the crew walked up, and was I glad to see them! Found out they had all landed pretty close together on top of the mountain, and it took them about all the first day to get down. They had been following my trail all along, and the two left footprints sure had them puzzled. They had picked up the half chute I had left, as both the enlisted men had landed in trees and couldn't get their chutes down. They spent the first night hanging in the trees, too. None of us was hurt at all, so we were pretty lucky in that respect. We all decided to climb the cliff through the jungle; it was pretty difficult, but we made it O.K. Found some wild lemons around noon, and they were very good, almost the same as you could buy in the stores at home, except a little smaller. Made camp at 5:30 P.M. It rained all night and we were all very miserable and tired and it was impossible to sleep, being cold and wet. We dried out our clothes at dawn, and left camp around 7 o'clock. . . .

Fifth Day: Around noon the little rescue plane spotted us. The rest of the fellows were so happy that two of them fell in the river waving at it, but you know me, I didn't get very excited. Of course, I was happy about being found, but I wasn't about to fall in the river, so I stayed on the bank. We built a fire there and the rescue plane came back about an hour and a half later and dropped us some food and two blankets, also a message to stay on the river and they would keep us supplied. But for some reason or other (we never did find out why) they never dropped us any more food. We were all very hungry but couldn't eat much, not eating anything but chocolate for so long, and couldn't use a little can of corn willie. We took the rest of the food with us and made camp around 4:30 and ate again. By this time we could eat a little more. . . .

Eighth Day: Around 4:30 we came upon an old native and his two boys. It wasn't a village, just sort of a camp where the natives stopped on their way up the river fishing. The old native's hut was built upon stilts about twenty feet from the ground; also there were three or four bamboo lean-tos where they ate and slept. We conveyed to him the fact we were hungry, so he offered us some fermented rice and stuff that wasn't so hot, so we didn't eat any of that. Later on he fixed us a meal. Honey, I don't imagine you have ever eaten any, and I didn't think I would ever be eating it, but the best meal I ever tasted was fish heads and rice. The old native couldn't understand or talk any English, but he had seen Americans before and knew about the road I told you about before and promised to take us to the village and later the road. He made motions like a steam shovel to indicate the road. We got everything across by sign language; before we got back we were getting good at it. You would have died laughing at some of the motions we went through; in fact, we almost died at ourselves. We slept in the bamboo lean-to, which was just a little better than our tent, but we couldn't have as big a fire burning so we were colder. . . .

[The native took the crew of four to a village. They were then conducted down the mountain to another village and thence to the Burma Road on the twelfth day. Then they were taken to an American base hospital.]

LESLIE

Paul Howerton, of East Chicago, entered the Army Air Force on ————. He was sent out of the country in July 1943 to India, where he was attached to the Northern Air Service Area Command of the C.B.I. Air Service Command. Cpl. Howerton returned to the United States in October 1945 and was discharged. He is now a chemist in East Chicago.

April 20, 1944
India

My Dear Son:

Today you are five years old. You can't as yet read this but Mommy is undoubtedly reading it to you. You have a rare privilege in living in America. I doubt whether you will ever realize how lucky you really are. You live in a country where men are free. I know that is a very trite expression, and its full meaning is not apparent until you have seen what goes on in other countries. Americans tend to take this freedom too much for granted. Many years ago Grandma and Grandpa Howerton's ancestors fought for this country of ours. They didn't know why they were fighting except that they must be freed from the dominance of England. They were fighting for the freedom that you now enjoy. Every war that America has been involved in since has been to preserve that freedom. It is the spirit and heritage gained by our forebears that make us the proud and powerful nation that we are today. It has made us the envy of the world because we did not believe in the dog-eat-dog principle of Europe and Asia. We believed what was told us by Benjamin Franklin when he said "In union there is strength. We must all hang together or we shall all hang separately." God had said the same thing many hundred years before when He said, "Do unto others as you would have others do unto you." I hope that your life will be guided by this rule.

Your greatest privilege, though, was being the son of your blessed mother. I know that it is needless to tell you to always look after her. I am proud of you and Terry. You are the two finest boys in the world and the whole credit belongs to your mother. *Never forget that.* Your grandparents have given you something to live up to, and I am confident that they are as proud of you as I am.

I love you and some day we will be all together again. Happy birthday!

Love,
Daddy

Laverta Baldwin, of Jeffersonville, was inducted into the Army Oct. 4, 1943, and was attached to the Air Corps, 61st Air Service Group. Sent overseas in Sept. 1944, he served in India and Burma and earned two battle stars. Transferred to the 54th Air Service Group, Pfc. Baldwin returned to the States in March 1946 and was discharged March 17. He returned to work at Jeffersonville.

Sunday, July 29, 1945
India

DEAR MOM:

I received three letters from you today and was glad to hear all is well on the home front. If things keep going like they are over here, that will be the only front to worry about and I'll be home to do my share. My being here at Shamshanagro, India, is a big joke. I could be doing far more for the war effort if I were home. Before, we were doing a job (and a good one at that), but now—? What a joke it is. I haven't done a thing since coming here towards working on a plane. Due to a fire which burned down the mess hall I have been a carpenter for the past four days. Other than that I haven't done anything. If only we would get away from this base to a busy place, I would be happy again. Before, we worked like dogs "keeping them flying" seven days a week, ten to fourteen hours a day. Then I was happy but not now. Don't get me wrong, this is a swell base. It's almost like a camp in the States, but there just isn't any, or rather enough, work for the men. Of course, there are a lot of details to keep us occupied most of the time, but—I hate doing a job just to keep busy. If it had some goal then everything would be okay. All I can do is hope we can get away from here to a better place.

Well, so much for the griping. I just had to get it off my mind, that's all.

I think I told you about how much better looking the country is here in Assam than any of the other places I've been. The trees, grass, rice, and tea make this possible. They are all a beautiful shade of green. It reminds me of the late spring at home after the trees have donned their spring coats. Still, the typical Indian villages prevail. I'll attempt to describe one for you. First you walk up to what you would think to be a small woods, and upon going still farther you see it's more or less cleared out for a ways leaving anywhere from ten to twenty or thirty woven bamboo huts with thatched roofs. These have doors which are four or five feet high and you would have to stoop over a bit to enter. The scene inside would startle you. They have no furniture except maybe a bamboo platform which is used for a bed. The room is usually around eight by ten feet. They do their cooking outdoors, or some have a crude fireplace which smokes up the whole village. They don't need closets, dressers, bathrooms or any of that stuff. Why? Well, they only have a couple of rags for clothes which they wrap around themselves.

As for a bathroom—they have a man-made pond which we G.I.'s call "wog ponds." Most often they are of a perfect rectangle shape anywhere from fifteen feet by twenty to a hundred by two hundred feet. The sides are all straight and the corners square. If they were cemented they would compare with the best of the swimming pools at home. They don't do as we do back home when they bathe. They wear a cloth wrapped around them at all times. Don't ask me how they get clean all over because I don't know. I don't think they do. They use this "wog pond" for their laundry too. First they dip the clothes in the water then beat them with a stick or just beat them against a rock or board, whichever is the handiest method.

Yes, everything they do is done in a very primitive way. Even their means of farming is backward. It would take a hundred years to be as modernized as we are if we tried to help them. Let me tell you a story I heard from a man who tried to help them. He said, "When I came here and bought a large tract of land and hired the natives to work, they were a very backward people. They used a couple of oxen to pull a plow (which was made of wood), and one man could only plow a small plot in a day. I bought plows, discs, harrows, and tractors to pull this equipment with. But would they use it? No, they just wouldn't change over. 'It was good enough for my father so it is good enough for me' was their way of thinking. One day I finally got a young boy to drive the tractor after trying all the older men who wouldn't even climb up on the machine. He was doing all right for three or four days, but one day I went out and found them back at the old ox-drawn plow while they left the tractor parked out in the middle of the field. They had already plowed all around the tractor, not even taking the pains to move it or see what was wrong with it. I looked it over and found out it had run out of gas. Later on, after teaching them all about it, the natives finally decided it was a lot faster and less hard work to use the modern machinery. I now have a farm which pays good money and I have an agricultural school and the enrollment is picking up slowly but surely." He told this story just to illustrate how backward these people are. At times I feel sorry for them and still other times I am disgusted with them.

In America a woman is young looking even up to forty or forty-five, but here a woman twenty-five or thirty looks as though she were at least fifty-five. The best years of a girl's life here are between fourteen and nineteen. After that they are finished. Gee, but I'm glad I'm an American. We have anything and everything to make life a pleasure, while over here the Indians have nothing to look forward to except hard endless work, starvation, illness and death. What a worthless and miserable life they live. I am enclosing a picture of an Indian girl who is only about sixteen years old. To me she looks about twenty-three or four years old. What do you think? Yes, she is a typical Indian girl. The men? Should I have to tell you anymore? They are the same as the girls. A boy starts out at about eight or nine years old to help support the family. All that he makes is turned over to the family for food. It's a damned shame how these people live. Again I say, I'm glad I'm an American. Well, so much for the Indian and his way of living. I am getting disgusted just writing about them. On to more pleasant subjects. . . .

Love,
LAVERTA

Fred W. Fries, of Indianapolis, entered the Army July 25, 1942, and was commissioned a 2d lieutenant May 10, 1943. After serving as liaison officer for German prisoners of war at Fort Sumner, he was sent to India Aug. 30, 1944. There he served as assistant special service officer at three air depots in the Calcutta area. He was promoted to 1st lieutenant July 25, 1944. Discharged March 20, 1946, he returned to work at Indianapolis.

October 21, 1945
India

DEAR IRMA:

It is Wednesday night and my roommate and I have decided to run into Calcutta, to visit the Thieves' Market. You have never seen a city like Calcutta. It is in a class by itself.

We are going to town in a jeep, this being a very maneuverable vehicle and therefore the safest one in which to make such an excursion. We are just now proceeding down a very narrow road for about twenty miles. This road, they say, is the most densely populated area in the world, Brooklyn included. And I can believe it. As we go zooming along at twenty-eight per (the captain is driving), at every whipstitch a cow runs across the road in front of us, or an English lorry without lights looms up from the other direction, and we politely give way, because these lorries are very ponderous trucks indeed. Down either side of the road, moving in both directions, runs an endless stream of humanity. Just now it is quite chilly in these parts of an evening, and the natives have begun to burn cow dung in their huts, this being about the only fuel available. If you have never burned cow dung, you cannot imagine what a dense, black, impenetrable smoke it produces, and this smoke having a pernicious tendency to settle over the road, driving becomes doubly hazardous. By the time we get to town I have succeeded in wearing two big holes in the floor board where I have been pressing my feet.

The city itself is a madhouse. There are military trucks and jeeps, tiny European stock cars, innumerable taxicabs, horse-drawn carriages, ox-carts and rickshaws—all contending for the right-of-way. Times Square is a haunted house by comparison.

Ever since the Japs pulled a couple of token raids a year or so ago, there has been a dim-out in effect. To all intents and purposes it's a black-out. The main streets are infested with rickshaws. With their two tiny lights under the chassis, they give you the impression of so many beetles crawling in and out of traffic. Suffice it to say, I am one very relieved boy when we finally park the jeep and resort to pedicular locomotion.

Without further adieu, we head for the Thieves' Market, this being the primary purpose for our excursion into town. Let me state at this point that nobody ever goes to town without a specific predetermined purpose. It just isn't done.

As tradition has it, the Thieves' Market is so named because all the stuff sold there is supposed to be contraband or stolen. Normally, the place is off-limits, but under the auspices of a Red Cross tour one may go in. That benevolent organization, it seemeth, covereth a multitude of sins.

At first sight, the Thieves' Market strikes me as being the biggest collection of junk I have ever seen under one roof, if you discount the results of Brooklyn's eighth district in the 1941 scrap drive. Before I go any further afield, let me say that my companion is Captain Luty, from Philadelphia or Chicago or Atlantic City, I don't know which, but that fact alone should recommend him. Come to think of it, he hails from L. A., but that is neither here nor there and doesn't affect our story one way or another. Now that your mind is at ease with reference to my companionship, let us proceed with the narrative of our itinerary.

We stop at the first bazaar, this being a highfaluting name for a vendor's stand, just like Joe Venuzzio's fruit stand at the City Market. This duck is selling everything from salt and pepper shakers to bathtubs. You can't say they aren't above board; everything is on display.

I price the tubs, just for a joke. They are of the 1908 vintage, you might say. "Thirty rupees," he tells me, which adds up to about ten frogs in American dough, which I figure is dirt cheap for a bathtub, regardless of vintage. "Do you deliver?" the captain asks with a straight face, and, of course, this superfluous interrogation promptly throws me into a convulsion of laughter, which is exactly what he intended. The captain also is quite beside himself at his own joke. As a matter of fact, everybody laughs. Everybody, that is, but the merchant. He is in dead earnest. "No, I'm sorry, sahib," he replies in all seriousness, "we cannot make deliveries." We move on to the next vendor.

On display at this particular junk shop is a large variety of items, notably an old-fashioned coffee grinder, one of Tom Edison's original gramophones, a porcelain bedpan and a picture of Adolph Hitler. The captain examines the bedpan, but my interest reverts to the picture of Adolph, it being the first time I had seen such a picture with a frame around it. It is made up in a kind of bas-relief, as you might say, and this treatment tends to enhance the famous cookie duster more than somewhat. "How much?" I ask the merchant. "Five rupees," he quotes me, which, if you haven't figured it up already, is approximately $1.75 in real money. This strikes me as being an exorbitant price, albeit the character personified is very much in demand and carries a much higher stipend on his head, if you follow me. I finally manage to divert the captain's attention from the bedpan long enough to tell him what I am quoted on the aforementioned nightmare, *i.e.*, the Fuehrer's face. Both the captain and I agree that at that price it is a holdup, no less, and we don't mind telling him so. The vendor is more than a little upset and I might even say incensed at our attitude and threatens to call the M.P.'s. Figuring that the argument is not one that might be enhanced by the presence of the Military Police, we beat a hasty retreat, and forego the privilege of having a picture of Hitler to hang in our latrine.

At the next bazaar we find a very pretty WAC (a Pfc., I believe, though I didn't see much of her *sleeve*) looking at some baby shoes and other more intimate infant apparel that happens to be on display. Imagine her chagrin when her companion, a corporal, busts in on the scene and spying the proceedings, cries out in a loud, stentorian soprano (just as you expected) : "Why Jane, dear, why didn't you tell me?" Being in the same building and within earshot (anyone this side of the Victoria Memorial could hear it), we cannot help but overhear this unkind observation on the part of the corporal, but it strikes us as being quite funny, and we give vent to our natural risibilities. The Pfc. is more than a little disturbed, and our amusement only tends to increase her discomfiture. So we politely move on (the corporal is still hysterical), more strongly convinced than ever that rank has its undeniable advantages.

The next vendor is selling shoes. Shoes of every type and description, men's, ladies', children's, and horse. And now I am sure that the Thieves' Market comes by its moniker deservedly, for there smack dab in the front row, big as life, what do I see but three pairs of G.I. issue.

Finally, our excursion is over. I have bought a few useless items, but the captain, unable to get a decent price on the bedpan, walks out empty-handed. As we exit, we are dickering with the idea of a little reverse lend-lease in the form of shoplifting (in keeping with the name of the joint), but, as usual, virtue triumphs. There isn't anything worth stealing anyway. So we hurry back to get along with the war.

As ever,
FRED

→ XIII ←

THE RYUKYU ISLANDS AND JAPAN

THE assault on Iwo Jima was a naval operation, with the Marines making an amphibious landing on February 19, 1945. They met fanatical resistance from the well-entrenched Japanese. They captured Mount Suribachi on February 23, but the island was not finally taken until March 16. Iwo Jima afforded the United States a B-29 base, from which planes were launched to bomb the Japanese main islands. Following this air campaign, the American forces landed on Okinawa April 1. Fighting was light at first but soon stiffened, and the Marines and Army lost considerable men in the assault. Okinawa was secured on June 21, and the neighboring island of Ie Shima was taken. With the winning of these three islands, the American forces were just 500 miles from the home islands of Japan, and long-range bombers and carrier-based planes rained destruction on the main cities in the islands. Then, on August 6, the first atomic bomb fell on Hiroshima. Two days later another was dropped on Nagasaki. Russia declared war on Japan on August 8, sending armies into Manchuria and Korea.

Howard E. Claxton, of Paoli, enlisted in the Army July 1, 1940, and served with the 13th Armored Regiment, 1st Armored Division, until April 1941, and then with the 37th Armored Regiment, 4th Armored Division. He later served with the 706th Tank Battalion, 77th Infantry Division, participating in the engagements on Guam,

Leyte, le Shima, and Okinawa. Transferred to the 34th Engineers, Claxton returned to the U. S. on July 10, 1945, and was discharged Oct. 12. He is now employed in Paoli.

April 18, 1945
Ryukyu Islands

DEAR FOLKS:

The morning darkness gave way before the slowly rising sun to form a background of pale blue, etching our objective in clear, cold lines. Before us lay the island we had been briefed so much about; an island whose dangers were not solely those of guns and flames. Death might come from many sources, but we were ready and each man heaved a sigh of relief, unleashing a store of pent-up emotions. Ahead was Ie Shima, a part of the Japanese homeland.

Ie Shima! A rugged six-mile-long ridge of forbidding land that seemed to slope gently toward the sea; a ridge whose every crag, crevice and granite side held danger for us; a danger we could not see, but knew was there. The ridge gave way to gentle slopes, studded with groves of scrub trees, pine, and giant tombs, which resemble huge three-leaf clovers, hewn from solid limestone ridges and reinforced with concrete. It had well-placed guns, pillboxes and mines. Near the water's edge was a steel gray concrete seawall, behind which lurked death. In the isle's center, towards the northern tip, a massive mountain knoll of granite, half-covered by clinging vines and scrub trees, thrust up from a shaggy, wooded and heavily fortified ridge that formed the island's backbone.

Over all this lay a calm deadliness as the slight sea breeze brought a dampness that filled the morning air and crept into our veins. Darkness now gave way to bring a new dawn.

We had arrived, and our convoy consisted of hundreds of ships of all sizes. Huge wide-beamed battleships, streamlined heavy cruisers, rocket craft, sleek grey-bound destroyers, and hundreds of small craft. The big battlewagons sped shoreward, laying devastating blasts of explosives into the island's strongholds. Broadside after broadside was hurled into the island. The ground trembled and shook. The very mountaintop seemed to sway with the force of every explosion. The "swoosh" of rockets filled the air with eerie noises. Relay after relay smashed great holes and craters, leaving bright huge cuts as though a giant paw had clawed the land with bloody talons.

Destroyers lay close in shore, blasting the well-hidden and strongly built fortifications with blazing five-inch guns. Squadrons of bombers flew overhead to loose their first explosives from high altitudes. Then came the rocket-firing planes. Peeling off from formations, they came down in long single lines, gracefully sweeping to fire point blank into the mountainside, leaving traces of fire streaming in the air after each discharge.

While this was going on the convoy of ships moved closer in shore, soldiers climbing over the sides filled small boats, water buffaloes and amtracks, which circled the ships until the signal to go in. The sound of bombardment died; the signal was given. The water turned white under the driving power of a hundred screws and whirling tracks, and soon the first waves hit the beaches with guns spitting. Ramps of small boats were dropped, spilling soldiers ashore. Vehicles, like giant sea monsters, clamored ashore and clawed their way over the concrete defense walls, fighting to the tree-studded slopes. This was the morning of April 16. The battle had just begun.

The island was hit from two sides. The airstrip fell in the first day of fighting. The Japanese tactics seemed to be this: Use a small number of men in well-hidden trenches and gun emplacements on and near the beach; target their big artillery pieces, mortar and machine guns on the beaches which are hard to defend and take as high a toll of enemy dead as possible, while the majority of their forces retreated to the previously prepared and easily defended mountain ridges, valleys and tomb-studded slopes.

As the second day rose, the fighting stiffened. The enemy gave the lower ground reluctantly, and advances were measured in yards. Small gains were earned by sweat and blood as ranges became closer. The enemy was slowly but surely pulling back to the higher slopes of Mt. Iegusugu Yama, there to make his stand. After the advance reached the slopes, enemy fire of machine guns, mortars and heavier guns from the mountain stalked the doughboys.

On the morning of April 18, orders for tank support were received. Our 706th Battalion tanks clamored ashore and were rushed to the front. At midafternoon the Japanese counterattacked, but were stopped short as the heavy concentration of 75 mm.'s and 105 mm.'s broke loose. The tanks were placed in a semicircle around the base of this jagged, lone mountain peak. Here was encountered some of the heaviest emplacements—equal to those of Iwo Jima.

At the base of the mountain, on the eastward slope, was the town of Agarii-Mae. Its well-built houses, with walls of concrete two feet thick, were perfect pillboxes and offered the stiffest type of resistance. Beneath the houses were many tunnels, one of which crawled its twisting way through the mountain ridge some one-half mile to the westward slope. Many of the similar tunnels were large enough to drive a vehicle through. Some were so great in length, containing steel doors, that flame throwers, pole charges, and artillery fire had little effect upon them. Against these tanks were used very effectively with their 75 mm. and 105 mm. guns firing at point-blank range.

Sniper fire, combined with antitank guns, took a toll of tank commanders and their vehicles. At such close range, usually 75 to 100 yards, Japanese amidst the rock and coverage succeeded in crawling close enough to place satchel charges and mines that littered the fields and road crossings.

On April 20th, the doughboys succeeded in reaching the ridge, placing the American flag upon its crest. That night a counterattack by the Japs forced the doughboys to withdraw. Here again the Japanese succeeded in replacing many of their machine guns, pinning the doughboys to their holes. The tanks were again ordered forward. After the third counterattack, the combination of tanks and doughboys succeeded in smashing the Japs and took the ridge.

From here they continued to take the remainder of the town which wound itself around the base of the mountain. Many heroic and personal acts of bravery were displayed. Once again the artillery, bombers, artillery guns and tanks played an important part. The tanks and doughboys pushed their lines forward, smashing the final, fanatical resistance, to reach the mountain peak.

By noon of the 23rd of April the island was declared secure and the American flag was hoisted upon a pole next to a battered stone building, once a Jap headquarters on the high ridge. Thus ended our Third Campaign. Guam, Leyte, and Ie Shima! The last island taken was Okinawa! . . .

HOWARD

Walter Bodem, of Indianapolis, was inducted Oct. 2, 1941 into the Army and was assigned to the infantry. He was sent to Camp Wolters, Texas, and then to Seward, Alaska, from Feb. 1942 to May 1943 with the 153d Infantry, 35th Division. In July 1944 Cpl. Bodem served in the battle of the southern Philippines and the Ryukyu Islands campaign. He was awarded the Asiatic-Pacific theater ribbon with two battle stars and the Philippine Liberation ribbon with one battle star. Promoted to the rank of sergeant in June 1945, Bodem was discharged Dec. 25 and is now employed in Indianapolis.

April 28, 1945
Okinawa Shima

DEAR MARIE AND GOLA:

About all of my mail has caught up with me now. I keep getting letters from back in March every time that I get some written in April. I have all up to the 19th of April now and that is pretty good time. A combat division has a high priority on mail service. I have had so many letters from people that it is hard to keep track of them. I have a little more time to write now than I did for a while for we don't have to get undercover quite so early as we did.

Just a little after dark last night we had quite a show. The Jap planes came in and, of course, when that happens business picks up. We can first tell they are coming by the ack-ack of the ships in the harbor. They really pour it on up there and they don't aim at anything in particular but just fill the sky so full of flak that you can't see or hear anything but a roar. *If* they get through that, they circle over the island and then the guns on shore open up. They are smart enough to come in real low, just skimming the tops of the ships so the Navy can't shoot for fear of hitting other ships or us on shore. One got through and came in low over our tents, but he didn't get very far. He was just over our tents when the plane burst into flames and went a little farther and then spread all over the countryside. I have seen a lot of others do the same, but this was the closest any of them got.

When you see them coming you can't make up your mind whether to get in your hole and be safe or stay up and watch everything. I usually get under cover and then try to see as much as I can that way. I am not much scared during the air raids, but this artillery is what gets my goat. It is bad stuff.

We sure wouldn't eat so well while we have been here if the natives hadn't had such good gardens planted. They have everything that most of them have back home. All the farms that I have seen are just little garden patches, all terraced, and look like they have been worked by hand with very crude tools. There are a lot of horses running around loose, but they don't look like work horses for they are so small. They look more like riding horses, and it is possible that they might have belonged to the Jap soldiers. All the farms have a herd of goats and pigs, but I haven't seen any cows or dogs or cats. The people here are better situated and have better homes and seem to work more than those on Leyte.

I have been inside a lot of the houses and they have fancy woodworking and are fixed up funny. I have yet to see a bed in a house, either here or in the Philippines. I don't know just what they sleep on, but I guess on mats or something.

I have seen a lot of very nice mats around and I think that is what they sleep on. Some of the boys tried out the mats, but after one night they threw them away for it didn't take long to find out they were full of vermin.

I think we will be up in big tents in a few days so that will help in keeping dry. We have been very lucky in that it has only rained about three days since we have been here. It is pretty nasty when it rains.

Love,

WALTER

Dean R. Bahler, of Rensselaer, enlisted in the Naval Reserve in Nov. 1942 and was commissioned an ensign in April 1943. He was sent to sea on the U.S.S. "Monongahela" (tanker) and served in the Solomon Islands and New Guinea campaigns. In July 1944 he was promoted to lieutenant (j.g.) and given amphibious training. In October he returned to sea and served on several troop transports. He saw action again at Iwo Jima and Okinawa in 1945 and received two letters of commendation for his actions. Lt. Bahler was discharged in Dec. 1945 and entered medical school at the University of Chicago.

May 4, 1945

DEAR MOM, DAD AND KIDS:

Well, thirty days have passed so from here on I can preface all my remarks with an—"I was at Okinawa." You all seem to be waiting with baited breath for my thrilling personal episode. Remember I'm no Ernie Pyle, and since you've been following him and other columnists who are alive around Okinawa, I'm sure you have the full story there.

I'm just plain Dean and no hero and hope to remain so. Of course you knew we had been studying for and preparing for this invasion for over five months and guess that's the bad part of war—most of it consists of an endless nerve-wracking waiting for something to take place.

We all found out at the Russells where we were going and when. It did have to take place on Easter Sunday—seemed just a trifle ironical to me, but of course the operation orders for that blitz were written up actually a year ago. Can you imagine planning a major engagement that far ahead? We had about 8 or 10 various sets of attack orders to read through, they were all very confusing—we felt as though we were going into a final examination without having studied.

The big order was about the size of the Sears Roebuck catalogue and about the same kind of print. That was for all the forces involved except the Marines, who had their own individual orders. Then each individual task force, task group, and task unit right on down to individual ships took their part of the orders from the original. This just gives you a minor idea of how complicated it all was.

If it weren't for the typewriter we might have been licked long ago. We went from the Russells to Ulithi and hung around Ulithi for several days for last minute logistics, checkups and so forth. Those reports you read from Radio Tokyo about the approaching invasion were true, they probably knew to the hour and the minute when we'd arrive. We left Ulithi on March 27th and were to arrive at Okinawa just 325 miles from Tokyo early morning of April 1st. Guess that was the longest 5 days I ever lived through. We really were expecting the worst and we had every reason to expect it—look what had happened at tiny Iwo Jima; true enough, the surface units and carrier planes had been shelling and bombing the islands for several days before, but still we knew they had a pretty good army air force left and we would be just too close to Formosa and the Japanese mainland for combat. We began making bets as to when the first planes (enemy) would come out to meet us. We felt luckier every day that we got closer in without planes showing up. We were getting thoroughly disgusted and fed up with our enemy, the Japanese. On Saturday night, March 31st, I had the watch from 8–12—we were close enough on my watch so that we could see the shells bursting and the flares which our planes dropped.

We were all pretty much keyed up and it was really quite exciting—then I slept for about 4 hours (which was to be the most sleep at any one time for the next five days), then I came back up to the bridge around 4:30 A.M. All the crew and Marines were served a hearty breakfast of juicy steaks and eggs—how were your corn flakes that morning? We entered the transport area where the transports unloosed their cargo and troops about five in the morning. We were about 8 miles out from the beach and there was so much smoke from the bursting shells and also artificial smoke screens laid down by destroyers and special smoke boats, that it really wasn't much to see at first.

Several enemy planes tried to get through to the transport area but they never got beyond the screen of destroyers, cruisers, battlewagons and carriers. We would hear a report over the radio that an enemy plane was approaching—the next report was that the plane had "splashed." We started putting troops over the side at 8:30 A.M. Believe me, we held our breaths until we heard definitely that opposition was practically nil on the beach. We thought perhaps the Japs had pulled out for Formosa, but now since there is bitter fighting we know that they just retreated to the southern end of the island. The first day was a snap. We weren't scheduled to move to the inner transport area (about a mile from the beach) until the third or fourth day and things went so well the first day that we went on in that afternoon.

That way our small landing craft wouldn't have such long trips to make with the precious cargo and troops. Then in the evening about 5 or 6, before it got dark, we'd pick up the boats and crews which were near the ship at that time and the rest of the boat crews had to beach their boats and dig in on the beach for the night. Rest assured those boys always tried to get back around quitting time—they didn't relish the idea of staying overnight in a foxhole in no man's land. Then all the transports with suitable screening vessels would steam around during the night in a retirement area and then would approach the island again at dawn and continue unloading.

At night the Jap planes would sneak in, and we had all kinds of reports of various raids but our particular group of ships wasn't troubled much. One night one lone enemy bomber flew low the whole length of our division and each ship would open up on her as she approached just like some sort of a game. She was finally bagged by the last ship in our division and I knew then what was meant by the report, "Bogey has splashed." The next morning we started unloading cargo and troops again. It was all very interesting the first couple of days, but after a while because of lack of sleep and proper rest, and because of the constant nervous tension we all got numb and that unmerciful fatigue was the worst part of it all for us.

The second afternoon I was ordered over the side by the commanding officer. I expected something like this and was prepared for anything. Really didn't mind going into the beach, but had an awful fear of stepping on a concealed mine or booby trap. But I didn't go to the beach; instead I was to act as traffic control officer—was stationed on a little sub-chaser about 400 yards from our section of the beach. The small boats would come to us from the transport area and we would direct them into the beach as the beachmaster called for various cargo. Sometimes it was ammunition or maybe water or perhaps rations or gasoline or barbed wire, etc. Was interesting, wonderful change and relief, getting away from the powers that be and the big ship—worked like a trooper that day—no sleep and tried to exist on K-rations, but General Sherman during the Civil War days said that war is hell, and I'm beginning to believe it. Toward evening when I saw all the big ships leaving for the night I began to wish I were back on my transport—it's harder to hit a moving target than a stationary one.

But many large combat units stayed at anchor with us. That night I saw my first suicide planes—believe me they are terrible. When a nation gets that desperate I can't see why they don't call it quits. I saw one plane crash into a large ship only about a thousand yards from us and two others hit the water about 800 yards away. We were really petrified. Suicidal warfare in my opinion really isn't very successful. They didn't hit their mark often enough. There were some 1,400 of our ships of all types which participated and 1,600 aircraft. Gives one truly a wonderful feeling to look up and see our planes overhead dotting the sky like flies. . . .

Around the fifth day most of the ships were pretty well unloaded and I was getting uneasy and felt that I should get back to my ship as I knew they shouldn't hang around empty. Of course I wanted to get out of there at the very first opportunity. So I left the little sub-chaser and went back when my task was completed. The next morning those ships which were unloaded were ordered to depart immediately since there was a report that a mass air raid was expected. About twenty of our boys who had been on the beach were not aboard yet, and we hated to have to leave them to fare for themselves. About half of them started back in time and finally got aboard just as we were steaming at two-thirds ahead; the other half didn't make it. They finally rejoined us the other day—almost a whole month after we left the danger area.

Guess we got out in time, too. The fireworks really just started shortly after our departure—in the air, on the beach, and on the sea. Our boys have really been taking care of things. It seems almost unbelievable that so many enemy planes can be "splashed" all in a few minutes. It's a good thing because the enemy suicide missions really ran rampant whenever and wherever they did get through. And that big Jap battleship and several others were sunk out there about that time. Resistance is much stiffer on the beach now, I guess, and for once the Marines are taking it rather easy since they are taking charge of the less heavily defended north end and the army has charge of the southern end. I have lots of faith in the army—they did a miraculous job on the Philippines. So there you have it.

Once again we are waiting and wondering—and again strange as it may seem the most of us are getting anxious to get started.

May God bless and take care of all of you until my return.

DEAN

Gordon B. Enders, of Lafayette, was a 1st lieutenant in the Air Corps in World War I. After several years in China, he was commissioned a major in military intelligence Sept. 17, 1941. Major Enders was assigned immediately as military attaché to Afghanistan and concurrently assistant military attaché in Iran. In April 1944 he became military observer in India, then was returned to this country to attend a military government school and civil affairs school. Major Enders was assigned to the military government staff of the 10th Army Feb. 1, 1945, in Hawaii. He was transferred to Okinawa and then to Korea, where he served as director of the office of foreign affairs. Promoted to lieutenant colonel in Jan. 1946, Enders also received three commendations. He was discharged in June 1946.

August 22, 1945
Okinawa

DEAR —:

We arrived off the invasion beaches just after lunch on April 11th. All morning we had steamed in sight of land, and could see all manner of naval vessels systematically shelling enemy positions on the beaches and up the mountain ridges. It seemed a most leisurely affair, with the ships either anchored or steaming slowly up and down the shoreline. There seemed to be no Jap reply of any kind, and the men-of-war methodically let go with thunderous salvos. We could see the fire and smoke at the gun muzzles, and then see the fiery spouts where the shells hit their targets. We took an unholy pleasure in watching this.

The air that morning was full of our planes—little cubs directing our fire and almost standing still above the hundreds of smoke plumes which marked the Jap lines; and the noisy dive bombers and fighters which streaked through to their targets, dived and dropped bombs with all their rockets and guns blazing. Occasionally the Japs came out of their holes and caves to throw up same ack-ack at the planes, but the whole thing looked unhurried and haphazard. No particular pattern was discernable, and each formation went about its business without noticing other formations—like flights of abstracted birds. When we got near our beach, we could see the bombs coming away and striking the Jap lines.

The harbor was crowded with shipping in a variety scarcely imaginable. All manner of craft, each built in nightmarish shape for a special war job, churned up white wakes in the choppy harbor or lay rolling at anchor.

We had a difficult job finding our anchorage and spent over an hour circling amongst the crowded ships before coming to rest. One of the first things we saw was a Jap bomber shot down by our fighters, falling from about 20,000 feet in a ball of flame. We had hoped to get ashore quickly because we'd been cooped up for 21 days on our crowded ship and we could see jeeps and trucks scurrying about the muddy roads and between the tent bivouacs. It represented the freedom to move, the elbowroom we longed for. But immediately we ran into about 36 hours of air raids. We had experienced several as we came into "harbor," but had also missed many in the confusion. Once anchored, we got word of each raid and remained in a state of almost constant alert. This was bad on our own ship, for we were herded into our hot, crowded quarters when the gun crews manned their weapons. We had no portholes, and our doors were locked. Additionally, our ventilating system was closed down. We poured perspiration and either stood or lay down on our bunks. When our guns fired, the ship shook and rattled like a huge tin can. At first we just heard and felt the guns, without knowing what transpired. This was decidedly unpleasant. Someone must have said so, for at the third or fourth attack the ship's chaplain took the microphone of the ship's public address system and broadcast a blow-by-blow description to us. This was better. He was able to see well, apparently, and we'd hear something like this: "There are fifteen waves of four planes each coming in from our port bow. The ships farther up have opened fire. One Jap is down in flames"—pause—"Now they're over us"—pause, while all hell broke loose in the rattling ship from its guns—"Another Jap is down. He has hit the water with a tremendous splash." The chaplain spoke in a dull voice, very slowly. But it was better than nothing.

From that first day until we went ashore I arranged to see the raids from the deck. The outstanding event was early next morning when a suicide plane came for us. He was hit and afire for the last thousand feet of his dive, and it looked as though we were in for it. He came from the stern, diagonally across our length, and I confess I couldn't see any escape. But he wobbled and hit the water harmlessly about 200 yards off our bow.

We went through lesser alarms until noon of April 13th. We weren't allowed to debark during air raids. But a break came and the orders to leave were issued. I had practiced it plenty, but did not get into a small boat to be lowered over the side and to wade out onto the beach. I was put in charge of a jeep and rode ashore on a Seabee barge, driving off onto a sketchy pier and getting lost through helping out a stranded truck and missing my convoy. But I was only a few minutes late in finding our camp which was smack-dab between two airfields and within Jap artillery range. We were shown a long, narrow, terraced valley with several little offshoots and a number of fresh Jap graves. We were told to pitch our pup tents and dig our foxholes. It was four o'clock and supper was at five.

We named the place "Nightsoil Terrace" and worked like beavers to get set before dark. My bedding roll was in the mud, bearing the dark brown stains today. My foxhole was an empty coral irrigation ditch about five feet deep. I remained there two nights, through constant air raids aimed at the airfields. There were no bombs, but our own flak was dangerous and on the second night we were strafed. A tent some fifty feet from mine was hit; but I slept through it all like an innocent babe and had to be told about it at breakfast.

The morning of the 15th I went out to be with the Marines and was at once sent to my schoolhouse where I stayed for nine weeks.

The stuff I tell you is all mercifully in the past. None of us was particularly brave and dashing—mud and foxholes discouraged it. We just "sweated it out," and that's what we get our battle star for.

Now the radio is fixing the date for moving into Japan. I hope to go along, for sentimental reasons largely. For me it's the "end of the road" and so long as I have to stay out here for a while longer, it's the thing I'd choose to do. Also, it's a nice rounding out of my Oriental experience—from the Russian Grand Fleet in the Suez Canal, steaming toward Togo and disaster, to the entry into Tokyo. The rise and fall of the Japanese Empire.

GORDON

Richard Burns, of Rensselaer, enlisted in the Navy Dec. 29, 1941, and trained at Great Lakes. He was sent to Hawaii and to the Naval Air Station at Johnston Island. Being transferred to the Yard Mine Sweep 340, Burns helped sweep mines in both Atlantic and Pacific Oceans. Later he saw duty at Coco Solo, Canal Zone, and was then transferred to the LST 581, where he participated in the invasions of Luzon and the Philippines. On Aug. 9, 1945, Burns was transferred to the LCIL 329, which swept mine fields near Japan and evacuated prisoners of war. After serving 44 months overseas, Burns was discharged Dec. 19, 1945, and is now living in Lafayette.

Sept. 6, 1945
Buckner Bay, Okinawa

Dear Mom:

I was here at Okinawa on the initial invasion day. We brought a load of Sea-bees and their equipment up here to build air strips for the B-29 superfortress-es. In the first thirteen days up here we went to General Quarters 53 times. General Quarters is the manning of all battle stations.

My first job up here lasted five days. For the first day of the invasion and the next five I had charge of six small boats. I had to take the six small boats into ships along the beach, pick up a load of five-inch ammunition or eight-inch ammunition and fuses and take them back out to the destroyers and cruisers.

It was fairly rough duty. The seas were choppy and the waves lifted us up, dropped us, tossed us sideways and wet us good. It was a distance of 25 miles from the ships that were in close to the destroyers and cruisers we hauled to on the outer defense line. We ate K-rations for these five days. Food not fit for a dog. We were on the go for 144 hours without sleep. The wind was cold and the spray of water kept us wet all the time. Each time at night that we got near our ships they would shoot as us thinking we were enemy PT boats. We had several close calls.

We saw enemy planes crash many of our ships, crippling or sinking them. At one time nine planes attacked one destroyer; she shot down eight of them. The other crash-dived on her, causing considerable damage and casualties. Each time a ship was hit large fires would start illuminating other ships which were in turn hit. Each time our radar picked up planes we made smoke. It's terrible, it makes your throat raw and you gag.

We finally completed our five-day assignment and got back to the ship. We shaved, bathed, put on clean clothes and hit the sack. The G.Q. siren went off but we didn't care, we were going to sleep, even if the damn ship sank. We slept in our clothes always. We never were in the sack over a couple of hours.

After thirteen days of this we set sail for Leyte Island in the Philippines to get some rest and then bring up reinforcements. We stayed in Leyte ten days then back we came to Okinawa. Things had cooled down considerably when we got back. We unloaded and hauled troops to Ie Shima, where Ernie Pyle was killed. We had on a full load of ammunition this time. Several thousand tons.

A Jap bomber started to crash-dive us; we opened fire. It kept coming down at us, and we were scared terribly. I had my New Testament in my pocket. I clenched my hand on it and began to pray. Just then one of our fighter planes dove in at the bomber. It was forced to change course; it crashed the ship next to us, killing two men and hurting 26 others. Its bombs didn't go off.

We finished our job there then we went to a couple of small islands farther up. We picked up Marines who hadn't met any opposition on those two islands and hauled them back to Naha to relieve the guys at the front. Those Marines were scared and they sure had reason. The fighting on the beach was hard. There were considerable casualties. We then hauled troops back to the north end of the island to rest. All together we made eight trips.

Then I got transferred. I was supposed to come home. No luck. I was needed too badly out here. Too many men were dead or missing. Things calmed down. We made smoke each night. A few more ships were hit. We shot down several planes though.

Finally the news leaked out. The B-29 boys were betting every penny they could on the end of the war before the month was out. We have a new weapon, the atomic bomb. Japan sued for peace. Finally we broke down and gave it to them. As our favorite, Admiral Halsey, said, all we men want to go ahead and finish them off now. No, we are too easy. The big shots in the States with their chicken hearts. If they had been here with us, they too would have wanted to finish the job.

Well, the war is over now. Our ship will be sailing in a couple of days; it's either Japan or home. We don't know which, but we pray it's home. I have 32½ points. My enlistment expires December 20. We are to get some points for our overseas duty soon. Then I will have enough for discharge. I'll be home to stay December 20.

I am quite well and happy. And I pray all of you are the same.

As always,
Dick

William D. Patrick, of Indianapolis, was commissioned a lieutenant (j.g.) in the Naval Reserve on June 8, 1944. Lt. Patrick was stationed on the U.S.S. "Pitt" (APA 223) from Dec. 1944 to Oct. 1945 and saw duty on Okinawa and in the occupation of Japan. Promoted to lieutenant (s.g.) Feb. 1, 1946, he was discharged Feb. 7, 1946, and is now a budget officer in the Institute of Inter-American Affairs, Washington, D. C.

8 September 1945
At Anchor
Zamboanga, Mindanao,
Philippine Islands,
U.S.S. "Pitt" (APA 223)

DEAR MOTHER:

The lid is off!

With Halsey's fleet, MacArthur's troops, and Geiger's Marines in Tokyo, I can now tell for the first time many interesting things the censors would have snipped out before V-J Day. You will be interested mostly because these are the experiences of my own ship and shipmates. But, others will enjoy our story, too. It is typical of the daily sweat and danger of hundreds of unsung auxiliaries. They are the troop transports, cargo transports, oilers, repair ships, supply ships, troops and supplies, which help conquer and establish bases. These vital missions assure successful completion of tasks started by fliers, carriers, battleships, cruisers, and destroyers.

First, I want to answer one question everyone asks: "What is an APA?" Auxiliary Personnel Attack. The "attack" is right, too, for this ship doesn't pull up to a dock and discharge troops down a gangway. Our ship was specially designed and built, and our crew trained for one of the most difficult and dangerous jobs in war. We land marines (or soldiers) on strongly defended enemy beaches. On our deck we carry more than a score of landing craft weighing from 10 to 35 tons. Even if the ground swells are 10 feet high, we must lower boats over the side, fill them with troops, jeeps, tanks, guns, and pilot them through the surf. When you realize that this tough job must go off like clockwork under enemy fire and suicide attacks, you will understand why we drilled day and night for two months on our training and shakedown cruises off Southern California. Those cruises were backbreaking. Morning and night all hands sweated while we lowered our boats, climbed over the nets, ran into the beaches, hoisted boats back aboard, and gripped them down. After drills we turned to; chipped, painted, drilled, welded, peeled potatoes, splinted arms and legs, and groomed turbines and generators for those high speed runs ahead.

It was really a relief when, on February 10, we set our course on "two-seven-zero" and watched the amber-lighted arch of the Golden Gate Bridge fade into the haze. We were concerned, too; on board were hundreds of tons of the latest type high explosive rockets. Orders were to rush them top speed to a spot few of us and few of you had ever heard about.

That was Ulithi—in the Japanese Caroline Islands. There were palm trees and coconuts, colorful shells and devilfish. But the only natives we saw were men, and those through glasses! Here were floating dry docks, repair ships, sub-tenders, tankers, ammunition ships, refrigerator ships, LST's, LSM's, LCI's, a floating post office, and a dozen concrete barges, each carrying as much stock as a department store. Hundreds of ships were anchored in a coral-ringed harbor nearly 30 miles long.

This was the great secret anchorage of the Third and Fifth Fleets and the huge, floating "fleet train" that helped Admirals Nimitz, Halsey, Spruance, and Mitscher "cut loose" from their bases and push so quickly across the Pacific.

We had hardly rested when the big parade began. Back from Iwo Jima and the first carrier raids on Tokyo came the big ships—the "Hornet," "Franklin," "Yorktown"—the "Iowa," "Missouri," "South Dakota"—the "Indianapolis," "Guam," and "San Francisco." Soon all of "Task Force 58" lay at anchor, and we were talking with airmen who had been over Tokyo. We even had our own private "fleet review," steaming for two hours from one end of the armada to the other.

One day four brand new rocket ships came alongside, after two months steady steaming from Boston. All hands worked 39 hours straight, heaving 70-pound boxes into cargo nets, hoisting them up, and breaking open thousands of rounds of rockets. These rockets helped pave the way for the 10th Army to land on Okinawa. You may have seen them in newsreels, or in a full page picture in *Life* magazine.

Our loading job done, we had a few beers on Mog-Mog Island, a swim off the starboard gangway, and a movie called "Alaska." It was four months before we found out how that movie came out. In the middle of the third reel the "exec" yelled "Flash Red." We dashed to battle stations in earnest. To the north there were two flashes of orange flame. The "squawk box" told us that one Jap had crashed into an escort carrier, the other into a small island. No other Jap planes ever reached Ulithi.

The next day we steamed for Leyte Gulf in the Philippines. We felt important with three sleek destroyers for our own escort. Once again we worked "all hands" all night—dishing out more rockets. When we finished, orders came aboard to take army troops and cargo from a damaged transport. The brass hats gave us 48 hours to finish the job; hinted that it was impossible. Despite choppy water we did it in 48.

For four days we steamed north from Leyte in the first big troop convoy to invade the Okinawa Gunto. Six days before the 10th Army landed on Okinawa proper, we were putting 77th Division Army troops ashore at Zamami Shima in the Kerama Islands, 20 miles away. Only a few Jap planes challenged us the first day. They burst into brilliant balls of orange fire 10 miles away. We put our army infantrymen and their fighting gear ashore as smoothly as we could have done at Coronado or Oceanside, California. We stayed in Kerama Retto fourteen days; watched it develop into a full scale naval and air base—a pocket edition of the great fleet anchorage at Ulithi.

Caught off balance the first week, the Japs soon hit with all their dwindling air power. Before dawn and frequently several times each night, men jumped from their sacks, snatched lifebelts and helmets, and ran to battle stations. Between alarms we worked around the clock—running a combination hotel, cafeteria, supermarket, general store, waterworks, and filling station. Several hundred survivors and wounded came aboard. Two score smaller craft drew on us for stores, chow, fuel and water.

On April 6th we had a big scare. A long line of black ack-ack bursts traced the course of two skimming Jap torpedo bombers. As we raced to our guns, one crashed into a nearby LST. The landing ship poured out oily black smoke for 24 hours before it slipped into deep water with a dying breath of steam. The second Jap skidded through our antiaircraft fire and disappeared into "the wings" behind a nearby island. Two hours later a third Jap bored in through a gauntlet of black bursts. The range dropped—3,000, 2,000, 1,000. At 700 yards he rolled over and crashed into the bay. We were proud of the little Jap flag we painted on our bridge. Relieved, too!

With these suicide attacks over, we turned southward on the 10th. At sea we passed part of Task Force 58. We anchored at Saipan, standing by for weeks to carry reserves to Okinawa. They were never needed. Dogged sailors, soldiers, and marines had won the last great land, sea and air battle of the war. The way was open for the B-29's to polish off the Japs.

With our battle baptism over, the "Pitt" turned to shuttling men and materials forward. We visited many famous spots—Tulagi, Guadalcanal, Noumea in New Caledonia, Guam, Eniwetok, the Hawaiian Islands, and once again the Philippines.

Best of all, we spent V-J Day in 'Frisco. You've heard about that.

Yours, with love
BILLY

James F. Christie, of Indianapolis, enlisted in the Marine Corps Mar. 13, 1940, and was inducted for active service July 1, 1943. Christie went overseas in July 1944 and participated in the Battle of Okinawa as a stretcher bearer with the 22d Marine Regiment, 6th Marine Division. Returned to the States in April 1946, Cpl. Christie was discharged and is living in Indianapolis.

June 3, 1945
Okinawa Shima

DEAR FOLKS:

I'm pretty low on stationery again, but maybe if I write small you will be able to read it and I can say it all. For the first time in ages I've got a little time to myself; I'd better make use of it . . .

Lately, I've been wondering if you are hearing anything about our division back there in the States. If you run across anything of it in the papers I wish you'd send it out to me. I'll get a bang out of it and I'm sure a lot of the fellows will be interested, too. I guess everyone back there really knows more about this operation than we do here. As per usual, there are all kinds of stories and reports going around (scuttlebutt), but it's hard to separate fact from fiction. Did General Vandegrift make a speech? If he did and you got a chance to hear him, how's about telling a little of what he had to say.

Yesterday I had the opportunity of going forward on some business, so I got a little taste of what the boys are going through, and folks, hell is a mild word for it. Sugar Loaf Hill, where we had such a time of it, is just a lot of pulverized dirt, and the city of Naha is completely flattened to the ground. They haven't been able to evacuate all the dead from it either, and I've never smelled anything quite as strong or sickening as the odor of Jap bodies.

They have set up a reception center here to give the fellows going back to the lines from the hospitals a chance to draw clothing and get cleaned up. The thing I marvel at most is the way they go about as if they'd never been wounded and evacuated. Most of them will tell you that they'd like to stay here, but they say if they've got to go then it is okay by them. Many of them are shock cases, and shattered nerves are very numerous whether _Reader's Digest_ says so or not.

One boy I was talking to had been a corporal in charge of a mortar team. He told me of a shell landing as close to him as possible without hitting him. It exploded and as it did it picked him up and tossed him a good ten feet. The only mark it left was one tooth out and a cut inside his mouth. He'd had his mouth open luckily, for if he hadn't it would have been sure to have ruined his face for life. Lots of the fellows have been lifted out of their foxholes by the concussion of exploding shells. As one fellow said, "The Marines put me in them and the Japs blow me out." I used to think miracles were a bunch of hooey, but now I know different. The main thing in all of our minds now is to get the heck out of here!

One of the fellows was telling me of a Lt. Percy whom he is under. All through the battle he led his men in what we call "Gung Ho" fashion. He would stand up during intense fire and shout orders with complete abandon for his own safety. Bullets would pass through his canteen, etc., but they just seemed to pass Percy by. It so happened that the lieutenant has the handicap of poor eyesight and has to wear thick-lensed glasses. The boy told me that the only time Lt. Percy weakened was when a shell concussion knocked off his thick-rimmed glasses. Poor Percy couldn't see, so there he was on his hands and knees, pleading with the fellows, "Please help me find my glasses, please! I can't see without them." Finally, someone restored his glasses to him and in last reports the lieutenant was still going strong. I understand he was the only officer left to that particular outfit.

There are so many deeds of heroism over here, folks, that no one will ever tell about, that it's hard to believe. The saying that the real heroes don't return is perfectly true, though. It makes a person wonder, after all this bloodshed, if the world can or will regain all it's losing over here. People in the States don't seem to realize that the Japanese are a powerful nation and not a bunch of fanatical midgets. They aren't as good fighters as the Americans, that is true, but they are far from being the world's worst. I only hope that someday, someone will be able to bring that realization to the people at home so they'll wake up and do something "all out" to end this war. Okinawa is only a good start as far as I can see. From now on this isn't going to be an island war but a large, heavy job just like the European affair was. If the people who wonder at the immensity of production, and ask the old question, "What becomes of our War Bonds?" could spend five minutes after dark here listening to the artillery barrages and watching the antiaircraft fire; if they could see the wrecked tanks, the broken rifles, and immense piles of food and clothing, I don't think they'd have very much wondering to do.

Sometimes I'd like to try to write a book, but I don't suppose it would sell very many copies so I'll mark that idea off. Speaking of books, I'd like very much to get home and get started in school. I haven't quite made up my mind as yet where I want to go, but it's got to be a small place with lots of girls! There are times when I want to throw my arms up in despair. It's pretty hard to keep any dreams for the future alive out here. The days fly by and as each one passes the realization becomes more evident that nothing is being done to further myself for an occupation later on. My band work is very small compared to my other duties. It seems that about the time we do begin to progress some there's always something that comes up to take us away from it for a few weeks. You know yourself, Mother, that you can't just pick up where you left off. . . .

Folks, it will seem so different getting out of service. I'm thinking that I won't be able to conduct myself rightly for some time. It used to be that if I didn't care for a person I could ignore him, but in here you live and eat with them. Not that I don't get along, but some of these guys are hopeless cases. When I do come home I think I'm going to talk for about three solid days and get it all off my chest and then forget about it. I don't want you to try to handle me like a problem child, though. I really would like to have an interested audience to tell some of my experiences and viewpoints to. Sometimes I begin to believe that there is no one who has the same ideas about things that I do. And then I meet that rare character and we tear people apart and put them back together again.

Well, folks, this is all the writing paper I have so I guess I'm going to have to cease writing whether I like it or not. Don't forget the clippings and drop me a long letter soon. Be good and take care of things. Oh yes, I've got about seven months' pay coming to me after this operation is over so I ought to be able to send home a pretty nice lump of pecunia. Bye.

Your loving son,
JIM

Darrel H. Wagner, of Berne, enlisted in the Marine Reserves June 20, 1944, as a private in the infantry. Going overseas in April, 1945, Wagner reached Guam and joined Company A, 1st Battalion, 7th Marines, 1st Division. He fought with this group on Okinawa. In July 1945 he was stationed on Kume Shima, and from Sept. 1945 to Aug. 1946 he was in China. Discharged as a corporal on Sept. 26, 1946, Wagner is an insurance agent in Angola.

June 20, 1945
Okinawa

DEAR MOM:

I haven't forgotten you, but I've been very busy up until yesterday afternoon. Now I am at least a thousand yards behind the lines. I've had a bath, shave, and all new clothes. My buddy, Frederick Jones, Daytona Beach, Florida, and I have a tent fixed up and we sleep on top of the ground once again and just have a hole nearby to get in, in case mortars and artillery start hitting around the area.

We got some good chow again, 10-in-1 rations—ten men for three meals.

I'm just about 300 yards from the beach on the China Sea side. At night the moon makes everything look nice. That is the only time things look nice. The shelling and fighting have everything wrecked and ruined.

I guess my fighting is over for a while. I am well and in one piece yet. By the grace of God I am one of the lucky few who walked back. Without His help I don't see how anyone could live. It is a terrible mess. The enemy has these hills hollowed out and uses them as perfect defenses, coming out at night to throw hand grenades and knee mortars.

About all my action was with grenades at night. I didn't use my carbine much. They have long range snipers who just don't miss. In some ways it is just like a ball game at home. Before you start you are a bit scared and excited and when things start popping you forget about being scared a little bit, and when things quiet down you talk over particular bits of action, etc., just like we used to over each basketball game, play by play.

In another way it is like hunting at home. When you shoot a rabbit, the guy out of the group that shoots it gets it. Well, here when you get a Nip he is yours. That is, anything in his pocket you want. Lots of civilians get killed. It is the enemy's fault for the most part and lots of them cannot be trusted. Any kid big enough to pull the pin in a grenade might be your enemy.

Believe me or not, a guy is happy when he gets a little wound. He gets to go back, and you are still up there waiting yours. There is a lot of talk about foxhole religion. But no one prays in more earnest than when you are there. I know there is no better comfort than when you have trust in Him and have faith in His power. Don't worry about me. I'm O.K. We are near a pure water spring and it is really nice to be able to drink all the water you want. I haven't picked up any souvenirs. It is best not to fool around—I think. I lost my ring. I guess my finger got too skinny and I felt pretty bad about that, but I guess I should be thankful that that is all I've lost, and it can be replaced.

I'd sure like to have a little of that fresh milk, fried chicken, etc. We have fun just talking about the kind of chow we like and some day we are really going to have it.

I remember how everyone used to run their tractors all night and we thought it was lots of noise. It seems quite a joke now when you mention it. Here you get so tired that noise doesn't bother sleeping—neither does it matter what position one is in—or where you are, you *just sleep*. I know!

These Nips are a desperate bunch. Each one seems to fight a war of his own to the end. You should see the pile of ration books these civilians have to have— worse than yours could ever be—if you can imagine it.

When a guy gets hit on the line he can really get a corpsman in a hurry— here the corpsmen are the regular troops. The Nips have no regard for corps- men, in fact they try to spot them. That blood plasma is sure wonderful stuff.

Don't worry about me. I am O.K.

Love,

DARREL

Robert C. Barker, Jr., of Lebanon, enlisted in the Navy May 4, 1942, and received the rating of radio technician 2/c. He served in the Aleutians for 17 months and served his first sea duty en route home from Adak, Aleutians, aboard the U.S.S. "Kimberly." He was then assigned to the U.S.S. "Indianapolis," flagship of the 5th Fleet, on Nov. 30, 1944. This ship participated in two air strikes on Tokyo and the preparation for the landings of troops on Okinawa. When the "Indianapolis" was first hit by Jap sui- cide planes, Barker was transferred to the U.S.S. "New Mexico," which also was hit by suicide planes. Being assigned again to the "Indianapolis," Radio Tech, 1/c Barker lost his life when the ship was torpedoed July 30, 1945. He received the Purple Heart and Victory Medal posthumously.

1945—On U.S.S. "Indianapolis,"
Flagship of the 5th Fleet—

DEAR MOTHER AND DAD:

. . . Left Ulithi March 14th and we didn't know to where. Well, March 18th, we were near South Japan. Had an air alert earlier this morning. We shot down 3 Japs—midmorning a carrier got a hit very near us. March 19th early A.M. saw "Franklin" receive several hits—about two miles from us. So many explosions and smoke we thought her gone—a few destroyers and a carrier stayed with her and we went on. Planes from our carriers attacked Kyushu early next morning, March 19th. Next few days we were up and down this one area and arrived in sight of Kerama Retto—off Okinawa 24th of March. Next few days we bombarded by day and patrolled by night till March 31st. We were approaching shore again for bombardment, we had another air raid—we had had the regular dawn G.Q. alert and had secured supposedly with no enemy planes near, for breakfast. Being Saturday and beans for breakfast, I hit my sack.

A few minutes later the air alert was sounded (I have no A.A. station but thought to myself maybe I'd better get up and see what was cooking), but before I could really make up my mind our 20 mm. guns opened up—then I knew a plane must really be close, but before I could move we were hit. The ship shook and bounced and I found myself on the deck, covered up with bunk and mattresses and stuff. I was scared, of course, but determined to be calm, so calmly dug myself out—found my glasses hanging on my bunk unharmed, moved a few bunks and found my shoes. There were maybe six of us in my compartment and all ran up the ladder and out immediately but me and one other guy. This other guy had been in an upper bunk and he bumped his head on the ceiling and knocked himself out—I didn't even know he was up there! I tried to be so calm that later I realized how silly I was. I went over to my locker on the other side of the compartment from my bunk and got clean clothes, put them on—got out my toothbrush and put paste on it and then went topside to the "head" and washed my teeth. Then up to the radio shack where I looked myself over and found a nice cut on my left leg just above my knee, my elbow skinned up and 3 cuts on the bottom of my toes. I went to the first aid kit and painted them with iodine. I knew that the sick bay must be pretty busy. And it was, I later learned. Well, I went down then to look over the damage—even then we were under way as fast as we could go. Well, the plane had come in on the starboard quarter, went barely over and then smack down through the port quarter. Parts of the plane went through the main deck into one corner of the mess hall—some of it and the bomb on through the mess hall deck into a sleeping compartment and the bomb on through that, through the evaporator room (evaporator room pumps in salt water and makes fresh water) on through the hull of the ship and then exploded underneath the ship in the water and buckled the hole it had made upwards, knocking off two of our four screws (propellers) and the supporting yoke of one of the shafts. As soon as all the men that could got out of that living compartment it was dogged down and shut off to prevent flooding of the ship. Later learned that 8 men were trapped in that compartment—either instantly killed by the debris falling in there or drowned while unconscious in the oil that filled it. Oil tanks burst and flooded it and oil being heavier held the water out.

For lunch this day we had Spam sandwiches and for supper—the same thing—no fresh water! Next day—Easter—breakfast—bacon and eggs—Easter services—I attended as did almost all others except those actually working in the salvage crews. A salvage boat came alongside and divers welded a patch on the ship's bottom and we started pumping out the flooded compartments. Six of the trapped men were pulled out and we had burial services for them. They were taken by boat to land and buried. For lunch we had cold meats and Spam, salad and fruit juice. Still no fresh water for washing and rationed drinking water. Drinking fountains turned on for 15 minutes at the change of watches—1200–1600–2000–2400, etc. For supper we had ham sandwiches and ice cream. That night 0030 (thirty minutes past midnight) we had an air raid alert lasting till 0630. Fired at enemy planes at 0330. There we sat unable to move—being repaired—but several fighting ships in same harbor. Breakfast this Monday morning—Spam, gravy and baking powder biscuits. Two more of the missing men found and burial services for them in afternoon. That night—another air raid alert from 0130 to 0800. During the night we heard some Jap commandos boarded an LCM ship in our harbor and cut up four men before overcome. Think maybe they were trying to get to their radio transmitter to call the planes in this harbor!

Tuesday, April 3d (next morning), Admiral Spruance conducted a Purple Heart ceremony for 15 men on the quarter-deck and 7 men in sick bay—5 men had left our ship to go to hospital ships the day we were hit. One of them, an aviation radio man, was up in a plane on the catapult working on its radio when we got hit. The plane fell off its perch and this kid fell on his head. I had helped him the day before and was going to help him some more that morning, but since up all night on G.Q. I put it off for a little shut-eye till later in the morning. Fate? I guess so! Heard that the Flag was leaving the ship and the ship to go back for repairs. Back to where, we didn't know yet, Guam, P. H. or States. That night I was on watch and most of R. T.'s sitting around the radio shack when an announcement at about 2030 came over the system for all hands to dog down all hatches, and turn on all lights below decks and set a watch on all compartments, as there was a possibility of a Jap being aboard. A Marine guard had been found at his outside guard post with his throat slit—he didn't die, however! Well, we about passed out but weren't worried about the Jap himself getting to us—too many guys on gun watches outside our shack and I put on a .45 pistol—but we worried about what the bastard might do—such as put a charge of dynamite in an ammunition "ready box" or something like that—so we stayed up all night and next morning but no Jap was found, he either got scared off or was never on and the Marine cut up by a personal enemy in the crew! This day—in the afternoon I was told I was to be transferred into the Flag Allowance and to move the next day (Thursday, April 5th) to the U.S.S. "New Mexico."

We moved early next morning. While transferring our gear to an LCI, I barely got my foot caught between a railing and the wooden plank we had across the two ships, when the LCI rolled a little; I jerked it out quickly and wasn't hurt! Two minutes later a kid of the crew of the LCI did the same thing only he didn't get his out and got a crushed foot out of it. Fate! I guess so.

Well, while transferring to the "New Mexico" it started to rain a bit so we had a nice job moving all our stuff aboard. We worked like mad all day hooking up our receivers, but that night was the first really big air raid over Okinawa. The C.A.P. shot down over 100 enemy planes, a few got in to our part of the fleet just off shore of our landing place off Okinawa. The "New Mexico" shot one down. The next day Task Force 58 met a Jap force north of us and sank one of their battleships and two cruisers and others. Task Force 58 is the fast carrier force and their battleships (latest class), cruisers and destroyers that were on the Tokyo strikes and patrolled up and down north of Okinawa all the while protecting us. The next few days were spent working till late at night installing our equipment and some new stuff, with air alerts each night.

Roosevelt died, Ernie Pyle killed—but so were thousands of plain G.I.'s all around us! No mail received from March 26th till April 17th. All these days we were bombarding with our 14-inch guns most of the day each day and sometimes all night—then take a day off and go around to Kerra Merrato harbor for supplies and ammunition.

April 22d Admiral Nimitz came aboard to confer with Spruance, spent night aboard and we had a good air raid that night to show him. April 26th Admiral Halsey was aboard. Flew in from Guam. April 27th a liberty ship sank about a mile from us from a suicide plane. And two tin cans sunk out on patrol by the same. April 28th we were at G.Q.'s for five and one-half hours. C.A.P. shot down 88 planes but one of our hospital ships (U.S.S. "Comfort") was hit by a suicide plane—forty killed. Two cans hit but not sunk! The next few days or rather nights were interrupted by air raids—all track of time was lost—although I did record the times of G.Q.'s. May 1st. We were bombarding in daytime, at 1330 we went into G.Q. and got underway quick as a Jap shore battery started firing at us. We retired and some of our dive bombers saw the flashes and went in and got 'em—quick!

. . . On May 12th a few enemy planes got through Task Force 58 and two came in at us—one port, one starboard; the starboard one was shot down but not before he strafed the quarter deck and hit some of the gunners back there. But the port one came right on in midship, mowed off the "Jap-Trap" (a tub containing 4–20 mm. machine guns) and went on in to the smokestack and then down. He, too, strafed all the way in—several men were lost due to this—which is unusual for suicide pilots to do.

Well, my G.Q. station on the "New Mex" was in the radio transmitter room—three decks down and center of ship—two-thirds way back. So we hardly felt the crash. But, of course, fires were started and some ammunition boxes went off. But we couldn't leave our posts to go see. I did go to the "head" about one hour later—and to go there had to go through one of mess halls and they had the injured on stretchers all over the place. It was terrible, most of these burned badly, some with shrapnel in them, some with limbs missing. One of the Flag R.T.'s was up on bridge and just started down—came down to decks and just started outside—and got blown back in, receiving a flash burn on face and one piece of shrapnel in his leg just above the knee. An LCM came alongside and took some of the most serious casualties to the hospital ship. At 0030 next morning we had another raid lasting till 0110 A.M. and another from 0250 to 0432. At 1030 next morning—Mother's Day—we had burial services for 52 men. Later we knew that some men taken from the ship had died en route to or later on the hospital ship—making the total killed 67. All day, Mother's Day, salvage crews started cleaning up the mess and it was a mess but the ship had no holes in the bottom so no danger of sinking. All but one of our antennas were either down or their trunks flooded. The Flag radio intelligence shack was a wreck—we lost a radioman chief in there, shrapnel went through his radio and then into his heart. Another shack up higher, where we had two small transmitters, was riddled beyond repair. A salvage repair ship came alongside and started repairs. The rubble that went down the stack got into two of our boilers, damaging them badly. Two days later men had arrived by air from Pearl Harbor to repair the boilers—specialists on that type of work. The stack was patched with huge sheets of steel welded in place. A canvas hood put over it and the welders worked at night—but had to quit several times each night for more air raids.

We did receive mail the afternoon of Mother's Day which helped our morale until one stopped and thought of how many of those letters were not delivered—but marked, deceased. Next two weeks was same old stuff with that one break of May 21st when I went ashore on Okinawa. May 24th the usual air raid but heard it was to be a big one—started 1830 the 24th to 1405 next morning and again after breakfast 0800 to 1150. And during that period 111 Japs were shot down. May 27th Halsey's flagship came within spitting distance and next morning at 0530 we were underway for Guam, even though we had a raid starting at 0510—lasting till 0900. Later heard a tin can sitting 100 yards aft of where we were anchored got sunk! Fate? I guess so! May 31st—we moored at Guam. Next morning the Flag left the "New Mex" to set up headquarters ashore at Guam.

The rest you know. . . .

Robert A. Chesnut, of Columbus, was commissioned an ensign May 1942 in the Naval Reserve, and was attached to U.S.N. Armed Guard Center. He served on the M.S. "Peter Hurl," S.S. "Clifford D. Mallory," U.S.S. "Lash" (PYC 31), and the U.S.S. "Titania" (AKA 13), in the Pacific-Asiatic and European-African theaters. Returning to the U. S. Aug. 1945, Lt. (s.g) Chesnut was discharged Nov. 1945 and is now service manager for the Noblitt-Sparks Industries, Inc., Columbus.

May 15, 1945

DEAR JOHN:

Your letter of March 22 came as a complete—and completely pleasant surprise. You did ask a lot of questions—or rather, such big questions, that I've tried to save my answers until I had plenty of time. Not that I believe you'll find my answers particularly worthwhile, but I did want to do my best. You have the advantage of me, of course, with your Ediphone and your secretary. I envy you both for various reasons. I try to keep up a fairly extensive correspondence and find that in this climate it entails considerable actual labor, physical as well as mental.

Some of these big questions of yours—that you would ask if I were there—I can't answer, not being there. Where I've been is one of those, but you could guess pretty closely, I imagine. Two places I haven't been, and haven't especially regretted, are Iwo and Okinawa. I guess they've been without a doubt the toughest campaigns of the Pacific war, although our great power has never at any time left any doubt as to their outcome. We move around a great deal. Never stay in any one place very long, although we frequently return to old scenes. Of course the war has moved on and completely left many of the places which used to be familiar to "Titania." Our business is pretty strictly war, so we move with it. Actual combat operations come at fairly long intervals, although they do grow shorter as our strength makes it possible to speed up the timetable. We usually are there on D-Day (or Sugar-day, or Peter-day, or whatever they choose to call it), and then follow up with a support load for the same spot. Then somebody is clamoring for us for the next one, and we start preparing for it at once.

Another question you would ask is—what do I do? I sometimes wonder where my time goes. I'm not overworked, although it gets pretty rugged at times for a few days. As gunnery officer, I'm head of one of the ship's six departments. My first responsibility is for the maintenance of her several guns of various calibres and the training of gunnery department personnel, as well as most of ship's company, who are required to man the guns. My battle station is on the control bridge, the highest level on the ship, from which I control all guns. A Jap plane boring in looks pretty big from up there, and I've heard the swish and whine of other ship's projectiles passing by while the air was full of tracers and our own guns were blazing and clattering for all they were worth. Still, it's a good place to see the sights, and sometimes they are most spectacular. It's something to see when a Jap comes in at dusk over a big formation of ships, and they all open up with everything that will bear. You think there's no place in the whole surrounding sky where that plane could be without being hit. And maybe you're right, but he keeps coming with his throttles, and maybe his bomb bay, wide open, until at last somebody's fire takes effect and he spins down in flames or drops like a stone, raising a geyser of water and leaving a patch of flame and dirty water. That's if we're good enough or lucky enough. It doesn't always end that way, but I won't go into that. You think you must have been throwing everything but the galley sink at him for at least an hour—and then you realize it was a minute or maybe a minute and a half.

My other duties are those of the officer of the deck, which includes conning, lookout, seeing that ship's work is carried out according to the Plan of the Day, etc., member of the Summary Court Martial Board, Ass't. Educational Officer, Reviewing Censor, and other minor details. I also play a good deal of bridge and see a good many movies, most of them out-and-out stinkers.

What's it like to land on this or that island?—you wonder. Thanks to the unfathomable and unpredictable Jap, it's never quite the same. Sometimes he'll fight like the very devil on the beaches, but more often nowadays he withdraws and does his fighting and dying back in the brush or in his caves and tunnels.

The latter practice is doubtless due to the indescribable, overwhelming blasting we've learned how to give the beaches before our boys land. And, of course, it's fatal for him to pull back and let us land. He's never (yet) been able to push us off or hold his ground once we got a beachhead. Anyway, he's the world's most hopeless fanatic (and plenty clever, too), so there's always a certain amount of tension built up before H-hour.

You ask how we like the natives and how they like us. We don't stay long enough to get very well acquainted. The infantry or Marines could give you a better answer to that one. Generally, the ones I've seen are a pretty sorry lot. Part of this is natural; a good deal of it is due to the Jap robbery and ill-treatment. We always try to warn the natives away from the beaches beforehand, but sometimes they either don't have sense enough to move or the Japs won't let them. So they're caught between our own bombardment and the enemy's counter fire. The results are not nice to see. It's hard to tell in many cases whether they really like us or not, but they're keen enough to capitalize on the American's wealth and free-handedness. The Filipinos, of course, have known the freedom of American rule, so most of them are glad we have returned. They, too, have an eye for business—not always of the highest type. In fact, the so-called "oldest profession" is the most thriving, sometimes doing business on a waiting line basis and at very good prices. Just in case some of the office wise guys get hold of this, I'll state here that my information is strictly hearsay. But it's pretty well substantiated. As an interesting contrast, you may be surprised to know that the New Guinea natives, supposedly among the world's most primitive, have a very high moral standard. The young men buy their wives, usually with pigs. Sometimes it takes quite a while to accumulate the purchase price in this medium, and a long engagement results. If the intended bride meanwhile kicks over the traces and gets involved sexually with someone else, she gets her head cut off. The swain is dealt with somewhat more lightly.

Most of the places I've seen are definitely poor prospects for Arvin merchandise. To many island natives an empty tin can is a treasure. However, I do think there are great possibilities in New Zealand and Australia—at least potential possibilities. Whether they become real ones depends on many things; the kind of job we do on keeping the peace, whether world trade is unhampered, whether we can avoid a postwar depression, so that people will have money to spend, the speed and cost of transportation, etc. The Australians and New Zealanders are very much like Americans, I find. We're frequently in contact and cooperation with them, and I like them. Just the other day I was talking with an Aussie captain who had a radio business and various other enterprises before the war. He handled Sonora and Radiola and was selling about five hundred sets a year. He was a real promoter. Of course I told him I had worked for a radio manufacturer and put in a plug for Arvin. He was much interested, so I got his name and address, just in case.

Your most difficult question, obviously, is what do I think? But it's certainly a fair question, because everyone should be thinking to the limit of his ability these days. As to the outcome of the war there has been no room for doubt since we weathered the first bad months. Germany's defeat seemed to come as an anticlimax to most of us out here. I'm sure you folks at home feel a tremendous relief, since the German war has always been the main event in the eyes of most Americans. We can feel the relief too, although our war must go on, and V-E Day means no discharges for the Navy. The defeat of Japan is just as certain. Nobody can guess the time it will take or the price we'll have to pay for it, but still it's as certain as death.

How to win the war is no longer our main problem. How to prevent another one is. The answer must be found soon. I doubt if we have it yet. What's your opinion? And what's to be done to Germany? Or with Germany? Or for Germany? I suppose it will take a hundred years, or a thousand perhaps, for her to outlive her disgrace, not for having lost the war, but for having fallen to such depths of depravity as are indicated, for example, by the April 30 *Time*, which I just received today. I've heard people trying to devise punishments horrible enough for the perpetrators of her crimes. But all that is useless and impossible. Certainly they deserve no sympathy and must be removed from world society as we remove murderers from our own. But I hope it will be done quickly and quietly, so the world can begin to recover from its degradation.

Best regards to you and all the gang.

BOB

Norbert Henry Ertel, of Spades, was inducted into the Navy Jan. 15, 1944, as an apprentice seaman. He was attached to the crew of the U.S.S. "Compton" and participated in the Battle of Okinawa, did convoy duty from Okinawa to Guam, and served in Japan. He was promoted to the rank of ship's cook 2/c and was discharged Jan. 15, 1946. Ertel returned to Spades and is an owner of a store.

August 30, 1945
Tokyo Bay

DEAR DAD AND MOM:

You have already noticed on the envelope, no doubt, that the Destroyer "Compton" and I are helping Admiral Halsey end the war right smack in Tokyo Bay. And maybe you'd like to hear some of the details on what we've been doing.

We left Okinawa on the 25th of August and headed toward Japan. A couple of typhoons were apparently going the same way, but we managed to ride through them. Came the dawn on the 27th and we could see the big battlewagons, the "Missouri," the "Iowa" and the "Duke of York" dead ahead, leading the parade as the fleet steamed toward Japan. Battleships, carriers, cruisers, destroyers, DE's, transports—we were much impressed, and any Nips who saw that parade must have been flabbergasted for it gave them thoughts to think about, no doubt.

About midafternoon on the 27th, the "Compton" slipped into formation ahead of the transport group, and entered the outer harbor. We picked out a good spot between the "Missouri" and the "Iowa" and dropped the "hook." We couldn't see Tokyo or Yokohama, because we were still about twenty-five miles away, but we took a good look at Mount Fujiyama, with her peak showing above the clouds, and we looked through binoculars at the Jap houses and civilians on the beach.

Two Jap submarines which had surrendered went past us one morning, with the Japs lined up on deck under American guards. All day long we could see the Navy fighter planes wheeling overhead, just waiting for a Jap to try anything funny. And all around us were the American and British fleets, with all guns manned.

By the second night in the outer harbor, the fleet and the Marines had the situation well in hand, because all the ships showed movies on the main deck and there were lights all over the harbor. Finally, on the 30th of August, the minesweeps had made sure the inner harbor, Tokyo Bay itself, was safe for important characters like the "Compton," and so in we came and anchored near the city of Yokohama and the naval base at Yokosuka. And that's where we are right now. On the shore we can see the fire-gutted factories and plants of Yokohama. And around us the transports and cargo ships are pouring men and supplies ashore while the fighting fleet keeps an eagle eye on proceedings. In a day or two the Japs will sign the surrender on the nearby "Missouri." It's too bad that Jap admiral who was going to sign the peace in the White House can't be here to witness the ceremony.

Yours,

Nob

James Robert Galbreth, of Rockfield, enlisted in the Navy on Aug. 24, 1942, and was sent to radio school at Northwestern University. Leaving the country in Mar. 1943, he participated in the invasions of Normandy and Southern France in 1944, and later in the invasion of Okinawa and the occupation of Japan. Radioman Galbreth served aboard the U.S.S. "Ellyson" (DD 454), and in Task Group 80.6 in the invasion of Southern France. He received a commendation from the group commander. Discharged Nov. 9, 1945, RM 1/c Galbreth is now co-owner of a general store in Rockfield.

September 1, 1945
U.S.S. "Ellyson"
Tokyo Bay

Dear Garth:

With the closing of the war, the Navy has relaxed its censorship almost entirely, and so I am now able to tell you most of the things that have happened to me since the fateful day of August 10 when the Japs decided to sing, "I Surrender Dear."

Since that day the Navy has been preparing itself for the task of taking over the naval installations and naval occupation of Japan. We being in the Third Fleet were immediately faced with the prospect of taking over the capitol itself. For us it meant that before we could call the war all over it would be necessary to sweep the entrances and channels to Tokyo Bay; this was to be accomplished by a fleet of minesweepers. The ship was assured of a "front" seat as the "Ellyson" is the flagship for the commander of all mine-sweeping forces in this area.

On about the 12th of the month we were sent to sea to rendezvous with other units of the occupation forces and for instruction. All this was to take a lot of time, more than we thought, and naturally as the days went by we got very impatient to get in there and get it over with. Finally we got the go-ahead signal—we thought—but at the last minute the day we had been waiting for was pushed ahead another forty-eight hours because a high wind was misconstrued by the higher-ups as a typhoon. Finally, however, on the 27th we picked up our Jap pilot and headed towards the entrance leading to our objective. We arrived at the destination of our voyage on that day about 4 o'clock which was the entrance to Tokyo Bay. We stayed there that night, making preparations for the final step in the morning. During the remaining light hours of the 27th we spent most of the time on deck viewing the sights of Japan; a truly beautiful sight and one that all of us will remember longer than the kamikaze attacks we had previously gone through at Okinawa, was the sun setting behind the famed Mt. Fujiyama.

The morning of the 28th dawned bright and sunny. About 11 o'clock that morning we started up the channel which would give us entrance into Tokyo Bay. All of us on the ship had always hoped that we would be the first ship to enter this bay, but we were preceded by a group of small minesweeps, and so have only the distinction of saying that we were the first major war vessel to enter the anchorage. We were followed by other units of the occupation force. All of this came off without incident, I am happy to say. It almost had the aspects of an excursion boat, lunch being served topside so that none of the sights on the way in would be lost by those who wished to see them. About 1 o'clock that afternoon we were far enough in the bay to view the wreckage of Jap ships and see parts of the naval base at Yokosuka, and farther up the bay the burned-out city of Yokohama. That night we anchored in the bay and again I spent the rest of the light hours in seeing the new sights of this anchorage.

The next morning we returned to the outer bay to pick up some more of our fleet and to escort them into the inner harbor. After this chore we proceeded far enough up into the harbor to get a good view of the burned-out city of Yokohama. At first sight the city seemed to be in fair shape, but as we got closer it was easy to see it only looked like that. The buildings were just skeletons, their chimneys remained standing and were just about the only whole thing left in the area.

The fact that the Japs actually did use American prisoners of war as hostages against our bombings of their industrial cities was proven by the fact that a large number of them were quartered at the waterfront of Yokohama, and had evidently not been moved even after Japan's capitulation. Those men had painted a large white sign on one of the buildings which read "3 Cheers for the U. S. Army and Navy." Our signalmen talked to them and reported that they were very cheerful, but could hardly wait until the signing of the formal peace treaty as then they would be officially turned over to us.

There is very little more to say about our entry, but they have promised us a good show on the day they sign the formal peace treaty, and if it is anything like the sneak preview we had one day at sea when over 1500 carrier planes flew over us in a space of a few minutes, it is going to be well worth watching. Tomorrow is the day for the formal ceremony and I hope that the weather is clear so the aircraft can give us a good show. Incidentally, these are carrier-based and strictly a navy affair.

Doubt very much if I will ever get liberty here, but one never knows.

As ever,
JIM BOB

Robert Edward Hougham, of Franklin, enlisted in the Navy as a radio technician 3/c, Aug. 3, 1942, and was commissioned an ensign Jan. 7, 1944. He served on the U.S.S. "Seid" (DE 256) from June to Dec. 1943, and on the U.S.S. "Reeves" (APD 52) from Sept. 1944 to Nov. 1945. Engagements participated in were the Solomon Islands, 1943; liberation of the Philippines, 1945; Okinawa, Mar. to Aug. 1945, and the occupation of Japan. Promoted to lieutenant (j.g.) in 1945, he was released to inactive duty Nov. 27, 1945, and is employed as a state representative for a publishing firm.

August 31, 1945
Tokyo Bay, Japan

Communique Number Two

After lying off the shores of Japan with a number of other Allied ships for about a week we proceeded in and anchored in Sagami Wan. We were one of the first ships to enter Tokyo Bay and the fourth one to Tokyo. You all probably know quite a bit of what is to follow but I will give you as much as I can.

Our first job after our arrival was to evacuate ex-prisoners of war. I went in with the second group of boats. My trip was a very interesting one. Riding with me in my boat was Commander Stassen, with whom I spent ten hours and got fairly well acquainted. On our return trip we had a commodore who was in charge of evacuation. We picked up the first prisoners in the Tokyo area on the 29th. We started in about eight o'clock and got back about six the next morning. The boat I had did not actually bring back any P.W.'s but had staff men in it. We made the Hospital Camp and then worked our way through the numerous inshore canals down the bay to Camp Omori. When I get back I will be able to tell you several interesting tales, but for now that will have to wait. The stench of those inshore canals was unbearable. We ran aground once and churned up the bottom, it smelled terrible. About the best thing I know of to compare it with is a cesspool; it actually was worse though. These canals were very numerous, therefore we got lost a couple of times but finally got back.

You cannot realize the joy that engulfed the men that were picked up. After returning to the ship, I found that we had several celebrities aboard. Many of those picked up were listed as dead or missing. We had Major Boyington, the Marine ace and winner of the Congressional Medal of Honor aboard, Comdr. O'Kane, a submarine captain, and many others including men from Corregidor (one had been with Lauchner for a year and a half), men who made the Death March from Bataan, men from Wake Island, men stationed in China, and many pilots, including B-29 crews. They ranged from the first day of the war to having been prisoners for only a couple of weeks. There were some correspondents aboard who interviewed most of the men. Broadcasts were made from the ship to the States and recordings were made. One of the newsmen was the managing editor of the South Bend paper. I had quite a nice talk with him and helped him interview some of the men from the Midwest. The only man from Indiana that we had aboard was the one who knew Lauchner and he was from South Bend. We all worked without sleep for a couple of days, but no one minded as we knew that we were really doing something. Every minute counted. The sooner we could get a man out of the awful surroundings he had been in for so long, the better. The expressions they had on their faces and the funny little things they said are inexpressible in words. They were all given a good meal of ham and eggs on a hospital ship before they came aboard our ship.

I ran into a fellow that looked familiar so I asked him who he was. He told me and it turned out that he had been one of my company officers at Treasure Island. When we got through there he had gone to a sub. His sub had been sunk and he had been a prisoner for about ten months. He could not swim or float, but learned very soon after his ship went down. He was in the water for about eight hours.

The biggest trouble that we had with the men while they were aboard was that they ate too much and it made some of them a little sick for awhile. It really was quite an experience to be able to help liberate the first prison camps in Japan. As it is midnight now and I have only had about seven hours sleep in the past three nights, I think I will take a well-earned nap.

I'LL BE SEEING YOU!

BOB

Phyllis Zimmer, of Pleasant Lake, was commissioned a 2d lieutenant in the Army Nurses' Corps Feb. 22, 1945, and departed for overseas duty in July 1945. Lt. Zimmer served on Luzon and later was sent to Japan, where she received a unit citation for processing prisoners of war on Honshu, Sept. 1945. Promoted to 1st lieutenant in Nov. 1945, Lt. Zimmer is now stationed at Fitzsimons General Hospital, Denver, Colo.

September 7, 1945

DEAR FOLKS:

I suppose by this time you know I am in Yokohama, Japan, and that is about 18 miles south of Tokyo. We will move to Tokyo as soon as it is occupied.

I don't know whether I told you, but we were the first women (Allied) to set foot on Japanese soil since 1941. We were also the first ship to dock there since 1941. We like to tease the Marines about landing before they did—it makes them boil.

The Eleventh Airborne arrived here the afternoon before us. They made a sign "Welcome, First Cavalry" and put it on the shore. That was a cutting blow. Since then other hospital ships have arrived, but we make sure they all know we were here first. We arrived on Friday. By Sunday we had possession of all the ground around us, and as we had not started to work yet, we had a good old American baseball game, after which we went through several buildings and picked up a few souvenirs.

Work started in earnest about three days ago. The P.W.'s arrive by train from all over—about 1500 to 2000 patients per day. Our hospital unit is the only one here and it is more or less like an induction center. All patients go through us. We feed and clothe them, give them a medical examination and classify them to send home.

B-29's have dropped food to the patients about three weeks now. We (the nurses) work on shifts and go down to the trains to meet them. We fill our musette bags with candy, gum, cigarettes, etc., and pass them out at the train. I think the biggest moment of my life was when the first trainload of fellows pulled in. They had spotted us long before we could see them. They said the last thing in the world they expected to see was American women—and it was also the best thing. At first they didn't know what to do or say. Most of them have not seen or spoken to a woman in four or five years. You have no idea how those patients look or act. It's worth living a lifetime to see. They expect so little and are grateful for anything. All they want is to know that someone cares. They are so hungry for affection.

We are set up in an old warehouse. It's rather crude and our supplies are practically nil—but the boys are in heaven. They have not had coffee for years, and cookies and doughnuts are unheard of. We have supplies of mirrors, toothbrushes, etc., and they are crazy to see them. Even soap is a treat. Reading material is so welcome to them. It's great to see them all. There are Dutch, Australians, French, English, Italians, Indians; black and white, and all so nice and so glad to see us and they never can stop talking about B-29's.

Love,
PHYLLIS

→ XIV ←

AFTER V-J DAY

FOLLOWING the surrender of Japan, August 14, 1945, treaty-signing ceremonies were arranged to take place aboard the U.S.S. "Missouri" in Tokyo Bay, September 1. American forces under General MacArthur occupied the islands of the homeland. The emperor was untouched, but all authority stemmed from U. S. headquarters. Preparations were made for the trial of Japanese leaders as war criminals. Rebuilding began in the Philippines, and hard-won island bases in the Pacific were retained temporarily by the United States.

George B. Ciboch, of North Judson, enlisted in the Marine Corps and was assigned to a machine gun company of the 4th Marine Regiment, Nov. 4, 1940. He was stationed in Shanghai, China, from Jan. to Nov. 1941, and was then sent to Olongapo, Philippine Islands, arriving there on Dec. 2, 1941. He participated in the defense of the Philippines, Bataan, and Corregidor. He was a prisoner of war from May 6, 1942, to Aug. 1945. He was in Cabanatuan Prisoner of War Camp III until Oct. 1942, when he was taken to Hoten, Manchukuo (Mukden, Manchuria) for the duration of the war. Attaining the rank of sergeant in Feb. 1946, Ciboch was discharged Apr. 26, 1946, and returned to North Judson where he is a photographer.

August 25, 1945
Hoten, Manchukuo

Dear Mom and Dad:

By the time you receive this letter I hope to be on my way back to America. Gee, I can hardly believe it! But don't expect me home too soon, Mom. It may be several months yet. Some of the serious hospital patients have left by plane already and they may soon start flying us back, a couple of planes every day till we're all evacuated.

I am pretty sure I will be home by Christmas, if not sooner, but don't get impatient, Mom; after all, it will take three months at least to return, receive medical treatment, reorganize the organization I am in, and straighten up all my papers, etc., before I receive my discharge and start for home.

On the 15th of this month, at noon, we quit work at the factory a short distance from our camp. It is known as the Manchu Kabushiki Kozaku Karsha something or other. We had a hunch something was happening, but didn't know exactly what. Through the Chinese workers we had heard about a week previously that Russia had declared war upon Japan and was making rapid progress in the invasion of Manchuria. We heard that the Russians had penetrated from the north, captured Harbin, which is 300 some miles from here; the Yanks were coming east from Mongolia, American and Chinese troops were cutting Korea off by driving north from the southern border of Manchuria. Russian paratroops had landed in the northeastern part of Manchuria and were heading south cutting into Korea and holding all the coast. Mind you now, these were only rumors.

We did not go to work on the 16th and in the middle of the afternoon there was quite a bit of air activity around and over our camp. About 10 Japanese fighter planes and a large plane thought to be an American B-24. Parachutes were seen dropping from the American plane. They were colored red and yellow. Something was up. Our out-camp details were returning to this camp. We all knew something was in the wind . . . but what?

Later in the evening six American paratroopers were brought into camp by Japanese M.P.'s. We were not supposed to see them, but some did. It was noticed they still retained their pistols and other gear. They also carried many documents and official looking papers. One of the Japanese camp staff officers walked up to the American in charge, took his cap off and bowed to him. The American officer accepted his greeting sternly. Two trucks loaded down with radio equipment and other gear and covered over with open parachutes, red and yellow in color, came into camp.

What the h—— was going on anyway? A little later the men were seen in Japanese headquarters. They had removed their flight clothing and were dressed in clean, pressed khakis. One happened to be standing near a window and his attention was attracted by an American prisoner who signaled him by deaf and dumb language. American? He nodded his head. Prisoner? He shook his head negative. Then all kinds of stories came into camp.

In the afternoon of the next day General Parker, who had also been a prisoner, made a speech to all the assembled prisoners stating that there was an armistice between the United States and Japan, and we were no longer prisoners of war. You can imagine how we felt! We were advised to stay within the walls of the camp for our own protection. A few days later a Russian Red Army officer and his staff came into camp. Again the men were called to assembly and were told they were made free men by the Russian Red Army.

I went to Mukden yesterday, for the first time a free man. There isn't much to see except Russian soldiers who are occupying the city. There is scattered rifle and machine gun fire but most of it is being quelled by the Russian and Chinese Communist troops. I saw many dead bodies, some Japanese soldiers and others Chinese coolies. A lot of the killing seems to have been done wantonly and for no reason at all. I guess it's a form of celebration. There has been much looting of warehouses, factories, stores and even private homes.

The Russian soldiers are war-wearied and tired. They covered 1,500 miles in 10 days. They all want to celebrate and you just MUST get drunk with them. They are pretty well-built fellows and it's no use to argue with them. Many men have trophies of war, pistols, sabers, rifles, bayonets, helmets, etc. I didn't much care to get them because we probably won't be able to keep them.

Before I close, I want you to know I received many letters a few days ago. I somehow knew I would never see Grandmother again. I shall always remember her as I saw her the last time.

I received many pictures of you folks. I must say, Mom, that you and Dad look younger than I expected. Joe and Lavergne look different. Joe looks more like a family man now. I guess you know that I'm just as proud of my two nephews as you are of your grandsons, and Joe and Lavergne of their sons. . . .

Give my best wishes to the home town and the people of Judson. God bless you, everybody.

Love always,
Your son,
KID

Richard Blackwell, of Franklin, enlisted in the Naval Reserve July 3, 1942, and was assigned to the V-7 naval training program at Northwestern University. Commissioned an ensign Apr. 23, 1943, Ens. Blackwell reported aboard the U.S.S. "Colorado," and on this ship he participated in the Gilbert, Marshall, Marianas, Philippines, Okinawa, and Japanese engagements. For this action he was awarded six battle stars and the Purple Heart. Separated from active duty Mar. 1, 1946, Lieutenant (s.g.) Blackwell returned to Franklin and is an adjustor for an insurance company.

September 18, 1945
Tokyo Wan, Japan

DEAR FOLKS:

Instead of going to the movie this evening, I will write this letter. With a mid-watch coming up, I do not need much encouragement for retiring early.

Sunday I went with the liberty party over to Yokohama. We did not spend much time there, since there isn't much of a city left. That is, the business districts have been completely leveled with the exception of a few buildings.

We got on an electric train and rode into Tokyo. The trip takes about an hour and ten minutes. Bagot, Samuels, Proudfoot and I stayed together. With the exception of three other Navy officers, we were jammed in a car with a thousand Japs. You have heard of the crowded New York subways just after working hours? That is the way these trains were loaded with Japanese commuting between Yokohama and Tokyo.

Factories and homes had been burned out all along the track. We passed a large Mitsubishi aircraft plant which had been demolished. We had about an hour and a half to look around Tokyo, so tried to see the important things. The first building of interest was the Imperial Hotel. This hotel has been rated the finest in the Orient, barring none. A sign saying "Off Limits" kept us from going in. Across the street was Hiubya Park. We found a bench away from the Nips and broke out our K-rations. Before we had them opened, we were surrounded by a throng of hungry Japs. I felt like Louie the Fourteenth eating a steak in luxurious surroundings, with his starved subjects watching him from outside the gates. The park had been converted into gardens and was filled with trenches and air raid shelters. After our lunch we crossed the street to a walk above the moat of the Imperial Palace. We followed it around to the main entrance. No Americans were permitted to enter the palace grounds. We could see some of the buildings through the gate. It looked just like it does in pictures.

We wandered about the streets for about forty-five minutes. Tokyo had been hit hard, but not quite as bad as Yokohama. The buildings were about like those you see in Chicago or New York of 16 stories. Most of them if not completely gutted, had the top six or ten stories burned out. It being Sunday, the six or seven department stores left were closed. They were too far from the station to walk over to. The Tokyo railroad station is a large brick structure about two blocks long and a block wide. There was nothing left of it except a huge shell. The rails had been repaired, but the building had been completely demolished, except for brick walls. We saw Radio Tokyo from the train.

On our return trip to Yokohama we found an interpreter. He said he had a warm spot in his heart for America. I wanted to say "bosh." He had taken post-graduate work at the University of Chicago several years ago. Anyhow he was interesting to talk to. We arrived back in Yokohama without any mishaps, and returned to the ship safe and sound.

Today all small craft stayed tied up. A typhoon has been passing over all day long. The waters in the bay were rough and I imagine much rougher out at sea. The strongest wind up to now was 60 knots.

We may be pulling out in the next few days and start making our way toward the States. We may sail in 'most anywhere on the West coast in the next few weeks.

Good night, Mother and Dad.

Cheerio from Tokyo,
DICK

A sketch of William D. Patrick will be found on page 308.

September 28, 1945
Aomori, Japan

DEAR MOTHER:

They tell me that if I wait a couple of days the things I have seen will assume their proper relative importance and will be easier to write about. However, we probably will be getting under way tomorrow, and I usually find it easier to write letters in port than at sea. Moreover, I imagine you would prefer to get a letter written in Japan to one saying I had been there.

We arrived here about dawn the 25th. The night before I had the watch from eight o'clock until midnight and was on the deck most of the time we were passing through the straits, called Tsugaru-Kaikyo, which separate the islands of Honshu and Hokkaido. I hate to think what that passage would have been like had the war not come to an end before we got here. Mountains on either side of us and a channel so tortuous it seemed we were not on the same course more than fifteen minutes at any one time. It was difficult enough keeping station on the other ships in our column with their red and green running lights turned on and bright white lights ablaze atop each mast. Under black-out conditions I should think there would have been as much danger of collision as of fire from shore batteries or torpedoes, or even suicide planes. Nevertheless, busy as I was, taking bearings on the ship ahead and trying to keep our ship in column, I had time at least to see and be impressed by the show we were putting on. Ahead of us were our escort ships, or "screen," searching the water carefully with great floodlights, to detect any mine which might be drifting our way. And astern of us, as far as I could see, were the lights of the two long columns of transports.

I turned in at midnight, just as soon as I came off watch, because reveille was held at three-thirty the morning of our arrival. We had to get up early because it takes a long time to serve breakfast to fifteen hundred troops, and ship's company always eats first so that they can go about their work while the troops are at "chow." At six o'clock we manned our boats and were ready to be lowered into the water. It was daylight then, and we were about three miles off shore in Mutsu Wan (or Mutsu Bay). As you can see on a map, this bay is completely landlocked. Consequently, there was no surf to contend with—just enough of a swell to facilitate beaching and retracting the landing craft, although there was enough of a wind blowing that we were constantly being covered with a salt spray.

I was salvage officer for the operation, so I went in with the first assault wave, lying a short distance off shore throughout the day and night while the other boats plied back and forth between the ships and shore. Because there was no surf, the salvage work was light and about all I had to do was pump out a couple of boats that had not run up high enough on the beach and consequently had been swamped when their ramp was lowered.

We had K-rations in the boat, but nothing to drink other than the water in our wooden breakers, so about eight o'clock at night I beached my boat and let my crew warm themselves by the camp fires. Hot food had been sent in from the ship to our beach party, and the assistant beach master had very generously (and by prior previous arrangement) saved some for us. They had frankfurters, sauerkraut, potatoes, and bread. Unfortunately we had no plates or utensils so we could not do anything about the potatoes or sauerkraut. However, we made sandwiches of the bread and frankfurters, and altogether it was very much like a Boy Scout picnic back home—especially since our landing happened to have been made in a park! Coffee was scarce, however, as the ship had not sent any in, and the beach party was having to brew their own, using their precious ration of fresh water and some coffee grounds one of the boys had pilfered from the ship's galley. I offered to exchange a breaker of water for some hot coffee, so we all had a drink before we went back to the boat.

The following morning we were relieved by the salvage boat from another transport. I hit my sack about ten o'clock and slept through until six the next day, only getting up for my meals—which I never miss, regardless of how tired I may be.

Perhaps I have gone into too much unnecessary detail in telling about this landing. Actually it was carried out in every respect as though fighting was still going on. We even had planes overhead—but only American planes this time!

Yesterday and today we were permitted to take small groups of men ashore for sightseeing. I accompanied two such parties. Actually there is not much to see. The central part of the city has been completely levelled. There are no bomb craters, so apparently all the damage was done by incendiary bombs dropped from planes of Admiral Halsey's fleet. If many of the Japanese cities look like this it is likely that the atomic bomb had little to do with Japan's surrender. The walls of some half-dozen buildings are still standing, and there is a large Buddhist shrine which was unharmed, but that is all.

We walked back into a residential section. The people there seemed to be living just as they must have been living before the war. Their houses are made of wood, of very simple design. We were not permitted to go into any of them, of course, as it is a court-martial offense to have any dealings with the natives. Most of them had large glass windows across the front, but the view of the interior was obscured by the characteristic paper partitions.

In the burned-out section several new huts have been built of wood and scraps of metal, and already families are moving back down from the mountains. Some of the older Japanese either looked at us quietly or paid no attention to us. But the younger Japs, particularly the little children and their parents, appeared to want to be friendly. This was especially noticeable the second day, probably after they realized our sightseeing parties meant them no harm. Little children ran after us wanting to give away coins and paper money, photographs (apparently out of family albums), prayer sticks, etc. I didn't get any for the simple reason I was responsible for seeing that no one in our group did any bartering or took any souvenirs. A few of the fellows did accept the gifts, however, when I "wasn't looking." We all got a laugh from a little fellow, probably four or five years old, who, after giving away the one picture postcard he had in his hand, went into his house and a few minutes later came running down the street after us, both fists full of family photographs.

I don't know what was the reason for these gifts, which in many cases were obviously sponsored by the adults. Possibly they did it to forestall any looting that might have taken place. Perhaps they know that Americans just naturally like little children and thought by appealing through them they might avoid harsh treatment. Or perhaps they were afraid we would treat their little ones the way the little Zamboangans, whose grin is as much a part of them as their monkey-like way of sitting, were treated by the Japanese soldiers, who thought they were being made fun of. At any rate, the little slant-eyes were having a lot of fun with their game, and their parents appeared to be genuinely happy when their children's gifts were accepted.

These, of course, were the common people, obviously poor and used to hardship. They are quiet and dignified, though obviously capable of laughing and having a good time. My chief thought all the time I was ashore was, "Suppose this had been my home town." I know some, if not all, of the other men were thinking the same thing. War is bad enough when it takes men from their homes, but one can't help feeling sorry for the people who live in those homes when the war comes so close to them.

The Jap soldiers who were drafted to unload our boats at the beach showed signs of great surprise when they saw the rubber tires on our jeeps and trucks. Apparently they had been led to believe that we had no rubber, because many of them came up to feel the tires, as if to see if they were real. I saw the charred remains of two automobiles still in the streets (one of them was a Ford), but bicycles seem to have been the chief means of locomotion, for everywhere I looked were heaps of rusting frames and wheels. I saw a couple of rickshaws, but no one was riding in them at the time. The railroad is in operation—but it is carrying American troops now.

The policemen wear blue uniforms with brass stars on their shoulders that make them look like admirals. The other men wear ordinary shirts and pants, though some also wore a short waist-length kimono in addition. I saw a few men in business suits and felt hats—probably professional men. Most of the women were dressed in trousers of a soft type of material, full at the waist but gathered at the ankle, and long-sleeved blouses of the same color and material, so that at a distance they appeared to be wearing ski-suits! Nearly everyone wore flat wooden clogs, supported by short pegs, on their bare feet.

October 3

It has been some time since I started this, but we left Aomori on the 29th and have been underway ever since. We are scheduled to arrive at Saipan to-morrow. From now on we will be a part of the "Magic Carpet" fleet—taking soldiers, sailors, and marines back to the States. That will keep us pretty busy, and I doubt if we will be at any one place very long at a time. I hope our mail catches up with us soon! It has been a month since I have had a letter, and it is getting a little monotonous.

Love to all,
BILLY

V. James Rizzo, of Indianapolis, enlisted Nov. 20, 1942, in the Army Air Corps and was assigned to the Scott Field Radio School until June 1943. From that time until his date of discharge, he served with the Army Airways Communication System, first at Westover Field, Mass.; then Dover A.A.B., Del.; and later at Maxwell Field, Ala.; Columbus A.A.F., Miss.; and Stout Field, Ind. In Dec. 1945 he attained the rank of staff sergeant and was discharged Jan. 29, 1946, returning to Indianapolis where he is studying law and working as a license examiner at the State's Bureau of Motor Vehicles.

August 1945
[Dover Air Base]

DEAR—:

I've written you many times telling you of very grand evenings I have spent and I've gone into long narrative paragraphs describing some very good times (although few). Well, I'm going to tell you about another evening . . . but this evening wasn't so terrific. In fact it wasn't terrific at all. To put it very mildly, it was boring and (more than you can possibly imagine) overwhelmingly disappointing and disheartening.

About 6:30 P.M. I was resting on my bunk in the barrack and feeling very very good about everything in general and nothing in particular. The evening was cool, clear, and unusually quiet, except for the intermittent shouting of a few fellows in the street and our hum of conversation in the barrack. It was evident that everything was in order and that everyone was feeling pretty good. You could detect it through the ensuing conversation.

"Hey, Sam! Does that USO show start at 7:00 or 7:30?"

"Look at Ziggy over there. You'd think he had a date with Lana Turner."

"I don't know about you, Fred, but this is one night I'm going to remember for a long time."

"Something tells me I'm gonna regret tonight tomorrow."

Big plans were being made for an equally big evening . . . some were going to the NCO Club; others were going into town. Those who had dates were going to the USO show in the gymnasium at 7:00 P.M. or 9:00 P.M. Those who didn't were going to meet the bus scheduled to bring the girls down from Aberdeen and Prairie around 8:00 P.M. It was bound to be a good evening on the base together with a civilian dance band at the Club and a USO show in the gym.

The next half hour was spent doing those little things that always add to one's personal appearance . . . polishing belt buckles, shining shoes and deciding which uniform was the cleanest. Gradually the barrack emptied and one by one the fellows walked through the door and out into the street, lightheartedly whistling and still carrying on that steady hum of conversation . . . everyone talking at once.

"Come on, Jack. Fix your tie while you're walking. This is one evening when we don't want to be late."

"Let's stop at the P.X. first for a beer."

"Hey, George, you've got a date with Sue. Suppose Alice shows up?"

"Boy, I *know* I'm gonna have a good time tonight!"

"Wait up, gang. Mac forgot his cap."

Yes, I had plans, too. Dick and I were going to the P.X., have a few beers and then catch the USO show. After that we were going to spend the rest of the evening at the Club.

We walked down the street toward the P.X. and couldn't help noticing how unusually quiet everything seemed. The sun was just beginning to hide below the top of a dark towering cloud and a slight breeze was blowing from the west.

Walking into the P.X. Dick and I brushed by two other G.I.'s who were mumbling some uncomplimentary remarks about something being unfair. Inside the P.X. the silence rang in our ears. The usual crowd wasn't there and only a handful of soldiers were sitting around the tables in the center of the floor. Something just didn't seem right as Dick and I walked up to the beer counter.

We realized what was wrong as soon as we spotted a sign on the cash register: NO BEER SALES FOR 48 HOURS OR UNTIL FURTHER NOTICE. The only alternative was the Club.

On the way out of the P.X. we stopped to talk to another G.I. who had just returned from the main gate. On his way into town, just one-half hour ago, he had been told at the gate that everyone was restricted to the base.

Out in the street once again, Dick and I talked to several other fellows on their way to the Club, who, by this time, were anything but happy. Once inside the Club the bottom fell out of everything. We were told that the sale of beer was also stopped at the Club. On top of that, the band had been cancelled and the girls from Aberdeen and Prairie would not be down. Rumor had it that the 7:00 P.M. USO show had also been cancelled. Later this rumor developed into reality. It all seemed like a bad dream.

By now it was 8:00 P.M. and there was absolutely nothing to do. No beer was on sale. The dance had been cancelled. The girls weren't coming down to the base. There would be only one USO show. No chance of going in town. We were restricted.

Now this has happened before, but it didn't seem to hit so hard or hurt so much as on this particular night. You see, this was a very special night—one that everyone looked forward to for so long—one that just didn't seem right without even a small celebration. It was August 14th.

At 8:30, back on my bunk in the barracks, I did a lot of thinking. Why was *I* so disappointed? Why did *I* want to celebrate? Perhaps it was because everyone else wanted to do the same thing and I just had a desire to follow the crowd. But, by now, I wasn't thinking of myself. I was thinking of a lot of other fellows here on the base—the fellows who were wearing what we term "fruit salad"—the Distinguished Flying Cross, the Presidential Citation, the Purple Heart. Those boys were called returnees. They're the fellows who have been over and back already. They're the fellows who made the news of August 14th possible. They're the fellows who should have done the celebrating. They're the fellows who stuck around the barracks that night—all night—listening to radio broadcasts of V-J celebrations in New York, Chicago, and San Francisco.

I wondered what their thoughts were.

JAMES

A sketch of Forest E. Collins will be found on page 168.

August 14, 1945
1st Base Air Depot, Eng.

Dear Loved Ones at Home:

The radio has just announced that the world is at peace. The war is over. We have won the long fight.

I had just got in bed; almost everyone was in bed with the radio on. Boys are running around with only shorts on. Flares and fires are beginning to appear. Factory whistles, fire alarms and sirens are adding their peals. Some of the boys are running around so happy they hardly know what they are doing.

At this time I put on my clothes and join the crowds. An hour before you could not have found enough kindling to fire a grate. Now there are bonfires that can be seen for many miles. What is burning—foot lockers, tables, chairs, fences, signs, bulletin boards, bicycle racks, and anything and everything that will burn and can be torn loose from its mountings. Large signs with posts 4×4 and 6×6 timbers are actually pulled from the ground by force of numbers and thrown on the great fires in their entirety. Heavy lattice fencing is being thrown on in 20-foot lengths, torn from the ground, posts and all.

Civilians are coming to our camp. Masses of people not drunk with drink, but drunk with happiness. No one has had time for drink. The great displays in the sky are bringing people on foot, bicycle, and automobile from miles around. The G.I. band is out parading. So great and forceful is their music that it can be heard for two miles as they circle around the road.

This large Base Air Depot must be visible for many miles about tonight. The rocket and parachute flares are so numerous that the tiny little smoke puffs from each one make designs in large clouds in the multicolored flashes. The display is a constantly changing, living exhilaration. It is something alive. It is the very manifestation of freedom in a democratic republic.

There is no arrogance. It is a place where freedom rules without any law, for the law is as powerless as it is unnecessary. I cannot conceive of a Nazi-dominated public being able to demonstrate a victory in such wholehearted carefree terms. This good will and love for your fellow man can come only from the inside out. It cannot go from the outside in. It is hard to explain a love and friendship as exists between these American soldiers and English civilians, as being so personal without being intimately personal. It exists here. Every face, soldier and civilian, man, woman, and child is a radiance of love, joy, and thanks-giving bound into one expression and punctuated by laughter, tears and song.

Automobiles filled with people are picked upright clear off the ground with engines running and wheels turning. So a world of people echoes and re-echoes the phrases. The war is over. Now our homes can be reunited.

May peace be everlasting,
FOREST

INDEX

Admiralty Islands, 205, 217, 228

Albert, Mrs. Charles. *See* Popp, Norma F.

Aleutians, 199, 200, 202, 316

Alexandria (La.), 40

Andersen, Hans C., 5

Anderson, David, letter from, 2–3

Anderson, James, 47

Anderson, John, 277

Angola (Ind.), 154, 314

Aomori (Jap.), 337, 341

"Aquitania," 85

Ardennes, Battle of, 145–146

Ardennes Forest, 131, 135

Argos (Ind.), 81

Army Nurses' Corps, 65, 330; letters
    written by members of, 65–66,
    330–331

Attica (Ind.), 214

Atwood (Ind.), 65

Avellino (It.), 58–59

Ayres, Lew, 224

Bad Ems (Ger.), 135

Bahler, Dean R., letter from, 300–303

Bailey, Charles V., letter from, 133–134

Baker, Robert, letter from, 117–118

Baldwin, Laverta, letter from, 289–291

Bales, Jack, 248–250

Barker, Robert C., Jr., letter from,
    316–321

Bartow Army Air Field (Fla.), 30

Bastogne (Belg.), 90, 131, 173

Bataan, 1, 10, 250, 329, 333

Bavaria (Ger.), 131, 189

Bedford (Ind.), 241

Belgium, 75, 79, 83, 95, 131, 133, 137,
    143, 145, 150, 158, 162, 166, 173, 176,
    181, 186

Benevento (It.), 58

Bennison, M. S., 7

Bentley, Joe, 51

Berkheiser, Myron, letter from, 96–100

Berlin (Ger.), 38, 119, 131, 133, 157, 165,
    176, 181, 182, 184–186

Berne (Ind.), 314

Bismarck Sea, Battle of the, 206–210, 231

Bizerte (Tunisia), 43, 44

Blackwell, Richard, letter from, 336–337

Blatt, A. Ebner, letter from, 100–103

Bloomington (Ind.), 117, 217

Bobbitt, Jesse Trinkle, letter from, 107–108

Bodem, Walter, letter from, 299–300

Boonville (Ind.), 4

Bougainville, Solomon Islands, 205, 211, 212, 214

Bowen, Frank, 2

Boyington, Gregory "Pappy," 329

Brimfield (Ind.), 173

Bristol (Eng.), 76–79

Brooklyn (N. Y.), 39, 85, 291, 292

Brooks, Ensign, 6

Brothers, Stanley N., letters from, 231–233, 258–263

Brown, Dawson Jack, 140, 141, 142, 143

Brown, Dota Claudius, letter from, 275–276

Brown, John Hays, letter from, 44–45

Buchanan, Vernon Clayton, letter from, 229–231

Buckner Bay, Okinawa, 307

Bulge, Battle of the, x, 25, 90, 131, 132, 135, 137, 145, 154, 160, 186

Burkenpas, Myron G., letter from, 158–160

Burns, Richard, letter from, 307–308

Caen (Fr.), 95, 105

Cal-Aero Flight Academy, 27, 29

Calcutta (India), 291

Camp Butner (N. C.), 18

Camp Croft (S. C.), 22, 24, 26

Camp Hood (Tex.), 34

Camp Kilmer (N. J.), 79, 92

Camp Mabuhay (P. I.), 276

Camp Omori (Jap.), 328

Camp Shanango (Pa.), 79

Canine, Ralph J., letter from, 144–145

Canol refinery, 203

Cape Cod (Mass.), 38

Carentan (Fr.), 105

Carmel (Ind.), 50

Carroll, Madeleine, 196

Carter, Boake, 211

Cassino (It.), 69

Chaskel, James O., letter from, 79–81

Cheeseman, James K., letter from, 91–93

Cherbourg (Fr.), 95, 105

Chesnut, Robert A., letter from, 321–324

China, 22, 211, 231, 258, 259, 279, 280, 283, 284, 285, 304, 314, 315, 329, 333

Christen, James B., letter from, 45–46

Christie, James F., letter from, 312–314

Ciboch, George B., letter from, 334–335

Clark Field (P. I.), 10

Claxton, Howard E., letter from, 296–298

Clay City (Ind.), 38, 53, 70, 123, 168, 199, 231, 237, 253, 254, 263, 265

Clayton, George Thomas, ix, 108–111

Clements, Harold, letter from, 118–119

Coatesville (Ind.), 189

Coblenz (Ger.), 150

Cologne (Ger.), 164

Collins, Forest E., letters from, 168–169, 344–345

Collins, Red, 141

Columbus (Ind.), 104, 321

Compiegne (Fr.), 83, 86, 88, 89, 90

Compton, John H., letter from, 223–225

Concentration camps, Germany, 159–160, 161–163, 166–168, 174–176, 177–180

Corrigan, Douglas, 16

Corydon (Ind.), vii, 115, 117

Coventry (Eng.), 88

Crawford, Joan, 22

Crawford, John W., letter from, 250–253

Czechoslovakia, 145, 150, 173, 181, 186

Dana (Ind.), 108, 248

DaVie, William C., letter from, 152–154

Davis, John N., letter from, 150–151

Davis, Willis Read, letter from, 16–17

Decatur (Ind.), vii, 45

Deeters, Robert, 201

Des Moines (Ia.), 20, 21, 22

Doolittle, James, 41

Domfront (Fr.), 97

Dorsey, Jesse, 19, 36, 37, 225

Dortmund (Ger.), 157

Dover Air Base (Del.), 341

Dunkirk (Ind.), 169

Dupont (Ind.), 186

East Chicago (Ind.), 27, 75, 288

Eckerty, Gene, letter from, 148–149

Edinburg (Ind.), 193

Edmonson, Henry, letter from, 263–265

Eisenhower, Dwight D., 75, 81, 100,
    181, 182

Ellett, Ernest H., letter from, 189–191

Ely, John W., letter from, 67–68

Emmanuel, Victor, 71

Empress Augusta Bay, Solomon Islands,
    211, 213

Enders, Gordon B., letter from, 304–306

England, 25, 30, 43, 75, 76–79, 80,
    81–83, 84–85, 86, 88, 90, 91, 95, 96,
    99, 100, 102, 103, 104, 106, 108, 109,
    117, 124, 125, 133, 137, 152, 168, 170,
    172, 176, 181, 192, 288

Erlangen (Ger.), 104

Ertel, Norbert Henry, letter from,
    325–326

Evans, William R., Jr., letters from, 8–9,
    235–236

Evansville (Ind.), ix, 108, 109

Fairmount (Ind.), 176

Falaise Gap (Fr.), 97

Ferdinand (Ind.), 163

Ferriers (Fr.), 137

Fischer, Edward, letter from, 23–24

Fleischman, R. M., letter from, 76–79

Florence (Ind.), 79

Foggia (It.), 68

Fondouk (Tunisia), 44, 49

Ford, George Burt, letter from, 147

Fort Bragg (N. C.), 79

Fort Knox (Ky.), 189, 190

Fort Stotsenburg (P. I.), 11

Fort Wayne (Ind.), 135, 241, 284

France, vii, 30, 49, 50, 68, 75, 79–81, 83,
    86, 88, 90, 91, 93, 95, 96, 100, 104–
    105, 107, 111, 114, 115, 117, 118–119,
    120, 122, 123, 124, 125, 126–129, 132,
    133, 134, 135, 137, 138, 145, 148, 149,
    150, 152, 158, 160, 161, 166, 168, 171,
    173, 176, 181, 186, 189, 191, 193, 194,
    196, 250, 284, 326

Frankfort (Ind.), 150

Frankfurt (Ger.), 168

Franklin (Ind.), 228, 328, 336

Franz, Paul W., letter from, 4–5

Friend, Ansley Gordon, letter from,
    169–170

Fries, Fred W., letter from, 291–294

Frohman, Charles E., letter from,
    104–106

Frump, John A., letter from, 200–202

Galbreth, James Robert, letter from,
    326–328

Gary (Ind.), 75, 255

Germany, 27, 49, 50, 59, 75, 78, 91,
    93, 95, 100, 104, 117, 123, 131, 132,
    133–134, 135–137, 138–143, 144, 145,
    146, 147, 148, 149, 150, 152–154, 155,
    158–160, 161–163, 166, 168–169, 171,
    173–176, 177–180, 181, 182, 186, 189,
    191, 324

Gestapo, 118, 157, 158, 184
Gilbert, Paul, 253
Gilland, George C., letter from, 145–146
Goldsberry, Walter M., Jr., letter from, 211–213
Great Bend (Kans.), 39, 40
Greencastle (Ind.), 211
Greensburg (Ind.), 145
Gribben, Bruce D., letter from, 132
Griffin, John Alexander, letter from, 27–30
Guam, 1, 32, 235, 243, 295, 298, 311, 314, 318, 319, 321, 324

Hackenberg, Harold, 126
Haifa (Palestine), 48
Halifax (N. S.), 38
Halsey, William F., 213, 308, 309, 310, 319, 321, 325, 339
Hamilton, Harvey W., letter from, 55–61
Hardy, George, 12
Harrington (Eng.), 91
Hartfelter, Stewart William, letter from, 266–271
Hasselt (Belg.), 138
Hawaii, 1, 2, 3, 4, 31, 202, 231, 237, 243, 263, 266, 304, 306, 311
Helms, Doan, Jr., letter from, 214–217
Hermosilla, Catalino, 255, 256
Hickam Field (Hawaii), 1, 3
Hill 609 (N. Afr.), 45, 49, 50
Hitler, Adolph, 20, 119, 124, 167, 168, 176, 180, 185, 293
Hobbs, Vernon D., Jr., letter from, 10–13
Hobby, Oveta Culp, 21
Hope, Bob, 78
Horton, John H., letter from, 237
Hoten, Manchukuo, 333, 334
Hougham, Robert Edward, letter from, 328–329
Houston (Tex.), 40
Howerton, Paul, letter from, 288

Hudson (Ind.), 275
Hungerpiller, James, 207, 208
Hunter College (N. Y.), 36
Hussey, Edna, 77
Hyman, Lester E., letter from, 120–121

Ie Shima, 295, 296, 298, 307
India, ix, 22, 23, 46, 279, 283, 285, 288, 289, 291, 304
Indianapolis (Ind.), x, 1, 3, 8, 17, 18, 21, 24, 25, 30, 49, 67, 83, 84, 100, 122, 131, 132, 148, 149, 152, 154, 160, 181, 191, 202, 210, 223, 229, 237, 243, 271, 272, 279, 280, 291, 298, 308, 312, 341
Ipil (P. I.), 255, 256
Isle of Wight, 104
Italy, 17, 21, 43, 44, 53, 55, 56, 57, 62, 65, 67, 68, 70, 73, 120, 122, 123, 131, 132, 181, 275
Iula, Ralph F., letter from, 51–52
Iwo Jima, 32, 243, 295, 297, 300, 301, 310

Jackson, Thomas, letter from, 123–124
"J. A. McAndrews," 92
Japan, vii, ix, 1, 2, 4, 6, 9, 11, 12, 118, 187, 188, 189, 199, 201, 205, 223, 229, 231, 235, 243, 244, 245, 248, 249, 250, 251, 252, 254, 255, 256, 257, 259, 263, 266, 267, 268, 271, 279, 295, 296, 297, 298, 301, 306, 308, 310, 313, 316, 324, 325, 326, 327, 328, 329, 330, 333, 334–335, 336, 337, 339–340
Jasper (Ind.), 39, 205
Jones, Frederick, 315

Kamp, Floyd L., letter from, 81–83
Kasserine Pass (N. Afr.), 44
Kearney (Neb.), 41
Keitel, Wilhelm, 182, 183
Kelly, Helen, 171
Kerama Islands, 311, 317
Knox, Jean, 21

Kovachevich, Alex, letter from, 274
Kovas, Marchmont, letter from, 62–65
Kress, Hubert, letter from, 70–73
Krieble, Wymond W., letter from, 54–55
Kwajalein Atoll, Marshall Islands, 238, 243, 245

Lafayette (Ind.), 132, 158, 304, 306
La Haye du Puits (Fr.), 105, 106
Lanahan, Thomas A., letter from, 49–50
Lawrenceburg (Ind.), 118
Layton, Morris E., letter from, 161–163
Leap, Clifford R., letter from, 225–227
Lebanon (Ind.), 316
Lee, Ernest R., letter from, 182–186
Le Havre (Fr.), 124, 125
Leyte (P. I.), 235, 250, 255, 296, 298, 299, 307, 310
Liege (Belg.), 137
Lince (Belg.), 137
Logansport (Ind.), 119
London (Eng.), 75, 85, 92–93, 133
Long Beach (Calif.), 16, 17
Long, George, 253
Losey, Harold A., letter from, 246–248
Luzon (P. I.), 10, 12, 229, 231, 235, 261, 263, 274, 306, 330

Maas River, 155
MacArthur, Douglas, 205, 210, 228, 235, 251, 276, 309, 333
McKee, Arnold, letter from, 38–39
McKillen, James F., letter from, 155–158
McNeal, John A., letter from, 238–241
Madigan, William L., letter from, 243–245
Madison (Ind.), 55
Maierson, Meyer, letter from, 202–203
Maktar (N. Afr.), 44, 45
Manila (P. I.), 1, 223, 235, 254, 266, 268, 274
Mannheim (Ger.), 194

March Field (Calif.), 15, 16
Mariana Islands, 235, 248, 336
Marion (Ind.), 31, 32
Marshall Islands, 235, 237, 238, 336
Mateur (N. Afr.), 44, 50
Maye, Ernest S., letter from, 18–19
Meehan, Arthur William, letter from, 3–4
Meyers, Justin Gail, letter from, 135–137
Mickle, Gerald St. C., 140
Mill Creek (Ind.), *frontispiece*, x
Miller, Glenn, 128
Mishawaka (Ind.), x, 124
Mitchel Field (N. Y.), 46, 206
Mitchell, Raymond K., letter from, 32–35
Mitscher, Mark, 310
Moberly (Mo.), 37
Mog-Mog Island, 310
Mojave (Calif.), 32, 35
Montbury (Fr.), 133
Monte Carlo (Fr.), 129
Montgomery, Bernard L., 43, 156
Montgomery, Richard H., letter from, 138–143
Moore, Dwain E., letter from, 68–70
Mukden, Manchuria. *See* Hoten, Manchukuo.
Muller, Victor, letter from, 163–165
Mussolini, Benito, 69

Naples (It.), 17, 53, 59, 68
New Albany (Ind.), 43, 44
New Guinea, 199, 205, 206, 210, 223, 225, 226, 227, 229, 231, 253, 255, 263, 265, 266, 271, 300, 323
New Haven (Ind.), 220
New Orleans (La.), 33, 34, 40
New York (N. Y.), 16, 32, 38, 46, 80, 84, 108, 117, 152, 171, 261, 336, 337, 343
Nice (Fr.), 127
Nimitz, Chester William, 310, 319
Nino, Frank, 207

Noon, Harry B., letter from, 30–31

Norfolk (Va.), 2, 20, 39

"Normandie," 80

Normandy (Fr.), vii, viii, x, 49, 78, 79, 100, 105, 106, 108, 109, 112, 114, 118, 146, 186, 188, 191, 326

North Africa, vii, 43, 45, 46, 49, 50, 52, 53, 55, 68, 70, 75, 118, 122, 131, 132, 181

North Judson (Ind.), 333

North Salem (Ind.), 126

Norwich (Eng.), 92

O'Kane, Richard H., 329

Okehampton (Eng.), 80

Okinawa, vii, 32, 39, 41, 118, 243, 245, 250, 276, 295, 296, 298, 299, 300, 301, 304, 307, 308, 310, 311, 312, 313, 314, 315, 316, 317, 319, 321, 324, 325, 326, 327, 328, 336

Oklahoma A. & M. College, 37

Omaha Beach (Fr.), 79, 80, 95, 96, 105

O'Neil, Bryan, 206

Ormoc (P. I.), 255, 256

Pace, Alva B., letter from, 126–129

Paoli (Ind.), 106, 295, 296

Paris (Fr.), viii, 50, 89, 95, 120, 125, 126, 192–193, 194–197, 283, 284

Parker, George M., Jr., 335

Parks, John H., *frontispiece*, x

Patrick, William D., letters from, 309–311, 337–341

Patterson, Joe, 68

Patton, George S., Jr., 95, 104, 160

Pearl Harbor, vii, 1, 2, 6, 238, 245, 250, 263, 279, 320

Pearson, Marvin H., letter from, 114–115

Peleliu, Palau Islands, 32, 275

Philippine Islands, viii, 1, 10, 41, 118, 199, 229, 231, 235, 237, 245, 247, 250, 251, 252, 253, 255, 257, 258, 263, 265,

266–269, 271, 274, 276, 298, 299, 303, 306, 307, 309, 310, 311, 328, 333, 336

Pilsen (Ger.), 188

Pleasant Lake (Ind.), 330

Plymouth (Ind.), 135

Point d'Albe (Fr.), 105, 106

Popp, John Stanley, letter from, 19–20

Popp, Norma F., letter from, 36–37

Pozzuoli (It.), 60

Pribble, Donald G., letter from, 283–284

Price, Karl, letter from, 191–193

Princeton (Ind.), 148

Prisoners of war, letters from, 132, 149, 334–335

Procaskey, Carl J., poem by, 122

Pullins, Edward R., letter from, 111–114

Putnam, Charles D., Jr., letter from, 220–223

Pyle, Ernie, ix, 108, 248, 300, 307, 319; dispatches from, 108–111, 248–250

"Queen Elizabeth," 80

Randazzo (Sicily), 133

Red Cross, viii, 69, 80, 83, 85, 88, 89, 92, 102, 124, 127, 128, 129, 132, 170, 171, 193, 194, 196, 277, 292; letters written by members of, 83–91, 125–126, 171–173

Renneisen, Frank A., letter from, 39–41

Renneisen, Robert M., letter from, 206–210

Rensselaer (Ind.), 68, 111, 276, 300, 306

Rheims (Fr.), 182, 184, 191, 193

Rheinberg (Ger.), 155

Rhine River, 25, 95, 131, 132, 155, 156, 157, 164, 165, 168

Richardson, Elizabeth, letter from, 125–126

Richmond (Ind.), 5, 10, 91

Richmond (Va.), 12

Rider, Kenneth N., Jr., letter from, 228–229

Rimmel, Marion H., letter from, 173–176

Rizzo, V. James, letter from, 341–343

Rochester (Ind.), 95

Rockfield (Ind.), 326

Rockport (Ind.), 283

Roermond (Neth.), 155

Rogers, Meredith J., letter from, 186–188

Rome (It.), 53, 62, 69, 71, 120, 123, 149

Rommel, Erwin, 43, 49

Roosevelt, Franklin D., 27, 117, 319

Rosenbarger, James E., letter from, 115–117

Rudy, William B., letter from, 149

Ruhr (Ger.), 25, 131, 145, 157, 158

Russell Islands, 300, 301

Russia, 50, 59, 110, 131, 133, 145, 153, 159, 161, 162, 174, 175, 177, 181, 182, 183, 184, 185, 201, 263, 295, 306, 334, 335

Ryukyu Islands, 231, 295, 296, 298

St. Lo (Fr.), 90, 95, 96, 105

St. Sever (Fr.), 106

St. Vith (Belg.), 135, 136

Ste. Mère Eglise (Fr.), 103, 106

Saipan, Mariana Islands, 235, 241, 243, 245, 311, 341

Salerno (It.), 44, 53, 56, 57, 132

Sander, Harold, letter from, 25–27

San Francisco (Calif.), 154, 181, 275, 310, 311, 343

Santa Ana (Calif.), 29

Sendak, Theodore L., letter from, 255–258

Seymour (Ind.), 114, 137

Shamshanagro (India), 289

Sheppard Field (Tex.), 29

Sicily, 45, 46, 49, 53, 54, 123, 132, 133, 181, 275

Sidi-Bel-Abbes (Algeria), 44

Siegfried Line, 131, 146, 158, 173

Sinclair, Mary, letter from, 83–91

Sioux Falls (S. D.), 19

Snyder, Kathryn L., letter from, 65–66

Solomon Islands, 205, 211, 245, 300, 328

Southampton (Eng.), 79, 104

South Bend (Ind.), 22, 46, 62, 146, 274, 329

Spaatz, Carl, 182

Spades (Ind.), 324

Speed (Ind.), 19, 36, 225

Spencer, Margaret, letter from, 171–173

Spitalney, Phil, 22

Spruance, Raymond A., 310, 318, 319

Stalag XVIII (Ger.), 149

Stassen, Harold E., 328

Stillwater (Okla.), 36, 37

Stine, Robert E., letter from, 193–197

Storm, Harry, 38, 54, 70, 123, 200, 231, 237, 253, 258, 263

Strasbourg (Fr.), 194, 196

Stratford (Eng.), 83, 85, 86, 87, 89

Stumpff, Paul, 183

Sullivan (Ind.), 266

Task Force 58, 310, 311, 319, 320

Taylor, Paul E., letter from, 210–211

Tebourba (Tunisia), 45, 49

Tedder, Arthur W., 182, 183

Templehof airdrome (Ger.), 182, 184

Terre Haute (Ind.), 54, 123, 144, 231, 250

Thorne, William S., letter from, 241–243

Thunderbird Field (Ariz.), 29

Tiber River, 69

Tipton (Ind.), 237, 245

Tokyo (Jap.), 199, 245, 247, 250, 301, 306, 309, 310, 316, 319, 325, 326, 327, 328, 330, 333, 336, 337

Tunisia, 43, 44, 45, 53, 193

Turner, J. E., 102

Ulithi, Caroline Islands, 32, 301, 310, 311, 316
USO, 15, 90, 277, 342, 343
U. S. R. R. A., 126
U.S.S. "Antares," 245
U.S.S. "Arkansas," 118
U.S.S. "Bailey," 6
U.S.S. "Colorado," 336
U.S.S. "Comfort," 319
U.S.S. "Compton," 324, 325
U.S.S. "Ellyson," 326
U.S.S. "Enterprise," 245
U.S.S. "Franklin," 310, 316
U.S.S. "Hornet," 8, 235, 310
U.S.S. "Huse," 5, 6
U.S.S. "Indianapolis," 310, 316
U.S.S. "Iowa," 310, 325
U.S.S. "Jack Miller," 275
U.S.S. "Kimberly," 316
U.S.S. "Lash," 321
U.S.S. "Medusa," 245
U.S.S. "Missouri," 310, 325, 333
U.S.S. "Monongahela," 300
U.S.S. "New Mexico," 316, 319
U.S.S. "Pitt," 308, 309, 311
U.S.S. "Reeves," 328
U.S.S. "Salt Lake City," 118
U.S.S. "Scroggins," 38
U.S.S. "Seid," 328
U.S.S. "Tennessee," 7
U.S.S. "Titania," 321, 322
U.S.S. "West Virginia," 5, 6, 8
Utah Beach (Fr.), 84

Valone (Fr.), 133
Vandegrift, Alexander A., 312
Van Steenberg, Leslie J., letter from, 285–287
V-E Day, 84, 132, 145, 155, 181, 186, 324
Vecera, Guy Louis, letter from, 6–8

Vielsalm (Belg.), 136, 137
V-J Day, 309, 311, 333
Volturno River, 59
Von Friedeburg, Hans Georg, 183

WAAC, 15, 20, 22; letter written by member of, 21–22
Wagner, Darrel H., letter from, 315–316
Wagner, Norbert, letter from, 166–168
Wahl, Henry E., letter from, 217–219
Wainwright, Jonathan M., 1
Wake Island, 3, 329
Wangelin, William R., letter from, 280–283
Washington (Ind.), 15
Waterloo (Ind.), 166
Watson Lake (Yukon Terr.), 202
Watson, Vivian B., letter from, 21–22
Waveland (Ind.), 170
WAVES, 15, 36, 37; letter written by member of, 36–37
Waynetown (Ind.), 20
Wells, Bryson, letter from, 176–180
Welzheim (Ger.), 171
Wheeler Field (Hawaii), 4
Wiles, Edward, letter from, 276–277
Wilkins, Lloyd H., letter from, 271–273
Woltman, Frank H., letter from, 46–48
Woolsey, Russell L., letter from, 253–254
Wy (Belg.), 140, 143

Yokohama (Jap.), 325, 327, 330, 336, 337
Yokosuka (Jap.), 325, 327
Yukon Territory, 202

Zamboanga (P. I.), 309, 340
Zhukov, Grigory Konstantinovich, 182, 183
Zimmer, Phyllis, letter from, 330–331

HOWARD H. PECKHAM (1910–1995) was Professor of History and Director of the William L. Clements Library at the University of Michigan. From 1945 to 1953, Peckham was Director of the Indiana Historical Bureau and Secretary of the Indiana Historical Society.

SHIRLEY A. SNYDER (1924–1999) was an editor for the Indiana Historical Society. Previously, she edited for the Indiana Historical Bureau for thirty-one years.

JAMES H. MADISON is the Thomas and Kathryn Miller Professor of History Emeritus, Indiana University Bloomington.